Women, Creole Identity, *and* Intellectual Life *in Early Twentieth-Century Puerto Rico*

In the ***Puerto Rican Studies*** series,
edited by Luz del Alba Acevedo, Juan Flores,
and Emilio Pantojas-García

Women, Creole Identity, *and* Intellectual Life *in Early Twentieth-Century Puerto Rico*

Magali Roy-Féquière

TEMPLE UNIVERSITY PRESS

PHILADELPHIA

Temple University Press, Philadelphia 19122

Published 2004
Printed in the United States of America

∞ The paper used in this publication meets the requirements of the American National Standard for Information Sciences—Permanence of Paper for Printed Library Materials, ANSI Z39.48-1984

Library of Congress Cataloging-in-Publication Data

Roy-Féquière, Magali, 1957–
Women, creole identity, and intellectual life in early twentieth-century Puerto Rico / Magali Roy-Féquière.
p. cm. — (Puerto Rican studies)
Includes bibliographical references and index.
ISBN 1-59213-230-8 (cloth : alk. paper) — ISBN 1-59213-231-6 (pbk. : alk. paper)
1. Puerto Rico—Intellectual life—20th century. 2. Puerto Rican literature—20th century—History and criticism. 3. Puerto Rican literature—Women authors—History and criticism. 4. Nationalism—Puerto Rico. 5. Identity (Psychology)—Puerto Rico. 6. Feminism. 7. Social classes. 8. Race. I. Title. II. Series.
F1975.R69 2004
305.4'097295'09041—dc21

2003053130

2 4 6 8 9 7 5 3 1

À mes chers parents, Henri et Jacqueline Roy

To my loving husband, Konrad Hamilton

Contents

Acknowledgments

To all of those who have so generously nurtured me throughout the years go my deepest thanks because, as the proverb says, "It takes a village . . ." So many people have been a part of this project from its conception. The most valuable lesson learned in this process has been that intellectual work is made possible by the community that fosters and supports it. My family, friends, advisors, and colleagues have all had to bear with me as words turned into paragraphs, and then into chapters. To all of you I owe an eternal debt of gratitude.

This study is written in the hope that it will contribute to a critical dialogue and a questioning of cultural presuppositions and received values that, at times, have seemed etched in stone. My desire would be that it also go beyond the academy. For if we are to fashion a future that is mindful of all people and that is truly democratic in scope, comforting and comfortable notions of identity—national, racial, sexual—might no longer suffice to help us forge ahead.

In a sense, I started this project years ago as an undergraduate at the University of Puerto Rico. We had just read the Antillean poems of Luis Palés Matos for class, and a good friend and I continued the discussion outside under those wonderful trees in front of the university theater. Palés's poems were beautifully written, seductively musical, and astonishing in their refashioning of the word. We even felt represented and courted in the verses of "Mulata-Antilla." Yet, the poems also made me uneasy and somewhat of a resisting reader who could not help talking back to these poetic representations. Something was in the air at that time and place, and as young undergraduates we were swept up in discussions about imperialism, class, race, and gender oppression that might help us make sense of the colonial and geopolitical realities we experienced daily. My feelings of displacement and desire to belong were no doubt influenced by my reality as an immigrant whose parents had taken the hard march "por la encendida calle antillana" from Haiti to Puerto Rico. The national ground beneath my feet has never been too stable. In retrospect, this book is a step in an intellectual journey embarked on years ago *en las aulas de la Universidad de Puerto Rico* but that in actuality had started much earlier.

I wholeheartedly thank Mary Louise Pratt for her intellectual generosity and steadfast support of the project in its dissertation stage. Her solidarity and feminist ethos have guided me throughout my academic career. My thanks also go to Sylvia Wynter for her example and for her faith in the necessity of my work. Their thoughtful mentoring and commitment have helped me chart my own paths through the ongoing process of decolonization. I would like to express my appreciation to the Ford Foundation for a post-doctoral fellowship that provided me much needed financial support. I also want to convey my thanks to Julio Ramos for his very valuable comments at the dissertation stage, and especially for his thoughtful reading of the first three chapters. Thanks to Gregory Strickland, Susan M. Dever, and Tom Conville for their judicious editing and proofreading. I would also like to express my deep gratitude to Dean Larry Breitborde and to Knox College, my home institution, for their financial and moral support. My sincere appreciation also goes to our librarians, Jeff Douglas, Anne Giffey, Sharon Clayton, Laurie Sauer, and Irene Ponce, for their very competent and prompt answers to my myriad queries and loan requests. My colleagues, especially Fred Hord, and my students at Knox have given me much encouragement, instruction, and friendship.

A number of parts of chapters in this book have appeared in some form in earlier publications. My thanks to the following institutions and individuals for permission to use these materials. "Negar lo negro sería gazmoñería: Luis Palés Matos, Margot Arce and the black poetry debate" (now in Chapters 7 and 8) was originally published in *CENTRO: Journal of the Center for Puerto Rican Studies* VIII, (1–2): 82–91, 1996. Reprinted, with permission, from *CENTRO: Journal of the Center for Puerto Rican Studies*, Copyright © 1996. "The Nation as Male Fantasy: Discourses of Race and Gender in Emilio Belaval's *Los cuentos de la Universidad*" (in Chapter 5) was published by the Caribbean Studies Center of the University of Puerto Rico in *Ethnicity, Race and Nationality in the Caribbean*, ed. Juan Manuel Carrión (1997), 122–158. Sections of "Margot Arce y las paradójicas raíces de la cultura nacional" (in Chapter 1), originally published in Spanish in *Margot Arce de Vázquez: Obras completas*, ed. Matilde Albert Robatto, Vol. 3 (2001), 177–204, are reprinted here with the kind permission of the University of Puerto Rico Press and the Sucesión Margot Arce de Vázquez. "Contested Territory: Gender, National Identity and Intellectual Life in Early Twentieth-Century Puerto Rico" (in Chapter 2) appeared in a shortened form in *Callaloo*, Vol. 17, 3 (1994), 916–934, as part of a special issue dedicated to Puerto Rican women writers, and is reprinted with the courtesy of The Johns Hopkins University Press.

Additional thanks go the following people for generously allowing me to reproduce graphic materials: to Carlos Filardi for Carmelo Filardi's book cover art and the caricature of Emilio S. Belaval; to Carmen Vázquez Arce and Sucesión Margot Arce de Vázquez for graciously allowing me to use Dr. Arce's photograph, to Rafael Bernabé of the Seminario Federico de Onís at the University of Puerto Rico for access to the photographs at their library, to Luis Agrait of the University of Puerto Rico Press, to Idsa Alegría Ortega, and to the Proyecto de Digitalización El Mundo at the José M. Lázaro Library of the University of Puerto Rico.

Many, many thanks to my dear friends who have enriched my life immeasurably. *Mil gracias* to Nina Menéndez for her friendship and intelligent translation work. I gratefully acknowledge Susan M. Dever for her enthusiastic reading of the manuscript and for providing invaluable comments and suggestions. She has been my long-time collaborator through thick and thin since our days in graduate school. Her house is my second home and her unswerving friendship makes her my sister. Thank you to Juan Flores and Miriam Jiménez Román for the support and generosity they have always showed me. Many thanks also go to Kelvin Santiago-Valles and Gladys Jiménez Muñoz. My gratitude also goes to Arnaldo Cruz-Malavé for his helpful comments and critiques. To my editor Janet Francendese and the staff at Temple University Press, many thanks for helping me to navigate through the manuscript to book process.

Lastly, I want to express my deepest recognition to my family. My parents Henri and Jacqueline Roy, together with my siblings Rachel, Pascale, and Henri, offered their continual love and support. My mother has selflessly and intelligently collaborated with me in my intellectual endeavors as an indispensable research assistant, photocopier of texts impossible to find outside Puerto Rico, and as a perceptive reader. My father has been my moral guide and has taught me the value of a generous heart. Their faith and sacrifices have nurtured my hopes and dreams. Thank you to my husband, Konrad Hamilton, whose love, humor, and encouragement never faltered. May ours continue to be a marriage of true minds. In every sense my family has made it all worthwhile.

Women, Creole Identity, *and* Intellectual Life *in Early Twentieth-Century Puerto Rico*

Introduction

Much of what we understand today as Puerto Rico's national literature is inextricably linked to the intellectual projects of the *Generación del Treinta.* Credited with exploring the nature of Puerto Rican "character and personality," the writers and thinkers whose works were first published in the turbulent 1930s resolutely formulated the bases upon which to build a uniquely Puerto Rican literature. Essayists, poets, novelists, and short story writers such as Antonio S. Pedreira, Tomás Blanco, Margot Arce, Luis Palés Matos, Julia de Burgos, Juan Antonio Corretjer, Enrique Laguerre, and Emilio S. Belaval conceived their work both in aesthetic terms and as a gesture of cultural affirmation and nation-building during a time of great political, economic, and cultural upheaval. As inheritors of the historical changes triggered by the United States's political and economic sovereignty over Puerto Rico after 1898, they, and other Creole intellectuals, endeavored to respond to a new colonial reality, experienced, in different forms, by all Puerto Ricans during the first half of the twentieth century. From the vantage point of the writers of this intellectual generation, the crisis was not limited to the political and economic spheres alone, but had severe ramifications for the island's culture. To counter the all-encompassing sense of social and cultural dislocation, the intelligentsia proposed to discover anew Puerto Rico's "national character" *(personalidad puertorriqueña, personalidad como pueblo)* in order to affirm the existence of the nation and to provide the discourses that would buttress new political projects. Thinkers, writers, and politicians, most of whom were members of the new professional elite coming of age in the 1930s, set out to instill Puerto Ricans with a renewed sense of collectivity, and took it upon themselves to speak on behalf of all their compatriots.[1] Significantly, many important members of this intellectual formation were literary critics and historians, who played a fundamental role in setting the parameters of the discourse on Puerto Rican culture. Through their access to cultural institutions such as the University of Puerto Rico, the

Ateneo Puertorriqueño, and a number of publications, figures such as Margot Arce, Antonio S. Pedreira, Concha Meléndez, Manrique Cabrera, Nilita Vientós Gastón, Tomás Blanco, and many others were instrumental in delineating a Puerto Rican literary canon, with its attendant interpretations and authoritative readings, that would influence contemporary and future critics and readers. With minimal changes, the cultural proposals of this generation would be incorporated into the populist political undertakings of the 1940s and 1950s.

This book examines the underpinnings of race, class, and gender evidenced in the cultural nationalist projects of the intellectuals of the *Generación del Treinta*. Their embattled responses to the questions "What are we as a people?" and "Who are we?" were the result of complex debates and negotiations for cultural leadership in the midst of competing proposals from U.S. colonial interests, subaltern formulations regarding social justice, and a more politically militant nationalist activism. The resulting national identity discourse formulated by these liberal intellectuals, when understood as a project undertaken by multiple and competing voices, reveals its elements of "creation and invention," to use historian Eric Hobsbawm's now famous conceptualization. More often than not, cultural nationalists select, reconfigure, and reimagine the defining elements that constitute the nation, conceiving new relationships, reorganizing meanings, and creating a synthesis suitable to their purposes. In the nationalist context, this discursive practice is part of an effort to inculcate certain conceptual frameworks, values, and norms of behavior in order to "establish continuity with a suitable historic past."[2] This new understanding of the past is then written into the present and projected onto the future. In the Puerto Rican context, the discourse of national identity that coalesced in the 1930s sought to connect the nation to a highly contested Spanish colonial past that would stand in opposition to the difficult colonial present inaugurated by the American intervention. At best, this new historical narrative of the *Generación del Treinta* engaged, only to marginalize, Puerto Rico's multi-racial history and the painful legacies left by centuries of racial slavery. At worst, it perpetuated a racial hierarchy grounded in centuries of stigmatization and discrimination against the descendents of enslaved Africans, a considerable sector of Puerto Rican society. Colonial modernity was the stage on which Creole intellectuals rehearsed their scripts for national identity vis-à-vis working class militancy and North American colonial intervention. As a group vying for social hegemony in the midst of the social crisis of the 1930s, their challenge was to modernize social and intellectual discourses while still retaining, to a large extent, their society's paternalistic values.[3]

With very few exceptions, the very milieu of the writers who have come to form the Puerto Rican literary canon demanded that they deal with the theme of national identity and "Puerto Ricanness" in one way or another.

The *Generación del Treinta* firmly established this expectation, often understood to be mandatory, as the legitimate endeavor for every Puerto Rican writer. Accordingly, the Puerto Rican artist is charged with the awesome task of being a guarantor of the existence of his or her culture. Following this logic, writers worth their salt reaffirm the reality of a uniquely Puerto Rican literature and culture; they are called to act as the national conscience within strictly defined boundaries. Already the overarching, sempiternal theme is "our unique way of being." This enduring ethical dictum has nurtured the flowering of literary works, as well as scholarly endeavors directed at documenting the persistence of a cultural tradition. But as writer Ana Lydia Vega attests in a 1988 essay, the powerful legacy of the *Generación del Treinta* can overwhelm many writers: "Such is the magnitude of the project that one can easily end up in a formidable *writer's block*. . . . Because, in addition to Saving the Fatherland, Affirming the Culture in Crisis, and Accelerating the Advent of the Great Popular Dawn with the utmost originality and within the utmost orthodoxy possible, one is also asked to denounce, with every touch of the key, the Vile Machista Oppression, a somewhat *risqué* variant of the dear class struggle. No, even in literature we are pursued by the double shift!"[4] (Tal es la magnitud del proyecto que podría fácilmente desembocar en un formidable *writer's block*. . . . Porque, además de Salvar la Patria, Afirmar la Cultura en Crisis y Acelerar el Advenimiento de la Gran Aurora Popular con la mayor originalidad y dentro de la mayor ortodoxia posible, se le pide también que a cada tecleteo de máquina denuncie la Vil Opresión Machista, variante algo *risqué* de la querida lucha de clases. ¡No, si hasta en literatura nos persigue la doble tarea!) Vega argues for the freedom to explore topics and genres other than those sanctioned by what has become an established tradition. Although the author takes a jab at the ensuing literary endeavors of the 1950s and 1970s, her irreverent and humorous declaration of independence is an oblique homage to the success of the cultural nationalist project to write the nation and, in the process, usher it into being.

Puerto Rican cultural nationalism was forged in the heat of political opposition and state repression of the more radical and militant nationalism promulgated by the Puerto Rican Nationalist Party. The Nationalist Party's call for sovereignty and total independence from the United States threatened the grip that North American sugar and other corporations had on the island's economy. In an effort to gain actual as well as symbolic terrain, militant nationalists defended the Spanish language and a Spanish-derived identity, promoted the use of a Puerto Rican flag, spread Catholic dogmatism, raised an unarmed liberation army, and organized marches and political meetings all over the island. The most ardent apostle of Puerto Rican independence and the leader of the movement, Harvard-educated Pedro Albizu Campos, suffered harassment and, later, incarceration and torture at the hands of the colonial authorities. A great admirer of Irish nationalism and in particular of

Sinn Fein, Albizu Campos believed that activism and confrontation would lead to an ebullient raising of consciousness among Puerto Ricans and to mass opposition to colonial rule.[5] Other nationalist-leaning groups were not so willing to go the route of militant confrontation with the regime and opted to struggle within the system. However, given similarities in class background, there were many points of agreement between the liberal young intellectuals who comprised the *Generación del Treinta* and the militant nationalists. They all agreed that imposition of colonial capitalism had been ruinous for the hegemonic aspirations of Puerto Rican landowners and for society as a whole, and that political independence was a way to solve the crisis. They also coincided in their conservative defense of Hispanic culture and the Spanish language as a way to reclaim cultural and political space. Their assertion of Puerto Rico's cultural difference vis-à-vis the United States was a way of approaching the greater issues of political sovereignty. In this, Puerto Rican cultural nationalists were not alone. Underscoring cultural difference was a practice widely used by other Caribbean and Latin American countries under the massive weight of the United States's economic and political influence.

In their efforts to establish the uniqueness of Puerto Rican culture and, thus, the separateness of Puerto Rico from its new colonial master, the *Generación del Treinta* would enlist the aid of a number of paradoxical strategies. They chose to combat one colonialism with another, and to formulate their idea of the nation using racialist discourses that were in contradiction to the heterogeneous racial reality of the island. This was not a simple matter, given that elite intellectuals were strongly invested in their identity as white descendents of Spaniards. Puerto Rican "whiteness" was further brought into crisis as it encountered the intransigence of the United States's racial hierarchies in which white Latin Americans occupied a lower position in relation to white Euro-Americans. Let us not forget that "whiteness" is a form of social capital jealously guarded in all societies that have experienced white supremacy. This was one of the many dislocations faced by the Puerto Rican intelligentsia in the early twentieth century. The Spanish conquest and colonization of the Caribbean and the Americas had put in place complex and highly fluid systems of classifying people by race, a legacy still remaining with us today. From the inception of Spanish colonialism, the ongoing process of race mixing was codified in a system of racial castes or *sistema de castas* with social privilege and life opportunities available according to a person's Spanish, Indian, or African parentage. *Mestizo, castizo, morisco, mulato, lobo, saltatrás, tente en el aire,* and *chino* are some of at least sixteen designations used at one time in eighteenth-century Mexico, for example. Each country developed its own cataloging systems based on the ratio of the races and the particular economic conditions of the time. For centuries the highest colonial and religious offices, as well as the best economic opportunities, were reserved for peninsular Spaniards, a practice resented by the Creole elites whose hegemonic aspirations would, in time, lead them to spearhead the various independence struggles of the early nineteenth century. As defined in this book, Creole or *criollo* are terms used to categorize the white descendents of Spanish and other Europeans born in the Americas. Yet in common parlance, *criollo* also refers to anyone or anything native-born. These two usages are interrelated, as we see in my later discussion of race.

Even as race mixing has continued uninterrupted in most of Latin America, it is vital to understand that the prevalence of *mestizos*, mulattos, or people of mixed race, does not imply an absence of racial hierarchies. Economic status, life opportunities, ideals of beauty, social desirability, and political power are constantly being negotiated within an elaborate system of white supremacy, where the most "European" in phenotype remain at the top and the most "African" and "Indian" remain at the bottom. People of many shades of brown, facial features, and hair types represent the broad middle of the scale. Race and class are interlocked—one category can at times supply what is perceived as lacking in another. For instance, money or circumstance can socially—though only up to a certain point—"lighten" or at times also "darken" a person, influencing his or her placement in the social hierarchy. Self-identification, phenotype, economic status, gender, ancestry, and social context all help define race. In Puerto Rico today, as in most of Latin America, social pressure toward *blanqueamiento* or "whitening" of one's bloodline by marrying a lighter-skinned person continues undiminished. For centuries race mixing occurred independently of formal legal marriage and was strictly forbidden among the upper classes by custom, and at times by law. Among the working classes race mixing has followed its own variegated logic.[6] Notions of race have been integral to questions of national identity and will be examined at length in this book.

By the end of the nineteenth century, the island's elite had a vested interest in internally and externally projecting an image of Puerto Rico as the whitest of the Antilles. The main points of comparison were the Anglophone and Francophone islands, with their obvious predominance of people of African descent, and Cuba, viewed by Puerto Rican intellectuals with both admiration and ambiguity. In the case of Cuba, the Creole elite's formulation of discourses of nationhood were powerfully informed by the massive presence of black Cubans who had provided the manpower for the sugar plantation and tobacco booms of the nineteenth and twentieth centuries. Popular involvement in the War of Independence, a developing Afro-Cuban consciousness, continuous race mixing, and the United States's political and economic intervention would shape discourses about "Cubanness" or *cubanidad*. In Puerto Rico conditions were somewhat different, given its lesser integration into international markets and a greater preponderance of small *haciendas.* As with Cuba, nonetheless, there had been an ongoing process of race mixing and repeated immigrations of whites from the newly independent Spanish colonies and from Spain at various moments in the nineteenth century. And even though at the time of abolition in 1873 most Puerto Ricans of African descent were not enslaved, the stigmatization of blackness was, and remains today, part of the fabric of life in Puerto Rico. To the proponents of nationalism writing in the 1930s, scarcely sixty years after abolition, the population's racial heterogeneity was a thorny question.

With the North American intervention, Puerto Rican elites came face to face with a new version of white supremacy that placed even the whitest and most educated islanders in a subservient position to the Euro-American. In 1898, most Puerto Ricans were not considered white by the invading troops, nor by the photographers and journalists who came to document life in the newly acquired colony. Nonetheless, the majority of Puerto Ricans, though "colored" in North American eyes, did not see themselves this way. In the new colonial economic and political context, the Creole intelligentsia underwent a crisis of legitimacy that led to anguished questioning of its role as a demoted white-identified elite intent on leading a racially heterogeneous populace.

The complexities of Creole responses to these new challenges are exemplified by literary critic Margot Arce de Vázquez, a figure I have chosen to highlight in my study. As she strives to construct a narrowly conceived Spanish foundation for Puerto Rican culture, concepts such as "race" and "cultural tradition" are appropriated by the author and invested with new meanings. Arce would glorify the Spanish colonial past as a way to combat the present colonial impositions. Similarly, her exegesis of Luis Palés Matos's *negrista* or "black poetry" is deeply embroiled in polemics about the nature and extent of the nation's racial heterogeneity. My analysis of the *Generación del Treinta* privileges the figure of Margot Arce as paradigmatic of the profound interconnectedness of race, class, gender, and sexuality in cultural nationalist discourses. While she is often mentioned as a contributor to the cultural nationalist projects of the time, my study places her squarely in the midst of the projects of this generation as one of its principal authors and interlocutors.

Margot Arce's long career as teacher, critic, and political activist spanned more than fifty years. Born Margarita Arce Blanco in Caguas in 1904 (a tobacco producing town at the time), Arce attended high school under the newly established U.S. public school system, whose expressed aim was the acculturation of Puerto Rico's youth into a specifically American way of life.[7] After attending the University of Puerto Rico and teaching there for a short time, she traveled to Spain in 1928 where she completed a doctorate in Spanish literature. Her career as a Hispanist began with the publication of her doctoral dissertation, by the famed Centro de Estudios Históricos, on Spanish Renaissance poet Garcilaso de la Vega. While in Spain, Arce traveled extensively and had contact with members of the Spanish intelligentsia, experiences that would greatly affect her later intellectual and political endeavors. She also became a close friend of the Chilean poet and ambassador to Spain, Gabriela Mistral. Yet in contrast to a number of Latin American intellectuals (Alfonso Reyes, for example) who visited Spain in the 1910s and 1920s and partook of the more avant-garde aspects of Spanish intellectual life, Arce went to Spain in search of a Spanish tradition, not in search of modernism and avant-garde culture. Her aim was to connect with a literary and cultural heritage, personified especially by the writers of the Golden Age and the Spanish Generation of 1898, and later the exiles of the Generation of 1927.

Upon her return to Puerto Rico, Margot Arce resumed teaching at the University of Puerto Rico in the Department of Hispanic Studies and was very active in the intellectual scene. She served on the editorial boards of professional journals such as *Revista del Ateneo Puertorriqueño* and *Brújula* (the journal of the Circle of Spanish Teachers), published in *Índice*, and edited the *Revista de la Asociación de Mujeres Graduadas de la Universidad de Puerto Rico* (Journal of the Association of University of Puerto Rico Women Graduates). In 1946 Margot Arce became a founding member of the *Partido Independentista Puertorriqueño*, a party dedicated to the attainment of political independence from the United States through the ballot and by appeal to the United Nations. As director of the Department of Hispanic Studies at the University of Puerto Rico from 1943 to 1965, Doña Margot, as she was respectfully known, trained generations of students and critics.

One could argue that Puerto Rican women of the *Generación del Treinta*, such as Margot Arce, identified more strongly with the concerns of their class and race than with interests stemming from their condition as gendered subjects.[8] Yet, such an additive model of these systems of domination does not capture the fluidity inherent in the construction of social subjectivities and the radical interconnectedness of these categories. As feminist critics have amply demonstrated, these social categories function in co-constitutive ways, each acquiring meaning and salience in the presence of the other. One is designated as a woman differently because one is a white woman whose very classification as white becomes intelligible and possible only in the presence of the non-white—the mixed-race and black women. Elite white women's gendered interests, in effect, only gain meaning when understood as inseparable from these women's race, class, and sexual identification. This interconnectedness could account for the apparent paradox that women intellectuals faced during this period. While participating in the propagation of a discourse of national identity, they both challenged and acquiesced to its patriarchal and paternalistic tenets, thus simultaneously advancing and limiting their options as social subjects. My argument is that discourses of national identification presuppose certain gender relations that have complicated ramifications for those they address as well as for those they marginalize. Women intellectuals are often excluded as the addressees of the texts of national identity that are almost invariably male, or imagined as generically male. Moreover, the women intellectuals of my study often do not—or cannot—escape the dominant practice of inscribing the subject as male and white. This is not just a question of adhering to correct grammatical usage. Women writers such as Margot Arce at times attempt to minimize their female self-representation, and the demotion of authority that accompanies it, by deliberately effacing a gendered presence. Nonetheless, they strategically stress gender when it helps their case. This is further facilitated by the protection that their identification with light-skin privileges affords them.

An overview of the two competing versions of feminism during the decade of the twenties shows the term "woman" to be a hotly contested one. The unequal access to power available to working-class feminism versus the elite suffragist movement may account for the way each group appropriates and redefines the category "woman" in relation to other social identities.[9] Intellectuals of the post-suffragist generation such as Margot Arce were poised to participate in the formulation of cultural nationalist discourses by continuously repositioning themselves within existing social categories and discourses. As a woman who aspired to be a protagonist in the intellectual life of her country, Arce left her mark in many areas during her lengthy career. In a fiercely androcentric milieu, she distinguished herself as a prolific essayist, a scholar, and a highly regarded professor of literature. She indefatigably struggled to escape the ancillary position to which women's intellectual work is often relegated.

The frankly male-dominated canon of the Latin American essay has led some critics to brand the production as a "masculine monologue."[10] The problem that this represents for the history of literature is complex. Literary tradition has valued the writing of masculine authorship and has overlooked the contributions of countless women writers. Canadian scholar Mary Louise Pratt points out that, in the case of the Spanish-American essay, the women authors that are included in the canon such as Clorinda Matto de Turner and Gabriela Mistral, for example, only represent a minuscule number among the copious production that still lies unvalued in newspapers, journals, and public and private archives. Pratt proposes that the essays of cultural identity be read in a dialectical relationship with what she calls the gender identity essay whose central theme is the fight for women's civil rights. A more representative reading of the diversity of the genre requires as fundamental that dialogic relationship that Pratt assumes between the essay of cultural identity and the gender essay. "The criollo identity essay," notes Pratt, " . . . must also be read as a response to the demands of women and other marginalized groups for full inclusion in society. . . . It requires reading the claims of the criollo essayists not as sui generis expressions of a particular imagination but as *contested* claims arising out of a profound and ongoing legitimation crisis."[11] It would be worth asking the reason for these omissions, and under what conditions the women writers that did form part of the corpus of our national literatures came to be a part of it. It is within this controversy that I situate Margot Arce's work.

Chapter 1 places the nationalist rhetoric of *Generación del Treinta* in the context of the great social changes that resulted after 1898. A review of the period reveals the underpinnings of a discourse of national identity aimed at curtailing the loss of hegemony suffered by the Creole elite in the wake of the American intervention. Colonial modernity was implanted on the island, giving rise to new social subjects and shifting class alliances. An examination of cultural and literary institutions shows how they provided the means by which class, racial, and gender interests were played out in the context of the United States's political and economic hegemony over the island. The Creole intelligentsia sought empowerment in the formulation of a rhetoric of national identity that recuperated, to a large extent, Spanish cultural models and elite sensibilities. In so doing, it failed to engage adequately Puerto Rico's multi-racial history. In addition, such a project did not envision women as co-authors of the discourse or as enfranchised historical agents. The chapter ends with an analysis of the concept of "roots" as interpreted by nationalist intellectual Margot Arce.

With increased educational opportunities after 1898, diverse sectors of women tried to promote their advancement and interests. Chapter 2 argues that the suffragist movement was fertile ground for the development of women's professional and intellectual institutions. Women's suffrage, as an expression of modernity, was often interpreted by the male elite as a potentially destabilizing force and a threat to Creole hegemony. White middle-class and elite *criollas* were confronted with the option of aligning themselves with the male elite in order to gain a measure of access to the power structure, ultimately strengthening the future cultural and political projects of this class. An examination of the work of suffragist and educator Mercedes Solá gives us clues about the articulation of Creole feminism. This chapter's aim is to explore the possibilities and limits of inter-class gender solidarity.

The projects of university-educated Creole women professionals are the subject of Chapter 3. To this end, it analyzes the *Revista de la Asociación de Mujeres Graduadas de la Universidad de Puerto Rico* (1938–1942), the publication that expressed and promoted their vision. This eclectic journal provided a vital space for women intellectuals and professionals in training to test their ideas and showcase their talents. Under the direction of Margot Arce, an ethos of service is coupled with a discourse of competence as a way to gain a voice into the affairs of the nation. As a university-based publication, the journal positioned itself vis-à-vis more male-oriented forums.

Chapter 4 presents responses to Pedreira's *Insularismo* by Tomás Blanco, Emilio S. Belaval, and Margot Arce. These writers contest and amplify his proposals via the *mestizaje*, *criollista*, or telluric road. Their dialogue illustrates the diversity of positions within the group. Blanco seeks to be more racially inclusive within the limitations of a discourse of white supremacy. Belaval wants to rally others around him to transform and amplify the Creole nationalist project. His discourse is in marked contrast to the pessimism of Pedreira. Arce, for her part, tries to apprehend her subject via the lyrical voice. The chapter examines both the aesthetic and the ideological import of their interventions.

The humorous short stories of Emilio S. Belaval, *Los cuentos de la Universidad*, are the topic of Chapter 5. Belaval's mordant comments on the new gender roles adopted by women in the late 1920s are interwoven with his valuation of the role of racial diversity in the island's culture. His is a decidedly masculine perspective on the conjunction of gender and race in this example of the Creole imaginary. The figure of the mulatto as symbol and social agent is of great importance in Belaval's collection. The stories provide us with the opportunity to inquire into the practice of the renewed *criollismo* expounded in Chapter 4. Formally and thematically, these stories challenge accepted notions and themes cultivated by his contemporaries. The chapter closes with an examination of complications surrounding the uses of irony.

Chapter 6 analyzes the work of María Cadilla de Martínez, a suffragist and mentor of many women intellectuals. The argument of this chapter is that as the author rewrites specific events and episodes of Puerto Rico's history, she becomes both interpreter and proponent of a cultural past devoid of racial conflicts. A number of anxieties surround questions of racial heterogeneity in the short stories of folklorist Cadilla de Martínez. She represents the Indian conquest and decimation by the Spaniards not as an act of war but as a story of devotion. Likewise, the slave past is reinterpreted from a Creole perspective that is unmindful of its responsibility in the history of enslavement. Cadilla de Martínez's literary treatment of the subaltern subjects of Puerto Rican nationalism reaffirmed a vision of national identity which includes, but only to subordinate, mixed-raced Puerto Ricans in national culture.

Chapters 7 and 8 interrogate the efforts of critic Margot Arce in the promotion and propagation of the *negrista* poetry of Palés Matos. Attention to Arce's role in the controversy over Palés Matos's poetry and her part in the canonization of his works allows us a better understanding of the interconnected nature of the race, class, and gender discourses that inform the *Generación del Treinta*'s ideas of national identity. While Pales's *negrista* poems might argue that blackness gives Puerto Rican culture its difference, making it part of the Caribbean, many readers resisted their Afro-Caribbean perspective and social implications. To grasp the enduring impact of this poetry, we need to take into account the history of its reception and the social context in which these poems were first received. Their meaning is inseparable from the ways in which they were read and later promoted.

Ultimately, Chapter 8 questions whether *negrismo* contributes to the stereotyping of people of African descent and the demotion of Afro-Puerto Ricans and their historical contributions.

Nationalism, perforce, calls into play race, class, culture, and gender in its service. All of these structures of domination are typically made invisible or subservient to the discourse. Yet my exploration of the discourse of national identity does not seek to minimize its primary oppositional role. The cultural nationalism of the *Generación del Treinta* was a valiant response to the presence of a new hegemonic power in the lives of Puerto Ricans after 1898, and as such its status as a statement of anti-colonial resistance cannot be understated. It was an effort to create a distance between the new colonizer and the colonized. In this aspect, the discourse of Puerto Rican national identity takes its place among other literatures of anti-imperialist resistance that, as Edward Said has said in a similar context, developed "quite consciously out of a desire to distance the native African, Indian, or Irish individual from the British, French or (later) American master."[12] He stresses that before this overt anti-imperialist literature can flourish, however, "there is a pressing need for the recovery of the land, which, because of the presence of the colonizing outsider, *is recoverable at first only through the imagination.*"[13] It is this recovery and, as I hope to show, the reimagining of the national space that—all while strategically responding to their own social, racial, and class interests—the members of the *Generación del Treinta* most poignantly tried to achieve.

CHAPTER 1

Nationalism Revisited: Deciphering the Creole Imaginary

The only way to vigorously counter our bewilderment is by projecting a cultural nationalism where we could all coincide in a consistent vision of Puerto Ricanness. (La única forma de contrarrestar vigorosamente nuestro desconcierto es mediante la proyección de un nacionalismo cultural donde podamos coincidir todos en una consistente visión de lo puertorriqueño.)
—Emilio S. Belaval, 1935

During the third decade of North American domination in Puerto Rico, the contradictions of colonial modernity had come to a head. Signs of social discontent were evident in the many marches and protests of striking workers, in the tracts and declarations of outspoken suffragists, and in the renewed militancy of nationalist activists. As a result of the implantation of colonial capitalism—with its concomitant imposition of descending social mobility for large numbers of citizens and the vertiginous socio-cultural changes it brought about—people from all walks of life experienced an ongoing sense of dislocation and uncertainty. Three decades of American domination had profoundly affected the survival strategies of the poor, who struggled with rapacious sugar corporations, loss of land, and hunger. Young Creole intellectuals, for their part, interpreted this societal and economic upheaval as a crisis of representation, demanding discursive remedies. Essayists and writers of the period channeled their class and political angst through a cultural nationalist ideology that cast their group as the defenders of the homeland's culture and "character." Perhaps no one better than Antonio S. Pedreira expressed this vision of Puerto Rican culture and the plight of the nation. In his 1934 book-length essay *Insularismo: ensayos de interpretación*, the university professor, essayist, and intellectual trailblazer offered a systematic analysis of the imperiled Puerto Rican national soul.[1] In short, Pedreira set out to map the parameters of the Puerto Rican "personality" in an effort to make sense of the country's many problems and to sketch some solutions. He found the causes of the contemporary crisis in the island's colonial history, geography, and racial composition. Accordingly, in Pedreira's view, both internal forces (the island's climate and geography, centuries of race mixing) and external forces (its geopolitical position for Spain and the United States) had thwarted national development. In spite of these obstacles, a difficult birth of the Puerto Rican way of being had taken place in the nineteenth century, the high point of the *hacienda* economy. The period saw the rise of a Creole liberal reformist tradition that would culminate in the granting of political autonomy to the island in 1897, a process abruptly interrupted by the U.S. invasion. Another obstacle was the lack of homogeneity amongst the island's populace. According to Pedreira: "In the depths of our population we can easily find a biological struggle of disintegrating and contrary forces that have retarded the definitive formation of our ways of being a people."[2] ("En el fondo de nuestra población encontraremos sin ardoroso empeño una pugna biológica de fuerzas disgregantes y contrarias que han retardado la formación definitiva de nuestros modos de pueblo.") In this narrative of origin, the assumption is that only a racially homogeneous group of people can give rise to the national body. Race mixing, viewed by Pedreira as miscegenation or the ill-advised merging of disparate and antagonistic human lines, was responsible for too much unsettling heterogeneity. For Pedreira, the island's brave Hispanic heritage was still very much alive, though encumbered by racial mixture with Indians and Africans who had left a legacy of irrationality and fear. Further, the Spanish-American War had traumatically ruptured the slow but ongoing process of spiritual differentiation and collective self-determination of the nation. Puerto Ricans, in spite of these difficulties, never gave up the sense of being Spanish. As the author explains, "In moments of historical transcendence that allow for the flowering in our gestures of the martial rhythms of European blood, we are capable of the highest enterprises and most glorious heroisms."[3] ("En instantes de trascendencia histórica en que afloran en nuestros gestos los ritmos marciales de la sangre europea, somos capaces de las más altas empresas y de los más esforzados heroísmos.") This noble Hispanic heritage was unfortunately commingled with many mismatched elements, evident in people's behaviors and ways of thinking, responsible for "our permanent docility." Pedreira listed as unhappy elements of the Puerto Rican character the fear of the foreign, the lack of resolve to act, and the pernicious presence of the black "soul" among the mulatto sectors of the population. As the essayist asserts, "But when the gesture is drenched in waves of African blood we remain unsure, as if stupefied by the sight of glass beads or frightened by the cinematic vision of witches and ghosts."[4] ("Pero cuando el gesto viene empapado de oleadas de sangre africana quedamos indecisos, como embobados ante las cuentas de colores o amedrentados ante la visión cinemática de brujas y fantasmas.") For the author, blackness is a deeply troubling presence both in the text and in social life. Examination of the images used by Pedreira is quite revealing of the placement of people of African descent in this national narrative. The drowning metaphor suggests both the fear and powerlessness of being overcome by a menacing black presence. Yet, such a presence is subsequently mastered by deriding it as childishly primitive.

For Pedreira, the racial heterogeneity of Puerto Ricans interrupts the discourse of *one race, one language, one nation* so dear to nationalist thought. His acceptance of the myth of a profound biological antagonism between races can only lead him to despair as he looks to provide essentialist explanations for historical questions. Subscribing to notions of racial purity, Pedreira declares that "the Spanish element lays the foundation of our people and merges with the other races. Out of this *fusion* comes our *confusion.*"[5] ("El elemento español funda nuestro pueblo y se funde con las demás razas. De esta *fusión* parte nuestra *con-fusión.*") One wonders if there is not a certain amount of frustration on the author's part at the Spanish founding fathers' acts of fusion with other races, given the text's almost impossible mission of finding continuity and purity in an environment of change and hybridity. Pedreira is intent on portraying the vast majority of Puerto Ricans as descendents of purportedly pure Spaniards who had adapted to the rigors of the tropical climate, accounting for the upper classes and the mass of the peasantry. Yet Pedreira's characterization of the peasant, or *jíbaro*, is double-edged. On one hand, he insists on portraying the *jíbaro* as invariably male, white, generous, cordial, fun loving, astute—all desirable traits for him. The peasant is to be pitied as a victim of urban inequities and black competition in the coastal regions. Nonetheless, like most intellectuals of his generation, Pedreira rebukes common folk for their supposed apathy and faintheartedness when it comes to the nation-building projects. But the docility of poor and working-class people is more a projection than a reality, given the very obvious acts of personal protest and social "disorder," class-based militancy, and democratic aspirations that the colonial administration tried to discipline out of existence and that the Creoles feared and condemned. There is a contradiction here. Conceptualizing the *jíbaro* mainly as a "docile peasant" allows the author to attempt to contain this group's other identity as "displaced and unruly agricultural proletariat." As for inclusion in the national body, however, our author argues for the unquestioned acceptance of the supposedly racially pure mountain *jíbaro*, and disdainfully relegates the uppity population of people of African descent, *grifos parejeros*, and resentful mulatto artisans to marginality.[6] For Pedreira the new colonial reality of his times was one of great bafflement, of push-and-pull between Puerto Rico's enduring Spanish and Creole heritage and the new North American way of life. His examination of the successes and shortcomings of the nation-building projects ends with an appeal to other young intellectuals to add their efforts to his, so as to provide guidance to a bewildered country.

And respond they did. Pedreira's formulations held enormous sway with the Puerto Rican intelligentsia of his time. *Insularismo* helped to set the dimensions of the intellectual dialogues among Creoles, becoming an obligatory reference point for the writers of his generation as well as for later expressions of Puerto Rican cultural nationalism. His most noted interlocutors were all fellow members of the prestigious *Ateneo Puertorriqueño,* including Tomás Blanco, Emilio S. Belaval, Margot Arce, and Luis Palés Matos, to name just four. I will examine their responses in later chapters. First we must place Pedreira and his cohort in a historical context and direct our attention to the intellectual field that nurtured their cultural nationalist dialogues.

Rethinking the Intellectual Field: A Historical Perspective on National Identity

> *The image that we have of Puerto Ricans is white; thus, to identify whites we simply hear people use "Puerto Rican," and to identity blacks we hear "black Puerto Rican." But this justifies nothing, merely describing one more injustice: portraying all Puerto Ricans as white when they are of all hues imaginable. (La imagen que tenemos del puertorriqueño es blanca, de ahí que para identificar al blanco se escuche llana y simplemente "puertorriqueño" y para identificar al negro, "negro puertorriqueño." Pero esto no justifica nada, meramente describe una injusticia más: hacer blanca la imagen para todos los puertorriqueños, habiéndolos de todos los matices imaginables.)*
>
> —Isabelo Zenón Cruz, 1974

During the 1970s a new understanding of Puerto Rican culture and social history came to replace the widely accepted view that had been put in place by the intellectuals of the 1930s. Aided by the critical lens of Marxist theory, social historians and literary critics would reexamine the class, racial, and political interests and biases that informed the discourse of national identity as construed and popularized by the Puerto Rican intelligentsia during the previous four decades.[7] This shift in critical perspective provided new answers to old questions, also pointing the way to research in previously unexplored areas. The pathbreaking studies of sociologist Ángel G. Quintero

Rivera on the Puerto Rican working class in the first half of the twentieth century were directed at uncovering a previously obscured "other face of history." Quintero Rivera argued that the discourse of national identity was the creation of the displaced descendents of the *hacendado* class and that, as such, it was a class-based defensive strategy. One of the effects of the United States's intervention in Puerto Rico was to interrupt the historical development of the planter class on its way to social and political ascendancy. For these children of generations of landed gentry, the land—and by extension, national territory and the very nation—had enormous symbolic importance. Their forebears had derived their power and prestige from land ownership and agrarian exploitation during Spanish colonial times. Dispossessed of their inheritance by the 1930s, the new generation would strive to recuperate their hegemonic potential in the professional and intellectual arenas, pressuring and negotiating with North American colonial institutions for political control.[8] The emerging artisan/working class, for its part, contested the claims of elite cultural nationalism with political and economic demands of its own, and did not necessarily see political independence for the island as a guarantor of democratic social progress. Moreover, the proletariat, together with its intellectuals, would actively contest what Quintero Rivera called the "culture of deference and paternalism" that had developed around the *hacienda.* They organized labor strikes and political groups, and created their own press, literature, and social clubs, which sought to popularize alternatives to the elite's political proposals. Gender relations and sexuality also became subject to controversy, as the emergence of working-class feminism amply attests.

The socially conservative cultural and political nationalism that developed among the descendents of the *hacendado* class, plus small landholders and the petite bourgeoisie who identified with it, found expression in many of the cultural and literary works produced by this intelligentsia in the 1930s, 1940s, 1950s, and even beyond.[9] Literary critic Juan Flores has studied the intertextual and ideological relationship between *Insularismo,* José Ortega y Gasset's influential *The Rebellion of the Masses,* José Enrique Rodo's Latin American classic *Ariel,* and Oswald Spengler's trend-setting *The Decline of the West.* In his still-unsurpassed study Flores shows that these texts share similar essentialist and static notions of culture, and strong biases against working-class empowerment. Theirs is a vision of the intellectual as hero and rightful interpreter and leader of the national destiny, conceived of in narrow class terms. Flores's rigorous critique of the ideological tenets of Pedreira's work has led him to conclude that *Insularismo* should be read as a (white) middle-class utopia. The limited social and intellectual vision of Pedreira corresponds to the political and economic travails of the colonized bourgeoisie and petty bourgeoisie seeking to assert themselves.[10] In addition, Flores calls into question *Insularismo*'s sweeping appeals to "Spanishness" as a buttress to claims of cultural belonging. Perhaps unaware of the fascist slant that racial and geographic deterministic theories were taking in Europe, Pedreira chose to stress the feudal and patrimonial legacy of the old colonizing power with the concomitant myths of its civilizing mission. Flores argues that such a choice disregarded the progressive and revolutionary tradition of modern Spain and the Spanish Civil War struggle, an important political and cultural referent all over Latin America at the time.[11]

The critical clarity that Marxist analysis brought to the class dimensions of national identity is further enriched by studies that explicitly question discourses of race in Puerto Rican culture and scholarship. Whereas Pedreira was enshrined in previous decades as a disinterested critic of the Puerto Rican character, it is more accurate to see his works, and most of the literature produced by his contemporaries, as a deeply felt Creole vision of a nation divided by race. Arguing that a profound anti-black racism still informs the daily experience of all Puerto Ricans, critic Isabelo Zenón Cruz's 1974 study of Puerto Rican culture examines language usage, popular culture, and literary works to support his argument that Puerto Ricans of African descent have been estranged from the discourse of Puerto Ricanness and from the national imaginary.[12] As the *Generación del Treinta* tenaciously held to the view of the essential Spanishness of Puerto Rico, their works contributed to the caricature and effacement of black Puerto Ricans. In Zenón Cruz's examination, power relations are the key to deciphering the social status ascribed to those marked as black and as white on the island. One fundamental contribution by Zenón Cruz was to bring to Puerto Rican audiences a sustained application of the revolutionary ideas of Frantz Fanon and Albert Memmi about the psychological effects of colonialism for those who live in colonized societies. Following Fanon, he rejects the theory of the "racial soul" and the "collective unconscious" utilized by white supremacist literature to advance ideas about the atavistic backwardness of peoples of African descent. Zenón Cruz's ambitious work offers readers a roadmap to understand the history of Puerto Rico from the perspective of Afro-Puerto Ricans, bringing to the fore the many colonial laws and edicts that enforced slavery and—most importantly—policed free blacks and mulattos for over 370 years on the island. His multi-facetted analysis convincingly traces the development of the devaluation of blackness in literary and historical discourses produced by the Creole intelligentsia during the nineteenth and the twentieth century.

Zenón Cruz's bold critical intervention regarding the complex question of the past and present racial divisions of Puerto Rican society convulsed the Puerto Rican intelligentsia when his two-volume study was published. Nonetheless, many have yet to engage its proposals with the seriousness that they continue to deserve. One of the intellectuals to do so was writer and literary critic José Luis González. In a germinal essay on literature and national identity, González further elaborated the idea that the literature produced in the first half of the twentieth century was strongly motivated by Creole nostalgia. Their project was to reconnect with a past in which the *criollo* elite held a quasi-hegemonic control over the class and racial societal structures.[13] Whereas, during the nineteenth century, the intellectuals who gave voice to the progressive and liberal sector of the elite passed harsh judgment on the peasantry and the conditions on the island, their descendents' material and psychological loss led to an obsessive tellurianism and idealization of the Spanish/Creole colonial past. In marked contrast to the mythical and conservative representations of the writers of the *Generación del Treinta*, nineteenth-century intellectuals did not see their country, and its social reality, as a paradise lost. Many, after all, had to labor under the vigilant eye of a Spanish colonial system that was not interested in furthering the freedom of Creoles in the nineteenth, or any other, century.

Puerto Rico's culture during the first three hundred years of Spanish rule could be characterized as heavily Afro-Caribbean, according to González. An 1812 census stated that 93,623 "whites" and 89,391 blacks and mulattos were living on the island. Of the non-whites, already 58,983 were mulattos, 12,872 were blacks. The official slave population was 17,536. It should be stressed, however, that racial identification is not totally dependable, since we can infer that social pressures to pass as white, once a certain degree of phenotypic traits are present, were the norm. Fearing a repetition of the Haitian slave revolution, the Spanish crown made a concerted effort to augment the number of whites on the island.[14] Of course, the Spanish were also seeking to capitalize on the disarray of the sugar industry that had resulted from the French defeat in Haiti. Be that as it may, the 1815 *Real Cédula de Gracias*, and other similar provisions, set a deliberate "whitening" process in motion. This decree permitted refugees of the Spanish-American Wars of Independence and numerous other Europeans (French, Dutch, Irish) to settle on the island, predominantly in the coastal regions. Also incorporated into the elite, but not really seeing themselves as Puerto Ricans, were the "uncultured, conservative, and arrogant" immigrants from Corsica, Catalonia, and Mallorca who settled in the central mountainous regions.[15] The foreign entrepreneurs who settled on the island as a result of the relaxation of Spanish immigration and trade policies had a great impact on the Puerto Rican elite. They aimed at establishing trade relations with other markets in Europe as well as with the United States. This new economic activity helped foster among the island *criollos* a consciousness of the need to control foreign trade, which was in the hands of the colonial bureaucracy. But the *Real Cédula*, as Zenón Cruz clarifies, "officially fomented prejudice against (blacks) by adjudicating land without equity, imposing tributes on blacks that it did not impose on whites, and above all, stimulating the trade in black and mulatto slaves by allowing for their tax-free importation."[16] Moreover,

Miriam Jiménez Román points out, it was not until 1860 that "whites" would feature as 51.5 percent of the total population, putting in question the commonly accepted numerical significance of the European immigration to the island and the predominance of the "white" population.[17]

In essence, Zenón Cruz and González challenge the claims that equate Puerto Rican history with the concerns of *hacendados*, their descendents, and a supposedly white peasantry. What emerges from their proposals is a much more nuanced idea of the ideological divisions among the pre-1898 Puerto Rican/Spanish elite, and between this class and the rest of the population. The mercantile and agrarian elite did not, in all probability, harbor the nationalist sentiments that the later generations ascribed to them. As González explains, "Still at the end of the century, the Mallorcan coffee *hacendados* spoke Mallorcan amongst themselves and only used Spanish to address their Puerto Rican peons."[18] Loyal to the colonial regime, these nineteenth-century white immigrants espoused a Eurocentric and seigniorial worldview. The literature and thought they produced were no match for the liberal culture generated by the coastal professionals represented by Manuel Alonso, Alejandro Tapia y Rivera, Salvador Brau, Manuel Zeno Gandía, and Eugenio María de Hostos, whose progressive tendencies are best exemplified in their literature and in the cultural institutions they developed. The elite also had among its ranks revolutionaries such as Ramón Emeterio Betances and Pachín Marín, although they were a minority.[19] A number of these intellectuals were mulattos and blacks, as in the case of Betances, and later, Sotero Figueroa and José Celso Barbosa.

Representatives of the liberal intelligentsia within the *hacendado* class physician Manuel Zeno Gandía and sociologist Salvador Brau were not shy about portraying the *jíbaro* and the peasant world as "an ailing world" much in need of modernization. In sum, as part of a class on the rise in the nineteenth century, the forward-looking coastal professional elite was interested, to a certain extent, in modernizing Puerto Rican society.[20] It was only after 1898, when the landed gentry's social and cultural hegemony came under attack by colonial capitalism, as we have seen above, that, in the main, this class would become defensive and conservative. For his part, Quintero Rivera also stresses that the national bourgeoisie-in-the-making was a "very contradictory seigniorial class" whose power was based on exporting goods produced by pre-capitalist forms of exploitation to the world capitalist market.[21] By 1898, *criollo* patricians had increasingly wrested control from the hands of the Spanish colonial state and positioned themselves as the putative rulers of a racially heterogeneous people.

When the United States began its colonial ventures in Puerto Rico, a fundamental restructuring of Puerto Rico's economy and society was set in motion. The changes that gave rise to agricultural capitalism had a tremendous impact on both the working classes and the *hacendado* bourgeoisie.[22]

At first, the large landowners reacted positively to what they understood to be a beneficial change of colonial metropolis and an opportunity of having a share of the North American market for their coffee. The policies of the United States, however, were directed toward breaking the hegemony of the *hacendados.* These measures included limiting male suffrage, controlling customs and the levying of tariffs, and determining the value of currency conversion. In addition, the U.S. Congress reserved the power to veto any Puerto Rican legislation and to decide what federal legislation would be applicable to the island.[23] Washington designated a governor who had the power to make judiciary appointments. In short, these measures were meant to support huge corporate investments in land and sugar production. Together with these concrete policies, the new colonizers brought with them a host of white supremacist attitudes that were projected onto the Puerto Rican population. A United States army Brigadier General had this to say about the people of the new colony: "About one-sixth of the people of Porto Rico *[sic]* are educated and of Spanish blood, of the rest perhaps one-half can be molded by a firm hand into something approaching decency; but the remainder are . . . ignorant, filthy, untruthful, lazy, treacherous, murderous, brutal, and black."[24] This disparaging appraisal set the tone of racial relations that would characterize North American rule.

North American sugar interests controlled 62 percent of the sugar cane-producing land by 1910. Coffee production dropped so rapidly that by 1930 it amounted to less than 1 percent of island exports.[25] The *hacendado* class was forced to assume a defensive posture. There was, nevertheless, a sector of this class that was able to reposition itself as sugar investors (an anti-national bourgeoisie), or as importers of U.S. goods, which by the mid-1920s already accounted for 90 percent of Puerto Rican imports.[26] Aside from these economic and political measures, others aimed at debilitating the cultural hegemony of the *hacendado* class were promulgated by the colonial government: the establishment of a public education system and the growth of Protestant proselytizing. These two worked hand in glove, generating individualistic values, new attitudes toward manual labor, substitution of the minister for the *hacendado,* and some support for women's independence.[27]

The advent of agro-capitalism gave rise to an agricultural proletariat that developed a concept of nationhood markedly different from the one promulgated by the *hacendado*s. During the last decade of the nineteenth century, the artisans of the urban centers—in the main, mulattos and blacks—began to develop a distinctly radical consciousness, identifying more with an international proletariat than with the Puerto Rican elite. According to Quintero Rivera, "Their self-definition in terms of production—workers, among many around the world—their rejection of the life of the *hacienda,* and an openness to their daily experiences, fostered a strong sense of internationalism within the artisan world; a sense they incorporated in their struggles and traditions."[28] The workers organized the *Federación Libre de Trabajadores* (later affiliated with the Socialist Party), which advanced a universal and abstract concept of the fatherland: "The fatherland of man is the universe; his strength is solidarity and human and social fraternity."[29] ("La patria del hombre es el universo; su fuerza la solidaridad y la fraternidad social y humana.") They understood elite patriotism as a farce destined to perpetuate the workers' oppression.

As the proletariatization of the artisans and peasants in the sugar fields and tobacco factories accelerated, a more concrete conception of the "socialist fatherland" was advanced in direct challenge to the *hacendado* concept of the paternalistic "great Puerto Rican family."[30] The Socialist Party was committed to social changes that conflicted with the interests of the *hacendado* class whom it perceived as its most immediate enemy.[31] Yet we must not forget that workers' struggles for social justice that characterize the turbulent years of the sugar monopolies were a response to the North American economic policies directly aimed at transforming peasants and artisans into a malleable wage-dependent work force. Kelvin A. Santiago-Valles has studied the phenomenon of social "disorder" within the new colonial capitalist order imposed after 1898. He persuasively argues that the increasing labeling of the poor's conduct as illegal and immoral by those in power went hand in hand with the brutal coercion aimed at producing a surplus army of workers for the sugar and other U.S. economic monopolies between 1898 and 1947.[32] Early manifestations of this "disorder" were the spontaneous groups of peasants that, as the American troops were taking possession of the island, rose to avenge the ills suffered at the hands of *hacendados*.

Another such development occurring from 1900 to 1904 was the phenomenon known as the Republican mobs, or *Turbas Republicanas*. These mobs constituted an organized response to Creole *hacendado*'s political power in San Juan and other cities. Strategically using the modernizing citizenship-rights discourse of the United States's colonial power, and in alliance with a small group of sympathizers mainly from the professional elite, the artisan and working-class folk who comprised the "Republican rabble" struck fear in the Creole opposition during the earliest years of colonial domination. The socio-racial composition of the *Turbas* is instructive in an evaluation of the ways in which the U.S. domination affected previous understandings of white supremacy.[33] Many of those who composed the *Turbas* or *Comité para la Defensa del Partido Republicano* (Committee for the Defense of the Republican Party) were tobacco artisans and their leaders. They had the protection of the prominent Afro-Puerto Rican physician José Celso Barbosa, a promoter of mutualism among the racially mixed urban artisan class. The "Republican rabble" included displaced rural folk, the poor and generally unemployed, and permanent or occasional municipal workers, all of whom congregated in the streets of Old San Juan.[34] Also part of this group were poor, Puerto Rican whites who by virtue of their class position, sympathies, or family ties, cast their lot with this racially heterogeneous, urban proletariat that benefited, in some measure, from the social reordering taking place after 1898. As historian Mariano Negrón Portillo explains, the political events sponsored by the members of the *Turbas* were festive affairs with music, featuring marchers who carried provocative signs and addressed the opposition with derogatory and irreverent language. Often draped in the American flag when they paraded, they acted against their enemies with the help or complicity of the municipal police. The municipal government of San Juan, in the hands of the Republican Party, provided many members of the group with employment. In their heyday, the *Turbas* had felt empowered enough to dress up a marcher as *hacendado* politician Muñoz Rivera in the guise of a transvestite or *loca* and parade in the streets of San Juan in a carnivalesque spectacle that poked fun at the respected politician. The *Turbas* were also active in the city of Ponce, where they behaved in similar fashion. These incidents reveal not only irreverence toward this patrician figure, considered by the group to be a class enemy, but also unwittingly allow us to glimpse the heterosexist currency that underscores their harassment.[35] Furthermore, given that heteronormativity necessitates the presence of a homosocial/erotic other, this episode is fertile with clues that could help to map the historical presence of homosexualities on the island. Demoting the masculinity and honor of the noted patrician was only one form of assault. Continued attacks on Muñoz Rivera, as Negrón Portillo reports, prompted the leader of the party of the *hacendados* to move to the United States for a few years.

A reformist-democratic ideology and the historical experiences of the artisan sector influenced the ideology of the *Turbas.* They also adopted the term *pueblo,* the people, to refer to themselves, signaling a form of social presence that was antagonistic to the traditional Creole elite. Together with the provocative spectacles and marches arranged by the group, the *Turbas* also vandalized the property and physically harassed members of the opposition party, the *Federales,* who would later become the *Partido Unión.* Additional targets of their attacks were the members of the trade unionist *Federación Libre de Trabajadores,* and their leader Santiago Iglesias Pantín.[36]

By the late 1920s, two variants of nationalism would arise as one of the responses to imperialist capitalism. The militant version was headed by Pedro Albizu Campos, and the pragmatic/cultural (emotionally cathartic) nationalism was led by Luis Muñoz Marín.[37] These renditions responded to two distinct class positions in the waning *hacienda* world, but shared similar visions of the Spanishness of Puerto Rican culture. Militant nationalism was the desperate struggle of the small independent farmers and their impoverished descendents. They partook of the culture of the *hacendado* class and launched a losing battle for their survival as a class of independent producers. As their leader Albizu Campos saw it, independence was necessary to make Puerto Rico a nation of small landholders again.[38] The other nationalism, the cultural/pragmatic version, was the product of the descendents of the *hacendado* class led by the radical youth that had left *the Partido Liberal.* It is this group that would spearhead the populist movement of the 1940s. As a nascent social class made up of the new professional sector, they founded the *Partido Popular Democrático* (PPD) in 1938. Luis Muñoz Marín and its other leaders rallied supporters around a Manichean conception of the world.[39] In their political campaigns, those who comprised "the people" were pitted against "the enemies of the people": the huge sugar interests and their local allies. In populism, Quintero Rivera explains, "all classes must be represented in a government that must be directed, however, by a class that is not configured in terms of economic sectors or position in the productive structure, but in terms of governmental action that represents the people: a political or State class."[40]

Broadly speaking, the PPD would appeal to those sectors of Puerto Rican society who demanded land reform, social justice, and national independence as a solution to the colonial problem. The middle and professional sectors as well as the weak agrarian bourgeoisie, actual and ideological heirs of the *hacendado* class, organized the party that became an ample mass movement. Significantly, in their struggle for hegemony, the PPD enlisted and updated the old nineteenth-century idea of the "great Puerto Rican family." Their slogan "*pan, tierra, libertad*" (bread, land, freedom) expressed the aspirations of the great masses of the dispossesed who would give the party its electoral sweeps for three decades. The new trade movement *Confederación General de Trabajadores* (CGT) would provide trade union support within the coalition. The PPD were "New Dealers" who instituted a number of reforms—with the support of the United States. Politically and economically the projects of the populist coalition received the backing of North American capital. Among some of these reforms we find the creation of a board of minimum wage, the Land Authority, the Water and Sewer Authorities, the approval of 12-month salaries for school teachers, laws for the protection of working mothers, the Communications Authority, and the Bureau and Bank for Economic Development *(Fomento).*[41]

At the height of the economic and political crisis of the thirties, the *political* discourse of the descendents of the displaced landowning class sought to establish its legitimacy and to pacify the profound social antagonisms that polarized the island. In their campaigns, rallies, and radio broadcasts, Muñoz Marín and Vicente Géigel Polanco stressed that social harmony was possible under the aegis of the "defenders of the people" working against the voracity of the sugar interests.[42] With some modifications, many of the understandings that cultural nationalists put in place would come to inform the projects of the populist coalition. Poised to take control of the (colonial) state, the leaders of the populist coalition would spearhead the reorientation of the political and economic spheres, incorporating the cultural models of the nation that the *Generación del Treinta*'s essayists developed during the preceding decade. As María Elena Rodríguez Castro shows, the proposals of the 1940 forum of the *Ateneo, Problemas de la Cultura en Puerto Rico: Foro del Ateneo Puertorriqueño, 1940*, were a declaration of the maturity of the Creole elite who had been in disarray after 1898. By the beginning of the new decade, the role of the intellectual, epitomized by the late Pedreira and by Tomás Blanco, had become differentiated from that of men of state Luis Muñoz Marín and Vicente Géigel Polanco. As the elite leaders of the populist coalition, they set in place discourses about the "people" that featured the poor as historical protagonists in a new alliance of classes. The technical and intellectual elite join, explains Rodríguez Castro, "The plan of 'national reconstruction,' authored by the state, found in the plan of 'moral regeneration' of the intellectuals, the ideological support it needed for its legitimacy."[43] Additionally, meanings shifted around concepts such as culture and democracy, and by 1940 they were no longer seen as antithetical, according to Rodríguez Castro. This new technical governing elite incorporated the cultural proposals of the earlier decade with some modifications. This will be most salient in the case of the future (Puerto Rican) University Chancellor, Jaime Benítez. Under his direction the university expanded and modernized. He distanced himself from the more political tenets of *criollismo* and cultural nationalism and moved toward a "universalistic" cultural vision. Yet at the same time, some sectors of the university became bastions of cultural nationalism.[44]

When, a decade later in 1952, the populist coalition was formally installed as the *Estado Libre Asociado* (Commonwealth), they codified the vision of Puerto Rico's racial heterogeneity hashed out by the debates of the 1930s. The emblem of the *Partido Popular Democrático* features the silhouette of a peasant man wearing the *pava*, a large-brimmed straw hat. This was a necessary part of populism's symbolic appropriation, given the history of social and race relations on the island and the contradictory forces that informed this history after 1898. In fact, it becomes impossible to analyze the symbolism surrounding the *jíbaro* as a national-popular myth outside a discussion of race. Race mixing, the practice of social "whitening," and the dynamic socio-racial hierarchies specific to the island are not mere asides, but are fundamental to an understanding of Puerto Rican culture. Racism is an ideology and a practice that forms habits of being and modes of identification by the self and others, and limits or enhances life opportunities for those people marked and unmarked by it.[45] Rather than trying to define the culture as an aggregate of fixed components, as was done in the 1930s, detailed studies of the peasantry and its material circumstances have helped to reconceptualize the figure of the *jíbaro* and its attendant racial and other myths.[46] Far from being a pure descendent of Spanish settlers, the *jíbaro* gradually evolved out of brutal processes of conquest, colonization, enslavement, and ongoing flights away from the Spanish authorities. Flight, or *cimarronaje*, together with a loose and generalized process of retrenchment away from the Spanish authorities, encouraged the mixing of different cultural groups. What, by the nineteenth century, were described by Creole intellectuals as the *jíbaros* were the descendents of an amalgam of peoples who had resisted, suffered, and negotiated forced labor, decimation, and religious and social persecution. This group included the sparse population of the conquered Taino Indians, freed or runaway Africans, and racially or socially suspect Spanish soldiers who, more likely than not, were Moorish *conversos* and Jewish *marranos* forced to accept Catholicism after the final defeat of the Spanish Moors in the fifteenth century.[47] In order to preserve their freedom from the Spanish colonial authority's intrusions, these at-times seminomadic groups living in sparsely populated areas had to develop dissemblance strategies, adhering nominally to "Spanish" norms of behavior. In the context of the strict racial hierarchy of power enforced by the Colonial regime, race mixing was from the beginning a well-established and well-documented reality, where whiteness was valued over blackness. Foreign travelers, the Catholic Church, and the crown all attest to its enduring reality.[48] Although for most of the island's history people of African descent—classified by the crown as *pardos* or mulattos—comprised the majority of the island's population, countless court records and crown documents also make it very clear that mixed-raced people could neither be too socially aggressive nor penetrate too blatantly the higher echelons of society.[49] Given the association of blackness with slavery, to be a person of African descent meant that one had had enslaved ancestors. For example, in the late eighteenth century, Fray Iñigo Abbad y Lasierra reports in the memoir of his visit to the island that "there is nothing more affronting on this island than to be black or to descend from them. A white insults any of them with impunity with the most debasing expressions; some masters treat them with shameful rigor and enjoy raising their tyrant's staff, the result of which is infidelity, desertion, and suicide."[50] As we see, the colonial society developed under Spain was deeply divided by class and racial identification.

Historian Lilian Guerra proposes that the *jibarista* writings (writings about *jíbaros*) of the first half of the twentieth century were an attempt by the elite to incorporate certain aspects of peasant identity into the white *criollos'* concept of self. By construing the *jíbaro* as a passive and enduring white descendent of Spaniards, elite discourses could simultaneously find racial kinship with the peasantry and at once portray this social subject as idle, compliant, and in need of management. For Guerra, elite intellectuals' whitening of the working classes in their *jibarista* discourse should be seen as an anxiety-ridden response to the new racial hierarchies imposed in Puerto Rico by the North American colonial machine.[51] In this I concur. Moreover, as Guerra shows in her study of the J. Alden Mason collection of Puerto Rican folklore, subaltern conceptions of self and community, while contesting the class valuations of elite intellectuals, participate in the othering of blackness within their communities. And although the compilation Guerra studies contains certain examples of Afro-Puerto Rican pride and affirmation as well as some feminine responses to patriarchal rule, we need a more complete assessment of how Afro-Puerto Ricans constructed a sense of identity and negotiated racist assaults under both Spanish and U.S. colonial rule.

Historical divisions within the laboring classes caused conflicts as these groups increasingly coalesced in search of work in the cities and sugar regions. As Santiago-Valles explains, "A number of nineteenth-century cultural mappings, together with their respective socioeconomic foundations (particularly the incidence of slavery), still weighed heavily on the 'native' laboring classes during the first half of the twentieth century."[52] The majority of the population was composed of "whites" and mulattos from peasant backgrounds; they were less educated than their urban counterparts; they were historically landless or recently dispossessed small landowners, though attached to the coffee *hacienda*s. Artisans and urban coastal laborers, who were in the main blacks and mulattos, were generally more educated, and more dependent on wage labor than peasants. "After the U.S. invasion and however contradictorily," writes Santiago-Valles, "the mostly white and mulatto peasantry tended to continue appropriating the anti-artisan, anti-urban, and anti-coastal narratives of the large landowners."[53] Lilian Guerra also reports on the incorporation of landowner-sanctioned racial discourses in the peasant oraliture she examines. While in most of the folktales she studies the "Juan Bobo" (Juan the fool) or other *jíbaro* characters, using their wits, prevail over the injustices of the rich, a number of tales do reflect the possibility of alliances with paternalistic landowners. Still others express antiblack (and antiwomen) prejudices as a way of affirming class cohesion.[54]

The idea that Puerto Rico had an uncomplicated, homogeneous cultural trajectory has been effectively deconstructed by our discussion of the class and racial interests behind the 1930s discourse of national identity. These critical insights, however, need to be further reinterpreted through the lens of a feminist analysis that takes into consideration the tremendous changes that convulsed the *hacendado* gender system after 1898.

A Change in Women's Status after 1898: Working-Class and Middle-Class Feminism

The development of dependent capitalism on the island would propel an unprecedented number of women into the paid work force. According to the 1899 census some 47,701 women of all ages were engaged in salaried work. The majority were employed in domestic situations mainly as maids and laundresses (37,404), and only a small number (6,383) had jobs in manufacturing.[55] The percentage of women in paid occupations, such as the tobacco, garment, and cottage needlepoint industries, went from a low 9.9 percent in 1899 to 26.1 percent in 1930, representing a dramatic increase for an agrarian economy.[56] This rapid growth had important consequences in the development of a working-class ideology. It fostered the creation of both an agrarian and urban proletariat that would be organized around ideas of class solidarity and struggle.[57] For female workers, however, a feminist ideology with the consequent demand for women's rights became an integral part of their class consciousness. Women labor organizers and workers were adamant in their demands for their rights as workers and as women in open defiance of traditional roles and norms. Among the best known is Luisa Capetillo, who was a paid reader for tobacco workers, and who wrote for many trade-unionist publications. Strongly influenced by the international anarchist and suffragist movements, Capetillo wrote, lectured, and organized both male and female workers around issues of labor rights, education, equal opportunity, and health care.[58] Capetillo thought of her body as something she must have control over; she was a vegetarian, spiritualist, did Swedish gymnastics every day, and recommended that women bathe naked. In her plays, essays, and through her daily praxis she spearheaded the discussions on a new morality and new social mores, and radically criticized the institution of marriage.[59] Historian Eileen Suárez Findlay places Capetillo's emancipatory ideas in the context of the male-dominated labor movement and the working-class and Creole sexual politics that were a part of her daily experiences. As Suárez Findley notes, "Her play *Influencias de las ideas modernas* ends with a woman worker exhorting women to reject the institution of marriage, as a crowd of workers shouts: 'Long live free, loving unions! An end to exploitation! An end to the reign of the wage!'"[60] Capetillo's transgressive choices bore a high personal cost. She lost her children and was a "proscribed woman." Her biographer Norma Valle Ferrer reports that, though respected by many, Capetillo was at times harassed by fellow labor organizers who demanded sexual favors on account of her ideas about free love. Additionally, bourgeois women shunned her presence by hiding from sight when she was near.[61] Capetillo's efforts on behalf of worker's education incorporated practices very organic to the situation of the laboring class. Her writings, speeches, plays, and her early work as a reader in tobacco factories had the deeply educational function of consciousness raising. This was not learning at the service of amassing academic cultural capital, but education as a practice of freedom.

Education after 1898 became almost synonymous with change and opportunity for women. The new colonial school system would bring into play ever increasing numbers of women for the first time, affecting the balance of the *hacendado* gender system in significant ways. The public education system implemented on the island by the American colonial government was the source of great controversy. Its stated goal was to make "profitable citizens" out of Puerto Ricans. According to this logic, if Puerto Ricans were to be taught the "American Way," they had to learn to speak English. The new agricultural monopolies needed to transform laborers with a pre-capitalist ideology into workers who would serve the larger development of capitalist imperialism. Two areas were targeted: elementary education for the majority of the school-age population, and the technical training of professional cadres. Work in the capitalist sugar plantation required more intensive use of machinery and needed a labor force that would follow directions and function in an orderly and systematic way. The new economy also needed a professional faction trained in accounting, agronomy, engineering, law, and public and private administration. Intermediate education was de-emphasized because this would interfere with the state's ability to provide a large and stable young work force on demand.[62]

The concomitant stratification of the educational system resulting from the North American colonial venture affected working-class women and middle- and upper-class women in distinct ways. In the public school system co-education became the norm, putting an end to the rigid separation of the sexes previously mandated by the Spanish educational system. This did not mean that education for both sexes was absolutely equal, or that all children received the same education. Home economics and courses of needlepoint for girls became important components of the curriculum. "The growth of home economics," Yamila Azize explains, "was directed at an organized development of the traditional training that women had received in Puerto Rico."[63] World War I also favored the development of the needlepoint and garment industry by creating a huge demand for these goods in the States. Various U.S. corporations established sewing and needlepoint schools on the island. The 1920s would see the results of these experiments with the tremendous boom in the garment industry, coupled with the horrible exploitation of garment and needlepoint industry workers.[64] Middle-class women, for their part, entered the labor force as nurses, secretaries, or teachers.[65]

With the availability of higher education for upper- and middle-class women, there was an increased female presence in the work force, which made itself felt in the establishment of cultural and political organizations and in the struggles of the suffragist movement. Yamila Azize's study of women's suffrage in Puerto Rico carefully traces two parallel, and often antagonistic, movements: the working-class women's movement, which considered female suffrage together with its other objectives; and the middle-class and elite feminist movement, which concentrated efforts on suffrage exclusively for literate women.[66] Teachers became the vanguard of the bourgeois suffragist movement. Between 1903 and 1923, 74 percent of the graduates of the Teacher's College of the University of Puerto Rico were women. This increased visibility was resisted by the male intelligentsia, who often chose to interpret these women's struggles for autonomy as a sign of antinationalism. Antonio Pedreira's *Insularismo* expresses this alarm at middle- and upper-class women's intervention in the public sphere. For Pedreira, a university professor who saw these students daily, women—especially those in the teaching profession—were a dangerous and debilitating force that contributed to the lack of virility of Puerto Rican youth. It troubled him that those males destined to become part of the ruling elite would be molded, or softened, by women. It is important to recategorize the study *Insularismo* as the product of a class in decline that finds its gendered discourses and practices undermined by the new social protagonism of women, especially those in the professions. Its cultural nationalism-in-the-making is deeply imbued with misogyny (a question I examine further in the next chapter). Discussions of the links between colonialism and gender are far from academic when we consider recent feminist criticism that has argued, with limited success, that colonialism benefits from, as well as fosters, a subservient mentality in women.[67] As I will show in my later analysis, it is not a forgone conclusion that colonialism hinders the social progress of all women, nor is it always true that anticolonial ideology is, at the level of praxis, profeminist.

The University and the Intellectual Field of the 1930s

Citizens, this university must be our republic, a republic ruled our way, that would resemble us all! (¡Ciudadanos, esta universidad debe ser nuestra república, una república regida a nuestro modo, que se parezca a todos nosotros!)
—Emilio S. Belaval, 1935

Having a culture that expresses Puerto Rico's unique national character is very much part of the parlance of cultural nationalist discourses to this day. Also at issue is the sense that Puerto Rico's Spanish heritage and language are permanently in danger of being obliterated by the continuing presence of the United States in Puerto Rican life. The emphasis on culture, however, does not mean that cultural nationalism disregards economic and political discourses and fields of action. To the contrary, they are incorporated and translated into the arenas of literature, philosophy, and the visual arts, and invested with a different kind of prestige. Intellectuals of the period chose to distance themselves from the arena of "self-interested" politics in order to present themselves as outside direct political frays. This allowed them to claim a place from which to speak that was "above" petty politics, a strategy that nonetheless had potential political effects nationally and in the courts of world opinion. Conjoining culture with claims to nationhood (or national autonomy) made those demands intelligible to a potential international audience, without the nation builders having to adopt a language that implicated class structures or the legitimacy of the capitalist world order.

From the beginning of the North American presence on the island, the United States sought to facilitate its political and economic takeover by promoting the "Americanization" of the educational system, governmental structures, laws, production, and consumption. As we saw earlier, Puerto Ricans responded to these profound social changes in ways that often mirrored their changing class interests. The creation of a colonial school system responded to the needs of the new economy and sought the integration of the Creole elite as subservient partners in the new order. This fusion was not a simple matter, given that Creole intellectual life had charted its own, though troubled, course in the nineteenth century under Spanish hegemony. For the intellectuals of the *Generación del Treinta*, linked formally and informally to the (colonial) University of Puerto Rico, much was at stake in the discussion of the "contents" of a Puerto Rican national culture. The intellectual field of the 1930s was composed of established and aspiring writers, university professors, and other intellectuals who, to a large extent, shared an understanding that they should labor on behalf of Puerto Rican culture and, by extension, the nation. Journals and new publishing venues became the vehicles of lively debates and position papers that carried the aspirations of the new intelligentsia. "Literary activity gravitates almost totally to the University of Puerto Rico"[68] ("La actividad literaria casi gravita totalmente hacia la Universidad de Puerto Rico"), reports literary historian and *Generación del Treinta* participant Manrique Cabrera. At the center of this heightened activity were the Department of Hispanic Studies and the distinguished visiting Spanish intellectuals who taught there. Cabrera's reminiscence of the environment at the university in the late 1920s and early 1930s is quite enthusiastic: "This ebullient enterprise awakens the youth from the sleep in which the mediocre environment of a facile pseudopragmatism in all our educational institutions had immersed them. *It was refreshing to drink from the old sap of the language and thus enter the paths of self-rediscovery.*"[69] ("Esta arrolladora empresa despierta a la juventud del adormecimiento en que les había sumergido la mediocridad ambiente de un confianzudo pseudo-pragmatismo al uso dentro de todos los órganos educativos. *Refrescante fue aquel beber de las viejas savias de la lengua y con ello entrar en cauces de un auto-redescubrimiento.*") Cabrera touches only obliquely on some of the reasons that contributed to the university's centrality in the debates over Puerto Rican cultural life of the 1930s. He interposes the stultifying pragmatism of the colonial education against the excitement generated by the presence of Spanish and Latin American intellectuals who came to reinforce the students' connections with the Hispanic world. At a time of intense class and political struggle waged by the Creole elite for university control and autonomy, these lectures and courses by respected visiting professors struck a chord that had tremendous nativist resonance for young university students and intellectuals of the time.[70]

Yet developments such as this one could be interpreted not as a declaration of intellectual independence, but as a fulfillment and a greater integration into the North American colonial order. As Santiago-Valles argues, "This decade also witnessed an even greater expansion of the disciplinary functions of the Creole intellectuals and bureaucrats, concomitant with their looming place within the colonized political scene."[71] Creole intellectuals were able to rise to positions of influence because they collaborated with—or at least most did not radically oppose—the views that the colonial administration held of the working classes. Concessions were made to those who could position themselves as minor partners of the new economic order. "Regardless of its seeming insignificance and of the ostentatious manner with which it was announced," Santiago-Valles posits, "changing the official name of the Island in 1932 back to 'Puerto Rico' (that is, having the federal government recognize the pre-1898 nomenclature) signified the ascent of the privileged Creoles."[72]

Analysis of the specificities of the Puerto Rican "intellectual field" during the turbulent first decades of the twentieth century must underscore the part that the Creole intellectuals' bid for autonomy was already playing within the colonial context. Additionally, language—Spanish—would be a means by which nationalists could deliberately exclude those who used English. The intellectual field, as defined by Pierre Bourdieu, is that socially differentiated space in modern societies where producers and products of high culture interact. Comprised of universities, journals, newspapers, literary institutions, people, and ideas that hold sway at a given time, an intellectual field reveals the coexisting residual and emergent formations with respect to a hegemonic problematic.[73] Works, writers, and institutions are embedded in a complex and dynamic web of significance where all parts exert mutual pressures. The grid of social relations in which the author produces a work will color, for example, the very relation an author has to a work, and the work itself, in part, will be interpreted according to the acceptance of the author's past production.[74] The intellectual field, then, can be seen as a *system* composed not only of people, but of institutions and discourses as well. A writer's prominence or lack of favor is also determined by the ebb and flow of the tastes and fashions consecrated within the intellectual field, and by her or his relationship to the hegemonic problematic of the field at a given time.

Bourdieu's model stresses distinct and systematic aspects of an intellectual community, and its particularities within society as a whole.[75] In modern (capitalist) societies, the intellectual field has progressively achieved a certain level of autonomy with respect to intellectual matters and a considerable measure of power to define the parameters of the properly intellectual and, thus, of what is worthy of its consideration. Struggles for cultural autonomy in intellectual matters then are as much the product of historical reality as they are the pursuit of an ideal. Marxist critic Terry Eagleton, in turn, links the concept of autonomy to the emergence of the aesthetic as a theoretical category. In tandem with the rise of the capitalist marketplace, aesthetic autonomy is a profoundly bourgeois concept that was "hatched and nurtured" in the European Enlightenment. Leaving behind feudal absolutism, a new form of aesthetic judgement is made possible in which objects are seen as self-referential, "existing entirely and gloriously for themselves."[76] The intellectual field in highly developed capitalist cultures enjoys a high degree of relative autonomy. Yet in Latin America, as Argentine critics Carlos Altamirano and Beatriz Sarlo have cautioned, the relative autonomy of the intellectual field is more susceptible to pressures from the political and economic systems. Latin American countries also present another asymmetry in the cultural field not present in a nonperipheral situation: the question of the cultural metropolis functioning not only as a purveyor of intellectual and aesthetic paradigms but as a site of consecration.[77] In the case of Puerto Rican literature, consecration was sought not only on the island but also abroad, in Spain and Cuba, and to a much lesser extent in Latin America. Tomás Blanco, for example, published a number of essays in the *Revista Bimestre Cubana* and Puerto Rican intellectuals read about and commented on Cuban cultural affairs. In a 1936 issue of the journal we find interesting evidence of these exchanges. *Revista Bimestre Cubana*'s editorial note reads:

> The visit of Eusebia Cosme to Puerto Rico engaged the interest and commentaries of the most serious and prestigious critics and thinkers of the neighboring island. We reproduce here, taken from the *Journal of the Ateneo Puertorriqueño*, this very interesting polemic around Afro-Antillean art sustained by Tomás Blanco and Margot Arce. And the agile article by Lavandero on our great black performer.[78] (La estancia de Eusebia Cosme en Puerto Rico determinó curiosidades y comentarios de los más serios valores de la crítica y el pensamiento de la isla vecina. Damos aquí, tomados de la *Revista de Ateneo Puertorriqueño*, esta interesantísima polémica alrededor del arte afroantillano sostenida por Tomás Blanco y Margot Arce. Y el ágil artículo de Lavandero sobre nuestra gran declamadora negra.)

But it was the Spaniards who took the day. As we will see, Peninsular writers greatly influenced the *Generación del Treinta*'s cultural field. Modern

Spanish scholarship and literature as well as the Spanish classics functioned as templates to be emulated by Puerto Rican critics and writers in search of models other than North American ones.

Spanish Visitors and Teachers

In the early twentieth century, the idea of a cultural elite made up of well-bred, well-read peers, called upon to carry on the cultural legacy of Western Europe, had a powerful impact among the Latin American intelligentsia.[79] In this respect, the leadership of Ortega y Gasset and his *Revista de Occidente* provided inspiration and validation to many Latin American writers and thinkers.[80] In Ortega y Gasset's many reinterpretations of German philosophy and in his own works regarding the role of the intellectual and the educational system, cultural elites found confirmation and well-wrought theoretical justifications that, sparing some reconfiguring, could be assimilated to their own positions and projects.[81] Ortega's influence in Argentina and his dialogues with Victoria Ocampo and her journal *Sur* constitute a case in point. Yet, it is no mere coincidence that the penchant toward European thought takes place in the context of the ever-expanding economic and political presence of a United States bent on exporting its capital and securing markets and raw materials. In the Puerto Rican cultural field, Ortega y Gasset's ideas were especially welcomed by the young group of intellectuals who found in the writer support for their elitist cultural projects.

The influence of Spanish visiting professors and, after 1936, of Spanish writers in exile was an important cultural phenomenon that should not be underestimated. The Spaniards were instrumental in creating a certain atmosphere in which new authors were read and new ideas discussed. Puerto Rican intellectual and University of Puerto Rico professor Concha Meléndez recalls the readings shared at that moment among students, young professors, and writers. "Some books circulated among all," remembers Meléndez, "*Virgin Spain* by Waldo Frank, *The Decline of the West* by Spengler, the books of the Count of Keyserling, those of Ortega y Gasset and his *Revista de Occidente*, the essays of Gregorio Marañón and of Ramiro de Maetzu, and those of Unamuno."[82]

The Spaniards acted as mentors to the young professors and students, and one of them, Federico de Onís, organized the Department of Hispanic Studies and would be its first director in 1927. The methodology and projects of the *Centro de Estudios Históricos* of Madrid became known to young Puerto Ricans through their visiting professors and colleagues. From 1925 to 1929, in addition to de Onís, distinguished linguists, historians, and literary critics such as Tomás Navarro Tomás, Américo Castro, Fernando de los Ríos, and Ángel Valbuena Pratt, Amado Alonso, and Samuel Gili Gaya lectured and taught at the University of Puerto Rico. They provided an authorized discourse, a system that could be reworked locally "to explore what is ours." Following these mentors, the Creole intelligentsia represented this rethinking of their leadership role, and their repositioning in the cultural and political arena, as a meditation on the national character of Puerto Rico writ large. Furthermore, the Spanish visitors provided a critical language, a rhetoric whose ideological function would only come under vigorous questioning in the 1970s. This connection between the Spaniards and the project of the *Generación* is very explicitly acknowledged by Emilio S. Belaval, a student in the 1920s. In his "Los problemas de la cultura puertorriqueña" he asserts that "Studies, conferences, monographs, investigations multiply thanks to the orienting injection of the *Centro de Estudios Históricos* that guided the young faculty of our university and some extramural enthusiasts towards the theme."[83] ("Menudean los estudios, conferencias, monografías, investigaciones, gracias a la inyección orientadora del Centro de Estudios Históricos que puso al profesorado joven de nuestra Universidad y de algunos entusiastas de extramuros en marcha hacia el tema.") Belaval credits the renewed interest in things Puerto Rican to the guidance and impetus provided by the Spaniards. This serious reevaluation he differentiates from mere superficial emotional links to things Spanish, which he mercilessly pokes fun at, as we shall see in my later discussion of his essay. What is significant here is that the young author is heartened because "our Creole themes," previously considered insignificant, are now taken seriously by Puerto Ricans themselves.[84] The type of nativist impulse exemplified by Belaval is, according to Edward Said, a necessary, though not unproblematic, phase of nationalist writing. "The search for authenticity," Said explains, "for a more congenial national origin than that provided by colonial history, for a new pantheon of heroes, myths, and religions, these too are enabled by the land."[85] Or, one could add, by the idea of the land and who should own it. "Our Creole themes" ("nuestro tópico criollo"), or as it is better known, *criollismo*, now occupied center stage in the ideology and the poetics of Belaval's generation looking to reclaim lost territory.

In the Puerto Rican intellectual milieu, the intelligentsia's common assumptions regarding culture were profound and more binding than their ostensibly diverse political positions. The hegemonic problematic of the time as developed by authors and texts—the articulation of national identity—set the boundaries of the discussion; in turn, an author's participation in the discourse of national identity defined or redefined her or his status within the field. Appreciating this complex relationship helps us to clarify the exceedingly uncertain position of women intellectuals of the period. Given the unexamined gender biases of most male authors and critics who contributed to the canon, women's voices were belittled or muted, often to the point of invisibility for later generations. The common assumption that Puerto Rican women writers and intellectuals did not contribute much to the intellectual life of the time is belied by closer examination of the considerable number of works written by women starting at the turn of the century. The novel is a case in point, as Lizabeth Paravisini convincingly shows. From its inception on the island, the novel had dealt with broad social problems as its preferred themes, exemplified in the works of male writers Manuel Zeno Gandía, Miguel Meléndez Muñoz, Enrique Laguerre, René Marqués and many others. This thematic preference had the effect of excluding from critical consideration the many works written by women novelists who, within the social milieu and its limitations, tended to write about the domestic and sentimental sphere. This new paradigm helps critics to delineate and characterize a previously "hidden" alternate novelistic tradition, which has as its original initiators at the turn of the century the writings of suffragist and educator Ana Roqué de Duprey, Carmen Eulate Sanjurjo, and Eulalia Matos Bernier. When gender is used as an analytical tool recurring themes and images become visible to the reader.[86]

Women writers have engaged in intricate negotiations in the intellectual field in order to speak from a position of authority. This is true not only of the novel, but of all areas of intellectual activity. Theorists and writers such as Concha Meléndez, María Cadilla de Martínez, Nilita Vientós Gastón, and Margot Arce at times exerted considerable influence on the literary scene. Yet aside from honorable mentions, the works of these women writers are often treated not as part of the main story of that generation, but as asides that seem disconnected from the important events. As literary and cultural analysts, journal editors, and academics, women essayists of the *Generación del Treinta* need to be accounted for, because at any given time the intellectual field is much more dynamic than can be captured after the fact. We should also question the reluctance of critics to acknowledge women as co-participants in the task of clarifying and defining a Puerto Rican literary canon or notions about Puerto Rican cultural identity.[87] One way of escaping the arbitrary reductionism in the accounts of Puerto Rican literary histories is to see women's participation not as apart from that of their male cohort, but as engaging in a dialogue—however strained—with other generational members. Such was the case of Margot Arce and her intense work as an essayist (see Illustration 1).

That Puerto Rico's colonial situation was a constitutive element of the cultural field during the late twenties and throughout the thirties and forties is exemplified by the cultural nationalists' struggle to separate the University from direct control of the U.S. government, and by the bitter partisan politics that ensued because of these battles. *Reforma universitaria* would be the rallying cry for both professors and students who demanded greater control over all university affairs. In this context the struggle surrounding "bilingualism and its evils" and the pursuit of expertise in Spanish literature and culture had strong ideological underpinnings. To study Spanish literature was to take a political stance with regard to the "Spanishness" of Puerto Rico's culture (with the consequent repression of the African experience) in the midst of great pressures by the colonial government to "Americanize" and "modernize" Puerto Rican society. University professor Concha Meléndez recalls the intellectual environment that surrounded the *Departamento de Estudios Hispánicos* and its importance for herself and for her peers. Above all the department provided them with institutional empowerment. Its founding as a proper academic unit in 1927, "vivified the study of Spanish culture with courses offered by visiting professors who contributed to the definitive formation of many of us"[88] ("avivó el estudio de la cultura española con los cursos de profesores visitantes que contribuyeron a la formación definitiva de muchos de nosotros").

The creation of such a program of higher learning face-to-face with overt policies aimed at assimilation and acculturation has a complicated political significance for all parties involved: colonial administrators, university professors, the wider Creole block, and people with no access to the university. The U.S. government, through the *Comisionado de Instrucción*, implemented myriad assimilationist policies in primary and secondary education. Aida Negrón de Montilla has demonstrated that the public school system deliberately sought to acculturate and Americanize young Puerto Rican children who, through the public schools, would learn to become loyal American citizens. Yet students and teachers who spoke Spanish at home and conducted all aspects of their daily life in the vernacular, vigorously resisted mandatory teaching in English, the backbone of this policy.[89] Higher education, however, differed in important ways. According to historian Isabel Picó de Hernández, during the first two decades of the twentieth century the allocation of resources for higher education by the U.S. government spoke to the "school to field" interests of the traditional agrarian classes. The United States, in turn, favored the strengthening of the local managerial elite that would benefit from a system of higher education. Pico de Hernández's conclusions provide important insights for our discussion: "In other words, a considerable dimension of the educational policy was directed at coopting an important sector of the most powerful groups of the social structure in order to obtain their loyalty to the new hegemonic power."[90] The university was geared to serve the traditional upper classes—the *hacendados*, middle classes, small landholders, and merchants—in their integration into the new social order. Acquiring a profession was a way into the new economy dominated by the big sugar corporations. Toward the end of the 1930s, an increasing number of the university student body no longer had a direct connection with land ownership, which accounted for the significance of a course of study that stressed the professions and commerce.[91]

It is important to remember that the majority of the university student body studied education, liberal arts, pharmacy, and other traditional professions. However, a stagnant economy and high levels of unemployment in the 1930s fostered a sense of marginality and a growth in student political militancy. According to Picó de Hernández, "Many students were attracted to nationalism, the principal ideological movement of the time, because it was the first to denounce energetically economic absenteeism, imperialism, and cultural aggression."[92] Opposition to the new cultural and economic conditions would be most strongly expressed in the formation of the Puerto Rican Nationalist Party in May of 1930. Student demands for university autonomy and reforms during the 1930s were, however, conservative in matters of culture and class. They shared the same assumptions as their teachers regarding the role of the university in the training of students who were to become a *clase dirigente*, a cultured minority who would be intellectually prepared to take the reins of Puerto Rican society. In this specific regard, we also see a convergence between students, teachers, and the administrators, even if the colonial establishment's goal was to train a *dependent* elite.

According to Thomas E. Benner's memoirs of his activities as (the U.S.) Chancellor of the University of Puerto Rico, the Department of Spanish Studies (as he called it) of the University of Puerto Rico "had its roots in the summer courses offered primarily for teachers and other students of Spanish from the North which had been developed under the leadership of Miss Josephine Holt of the University of Richmond."[93] Spanish scholars attached to the *Centro de Estudios Históricos* were invited to strengthen the program, at first through the courses they offered during the summer session. By 1929 the first master's degree was awarded there to Carmen Gómez Tejera for her thesis on the history of the Puerto Rican novel, *La novela en Puerto Rico: apuntes para su historia.* The University would also send its junior professors abroad for graduate studies. Concha Meléndez and Antonio Pedreira went to Columbia University in 1925 and Margot Arce was sent to Madrid. In 1932, Meléndez would complete her doctorate in Latin American literature at Mexico's national university, reportedly the first woman to get such a degree even in Mexico.[94] As Benner records, the decision to reorganize the department properly came as a response to local criticism and charges that too much emphasis was put on the teaching of English, a charge he disputed.[95] Part of the interest and support for the reform came from Creole politicians, as well as from moneyed local Spanish residents intent on increasing the visibility of Spanish scholars on the island. Even after thirty years of American presence this pressure group was still influential. Moreover, sociologist Luis Ángel Ferrao finds very direct bloodlines between the intellectuals of the *Generación del Treinta* and the Peninsular and Balearic immigrants who came to the island during the late nineteenth century. A substantial number of these intellectuals had as their progenitors those who "had been part of the old Spanish elite who occupied positions of power and privilege in Puerto Rico up to 1898: military officers, professionals, wholesale merchants."[96] These family ties mattered in Creole society of the time. In 1938 Jorge Font Saldaña, interviewing Margot Arce Blanco for *Puerto Rico Ilustrado,* stressed her Castilian, Andalusian, and French parentage as well as her father's profession as a lawyer.[97] She was Tomás Blanco's first cousin. Tomás Blanco's father, in turn, was a pharmacist of Asturian ancestry. In 1942 Margot Arce Blanco married the exiled Spanish sculptor Francisco Vázquez Díaz—known by the pseudonym Compostela. Concha Meléndez grew up in the same family circle as Arce; she was goddaughter to Margot Arce's mother.[98]

The Spanish citizens' block was still an influential sector of the elite in the early 1930s, with their own exclusive social clubs, hospital, and until 1933, a newspaper. As Ferrao reports, the *Institución Cultural Española* organized festivities and lectures, and published books on Spanish themes. It even awarded annual scholarships to talented students, including Margot Arce and future linguist Rubén del Rosario.[99] By all accounts, Chancellor Benner had a cordial working relationship with the members of *Sociedad Cultural Española de Puerto Rico.* Its soon-to-be president, Rafael Fabián, offered a contribution of $3,000 to help bring Navarro Tomás to teach for a year. Though he never said this candidly, for Benner the Spanish contingent was there to perform a "corrective" function. It was Spanish models that his administration sought for his Puerto Rican students. Some Latin Americans visited the University, but they were a token few. Benner unwittingly allowed us a glimpse into this colonial magisterial function that the Spaniards undertook at the behest of the Americans, as he reports an "amusing" incident involving Navarro Tomás and a university bell-ringer called Don Demi. As the Spanish linguist carefully interviews his native subject, he shows Don Demi the picture of an owl. Benner reports the exchange this way: "He [Don Demi] said it was a *múcaro.* Navarro then asked whether he had ever heard the *correct* Spanish name. Demetrio replied: 'Sí, sí. Así lo llamaban en los tiempos atrasados de España.' ('Yes. Yes. That's what they called it in the backward days of Spain.') Navarro reported the incident with great delight."[100] This apparently banal reminiscence is rich in meanings, however. It would be fair to say that both the Creoles and the American Chancellor shared the vision that Puerto Rico's "Spanishness" needed to be rescued and amplified by further instructions from "correct" Spaniards. Ironically, this coincidence in the vision of Puerto Rican deficiency by all parties was negotiated to the satisfaction of both the colonial order and its subjects. Benner's activities indubitably resulted in the benefit of the young Puerto Rican scholars and students of the University. Yet at the same time, he was an American administrator helping to fulfill the cherished U.S. dream of Puerto Rico—in this case its university—as a "bridge" between North and

South America. He himself ends his recollections of that period satisfied with the mission accomplished: "The Department of Spanish Studies in the short space of three years had created new ties between the University of Puerto Rico and the universities of Latin America, the United States, and Europe."[101]

Spain in the Heart: Of Emotional and Other Mappings

The *criollo* sense of connection to Spain and its culture was almost universally shared by the *Generación del Treinta.* Poet Julia de Burgos, who was a more marginal figure at the time, describes this emotional attachment to what she understood to be Spanish culture. De Burgos was associated with the left wing of the *Partido Nacionalista* and was a supporter of the Spanish Republic.[102] Yet her vision of "Spain" was somewhat romantic at times. Marveling at the architecture of the old city as she visits Havana, for instance, she describes her emotions in a letter to her sister in 1940: "Inebriated with patriotic emotion, we proceeded to the Cathedral. It is something wondrous, *built by Spain* in the eighteenth century. Imagine, Consuelo, what a contrast of emotions and, up to a point, what paradox."[103] ("Ebrios de elevación patriótica, seguimos hacia la Catedral. Es algo maravilloso, *construida por España* en el siglo 18. Imagínate, Consuelo, qué contraste de emociones y hasta que punto qué paradoja.") The paradox of praising Spanish colonialism and the very Cuban heroes who fought for independence in the same breath is not lost on her. Nonetheless, her exaltation of Spain remains unabated. The poet seems to overcome her contradictory feelings after seeing the monuments to José Martí and Máximo Gómez: "From the heroes of the Revolution we went to admire and to drink in another monument of the land that moved these heroes of Independence. Cuba and Spain were fused in our eyes and in our emotions."[104] ("De los héroes de la revolución pasamos a admirar y beber en otro monumento de la tierra que dio motivo a esos héroes de la independencia. Cuba y España se fundieron en nuestros ojos y en nuestras emociones.")

But what is Spain in Julia de Burgos's text? More specifically, what is signified by the signifier "Spain"? "Spain" is a builder of cathedrals and monumental edifices. It is a spiritual entity that takes form in buildings, a fount where one drinks to replenish one's cultural soul. It is a permanent presence from which its former colonies can never separate themselves, "Because if Cuba, better still (Latin) America, freed itself from the arm or the yoke of Spain, it will never be free of its soul. For in art we also find the soul of Spain. If those institutions alone responsible for the protest do not still exist, why not admire the spiritual and artistic river that the Motherland deeded to us flowing on our lands *forever?*"[105] ("Porque si Cuba, no, América, se libertó del brazo o del yugo de España, jamás podrá libertarse del alma. Y en el arte también está el alma de España. Si las instituciones únicas responsables de la protesta, ya no existen, ¿por qué no admirar el cauce espiritual y artístico que nos dejó la madre Patria corriendo en nuestros suelos *para siempre?*"). De Burgos's metaphorically charged language recasts the struggle for independence as one aimed at oppressive Spanish institutions, not at Spanish culture or the "values" Spain embodied, nor, surprisingly, at the cruelty of the slave plantations that produced material wealth for a few. Though she was a light-skinned mulatta, she relied on the same racialist view of culture displayed in Pedreira's *Insularismo.* A very sophisticated poet, de Burgos questioned social conventions of her time, experimented with multiple poetic voices, and was not bashful about bringing her contestatory politics into her poems and progressive activism. Yet she seemed to forget that the values she ascribed to Spain were, in many instances, the same values that legitimated the subordination of black and non-white Puerto Ricans, and that Spanish colonialism was, above all else, a political and economic venture that left millions of casualties.[106] Monarchic and monumental Spain had been pointedly rejected by those same heroes who had defeated the Spanish government. Identification with Spanish grandeur on Cuban soil renders her speechless: "We left uplifted, impressed, mute."[107] ("Salimos altos, impresionados, mudos.") She accepts the Spanish colonial relationship by casting it as a spiritual, yet also familial, relationship in contrast to the present colonial subordination of Puerto Rico to the United States. The notion of Spain as a benign metropolis that bequeathed its civilization to its children/colonies is a favored trope of the writers of the *Generación del Treinta* and of political nationalists such as Albizu Campos. The very concept of Spain as the *madre patria* implies that the bond between Spain and its colonies is genetic or, in the parlance of the time, a blood bond. Accordingly, the mother-child metaphor suggests natural continuity, stronger than nationalist differentiation. De Burgos conveys some of the emotions regarding the word *patria*, buttressed by the notions of the illegitimate/unnatural colonial relationship with the United States and the new realities imposed by the hegemony of dependent capitalism. The poet's highly sanitized version of colonial reality enables her to access a sense of quite genuine patriotic euphoria, even though it is mediated in this instance by multiple mirrors: Puerto Rico—through Spain—through Cuba.

As we can see, defining patriotism vis-à-vis the new colonial relationship imposed by North American capital is a contradictory project for the intellectuals of Julia de Burgos's generation. We cannot discount their heartfelt search for clarification and preservation of the Puerto Rican national character. Many who were politically active—especially militant nationalists—paid a price for their affirmation of the separate identity of Puerto Rico as a nation. Yet if we understand national identity as a construct formulated and propagated by a besieged generation of intellectuals, we must interrogate their usage of the terms "personality," "identity," or "character" in their references to the nation. Undoubtedly, these are emotionally charged metaphors that seek to institute a discourse that has political effects, as anthropologist Richard Handler notes. Taking as his example the nationalist ideology of Quebec, he theorizes that ideas about nationhood are deeply rooted in Western individualism. Rhetorically, nationalists and theorists of nationalism endow the nation with some of the properties of the living individual.[108] This is why we can speak of a nation and a culture as having "rights" that need to be defended in and of themselves. While it is customary to speak of the *personality* of a nation, and tempting to see the nation as a biological organism, such accepted analogies, as we shall see, carry with them conceptual and ideological consequences. An examination of some of the workings of the rhetoric of "character," "identity," and "personality" used with respect to the concept of nation reveals that ideas about the nation and its culture are inextricably linked to individualism and, by extension, to property. This linkage between nation and culture—what it is and who has rights over it—is fundamental to the writers of the *Generación del Treinta.* Given the international currency of their ideas, their aim was to establish the existence of a cultural personality for Puerto Rico, guaranteeing in this way the existence of the nation and national/cultural rights.The works of cultural nationalism endeavor to build a scaffolding of cultural points of reference common to all the citizens, and accepted by those outside. What is understood as tradition is often the result of a particular interpretation, not of the historic past itself, but rather of a past portrayed as everyone's heritage.[109] The particular cultural memory of the descendents of the *hacendado* class is represented as a common historical and cultural patrimony and defined as "the Puerto Rican personality." Writers and scholars wage a symbolic battle to preserve and renovate a specific cultural memory.[110] Spain, as our discussion thus far shows, was inseparable from this process of re-membering the nation.

In the following section I want to examine an essay by Margot Arce, perhaps the key figure in this work of remembering through Spain. The recuperation of certain aspects of Spanish culture—the literature and art of the Golden Age, of the Generation of Ninety-Eight, and of the writers associated with Spanish Republicanism—would become more important for Margot Arce than it would ever be for any of the other members of her cultural formation. This project was so compelling in her case that she would restate its premises time and again in both her writings and her teaching. One such example is her 1956 essay "Las raíces" (Roots). In this later essay, published more than two decades into her career, the exemplarity of Spanish culture endures, as does Puerto Rico's cultural filiation to it. "Las raíces" invites the reader to share the emotive and ideological weight that Spain has for the author. Time, sentiment, and memory inform this journey to the metaphoric roots found in "race" and in Peninsular culture. Here, the racialist notions of Puerto Rican culture developed by Pedreira are corrected and expanded by Arce. Her "Puerto Rican passion" rests on an absolute conviction of the continuity and validity that Spain has, or should have, in Puerto Rico. To combat the North American offensive and to reduce the harmful effects of colonialism on the island, knowledge of Spanish tradition, through study and travel, is a must.

One revealing detail of "Las raíces" has to do with the voice of the speaker as a textual presence. The speaker is a female traveler who feels absolute freedom to come and go alone during her extensive stays on the Iberian peninsula, without the need for masculine support. This textual device assumes and amplifies corporal autonomy for women. Very early on, Arce assures us that the journey on which she is embarking is not one of tourism, much less the carefree ramblings of the *flâneur.* It is rather a journey of discovery, a pilgrimage with transcendental implications. Given her personal understanding of what Spain is, she will also be an interpreter who deciphers for the reader the profound meanings of these experiences: "I have enjoyed arriving in Spain with time; staying and staying again wherever I pleased, living free of the clock."[111] ("Me ha gustado llegar a España con tiempo; quedarme y requedarme donde me agradaba, vivir libre del reloj.") Time and its symbol, the clock, will become in this essay the privileged measure of culture. She will stress, "I was never in Spain as a tourist."[112] Time—in abundance—will allow for reflection and access to truth and revelation.

When the traveler narrates her visit to the cathedral of Burgos, she experiences Burgos almost as a mystical event, not just as another "attraction" that seduces tourists. The language used here is of transforming illumination. This is not surprising given Arce's wide-ranging knowledge of the mystical poetry of the Golden Age and her attachment to the Catholic tradition. Like the mystic in the presence of the divine, the traveler feels transformed by the spirit that permeates Burgos, where she has spent some weeks visiting the cathedral: "The air is transparent," she tells us, "the light is blinding; a golden dust rises from the plots surrounding the village. With the changes in lighting the gray rocks turn rosy; they reverberate into opals; they become translucent, almost immaterial."[113] ("El aire es transparente, la luz cegadora; un polvillo de oro sube de las eras que ciñen el caserío. Con los cambios de iluminación las piedras grises se tornan sonrosadas, reverberan en ópalos, se vuelven translúcidas, casi inmateriales.") This passage, where blindness is followed by otherworldly perception, preludes the ecstatic experience in which time stops. The narrative voice adopts the persona of the seeker who has to relinquish her will to receive guidance. She is impelled by something outside her, and has no power to control the presence calling to her: "I follow, dazzled, the willful impetus of the towers; quiet and silence remove me from time, from what is tangible, and I float in that imprecise place where the barber's bowl becomes Mambrino's helmet and Aldonza Lorenzo, Dulcinea."[114] ("Sigo alucinada el ímpetu voluntarioso de las torres; la quietud y el silencio me sustraen del tiempo, de lo tangible y floto en esa zona imprecisa donde la bacía se torna yelmo de Mambrino y Aldonza Lorenzo, Dulcinea.") We have entered the mystical experience where time and space give way to transcendental knowledge and emotional plenitude, at least for a while.

The profound meaning of Spanish literature and its transformative power illuminate her: "Yes, here in Burgos, in front of the cathedral, whether I look at it from the height of the castle or from the path from Cartuja . . . I understand Don Quixote; I discover the link that closely unites me with the culture and spirit of Spain."[115] ("Sí, aquí en Burgos, ante la catedral, ya la mire desde la altura del Castillo, ya desde el camino de la Cartuja . . . entiendo a Don Quijote, descubro el vínculo que me une estrechamente con la cultura y el espíritu de España.") The tropes of the Golden Age mystical tradition undergird the essay time and again, as we see in her choice of the motives of the pilgrim, the revelation of a secret truth, and the connection with the transcendent and eternal. Her models are Saint Teresa of Avila and Saint John of the Cross.

Access to enlightenment is available to her readers if they desire it too. Any Puerto Rican who travels to Spain in the right frame of mind "will begin to discover that there, on that ground, in those ways of conceiving God, man and the world, in those customs and gestures are established his deepest and most permanent roots. . . . He will perceive the strong blood ties and the full history that binds us to a common destiny."[116] ("Empezará a descubrir que allí, en aquel suelo, en aquellos modos de concebir a Dios, al hombre y al mundo, en aquellas costumbres y gestos arraigan sus más hondas y permanentes raíces. . . . Percibirá el fuerte lazo de sangre y de colmada historia que nos ata a un destino común.") However, her assertion that, for Puerto Ricans, the trip to Spain is a requirement that will lead to self-recognition, is tempered with a warning. She cautions that one must have patience, since the affinity with what is Spanish is no longer immediate or obvious for those who come from Puerto Rico. One must know how to look in order to see. As the author puts it, "In the first months after arrival, this need is not perceived; we feel strange and as though lost. Some things startle us: we must alter the image that is preconceived by the light of our readings, by propagandas, or by other people's tales. . . . The effort we have to make to adapt and to accept what is different fills us with impatience and irritation."[117] ("En los primeros meses de la llegada no se percibe esta necesidad; nos sentimos extraños y como perdidos. Algunas cosas nos chocan: debemos enmendar la imagen preconcebida a la luz de lecturas, de propagandas o de relatos ajenos. . . . El esfuerzo que hemos de hacer para adaptarnos y para aceptar lo diferente nos llena de impaciencia e irritación.")

For Puerto Ricans who have lived under North American influence on the island for decades, identification with Spain is no longer instantaneous. They require the mediation of the author/guide, as well as an effort of interpretation, or at least an examination of their conscience. Arce bemoans the reality that Puerto Ricans arrive in Spain with changed values, morally confused by North American consumer goods. If the traveler measures Spanish culture with the "gadgets" produced by the United States, "he will never understand the most genuine and permanent values of his own Puerto Rican culture"[118] ("jamás entenderá los valores más genuinos y permanentes de su propia cultura puertorriqueña"). Permanence and authenticity are contrasted here with the changing and false values of the culture of consumer goods that Puerto Ricans have learned to desire under American capitalism. The representation of the Spanish cultural legacy offered by Arce in "Las raíces" rests on a rather fetishist vision of Spanish culture. Spain is reduced to its art—"Las lanzas" of Velázquez—and its literature, which she cites often to illustrate or support her observations.

We should remember that this essay was published during the booming years of economic development under Governor Luis Muñoz Marín, and that the social panorama was changing by leaps and bounds with the country's accelerated industrialization-by-invitation. New consumer habits, the massive emigration of Puerto Rican workers to the United States, and the brutal repression of militant nationalism were the order of the day. Faced with the cultural changes that dependent industrialization brought, Arce countered with what she considered to be the *permanent* values of Spanish spirit incarnated in its art, its literature, and a way of looking at life. Historical reality was more complex, however. Spain was not frozen in the timeless void as many Puerto Ricans would have had it. In the 1950s, that country was undergoing an economic expansion similar to the one in Puerto Rico, which would culminate in the large student and worker demonstrations of 1958.[119] The sixties witnessed an intensification of these processes, and it has been argued that this contradiction between economic liberalization and political repression fed the anti-Franco movement. Anthropologist Yvonne Lassalle-López reminds us that the 1950s and 1960s witnessed massive migrations of Spaniards to more industrialized regions within the country and to the rest of Europe. For example, two million Andalusians moved to Barcelona, France, Switzerland, and Germany. The socio-cultural dynamism and the pronounced economic changes found in the Spanish context throughout these decades contrast greatly with Arce's vision of a Spain of eternal essences. The essentialism of Arce is strategic, however. It has more to do with ideological battles fought in Puerto Rico concerning dissimilar visions of national identity than with the Spanish cultural realities.

"Las raíces" rests on an intellectual tradition that identifies land, blood, language, "attitudes about love and death," and even the language of the body, as manifestations of immutable racial essences. Like Antonio S. Pedreira's *Insularismo*, "Las raíces"—and many of Arce's other texts on identity—partake of the type of discourse established by German "national soul" or *Volkgeister* nationalism.[120] Examples of the unalterable Spanish, and by extension Puerto Rican, spirit are "the nobility that obliges all Hispanics to be humble and generous in triumph . . . a profound respect toward men and things . . . Castilian modesty"[121] ("esa nobleza que nos obliga a todos los hispanos a ser humildes y generosos en el triunfo . . . un profundo respeto a los hombres y a las cosas . . . el pudor castellano"). Humility, generosity, respect, modesty, and moral freedom, insists Arce, are qualities proper to the Spanish *ethos* par excellence. Faced with these spiritual virtues, she contrasts the moral emptiness represented by North American industrialized culture in Puerto Rico. Culture is permanence. She clarifies: "He, who among us, betraying himself, surrenders or exchanges it (culture) for mirages of security, of power, of material goods, how profoundly he becomes a *déclassé* (or is denatured), what a foreign air he assumes, so awkwardly does he disfigure his Hispanic countenance and turn himself into a caricature!"[122] ("Aquel de nosostros que, traicionándose, la entrega o la canjea por espejismos de seguridad, de poder, de bienes materiales, ¡cuán profundamente se *descasta*, que aire tan ajeno, tan torpe desfigura su garbo hispánico y lo convierte en caricatura de sí mismo!") The Americanized Puerto Rican is represented here as a pathetic and degenerate being. Already in "El paisaje de Puerto Rico" (1939) the author had made reference to the metaphor of grafting to refer to this figure who, according to her, has adopted cultural mores that are fundamentally antagonistic. For this version of cultural nationalism the possibility of hybridism does not exist. Hybridity is the very negation of culture; it is the contamination of everything that, in order to exist, must remain purified. Just like in many other discourses of the national, a thing called culture is born and develops, yet it also remains integral, whole, and without internal contradictions.[123] A people can trace its genealogy almost from the beginning of time. Arce's essay also plays with the diverse meanings of the word *casta*, (caste, ancestry). We already saw how pathetic the *descastado* (denatured) Puerto Rican seems, a mere caricature of himself. This is an appeal to a classist discourse according to which the abandonment of one's class implies reprehensible conduct. The envisioned reader of "Las raíces" is asked not to relinquish the moral conduct of his social rank, not to be a déclassé. But for the working class, what can *casta* mean? Would it not be to its advantage to break with such a system? The presumed reader of this essay, invited to journey to the motherland, does not belong to the working class.

The vision of Hispanic culture that Arce presents in 1956 is somewhat reductionist, and historical conflicts are notably absent, as mentioned earlier.

Yet, the text is not able to mute them entirely. What is the essayist referring to when she mentions the "renewed disillusions" she has suffered? Perhaps this is an oblique reference to the defeat of Spanish Republicanism and to the Franco regime, which had very personal repercussions in her life. It could also be a reference to the events of 1898, but it seems rather paradoxical that Arce would have to resort to a Spain that politically betrayed her to find Puerto Rico's cultural salvation. To explain this contradiction one must examine both her ideas on the nature and function of cultures, as well as Puerto Rico's reality during the 1950s, especially the establishment of the Commonwealth or *Estado Libre Asociado* (ELA) in 1952.

The search for continuity and essential permanence is nuanced with Arce's admiration for regional diversity. This diversity, we might add, the Franco dictatorship tried to repress, but there is no mention of this in the text.[124] Instead, the plant metaphor that gives the essay its title—Roots—implies vitality and depth while also suggesting growth and diversification. From Cádiz to San Sebastián, from la Coruña to Barcelona, in contrast with industrial mass culture, "nothing repeats itself," and the multiple national cultures attest to the "vitality and persistence of a tradition"[125] ("nada se repite," "la vitalidad y persistencia de una tradición"). Mention of the already long years of the Franco dictatorship would perhaps deflect from her message of the enduring democratic "character" of the Spanish people. Instead, with great economy of words, Arce targets both the cultural and political aggression that Puerto Rico was suffering at that moment and the current industrialization program of the ELA. To achieve this, she recuperates the old critique of the deterioration of values that many saw in technology, the intensification of production, and mass culture. We have here a belated restatement of Spengler, Keyserling, Frank, and, of course, Ortega y Gasset, who, from different perspectives, theorized the effects of industrial modernization on culture. Arce chooses to retain what European and other cultural critics had left behind after the trauma of World War II.

The discursive journey through Spanish regional diversity allows the author to critique representative democracy American-style. She places democracy in a different context by recognizing, in the popular cultures of the Peninsula, the persistence of the Hispanic democratic spirit. As she enthusiastically puts it, "*In this true democracy* it is not the quantitative that counts, rather the qualitative, the intrinsic values of the person, of every particular person and not the brute force of numbers."[126] ("*En esta verdadera democracia* no es lo cuantitativo lo que cuenta sino lo cualitativo, los valores intrínsecos de la persona, de cada particular persona y no la fuerza bruta del número.") The term "democracy" is here redefined as a clearly Hispanic quality, the obverse of the false North American democracy: "Nowhere have we uniformity, mass production: nor democratic leveling, nor *live up to the Joneses.*"[127] ("Por ninguna parte la uniformidad, la producción en masa: ni la nivelación democrática, ni el *live up to the Joneses.*") Arce's invective against massive capitalist production is directed at the cultural situation of a Puerto Rico whose language, folklore, cuisine, and dance, as well as habits of being, were irremediably changing. But one must remember that these changes, due in part to dependent capitalist progress, responded also to their own internal forces that gave Puerto Rican popular cultures greater visibility and drive. The culture of deference and paternalism was long gone. Working-class migration to the States in search of a better future was the order of the day.[128]

In praising the "permanent" Hispanic democratic spirit, Arce is targeting the situation in Puerto Rico, as I mentioned before. These are the years of the repression of militant independentism during which, in order to keep the industrial peace at the center of the *Estado Libre Asociado* project, the shameful "gag law" remained in force.[129] This quelling of militant independentism touched the lives not only of the members of the Nationalist Party, but of supporters of independence in general. Any reader in 1956 would understand this. My textual analysis of "Las raíces" leads me to believe that this essay existed in an embryonic form years before its 1956 publication. Could this explain Arce's silence with respect to Franco's dictatorship and the depoliticized narration of her travels throughout the Peninsula? It is also possible that she only wanted to present her "deep Spain." Perhaps she interpreted the dictatorship as an accident that soon would be overcome. Note that in her criticism of consumerism and the culture of the masses Arce relies on a discourse whose terms were already passé in the 1930s in Europe and the United States. But in the Puerto Rican context condemning the attachment to industrialization and the new consumerism acquires a very particular meaning. The *descastados*, lacking in class, are people who live by imitation, senseless competition, and who willingly acquiesce to the system. To these momentous historical processes, the essayist proposes the following antidote: "to the leveling and 'massification' of peoples, respect and the conservation of national cultures; to the cult of worldly possessions, that ascetic ideal of Fray Luís"[130] ("a la nivelación y 'masificación' de los pueblos, el respeto y la conservación de las culturas nacionales; al culto de los bienes mundanos, aquel ideal ascético de Fray Luis"). While her criticism of dependent capitalism is in many of its aspects very valid, Arce's use of precapitalist and seigniorial concepts like *casta* and *sangre* needs to be interrogated.

If we grant that the study of things Spanish will allow Puerto Ricans to revive some kind of ancestral blood memory, and to recognize themselves as Hispanic, one should ask if, in fact, all Puerto Ricans have equal access to that memory and that blood. *Sangre* becomes a metaphor whose referents are fairly imprecise. We should further ask if even Spaniards themselves ever enjoyed this bonding element. By Arce's insisting on such a symbol, the history of Spanish colonization and its violence disappears. In the same manner, class divisions also vanish, as well as the gestures of cultural resistance against owners and bosses. I am not referring here to a supposed Spanish "blood" that would be different from an also supposed African "blood"; rather I am attempting to shed light on the ideological content that the word *sangre* carries in the context of Arce's essay. "Blood" and "roots" are signifiers whose effectiveness is guaranteed by their organic, vital, and connective referents. Blood in the context of Catholic cultures also has sacred connotations; it is communion and salvation. On her journey through Spain riding in third-class train cars and contemplating the view of Castile, the speaker tells us, "Among these people I find myself; I am aware of my roots. They are my people; as much mine as my generous *jíbaros* in the center of the Island, as my gentle blacks on the coast. They speak my same language, love what I love, believe in what I believe."[131] ("Entre estas gentes me hallo; cobro conciencia de mis raíces. Son mis gentes; tan mías como mis generosos jíbaros del centro de la Isla, como mis tiernos negros del litoral. Hablan mi mismo lenguaje, aman lo que amo, creen en lo que creo.") The connection is provided by the Spanish language, sentiments, and beliefs, which attempt to bridge the gap that could exist between people of different education, social prestige, and economic means. What is expressed here is desire, an integrative desire that feels capable of transcending differences: "I never feel like a foreigner nor excluded from their circle; we look at each other and we know of the bond that unites us."[132] ("Jamás me siento extranjera ni excluida de su círculo; nos miramos y sabemos del lazo que nos une.") What is interesting is that mutual recognition is claimed to take place even without the need for words. Finally, we are left with a discourse of class that unites the speaker to the experience of the subordinate when she imagines a communion free of contradictions.

Upon returning to Puerto Rico, the traveler has a layover in New York and heads to the Metropolitan Museum, where she again reaffirms the contrasts between Spanish and North American cultures. The Spanish exhibit hall of the museum is portrayed in this essay as a peaceful and ageless refuge, "a small cell without time." In it Arce is removed from "the modern Babylon" that "palpitates noisily, inhumanely, indifferently."[133] There, in this quasi-religious space, the enlightening contemplation of art produced by the Spanish masters helps her to reaffirm a fundamental unity. Spanish literature teaches her to appreciate the Spanish visual arts as she contemplates the *View of Toledo* by el Greco. The reader is invited one last time to go beyond, to perceive a profound unity. But this visual exercise, healthy for any person who approaches a work of art, becomes in Arce something more: the desire to resolve contradictions in art and life. The museum as sanctuary and preserver of art is privileged in the last part of her essay, given that it offers access to "culture." Never mind that this is a very decontextualized and reified access; one that takes place in a metropolitan institutional venue. Contemplation of Spanish art once again comes to the rescue of the lost

Puerto Rican, convincing her finally that one sensibility informs "every peninsular or overseas Spaniard"[134] ("cada español peninsular o ultramarino"). Communion becomes a possibility. The unity of the old Spanish empire is reestablished on the aesthetic and affective plane, and there is a return to a period prior to the rupture of 1898, when (some) Puerto Ricans were overseas Spaniards.

Rediscovery and reintegration are concepts that challenge the dispossession produced by the North American presence in Puerto Rico. "Las raíces" ends with an emotional profession of faith by the author. To the disharmony, rupture, and injustice of her present she offers the possibility of continuity, regeneration, and fulfillment. In studying and pondering what is Spanish, "I imbibe in the originating fountains of a culture that I have not invented, that I conserve and attempt to enrich and refine with my small works and my best intentions"[135] ("abrevo en las fuentes originales de una cultura que no he inventado, que conservo y pretendo enriquecer y afinar con mis pequeñas obras y mis mejores intenciones"). This is the paradox that supports her argument. The political independence or Puerto Rican affirmation that Arce seeks demands cultural continuity with the colonial reality situated before 1898. To combat one colony, she counters with another. Against the denaturalizing relationship with North America, the revitalization that stems from a reunion with the Spanish colonial past. Her profound nostalgia for the past leads to surprise, reverence, and the desire to emulate—impulses that are portrayed in the essay as a regenerative possibility.

The dedication of "Las raíces," directed "to my comrades in the task of our 'inventing' a Puerto Rican culture," acquires a heavy ironic weight.[136] ("A los compañeros en la tarea de 'inventarnos' una cultura puertorriqueña.") After all, the acknowledgment heads an essay that wants to make clear that Puerto Ricans have a definite genealogy, and that nothing about it is improvised. Her essay, as she underscores with her dedication, is a gesture of elucidation and affirmation, not a mere *invento*, not a lie. Taking into account that "Las raíces" was published in the newspaper *El Mundo* as well as in the university journal *La Torre* only a year after the establishment of the *Instituto de Cultura Puertorriqueña* (ICP) in 1955, we notice that Arce's essay was part of the burning controversy surrounding the character of Puerto Rican culture under the Commonwealth. If, for the ICP, the roots of the culture were found in the triple Spanish, Taino, and African legacies, it is interesting that for Arce the "raíces" were exclusively Spanish. But it is worth clarifying that even for anthropologist Ricardo Alegría, who directed the *Instituto de Cultura* for decades, the leading influence was Spanish. The legacy of the Tainos and of the descendents of Africans, although discernable, was limited. One of the purposes of the mid-century institute was to provide cultural coherence for the political projects of the ELA. It is true that the *Instituto de Cultura* offered a certain support to the pro-independence artists and intellectuals who partook of the limited opportunities that it often afforded them.[137] But the Puerto Ricanist projects of the *Instituto* could not satisfy the yearnings of supporters of independence like Arce. The battle for the nation and for national culture would always be fought by her at the University and in her role as a member of the Puerto Rican Independence Party, an institution that she helped found a decade earlier, in 1946.

As we have seen in this chapter, Puerto Rico's colonial links to the United States since 1898 had exerted pressure on the country's literary production in myriad ways. The class identification and biases of the writers of the *Generación del Treinta* were other constitutive elements of the intellectual field. Unanswered, however, are questions relating to the gender biases and gendered identity of both the men and women within this group. Chapter 2 returns to the 1910s and 1920s to examine the momentous changes that had occurred in the *hacendado* gender system. These are the years of suffragist struggles and women's rising demands for enfranchisement as social subjects.

Writing in the early 1930s half a world away in Italy, Antonio Gramsci theorized the explicit political role played by intellectuals in modern Western societies. From his prison cell he wrote, "Every social group, coming into existence on the original terrain of an essential function in the world of economic production, creates together with itself, organically, one or more strata of intellectuals that give it homogeneity and an awareness of its own function not only in the economic but also in the social and political fields."[138] Disputing the myths of the intellectual as a disinterested observer or outsider, Gramsci's essay, "The Intellectuals," argued that the traditional professional intellectual's existence derives ultimately from past and present class relations. Though specific to the Italian context, Gramsci's work serves as a model for the study of intellectuals elsewhere; in his view they are not distinct from society and independent of class, but perform a class-bound social function. Traditional intellectuals represent themselves as autonomous and independent of the dominant social group, a strategy that has important consequences for politics and ideology. Among other things, it obscures their "essential mediating function in the struggle of class forces."[139] Bearing in mind that Gramsci was interested in the creation of a new type of intellectual who would be organically bound to working-class projects, "The Intellectuals," nonetheless, lends itself to the study of the political role played by the Puerto Rican *Generación del Treinta.*

While his essay does not address questions specific to women intellectuals, Gramsci's discussion impels us to consider the relationship of these scholars and thinkers to their social groups. What is the relationship of gender to intellectual production and to class? Gender roles in Puerto Rico had undergone major changes after 1898; so we must ask what conditions allowed a group of women to become intellectuals, and to speak from a position of authority within the public sphere. Arguing that national identity is the product of gendered subjects as well as a discourse formulated by a class, Chapter 2 specifically looks at the rise of feminism among women of the literate elite and the fledgling middle class. I will show how the insights of suffragist feminism were interpreted by activists, many of whom were schoolteachers. Puerto Rican bourgeois suffragists, I posit, have a contradictory effect on *hacendado* hegemony: they challenge the gender system while maintaining and ultimately strengthening the class structure and the racial system. In effect, the empowerment of Creole middle-class women expanded the realm of action by the cultured sectors. Later chapters further explore these contradictions as they are played out in the discourse of national identity. My analysis of the cultural journal published by the Association of University Women, *Revista de la Asociación de Mujeres Graduadas de la Universidad de Puerto Rico,* further expands on the strategies of inclusion and exclusion deployed by women intellectuals of the *Generación del Treinta* as they strove to become part of a Puerto Rican intelligentsia. I look at some of the "blind spots" and silences in their projects in the hope of showing how their participation in the national identity discourse superseded any awareness of their condition as gendered subjects. Furthermore, these women failed to include in their vision of Puerto Rican culture any serious consideration of Puerto Rico's complex racial history. This "silence," consequently, helped to perpetuate the racial/social hierarchies in which blacks and their contributions to Puerto Rican culture were—and sometimes still are—seen as inferior to the Spanish and "white" heritage.

CHAPTER 2

Compromising Positions: Reconstituting the Creole Gender Hierarchy

I do not accept as loose or perverse any woman so considered by any historian who erroneously believes that women have no right to use their entire freedom. (No acepto como viciosa, ni perversa a mujer alguna conceptuada así por cualquier historiador que equivocadamente haya creído que la mujer no tiene derecho a usar su completa libertad.)
—Luisa Capetillo, 1914

The Puerto Rican woman, now educated just as men are, has the capacity of intervening, by both divine and human right, in the functions of her country's government, and her awakening is beautiful and imposing. (La mujer puertorriqueña, educada hoy al igual que el hombre, se encuentra capacitada para intervenir, por derecho divino y humano, en las funciones del gobierno de su país, y su despertar es hermoso e imponente.)
—The Twentieth-Century Woman, August 15, 1917[1]

Suffrage for Literate Women

Imagine for a moment the tremendous excitement present in that room of the Biblioteca Carnegie of San Juan, Puerto Rico, during the first organizational meetings of the *Liga Femínea* in August of 1917.[2] Present, according to the roster of the first meeting, were San Juan's most prominent women: intellectuals, school teachers, doctors, philanthropists, journalists. Dissatisfied with the rigidity of the gender system, these wives, daughters, and sisters of elite families had come together to organize the *Liga Femínea* in order to help Puerto Rico keep pace with the most "progressive" nations of the world. Their petition sent to the Puerto Rican legislature stated unequivocally that Puerto Rican women had a right to participate in the political process:

> The Puerto Rican woman, responding to the signs of the times and *conscious of the increased number of duties that go along with the increased number of rights* that deservedly and justly have been conceded to us, reclaims proudly her part of the responsibility for the arduous political labor of her fellow citizens, desiring to contribute with all of her loyal energies to the most perfect development of an ideal government for our beloved Island.[3] (La mujer puertorriqueña, respondiendo a los signos de los tiempos y *consciente de la mayor suma de deberes que apareja el mayor número de derechos*, que merecida y justicieramente se nos han concedido, reclama orgullosa su parte de responsabilidad en la ardua labor política de sus conciudadanos, deseando contribuir con todos sus leales esfuerzos a la realización más perfecta de un gobierno ideal para nuestra querida Isla.)

Their statement further stresses that political rights should be extended to all of humanity—not just to one half of it. Ironically, these forgers of equality arrogate the right to speak for *la mujer puertorriqueña* even as they advocate for only one sector of the female population. Creation of the league was no accident. The provisions of the Foraker Act of 1900 had allowed adult males the right to vote for the members of the island legislature organized in 1903. When the 1917 Jones Act extended (a limited) American citizenship to Puerto Ricans, the women of the *Liga Femínea* did not want to miss the opportunity to demand, in turn, the right to one of the most visible symbols of citizenship—the vote. As sophisticated women, and by virtue of their schooling and professional standing, they would participate responsibly in the political affairs of the country, promising to make judicious use of their increased rights. "Today we have women lawyers, doctors and pharmacists," the document reads, "professors, accountants, artists, writers, public speakers, and every year our schools graduate young ladies who honestly and nobly compete with the young men for the highest honors of the school."[4] ("Contamos hoy con abogadas, médicas, farmacéuticas, profesoras, contables, artistas, escritoras, oradoras y todos los años se gradúan en nuestras escuelas señoritas que disputan a los jóvenes en buena y noble lid, los más altos honores de la escuela.") These cultivated, professional women were proposing a redefinition of the concept of womanhood, and an education in the liberal professions was key to their new conceptualization and social aspirations. Many among the founders of the *Liga* were teachers, like Ana Roqué de Duprey and Mercedes Solá, editor of the *Liga*'s journal *La Mujer del Siglo Veinte* (The Twentieth-Century Woman).[5] The journal proclaimed that Puerto Rico's women were ready for the vote, and were capable of leading the nation. And women's awakening, *La Mujer del Siglo Veinte* announced, was beautiful and unrelenting.

This chapter examines a number of strategies used by white *criollas* of the middle and upper strata of Puerto Rican society to negotiate a space from which to speak with authority in the intellectual field of the early twentieth century. My observations draw on a wide range of materials: the essay, the opinion survey, the interview, the eulogy. I posit that Creole women's search for voice and empowerment was initially facilitated by a pragmatic and selective adherence to suffragist praxis. Later, when women intellectuals of the *Generación del Treinta* adopt a "genderless" tone, they do so in order to further establish authority and credibility in the male-dominated discourses on culture and the nation. What were the ideological and political maneuvers that sanctioned *criolla* utterances, allowing them to be heard, to be intelligible to those in power? First, taking as a case in point the specific way in which the elite suffragist movement formulated its class demands for the literate-only vote, I examine the female subject imagined by emerging elite women intellectuals. I propose that as social critique the feminism defined by their suffragist movement had serious limitations. These weaknesses—imposed by the narrow definition of its field of action—invited defections and hastened the waning of the movement after the suffragists obtained the vote and greater access to educational opportunities. Finally I explore why non-gender-specific political and cultural pursuits would become more appealing to Euro-Puerto Rican professional women after 1936.

As suggested in the Introduction, the program of a feminist organization such as the *Liga Femínea* did not envision the enfranchisement of all Puerto Rican women in their demands for the vote and other civil and political rights. Working-class intellectuals, regardless of gender, faced great opposition from the power structure, as evidenced in the life and writings of working-class feminist labor organizer Luisa Capetillo. Discursive agency was the result of arduous political struggles and hard-fought institution building. Julio Ramos's research on Luisa Capetillo sheds further light on the predicaments of the working-class intelligentsia and, specifically, on the precarious position of Capetillo as a working-class woman intellectual. In an agricultural country with very high levels of illiteracy, writing is a technology that bestows power on those who can wield it. Ramos reminds us that the elite tenaciously controlled the intellectual field. He writes: "It wasn't easy. Because rather than gently knocking on the closed doors of the discourse, Capetillo and her comrades burst into one of the most jealously protected centers of power: symbolic and cultural production, a territory where power produces the fictions of its law, the norms of its sociability. And the institutions of power, faced with the loss of their hegemony in this zone, responded with violence, often literally breaking heads and incarcerating the new discussants."[6]

Middle- and upper-class women, for their part, were not subjected to the same type of repression, indignities, and strategies of containment that the male middle-class, Euro-Puerto Rican elite used in order to block working-class access to the discourses and institutions of power. The dynamics of the struggle for elite women were different, in that access to cultural capital was limited, but not unavailable. Provided they did not go too far, genteel society was open to the education of its women. Moreover, the transmission of cultural capital, secured and maintained by the professional elite (to follow Bourdieu), does not depend solely on the mediation of the school system. Crucial familiarization with the discourses of high culture occurs, in part, in the home and in other non-educational institutions such as the theater, concert hall, museum, art gallery, and foreign travel. Ownership of art objects, access to the home library, and the everyday upbringing of a child by the parents increase that capital and, more importantly, naturalize it.[7]

As we saw in my earlier discussion of the establishment of monopoly agro-capitalism after 1898, the ensuing social and political changes under American colonialism affected virtually all aspects of life for Puerto Ricans of all social classes. Greater opportunities and choices became available for upper-middle-class and middle-class women, challenging and fundamentally transforming the gender system created by *hacendado* social hegemony. This is not to say that there were no women fighting for women's rights and advancement before 1898. The example of Ana Roqué de Duprey is a case in point. She was an educator who, in 1893, founded the newspaper *La Mujer*, printed by women typographers.[8] Capitalism had propelled an increasing number of women from all strata of Puerto Rican society into the paid work force. Within the ranks of the working class fervent women labor organizers increasingly sought to bring together a class-and-gender awareness that would better represent the real situation of poor working women. We should keep in mind that already by 1907 Luisa Capetillo had published her first book, *Ensayos libertarios* (Essays on Liberation). But there were other labor organizers who also gave their all to the cause. Genara Pagán, for example, worked as a tobacco stemmer (despalilladora) on the island and in New York. She was an active trade unionist who tried to register herself to vote in 1920, arguing that she was entitled to do so since American women had acquired this right that very same year. Juana Colón, another tobacco worker and mother of six, indefatigably defended women's right to enfranchisement. Though illiterate, Colón was a fiery orator and skilled organizer.[9]

Access to higher education for an unprecedented number of middle- and upper-class women opened up new careers and ambitions that found expression in gender specific institutions, such as suffragist clubs (including *Liga Femínea*, 1917; *Liga Social Sufragista*, 1921; *Asociación Puertorriqueña de Mujeres Sufragistas*, 1925) and professional organizations (*Asociación de Enfermeras*, 1916; *Asociación de Mujeres Graduadas de la Universidad de Puerto Rico*, 1936). Recent research has stressed that women teachers were in the vanguard of suffragist struggles in Puerto Rico.[10] Already by 1910 there were 928 female to 815 male school teachers. Nonetheless, a number of legal restrictions impeded female teachers from advancing in the school bureaucracy.[11] Women could neither be elected to nor participate in the election of members of school boards *(juntas escolares)*. "The suffragist school teachers," writes Yamila Azize, "acquire the awareness that in order to effect changes that would better the situation of women, women's active participation in the government of their country was fundamental."[12] Who were these teachers/suffragists? This group was composed of women from relatively well-to-do backgrounds, as well as a number of women whose families once owned a small amount of property, or from artisan backgrounds, including black and mulatto women. Many of the teachers from the latter group supported families and were in constant danger of losing their jobs and becoming indigent.[13] Such was the case of teacher, poet, and feminist Julia de Burgos.

The young poet wanted to pursue a bachelor's degree rather than a teaching certificate, but her precarious financial situation did not allow it. De Burgos had to work as a *maestra normalista* and sell her poetry door to door, a situation that greatly distressed her. As María M. Solá details in her biographical/critical essay on the poet: "In the face of every disadvantage, Burgos received in 1933, when she was 19 years old, the school teacher's diploma; she went from place to place, to Comerío, to Naranjito, to San Juan, wherever she was offered work, because there were very few job vacancies and she was partially responsible for her siblings' upkeep."[14] A number of de Burgos's poems attest to her feminism, especially in works such as "Yo misma fui mi ruta," and "A Julia de Burgos." These poems forcefully interrogate gender hierarchies and gender roles in Puerto Rican society. In the company of Dominican intellectual J. I. Jiménez Grullón, she traveled to Cuba and enrolled for a short period at the University of Havana, but she was unable to complete any degree there. De Burgos would shortly follow the road of Puerto Rican migration to New York where she later died destitute.[15] Though a feminist and a teacher, Julia de Burgos, and many other women in her social condition, did not have access to the opportunities that other, more affluent school teachers and professional women enjoyed. In the 1920s and 1930s neither women nor men of modest means would be able to travel abroad to complete doctoral degrees, or to enrich their education. Among the group of teachers and feminists, class background and race would also determine whether a woman could become a professional (doctor, lawyer, pharmacist, or philanthropist) or a low-paid teacher with a circumscribed future. Only a restricted number of women teachers went on to hold positions of power at the University, or to become secondary-school principals.

During the first decade of the twentieth century, women who aspired to study the medical arts had to go to the United States, because these fields of study were not available at the University of Puerto Rico at the time, according to historian María de Fátima Barceló Miller. In her study of the early incursion of women into the professions—medicine, nursing, pharmacy, law, and education—she explains that in the first decade the small number of women who studied medicine had to face hostile male colleagues. Nonetheless, these physicians had a significant impact in fighting tuberculosis, providing prenatal care, and health care for children.[16] Male doctors were equally hostile to nurses, considering them to be unqualified competition. The establishment of the first nursing school in 1903 prompted much growth in the field, and in 1917 nurses requested that the island's legislature give them official recognition. But, as Barceló Miller explains, "that petition was considered to be another one of those entertaining pretensions of Puerto Rican feminists."[17] Likewise, the School of Pharmacy, established in 1913, was not very welcoming. Nevertheless, 14 women pharmacists had graduated by 1920. Yet since these were women of means, not all educated women exercised their professions. Additionally, sexist attitudes also kept doctors and pharmacists from assuming any positions of power in their respective male-dominated professional organizations. The University of Puerto Rico graduated very few women lawyers, 7 in contrast to 149 men between 1920 and 1930.[18] This dismal record, Barceló Miller points out, helps us to appreciate the tremendous talents and achievements of Nilita Vientós Gastón, a 1926 law school alumna who went on to become very active in the law and in Puerto Rican intellectual and artistic life.

In spite of their modest numbers, the presence of increased cohorts of women in the public sphere threatened male monopoly and supremacy. Elite men were not so willing to let women—even of their same social class—share as equals in their power and symbolic capital. Though some parents might have been individually supportive of their daughters, there are many indications that the male elite did not voluntarily open its ranks to women. The bitterness of the struggle for suffrage is a case in point. From 1908 to 1929 twelve projects for women's suffrage were proposed to the legislature, but only one was accepted.

The Creole press of the time, according to historian Gladys Jiménez Muñoz, portrayed women's suffrage as a menacing part of the modernization of mores and social institutions. Journalists and politicians often linked the vote for women to the militancy and visibility of the laboring classes.[19] Elite public opinion in the late 1920s feared the "chaos" that new political protagonists would bring into the public sphere. Women's suffrage, in their view, could effect a blurring of boundaries at the symbolic level that would greatly destabilize *criollos'* hegemonic masculinity in the public and private spheres. As she explains, "Such fears immediately conjured visions of political cross-dressing and gender uncertainty among those opposed to granting women the vote and among mainstream representatives within the colony's legislature."[20] Embodying these anxieties were the suffragist and laboring women whom the vote would make too much like men, or "prostitutes," or "women of the streets."[21] Male privilege required strict controls over women's roles as mother/homemaker. Propertied men, and the women who agreed with them, saw sexual propriety threatened by the changing aspirations of women. The semantic slippage evident in the antisuffrage press analyzed by Jiménez Muñoz, links women in the public sphere to "public women" or whores. The foes of suffrage attacked gender equality with the specter of class equality (at least discursively). Furthermore, Creole men expressed great consternation over the perceived danger that the "masculine" voting woman would destabilize the heterosexual construction of hegemonic masculinity within their class. Consequently, the advocates of male privilege saw all these new symbolic and political areas of action for women as "disorderly."[22]

In the late 1920s in Cuba, a similar fear of the masculine woman gripped the intelligentsia. Cuban opinions on this matter varied greatly. On one hand, there were feminists who found themselves in the position of assuring their reading public that expanded rights for women would not transform women into the much feared *garzona.* As Nina Menéndez explains, well-known feminist Mariblanca Sabas Alomá wrote a series of articles that affirmed her groups' loyalty to heterosexism by pointedly condemning lesbianism. On the other hand, there were the much-publicized views of Spanish intellectual Gregorio Marañon who saw lesbianism as a biological aberration. Yet other voices, such as that of novelist Ofelia Rodríguez Acosta, would expand the social discourse about sexual freedom of choice. Rodríguez Acosta's 1929 best-seller *La vida manda,* featured an important character whose lesbianism is represented as a dignified life-choice, not as pathology. Menéndez's fascinating analysis of this novel leads her to conclude that, "Although Rodríguez Acosta does not explicitly condone homosexuality, there is clearly an absence in the novel of any ideal model of female sexuality or womanhood that would exclude a lesbian identity."[23] As Menéndez further underscores, the novel's critique of heterosexual romance, "is quite significant given the rampant homophobia of the mainstream feminist movement in Cuba at the time, and the generalized social invisibility of lesbians in Latin American society."[24]

For their part, working-class men writing in support of unrestricted suffrage and in defense of working women's dignity were not advocating the total dismantling of male supremacy. Feminine subservience was still a definer of maleness among all classes. Nonetheless, male trade unionists at times would turn on its head the elite's fear of the voting woman who assumed the role of men. Their tactic, as seen in a 1928 piece in *Unión Obrera* for example, was to asseverate that working-class women were decent and deserving of the vote because they worked outside and *inside* the home, unlike the well-to-do woman who leads a fashionable and parasitic existence, "sits idle not producing anything useful."[25]

The prostitution panic that targeted mainly poor white and Afro-Puerto Rican women vividly illustrates the ways in which female bodies—coded by discourses of gender, race, class, and sexuality—became battlefields or territories to be won over. Especially during World War I, prostitution was the object of the North American and Creole reformers intent on "rehabilitating" a mixed race population whose sexual practices (especially the preference for consensual relations) shocked the Northerners." But Afro-Puerto Ricans, as well as socialists," Eileen Suárez Findlay explains, "attempted to challenge the implicit linkage between blackness, poverty, and disreputability."[26] Black Puerto Ricans in the city of Ponce and elsewhere would respond to discourses that labeled working-class black women as prostitutes with what she characterizes as "a race- and class-blind presumption of female respectability."[27] This was explicit in the pages of the *Partido Republicano*'s paper *El Águila.* Moreover, the activities of the Socialist Party and the *Federación Libre de Trabajadores* trade union vigorously asserted worker's rights to decency in wages and respect for their persons.

In 1918, hundreds of poor women were arrested and charged with prostitution under the presumption that they were carriers of venereal disease. Many of the accused women contested their arrests on the street and in the courts by, in Suárez Findlay's words, "ensur(ing) that the state's violation of civil liberties remained in the spotlight; they thus played an important role in sustaining the opposition."[28] Impoverished mulatto, black, and white women became the target of the moralizing reforms of society women who swelled the ranks of philanthropic organizations. Well-to-do women, who perhaps saw this as an opportunity to assert their public presence, were more than happy to enter the prostitution or the prohibition of alcohol debates. As "decent" women who saw themselves exerting a beneficial influence on "fallen" women and their abused progeny, the reformers wrote on the subject, organized "charitable" ventures, and for a while visited the accused in jail. And although they were patronizing to the poor they intended to save, Suárez Findlay sees their response as more "woman centered" than that of their male counterparts.

The cases of progressive bourgeois activists Herminia Tormes and Olivia Paoli from the city of Ponce are instructive in this respect. "Ponce alone," explains Suárez Findlay, "out of the major cities in Puerto Rico, did not organize a squad of feminine police. In addition, the Ponce group focused on job creation and intensive literacy training, as well as instillment of labor discipline and moral reform."[29] Her study sheds further light on the factions that composed the suffragist reformists. Herminia Tormes, a light-skinned lawyer and the first Puerto Rican woman attorney, represented the victims of the antiprostitution campaign. Another interesting example is that of Olivia Paoli—a member of the progressive *Liga Social Sufragista* and the Socialist Party. Paoli raised nine children by herself after the death of her husband, Jacobin journalist Mario Braschi. "She eked out a living for herself and her children as a teacher and census taker," reports Suárez Findlay, "eventually becoming a journalist, renowned in the 1930's for criticizing the roots of poverty in Puerto Rico and the inhuman conditions of its prisons and reformatories."[30] Paoli was a white woman whose experiences and temperament led her to make common cause with the struggles of the poor.

Throughout the controversy, the U.S. colonial administration was ambivalent about the question of votes for women. On the one hand they acknowledged that since the franchise had been granted to women in the United States, Puerto Rican women now should logically have this right synonymous with citizenship. Yet the United States was not too keen on having more Puerto Rican political actors on the scene.[31] Suffragists would nonetheless plead their case with the federal authorities. In 1919 for example, in view of the stony refusals they received from patrician senator Antonio R. Barceló, a delegation from the *Liga Femínea*—Isabel Andreu de Aguilar, María L. de Ashford, and Milagros Benet de Mewton—went to Washington.[32] Famously, Barceló resisted women's suffrage even for those of his own class. In the end he would find it politically expedient to push for a literate-only vote. Leaders of the *Alianza* would incorporate the paternalistic discourses of the colonizers to promote the idea that the island elite was perfectly capable of deciding political and social matters for the illiterate masses. They were not unwilling to be in charge of the "civilizing mission" that North American colonialists were so fond of touting.[33]

Before going on to discuss what is perhaps the most important middle-class feminist manifesto of the 1920s in Puerto Rico, it is useful to make some remarks on the nature of the professional middle class as a whole in order to discern some of the functions, aspirations, and values of this peculiar elite. "This class can be defined, somewhat abstractly," Barbara Ehrenreich tells us in a parallel context, "as all those people whose economic status and social status is based on education, rather than on the ownership of capital and property."[34] In general, possession of a college degree and sometimes a graduate degree is required to be part of this distinct minority. Included among the middle class are people with such occupations as engineers, school teachers, professors, lawyers, physicians, government bureaucrats, middle management corporate executives, media and advertising people, scientists, social workers, therapists, architects, financial managers, and agronomists. Race, gender, and prestige further stratifies this group. "At the lower end," Ehrenreich writes, "there are hard-to-classify occupations like schoolteaching, which is certainly based on education, but which despite its aspirations, falls short of the kind of income and prestige awarded to professions traditionally dominated by men."[35] At the occupational level middle-class professionals have more autonomy than laborers, and are expected to be self-directing. These professionals often define—conceptualize and command—the work of others. To avail themselves of these opportunities, they must accept long periods of apprenticeship or study, which in themselves are elements of class cohesion and identity. Lifelong friends and future spouses often meet during the college and graduate school years. "Typically," Ehrenreich writes, "middle-class couples earn enough for home ownership in a neighborhood inhabited by other members of their class."[36] Education and consumption are used to establish status in relation to the working class. The middle class has access to "enriching experiences as vacation trips, psychotherapy, fitness training, summer camp, and the consumption of 'culture' in various forms."[37] Such professionals also enjoy a particular type of elite status that, while located well below the ruling class, is still elite in relation to the poor and the working class. But, Ehrenreich clarifies, this professional middle class constitutes an insecure and deeply anxious elite: "Its only 'capital' is knowledge and skill, or at least the credentials imputing skill and knowledge. And unlike real capital, these cannot be hoarded against hard times, preserved beyond the lifetime of an individual, or, of course, bequeathed."[38] Given that its access to capital is limited, an at times profound sense of insecurity permeates the lives of middle-class families intent on reproducing their status in the next generation. This explains the dictums of "discipline and effort" that this class propagates among its members and in its discourses about itself. Of course, the middle class passes on a certain amount of property and connections to offspring poised to benefit from this. But, while the middle class can welcome their children into a medical practice, the children cannot inherit diplomas, licenses, and skills.

The Suffragist Speaks: Mercedes Solá's *Feminismo*

Capitalism—even the dependent agro-capitalism exported to Puerto Rico—needed a certain level of literacy for its implementation. The suffragists/professional women were part of the skilled, literate work force, a necessary condition for the deployment of the new socioeconomic system. But changed economic conditions go in tandem with changes in the social subject. The feminists knew this and welcomed those social changes that they viewed as favorable. Suffragist leader and school teacher Mercedes Solá was among the professional women who, early in the 1920s, vied for acceptance as one of Puerto Rico's intellectual elite, a position that had the cultural clout to shape political feminist thought. In a conference paper read at the *Ateneo* in May 1921, Solá, *La Mujer del Siglo Veinte*'s editor, delineated what she understood by "feminism" and the "new woman." "Because feminism," says Solá, "is the doctrine that reveals and upholds the capacity and the right of women to use all of their energies and display their personalities just as men do, I believe that all women must feel an irresistible impulse in their hearts to embrace this cause, even if only for the conservation of their own personalities."[39] ("Siendo el feminismo la doctrina que expone y sostiene la capacidad y derecho de la mujer para desenvolver en la vida todas sus energías y ostentar su personalidad como lo hace el hombre, yo creo que toda mujer debía *[sic]* sentir en su corazón un impulso irresistible hacia esa causa, aunque sólo fuera por la conservación de su propia personalidad.") The suffragist school teacher believes that all women should realize that feminism benefits them, because it allows women's *personalidad* to thrive. What does she mean by this? Solá indicates that all working women de facto practice a *feminismo de acción* by their very presence in the paid work force. This feminist practice, unfortunately, goes unacknowledged by the *dependientes de comercio* or *empleadas de oficinas.* The working woman would do well to understand that, willingly or not, she has a relationship with the *raison d'être* of feminism. Men, for their part, have benefited from the work of the new woman in that they are paid more than a woman for equal work. Solá in fact unites her voice to that of other feminists around the world who even at that time demanded "equal pay for equal work."

Women, Solá argues, have successfully infiltrated a realm previously occupied almost exclusively by men. There are many areas where middle-class women's practical feminism is now triumphant:

> As proof of the triumph of our feminism of action, we have women working in stores, we also have them as merchants who direct and administer their own interests with complete success; we have them in all commercial and government offices doing a great job at shorthand, typing, letter writing, accounting. . . . In the professional arena we have female telephone operators, telegraph operators, nurses, pharmacists, dentists, medical doctors, lawyers. . . . In teaching they occupy a very central role, and they may even have the entire branch of Public Education in their hands.[40] (Como prueba del triunfo de nuestro feminismo de acción, tenemos la mujer dependiente en las tiendas del comercio, la tenemos también comerciante dirigiendo y administrando sus propios intereses, con entero éxito; la tenemos en todas las oficinas del comercio y del gobierno rindiendo un buen trabajo en taquigrafía, mecanografía, correspondencia, contabilidad. . . . En el campo profesional la tenemos: telefonista, telegrafista, enfermera, farmacéutica, dentista, doctoras en medicina, abogadas. . . . En el magisterio ocupa puesto principalísimo, y bien podía tener en sus manos todo el ramo de Instrucción Pública.)

Men no longer numerically dominated the public school system, and women entered this low-paying field shunned by men. Solá points out that women have taken the place in the educational system that men have deserted. This exemplifies the willingness, dedication, and generosity with which women serve their society, a central idea in Solá's defense of feminism. Women's selflessness and altruism, according to Solá, are unrecognized gender-based virtues that benefit all members of society. Even the wealthy woman, "she who only has to worry about governing her own home and taking care of her children,"[41] extends her realm of action through philanthropic work of a humanitarian and political character. (" . . . la que sólo tiene que prestar atención al gobierno de su casa y al cuidado de sus hijos.") Women are the ones who sustain religion and the ones who suffer the loss of their sons, brothers, husbands, and fathers in war. Solá reminds the audience of the price that all Puerto Rican women have paid in the World War. "Our women," says Solá,

> with a surprising level of civic consciousness and suppressing in her heart any expression of sorrow due to the sacrifice of her loved ones, march ahead with serene resignation. This, ladies and gentlemen, is a feminist triumph, because feminism implies the awakening of women to an awareness of their personalities, and to their *responsibilities* as well as to their *rights.*[42] (Nuestra mujer con un civismo sorprendente y ahogando en su corazón un grito de dolor ante el sacrificio de sus grandes amores, marcha adelante serena y resignada. Esto, señoras y señores, es un triunfo feminista, porque el feminismo implica el despertar de la mujer, consciente de su personalidad, a la vida de sus *deberes*, tanto, como de sus *derechos.*)

Inseparable from feminism, as understood by Mercedes Solá, is the dyad duties/rights. A woman's personality, that is, her "true" and "free" self, is molded by the biological call to motherhood. Motherhood, in the logic of her discourse, is inalienable from women. *La feminista* is by no means derelict in these duties. Solá's feminist is a responsible mother and wife who also participates, by economic necessity or philanthropic choice, in the public sphere. Solá's model of womanhood does little to promote the idea of freedom of sexual choice. It understands subjectivity, as bell hooks has written in another context, to be "mired by heterosexism, a narrative of selfhood contained within a paradigm of coupled relationships."[43] There is no space in Solá's discourse for the woman who does not desire to be a man's wife or the mother of children. Feminism, Solá takes pain to stress, need not be seen as alien to Puerto Rican reality. Her feminist subject will not clash in any fundamental way with societal expectations for women when it comes to sexuality.

Two societal conditions are indispensable for the triumph of feminism as Solá points out: "la escuela y el taller," schooling and remunerated work. She writes:

> Without education feminism can never prevail because feminism calls for women to be *capable* and to have *rights*, and the former cannot be obtained without an

> efficient preparation. That is why feminism demands not only equality between women's and men's activities but also a cultural level just as high for her as the one men receive. . . . In regard to the economic base, this too is indispensable. Women will not be able to achieve their emancipation without first achieving the economic independence that will substitute for men's tutelage.[44] (Sin la instrucción es imposible el triunfo del feminismo, porque éste sostiene la *capacidad* y el *derecho*, y la primera no puede obtenerse sin una eficiente preparación. Por tanto, el feminismo al demandar la igualdad de actividades entre el hombre y la mujer, demanda también la cultura para ella con la misma amplitud que la recibe el primero. . . . En cuanto a la base económica es también indispensable, pues la mujer no puede conquistar su emancipación, sin conseguir antes la independencia económica que la releva de la tutela del hombre.)

Yet here we see that Solá is critical of the society that allows men to wield such disproportionate economic power over the lives of women. Women are in the hands of men because they are not afforded the means to support themselves. She understands that women's other civil liberties are inseparable from her material or economic condition. On this account, her intervention is, indeed, unsettling for the gender-class-race system. In an oblique way she invites her audience to examine the new social reality of which women and men are *de facto* equal parts.

It would be unfair to look for absolute ideological coherence in Solá's text. Her discourse is predicated under precarious conditions. It is a defense and an affirmation of rights that women like Solá sincerely see as necessary. We should not forget that these suffragist/professional women remained a thorn in the flank of Creole hegemony at this time. Indeed, their mere existence represented a challenge to traditional *criollo* visions of femininity. The women themselves, as illustrated by the hesitation in Solá's discourse, harbored some ambiguous feelings about their new social status.

For the author, feminism is not a foreign import or fad propagated by outside feminists. It is an expression of the human desire for justice. Mercedes Solá very clearly states that "Feminism is coming because in these times of *world evolution and revolution* great human vindications will take place and women will have their share of these."[45] ("El feminismo viene, porque *en esta época de evolución y revolución mundial* han de tener lugar grandes revindicaciones humanas y entre ellas ha de tocar su parte a la mujer.") Faith in progress, that nineteenth-century teleological ideal, is co-opted by the women even if not originally intended for their usage. The new conceptualization of the subject as empowered social actor, which the Mexican and Bolshevik revolutions proposed, is also available as part of the rhetoric of progress that women's rights activists had access to in 1921. However, social upheaval has an ambiguous position in her discourse. For even though she appeals to evolution and revolution as ideological guarantors of the rightness of her cause, the class upheavals that convulsed Puerto Rican society in the first decades of the twentieth century are practically silenced in her text. Middle-class feminism feels compelled to present itself as collaborator and not as agitator. Solá assures her public that fundamental changes in the social, racial, and class structures of Puerto Rican society will not necessarily occur when feminists have the rights they desire. "The feminist woman as a social entity," Solá argues,

> is an excellent collaborator. *Feminism doesn't damage or disturb the social conglomeration;* on the contrary, a woman, by having a well-cultivated mentality, along with her renowned spirituality that is superior to man's, and her own special intuition that no one can deny, is adding an element of capability and utility to the social action she shares with her male companion.[46] (La mujer feminista como entidad social, es una excelente colaboradora. *El feminismo no daña ni perturba el conglomerado social;* por el contrario, teniendo la mujer su mentalidad bien cultivada, además de su reconocida espiritualidad superior al hombre y de esa clarividencia que le es propia y que nadie puede negarle, ella suma un elemento de capacidad y utilidad a la acción social en común con su compañero.)

With whom should the feminist collaborate? She is to help her mate in the better management and direction of society. Solá explains that since men have not always been enlightened in the management of world affairs—the horrible World War is an example of the debacle men can bring on the world scene—women's spiritual superiority, their "obra de amor," is a much needed *complement* to men's rule. Appealing to what is, in effect, a class discourse, she argues that the educated and spiritually superior (socioeconomically privileged) woman will make sure that she raises sons who will be more humane than their fathers, and, unlike their progenitors, will not be bent on the ruination of the world.

In a crafty rhetorical maneuver she goes as far as "congratulating" the all-male Puerto Rican Legislature for the beneficial laws they have passed on behalf of women (new laws of divorce, child custody, community property, minimum salary). But, though it is true that generous men exist, Solá insists that most men are not generous. Women need laws that will protect their rights as citizens. Nonetheless, Solá must have perceived her position as one of weakness, for she still feels obliged to cater to her male listeners. She illustrates with a number of examples how the home will benefit from the presence of an educated and empowered mother and wife. Solá takes great pains to show men what advantages they will derive from feminism. She states that feminism, ultimately, makes for a more pleasant wife and mother: "The dignified woman will feel happy in her home; she will be pleased to beautify it and to make it enchanting for her loved ones. She will be the center of attraction whom everyone looks to because at her side they delight in all of life's joys and in her they find solace."[47] ("La mujer dignificada se sentirá feliz en su hogar; se complacerá en embellecerlo y hacer de él un encanto para los que ama. Ella será el centro de atracción que reciba todas las miradas de los seres que le rodean, para disfrutar junto a ella todas las alegrías y buscar en ella todos los consuelos.")

Enfranchised women will not lose their feminine charms, nor will the home be endangered; Solá is emphatic on this point. As a preventive measure, women will be given a strong moral education. There will be no danger, the listeners are assured, of the proliferation of "fallen women" because only capable women need to be granted these political rights and freedoms. In Solá's words, "As feminists we reject that fear. *The danger would be in the freedom of uneducated women;* never in one who has been fortified with a severe moral basis and a broad mental cultivation."[48] ("Las feministas rechazamos ese temor. *El peligro estaría en la liberación de la mujer incapacitada;* pero nunca en la que está fortalecida por una severa base moral y un amplio cultivo mental.") Here Solá expresses the view held by most middle-class and upper-class feminists: suffrage need *only* be extended to schooled women. *La mujer capacitada* is a variant of the middle-class Euro-racial concept of the *by nature capable and incapable* races and classes. Not all women are *capacitadas*, she underscores, to handle freedom or the vote. In fact, such liberties would be harmful to those women who do not have a strict moral upbringing and plenty of education.

We should remember that in the eyes of the middle and upper classes the poor did not always observe strict and "moral" behaviors. The elite labeled as immoral the codes of ethics followed by the working class and the peasantry. Church weddings, for example, were not universal among poor people who might not have been able to afford such a luxury. Soon after 1898 the new colonial administration changed the juridical status of women, enabling them to initiate actions in their own name, testify, pursue an occupation legally, and be consulted in marital decisions regarding shared property.[49] Additionally, a woman could file paternity suits, have the right to keep her children, represent herself in business transactions (even if married), administer her dowry and share of family property (even if divorced).[50] Eileen Suárez Findlay's study of the politics of sexuality and race in Puerto Rico shows that American colonial administrators and elite Puerto Ricans were disturbed by the lack of interest in Church marriages among the working classes. To remedy what they saw as a lack of morality, the Americans instituted free civil marriages. Yet, as Suárez Findlay explains, "Many laboring Puerto Ricans were actively *un*interested in marrying—not simply prevented from doing so. It was the right to divorce, not access to marriage, that eventually provoked a popular explosion of interest."[51] The new legalization of divorce in the 1902 Civil and Penal Code had potentially enormous cultural impacts on the balance of power between the genders. It codified as grounds for divorce the cruelty by one's spouse, drunkenness, abandonment for a period of a year, and adultery. The code also weakened the power of the Catholic Church since all marriages became civil contracts. Suárez Findlay argues that divorce laws helped to create sympathy for the American regime among the popular classes and among liberal elite men and women.

But Solá's *caveat,* the desirability of strict moral upbringing, is also designed to assuage the fears that well-to-do feminists would support "free love" or *libertinaje* as its foes also called it. She overtly refutes this point: "There is no doubt that the woman with a strong education, Christian morality, and a well-cultivated mentality that create a balance between her heart and her brain, will always sustain the highest concept of personal dignity."[52] ("No hay duda alguna de que la mujer con una firme educación moral cristiana y su mentalidad bien cultivada de modo que equilibren su corazón y su cerebro, se sostendrá en todo momento, conforme al más alto concepto de su dignidad personal.")

Substantial passages of the conference paper are dedicated to the educational role of women in the family: as molders of children and of future citizens and patriots, as persons invested with the right and duty to "formar al ciudadano." The connection between women and nation is achieved by way of the mothering function. Solá specifies that: "Nationalities exist where man wants them to, because he is the one who must form them. But this is only done with love and, as the *mother* will give it, the son will want a country and will have a country."[53] ("Las nacionalidades existen donde el hombre quiere, porque él es quien ha de formarlas. Pero esto se hace sólo con amor, y como lo dará la *madre,* el hijo querrá una patria y tendrá una patria.") The supreme feminist achievement is, in the final analysis, to shape men. As Solá puts it, "The feminist masterpiece will be women's formation of men."[54] ("La obra feminista maestra, la hará la mujer en la formación del hombre.") This is women's great calling, the "gran misión de su vida." Feminism is not only about the vote, Mercedes Solá tells us, but about forging citizens through an enlightened motherhood.

Ultimately, Solá declares herself in favor of conservative feminism, and states that she became a feminist out of fear that radical feminism, favored by many working-class feminists, might gain popularity in Puerto Rico. She says, "I frankly declare that the fear that a radical brand of Feminism might take hold in our country had quite an influence on my decision to take part in the movement." [55] ("Con franqueza declaro que el temor de que se entronizara en nuestro país un Feminismo radical, influyó grandemente en mi ánimo para tomar parte en el movimiento.") Her conservative feminism had as one of its objectives the empowerment of the women of her class and the silencing of the women who did not belong to it. This conservative feminism that she professed needed to keep all the trappings of traditional femininity intact, "hacer ostentación de todos los rasgos de la feminidad."[56] It needed to conserve "nuestro tipo criollo," Creole femininity in accordance with the tradition and racial stratification of Puerto Rican society. She sums up her requirements of a conservative feminist:

> A delicate and beautiful woman; with a refined walk and an elegant carriage, who dresses in fashion with a refined taste and style, and who at balls dresses in lace, ribbons and flowers. Who in all her activities and actions is feminine; and in her heart holds a love of humanity and of the ideals that purify souls; whose character flows from her personal dignity and whose will from the strict realization of her duties. Who is the queen of her home. Whose intellect is exquisitely cultivated; who loves the sciences and the arts; who is aware of and contributes to overcoming her country's problems and who is her country's most complete *citizen* (rendered in Spanish as masculine) and most faithful *son.*[57] (Una mujer delicada y bella; de andar fino y porte elegante. Que vista a la moda, con gusto, recato y oportunidad y que en sus galas luzca encajes, cintas y flores. Que en todos sus actos y acciones sea femenina; que en su corazón tenga amor para la humanidad y los ideales que purifican las almas; que su carácter responda de su dignidad personal y su voluntad del estricto cumplimiento de sus deberes. Que sea la soberana del hogar. Que su intelecto tenga un cultivo exquisito; que ame las ciencias y las artes; que conozca y coopere en los problemas de su país y que sea de su patria el *ciudadano* más integro y el *hijo* más fiel.)

These attributes of the *feminista conservadora* are a blueprint for the making of the middle-class Euro-Puerto Rican woman. She has enough financial resources to be refined and elegant, fashionably dressed, but not ostentatious. She may not look "manly" in any way, but must be pleasing to the male gaze. She must be a homemaker who is highly educated. Finally, in an uncritical use of phalocentric language, she is made to be virile, but only as far as her duties as citizen are concerned. Thus her designation as *ciudadano integro* and *hijo fiel* is simultaneously a promotion and a demotion. Solá feels compelled to accept the terms imposed by the very gender hierarchy that she, as a feminist, opposes. Absent from her conservative feminism is a critique of racial hierarchies in Puerto Rican society. No mention is made whatsoever of the racial inequalities and tacit segregation that were then the norm in Puerto Rico. Solá speaks for *criollas*—white women—to *criollos*—white men. The *feminista conservadora* is not a *mulata* or black woman, for it would be hard to find a (self-identified) black woman in the social class to whom she speaks. Though it remains unuttered, race is crucial to her conceptualization of the "capacity" of the conservative feminist.[58]

Solá died in the mid-twenties, but the sector she so well represented carried her ideas to their logical conclusions. Educated and professional women joined in clubs and associations to promote and extend their bid for civil and economic rights. The position taken by the young Margot Arce on women's rights follows in the footsteps of Solá's suffragist ideals. Arce's position on universal suffrage is emblematic of the dilemma faced by women who already enjoyed important class, socio-racial, and cultural privileges. A rising woman intellectual during the decade of the twenties, Margot Arce plainly states in an interview (later published in the book *Mujeres de Puerto Rico,*

1935) that suffrage is not a right to be extended to all. The interviewer Angela Negrón Muñoz comments on Arce's ideas of restricted suffrage:

> Doctor Arce does not believe in the beneficence of universal suffrage. She assures us that the vote is a very dangerous weapon—double-edged blade—and she therefore demands absolute responsibility of anyone who uses it. Citizenship, the right to vote, should be a privilege acquired through civic merit and proven honor: it is an acknowledged myth that 'all men are equal.'[59] (No cree la doctora Arce en la bondad del sufragio universal. Asegura que el voto es un arma muy peligrosa—de doble filo—y exige por lo tanto absoluta responsabilidad de quien la utiliza. La ciudadanía, el derecho de votar, debería ser un privilegio adquirido por méritos cívicos y por probada honradez: ya que va siendo un mito que 'todos los hombres son iguales.')

University professor Margot Arce echoes Solá and adds a new wrinkle: Ortega y Gasset. She explicates and repeats Ortega y Gasset's ideas on the rights and functions of the talented minority. As with men, only a worthy minority of women should have the right to participate in self-government. Arce says, "I don't see democracy as the exaltation of the 'divine average' and, even less that almost superstitious respect for the majority. . . . For me, it's the 'select few,' not the 'rebellion of the masses.'"[60] ("No entiendo por democracia la exaltación del 'divine average' menos aún, este respeto casi supersticioso a la mayoría. . . . Para mí, las 'minorías selectas,' no la 'rebelión de las masas.'") Suffrage, as Arce sees it, should not be extended to everyone, because the right to vote should only be in the hands of those who are "responsible." In the wrong hands—that of the rebellious masses—the vote becomes a dangerous weapon. Citizenship should be a privilege accorded to people of recognized probity. The tendentious logic of Arce's argument suggests that there is a difference in the moral and intellectual capacity of the elite qua elite, which the masses—by nature—cannot hope to equal. The "rebellious masses" are without civic merit or honesty; their political actions are deemed irresponsible. She reflects the reluctance of her social class even to consider complete democratic participation of all races and classes in the affairs of Puerto Rican society. Arce's logic sets up a neat syllogism: as with children, the behavior of the masses is untrustworthy; only the privileged few can be trusted with adult decisions. Note that it is a white woman who is voicing these rules of exclusion and inclusion. She makes way for those women who—like herself—are in possession of literacy and, more importantly, high culture. But even as she asserts elite women's right to speak and act as citizens, she artfully assures her male peers that the *criollo* social hierarchy should be maintained, even strengthened.

Margot Arce takes pains to underscore the connections between bourgeois women's rights and the balance of power. Her brand of feminism assumes that women as a group have boundaries that cannot be breached. Moreover, this feminism must beware of leaving behind the thing called femininity, which must be compulsorily fostered to the maximum. Arce believes in a "Feminism . . . that tends to develop in women the highest level of femininity; giving them an acute awareness of the great dignity of our sex, of the privileges, and of the undeniable limitations."[61] ("Feminismo . . . que tienda a desarrollar en la mujer el máximum de feminidad; que sea conciencia plena de la gran dignidad de nuestro sexo, de sus privilegios y de sus innegables limitaciones.") Such a narrow desideratum over-simplifies the history of women's suffrage, de-emphasizes the importance of collective struggles, and downplays the role of militancy for women. As she puts it, "The conquest of political and economic rights that has concerned women since the last century is not, in my humble opinion, the essence of the female problem."[62] ("La conquista de derechos políticos y económicos que ha preocupado a la mujer desde el siglo pasado hasta hoy, no es, a mi corto entender, lo esencial del problema femenino.") If political and economic rights are not essential to "the woman question," then what is? Women must understand above all, Arce affirms, that they are not intellectually equal to men. Her experiences as a teacher are proof enough:

> The main thing is that the equality of the sexes does not exist even at the intellectual level . . . and so the woman question should be framed from this radical point of view. *Therefore I cannot defend co-education:* each sex requires a certain environment and certain methods in order to set in motion those different pedagogical solutions, since the objectives they pursue cannot be, in any way, identical for both. To be a woman means—if one is consciously a woman—to accept a certain destiny. This is what I consider to be the most serious problem for feminism.[63] (Lo esencial es que la igualdad de sexo no existe ni aún en lo intelectual . . . y por lo tanto, el problema de la mujer debe enfocarse desde este radical punto de vista. *En este sentido no puedo ser partidaria de la coeducación:* cada sexo requiere ambiente y métodos necesarios para poner en ejecución aquellas soluciones pedagógicas diversas, porque los fines que persiguen no pueden ser, en manera alguna, idénticos para ambos. Ser mujer significa—si se es mujer conscientemente—aceptar un determinado destino. He aquí, para mí, el más grave problema del feminismo.)

Biology as destiny had been previously used to sustain class and racial hierarchies by believers in social Darwinism. Arce too understands biology as destiny: women and men have different intellectual capacities.[64] This belief impels her to advocate separate educations for men and women, educations that would pursue different goals. To *be* a woman, according to Arce, one must accept the inevitability of that different destiny. She undoubtedly means compulsory motherhood, given the militant Catholic views she often expressed. Additionally, we should not forget that coeducation had been implemented on the island as a result of the new colonial educational system. In a deft way Arce is criticizing this particular colonial intrusion in the *criollo* gender system. She fails to mention that coeducation had facilitated her own education in the formerly male-only profession of university teacher and literary critic. When Arce traveled to Spain as a graduate student, she was able to study because Spanish universities had recently been opened to female students. She does not seem to recognize these facts, nor the privileges that she derived from a coeducational public school system.

Arce takes great pains to distance herself from militant suffragist politics. She seems to advocate education not in tandem with political militancy, but as an alternative to it. Her choice excludes direct action, one of the most powerful tools for social change that feminists around the world have used with a great deal of success. In this, the Puerto Rican working-class feminist movement also differed from the middle- and upper-class feminist expression. In many important ways what bourgeois suffragist movements demanded was to be included in the power elite. Their goal was to garner greater participation in those areas in which the men of their class held sway.

Yet it would be a mistake to underestimate the impact of the ostensibly moderate reforms of bourgeois feminism. In Puerto Rico, as in other countries, the white male elite bitterly opposed even moderate sharing of power across gender lines. Puerto Rican suffragists had hoped that the right to vote would be extended to them with the 19th Amendment, passed in 1920 by Congress. This was not to be, despite lobbying by Puerto Rican women with U.S. feminist groups. In an effort to bring the vote to Puerto Rican women, a delegation of the *Liga Femínea* from San Juan—which included renowned feminist activist Andreu de Aguilar—traveled as early as 1919 to the States to cement relations with their feminist counterparts.[65] Many influential *criollos* conveniently chose to see in women's suffragist struggles an undesirable intrusion of American ideas into the social life of the island at the cultural level, as well as at the level of colonial politics. Moreover, most of these men saw as natural the types of legal, economic, and emotional control they held over their daughters, wives, and sisters, and they were not eager to relinquish these powers.

There were important differences between the aims and tactics of Puerto Rican working-class feminism and the upper- and the middle-class Puerto Rican suffragists. Strategic maneuverings and alliances were the order of the day for elite women as they negotiated their way into the public sphere in the pursuit of their own interests. It is small wonder that working-class feminism had a contentious relationship with bourgeois feminism. Often during the 1910s and the 1920s, working-class feminists were in the vanguard of Puerto Rican feminism: they were the first to demand suffrage for women, and would not trust the good will of the legislators in the fight for women's rights.[66] In light of this dual history the struggle for the vote becomes a privileged conjuncture in the study of the interlocking gender and class dynamics of the first three decades of the twentieth century in Puerto Rico. Yet we must take care not to see simplistic correspondences between class background and ideology. As Jiménez Muñoz clarifies, the *Liga Femínea*, for example, was a group that harbored among its ranks diverse viewpoints, even as it also contained a majority faction that advocated limited suffrage (for literate women only). The *Liga Femínea*'s reorganization into the *Liga Social Sufragista* in 1921 signaled the increasing influence of socially progressive women professionals who sought the vote along with other social reforms. A year later the league would, in fact, promote several bills in the legislature that sought the vote for all women. Some elite Puerto Rican women proved willing to compromise in their demands and strategies, but most suffragists remained split in their support for universal suffrage. A faction of progressive women professionals from the *Liga Social Sufragista* was willing to unite its strength with the working-class feminists and the Socialist Party on the issue of the vote. In 1924 labor leader Mariana Morales Bernard and suffragist leader Milagros Benet de Mewton asked the courts to grant all Puerto Rican women the vote. This joint action caused a rift in the *Liga Social Sufragista.* According to Azize, "The most liberal sector of women, sympathizers of the *Partido Republicano Puro,* remained in the social league under the leadership of Milagros Benet de Mewton. But the most conservative sector . . . founded the *Asociación Puertorriqueña de Mujeres Sufragistas.*"[67] These less progressive suffragists identified with *la Alianza.* The Alliance was composed of the *Partido Unión,* which represented the *hacendado* ideology, and the wealthy conservative wing of the *Partido Republicano,* which represented the anti-national bourgeoisie linked to North American interests. "The conservative group," according to Azize, "united under the *Asociación Puertorriqueña de Mujeres Sufragistas,* decides to accept the proposal of the *Alianza* to legislate for restricted suffrage."[68] Even so, the *Alianza* was slow in approving even restricted, literate-only female suffrage.

At a number of levels the issue of women's suffrage was linked with partisan politics as well as colonial politics. The Socialist Party's coalition with the progressive wing of the Republican Party—the *Coalición*—could seriously upset *hacendado* voting blocks if working-class illiterate women had access to suffrage. The number of potential women voters—literate and illiterate—was estimated at 300,000, of which only 50,000 qualified to vote under restricted suffrage proposals. This left out 250,000 illiterate women voters who could shift the balance of power. In an effort to assuage the fears of the legislators, veteran suffragist leader Ana Roqué de Duprey repeatedly declared her support for the restricted suffrage measures. She writes: "If they are afraid that the illiterate classes will take political power as a result of giving the vote to women, the solution is to restrict the illiterate classes' access to the vote."[69] ("Si temen a que las clases analfabetas tomen fuerza política concediendo el voto a la mujer, la solución era *[sic]* restringir el voto a las clases alfabetas.") Women's enfranchisement, the *Asociación Puertorriqueña de Mujeres Sufragistas* argued candidly, need not include poor and uneducated women.

Working-class women had formed their own feminist organizations following a vision of class-based rights. In 1921 the trade unionist *Asociación Feminista Popular de Mujeres Obreras Puertorriqueñas* was advocating equal rights for all women, as well as fighting for better wages, labor protection, child protections, and access to food for their children. Most of the membership of this organization came from the tobacco workers' organizations. Though working-class and elite suffragists both made reference to a discourse of motherhood in their demands, they were tied to their material circumstances and class projects.[70] Jiménez Muñoz explains that a year later, "many of its members participated in pro-suffrage activities with the *Liga*—before and particularly after the formation of the *Coalición* in 1924."[71] This reflects some affinities between socially progressive urban professionals and working-class leadership. A rapprochement in 1926 between the *Asociación Puertorriqueña de Mujeres Sufragistas* and the working-class feminists in an organization called the *Sub-Comité Sufragista de Puerta de Tierra* was short-lived on the other hand. In the end the *Asociación Puertorriqueña de Mujeres Sufragistas* would go back to their conservative positions. This prompted working-class leader Pilar Pacheco to break her temporary alliance with the conservative suffragists, and to publicly announce the reasons for their incompatibility. Pacheco wrote in a letter to the daily *El Mundo:*

> I will never lend my energies to a cause I do not have faith in, in which I do not believe. That is to say that I do not believe nor do I have faith in *limited suffrage* for men or for women. . . . Women should make room at the public table for the dispossessed; the upper classes are already seated. A people is not uplifted through the destruction of their hopes nor by telling them *you are no good.* [72] (Jamás prestaré mis energías a una causa en la cual no tengo fe, en la cual no creo. Es decir no creo ni tengo fe en el *sufragio restringido* ni para los hombres ni para las mujeres. . . . La mujer debe abrir la mesa de la casa pública y hacer sitio para los de abajo, los de arriba ya están acomodados. No se eleva a un pueblo destruyendo esperanzas ni diciéndole *tú no sirves.*)

Here Pilar Pacheco is calling attention to the limitations of the closed feminism of the middle class, as opposed to the necessarily open, more inclusive feminism of the working class. For its part the *Liga Social Sufragista*, at this time under the direction of school teacher/activist Ricarda L. de Ramos, would remain steadfast in its support for universal suffrage. In 1927 the *Liga Social Sugfragista* would initiate a lobbying campaign in Congress on behalf of Puerto Rican women's suffrage. It was only with the impending concession of universal suffrage by the U.S. government that the patrician *Alianza* approved the restricted female suffrage project in April 1929 in order to avoid a loss of face in the game of colonial politics.[73]

Literate women voted for the first time in the 1932 elections, bringing a new variable into play in island politics. The literacy rate was low, so this measure excluded the majority of Puerto Rican women. Of the suffragist organizations only the *Liga Social Sufragista* protested against the literate-only vote, as did the Socialist Party. The socialists emphatically protested literate-only suffrage in a letter to the *Asociación de Mujeres Votantes* (the new name of the *Asociación Puertorriqueña de Mujeres Sufragistas*). Responding to this state of affairs, socialist trade-unionist leader Santiago Iglesias wrote, "We will not rest nor will we stop using all available resources until the law is rewritten to recognize the right of all the women and all the men of Puerto Rico to vote without qualifications or privileges."[74] ("No descansaremos ni dejaremos de mover todos los resortes legales y públicos hasta que la ley sea reconstruida reconociendo el derecho de votar a todas las mujeres y los hombres de Puerto Rico sin cualificaciones ni privilegios.") In 1935 the Socialist Party presented another unrestricted suffrage project to the legislature. A year later, in 1936, after more than two decades of arduous struggles, poor women with no access to education went to the polls to exercise this elemental right (as well as rite) of citizenship.

The importance of the variegated alliances and strategies that literate elite women engaged in during the 1920s cannot be underestimated, for they suggest a class-based identification over a gender-based solidarity. Sisterhood, as understood by the most important and powerful sector of the bourgeois suffragist movement in Puerto Rico, was limited to the sisters of one's class and race. Education was one of the markers of their difference. This is why it was prized, and why many among the *hacendado* elite wanted to limit its availability. Most importantly, a university education was patent proof of a woman's mental capacity and ability to be gainfully employed in the traditionally male liberal professions.

The women intellectuals of the *Generación del Treinta* had close ties with the suffragist movement of the 1920s. Even when these women intellectuals sought to minimize the importance of those connections, they were indebted to the strategies of empowerment that the suffragists made available to their younger sisters. They were students or soon-to-be professionals during the heyday of Puerto Rican suffragist struggles.

Works of fiction can also give us clues about the men's reaction to the women's challenge at a time when the gender system was in flux. Chapter 5 examines one such instance. Emilio Belaval's *Los cuentos de la Universidad* investigates some Creole reactions to the new woman at the university during the 1920s.

Gender, Racial, and Social Attitudes and Expectations

A survey conducted in 1926 and 1927 concerning the social expectations of students at the University of Puerto Rico allows us a rare glimpse into the racial attitudes and biases of this privileged sector of Puerto Rican society. Two hundred and thirty students responded.[75] The survey was particularly interesting in that it reflected clear gender-specific expectations of unmarried men and women regarding desirable qualities in a mate. Furthermore, the women's responses coincided closely with the men's. The Chancellor of the University at the time, Thomas E. Benner, summed up the results as follows: "In short, the ideal woman in the minds of the male undergraduates of 1926–1927 was of the Latin type (and here he means Euro-Latin), vivacious, with black hair and black eyes, five feet one inch tall, weighing 121 pounds, *comfortably well-off*, attractive but not necessarily beautiful, a university graduate who *knew how to take care of children and to prepare food*, who was *very feminine and not very demanding*."[76] As far as the expectations of the women regarding the ideal man, the results indicated that he should also have black hair and eyes (again, read Euro-Latin), be five feet nine, slender, enjoy sports, and have an active social life. At the same time the ideal male would be economically comfortable, university-educated, and completely debonair. One third of the women said that a man should be *exigente*, demanding, while a much smaller number disagreed.

Both men and women surveyed agreed that the ideal woman should be undemanding. Coming at a time when the debate on women's suffrage in Puerto Rico was at its apogee, these responses illustrate the gap (for some college-educated women) between their desire for political enfranchisement and the unwillingness to change in their sex-role expectations. The poll also suggested that some women desired to remain outside of all controversy. Benner himself comments on the significance of the results. He says, "It is not surprising . . . that three fourths of the men and a fourth of the women were opposed to women's suffrage which was at issue in the island in 1926 and 1927."[77] Of the women interviewed, 54 percent came out in favor of voting rights. The remaining women were uncertain. Benner does not clarify that of the women who favored suffrage, most campaigned for the right to vote for literate women exclusively. Literacy requirements at the polls, as we saw earlier, would preclude suffrage for most of Puerto Rico's working-class women, leaving political participation to those few women whose social class had made them especially "fit" for the job. In other ways, moreover, the survey results suggested that the university students maintained very conservative values. For example, three fourths of the men and two thirds of the women rejected the idea of marriage with a person of a different race. Benner does not elucidate this point, but "of a different race" here means black or mulatto. Almost 100 percent of the men said they would *demand* virginity in a mate. The majority of women did not seem to object to a man's sexual experience outside of the marriage bonds.

The literature and cultural institutions of the *Generación*'s cultural formation would construct an ideal of womanhood that would, if not explicitly at least implicitly, not interfere with the emerging anticolonial discourse. Women intellectuals, for their part, must have wrestled with the contradictions imposed by a supposed lack of capacities.[78] As women, their subjectivity was defined more in terms of what they were *not* rather than describing what they *were* in affirmative terms. When, for example, serious and rigorous thought is understood as virile (possible only when the best white male mind produces it), how could women intellectuals ever produce serious and rigorous thinking? Women's very bodies were seen as impediments, as defective vehicles. In this context it became imperative for women writers, critics, and university professors to forge networks with other women, often with an international component, in order to affirm, nurture, and support their new subject positioning.[79]

The suffragist struggles of the 1920s provided a model of empowerment for women that made possible the strong presence of a number of women critics in the intellectual field. Among the members of the 1917 *Liga Femínea* one finds women active as intellectuals during the decades that followed. Suffragist leader Isabel Andreu de Aguilar, who was a member of the very first graduating class of the University of Puerto Rico in 1907, worked in the high echelons of the University bureaucracy and, in 1936, rallied the support of a group of women professionals to form the *Asociación de Mujeres Graduadas de la Universidad de Puerto Rico.* Literary critic Concha Meléndez, who though younger than many of the other suffragists had also been involved in the formation of the *Liga Femínea*, would be a member of the new association. But most importantly, younger women were as vital to the existence of the *Asociación de Mujeres Graduadas* as were the older suffragists. Along with Margot Arce, lawyer and intellectual firebrand Nilita Vientós Gastón was also a young founding member of this organization. Steeped in the ideology of professionalism, the association sought to advance its women members professionally and socially. The association's charter, "Reglamento de la Asociación de Mujeres Graduadas de la Universidad de Puerto Rico," specifically states this as a goal:

> (a) Be certain to establish and preserve relations between the women graduates of the University of Puerto Rico. (b) Work for the improvement and growth of the University of Puerto Rico. (c) Offer its members opportunities for cultural improvement, such as scholarships, conferences, concerts and any other analogous activity. (d) Offer the members help and cooperation in case of merit.[80] ([a] Procurar establecer y conservar relaciones entre las mujeres graduadas de la Universidad de Puerto Rico. [b] Laborar por el mejoramiento y engrandecimiento de la Universidad de Puerto Rico. [c] Ofrecer a las asociadas oportunidades para su mejoramiento cultural, tales como la concesión de becas, la celebración de conferencias, conciertos y cualquiera otra actividad de índole análoga. [d] Ofrecer a sus asociadas ayuda y cooperación en casos meritorios.)

Almost in its entirety the association was composed of teachers, university professors, social workers, and other professional women who had benefited from the gains of the suffragist movement. They were also very much part of the perceived need for some kind of change in the discourse of the nation that characterized the 1930s. Paradoxically, the young members did not feel the obligation to allude to an explicitly feminist ethos as a project valid for their new circumstances. Yet in 1948, only twelve years after the foundation of the group, Arce and Vientós refer to the complex personal and institutional nature of the relationships among the members of the *Asociación de Mujeres Graduadas* in Isabel Andreu de Aguilar's eulogy. Arce and Vientós praise Andreu de Aguilar's work as a teacher, philanthropist, and matron of culture, but ambiguously comment on Andreu's work as a feminist. According to Arce,

> Isabel knew that being a woman is not just a gift we are given at birth, but rather our daily conquest; an art that demands, on the one hand, the acceptance of many limitations, and on the other, the free choice of sublimating sex through the purifying and regulating exercise of the spirit.[81] (Isabel sabía que ser mujer no es tan sólo un don que recibimos al nacer sino una conquista nuestra de cada día; un arte que exige, de un lado, la sumisión a muchas limitaciones, y del otro, la libre decisión de sublimar el sexo mediante la acción purificadora y ordenadora del espíritu.)

To be a woman, according to these statements, it is not enough just to be born a female: one has to *become* a woman. Arce's statement indicates some awareness that gender is a socially constituted reality. Her notions of gender as constructed are, however, very limited. She does not critique the narrowness and the symbolic (and physical) violence implied in this particular construction of femininity. She acquiesces to a "narrative of selfhood" geared to disciplining women's bodies and psyches. Womanhood, as understood by Arce, is an endeavor that requires some skills. This self-made woman has to submit to a large number of limitations, which Arce does not specify here. A woman must choose the spiritual over the sexual. She must rein in desire and subject it to the disciplining and purifying actions of the mind. The mind, with what seems like great pains, has to subject the female body to its will. Using the language of psychoanalysis, "sublimar el sexo," Arce describes this task as almost a willingly accepted physical torture. She strives to couple a discourse of gender to a discourse of professionalism. Women (and children), according to the popular psychology of the time, were supposed to be close to nature, undisciplined. Both had to learn deferment of pleasure. We should remember that the formation of the middle-class professional requires long years of schooling and discipline. Consequently, the ability to defer gratification is highly valued in the professional arena.

The eulogized Andreu de Aguilar represented the ideal type of Puerto Rican woman—educated, philanthropic—so unlike those false models of womanhood proposed by Hollywood.[82] Her "exquisite femininity" was combined with her dedication to civic and cultural endeavors. This is a very important point, for it safeguards all the women involved in the text—Aguilar, Arce, and women readers alike—from contamination with, and accusations of, overly "masculine" behaviors, accusations that would make any woman suspect of deviance.

Nilita Vientós explains the role of feminism for her own generation, and what she understands as Andreu de Aguilar's legacy. Vientós remembers her activist friend and mentor:

> I can still see her on the balcony when she would come to chat with me in the afternoon and we would hold passionate discussions about a theme that we would never agree on: feminism. Because that highly feminine creature was the most feverish defender of the right of women to participate in all activities; she felt as if any woman's triumph were her own. Now I realize that we were both right. *The women of my generation did not need to be feminists anymore; she had done it for us.* She had the thankless task of the initiator; she fought for what today in Puerto Rico, regarding women's status and work, everyone accepts and surprises no one.[83] (Aún me parece verla en el balcón de casa, cuando venía, en las tardes, a charlar conmigo y sosteníamos apasionadas discusiones sobre un tema en que jamás logramos ponernos de acuerdo: el feminismo. Porque aquella creatura tan femenina era la más fervorosa abogada del derecho de la mujer a participar en todas las actividades, cualquier triunfo de una mujer le sentía como suyo. Y ahora comprendo que las dos teníamos razón. *Las de mi generación no necesitábamos ya ser feministas, ella lo había sido ya por nosotras.* Le tocó la ingrata tarea del iniciador, luchó por lo que hoy en Puerto Rico, en cuanto a la posición y labor de la mujer, todos acatan y a nadie sorprende.)

Vientos's text, just as Arce's, is keen to emphasize the femininity of Andreu de Aguilar. "Aquella creatura tan femenina" was not a manly woman, even if she was "la más fervorosa abogada," a paladin of woman's rights. One can infer from the text that in those heated and "apasionadas discusiones" Vientós did not agree ("jamás logramos ponernos de acuerdo") that women had to struggle for gender-specific rights or for the usefulness of identifying oneself as a feminist. Vientós seems satisfied with the gains already made by bourgeois feminism, which in the text are characterized as a certain standing in society plus the right to work.

In 1948 this statement might have been true for a very limited number of the educated professional and upper-class women, but it had no resonance for the majority of Puerto Rican women then (nor does it now).[84] Vientós almost welcomes the demise of the first feminist surge. Moreover, her statements are a vivid example of this feminism's shortcomings. She refuses to speak from a position where the gender inequalities of her society might be acknowledged or examined. One could argue that her statement is more the deployment of a strategy than a statement of fact, as she would have the reader think.

Increasingly, the new woman intellectual's discursive strategy was one where gender-specific concerns were silenced. This dissociation was, at best, precarious and always threatened because it is never true that women's rights are stable in a sexist society. Furthermore, the instability of women's rights is inextricably linked to the thorny question of a difference often read in the physicality of the body, something that bourgeois suffragists did not fully recognize. Luisa Capetillo, unlike the middle- and upper-class suffragists, had stressed through her actions (recall her strategic use of drag) that the body should not be used as a marker of inferiority. This carries profound implications for the subject who is always gendered-classed-raced. The women literary critics of Vientós's generation labored to dissociate their professional persona from a gender position that could put in question their ability to tackle "universal" concerns. But as V. Y. Mudimbe explains, Eurocentric formulations of the "universal" as a norm camouflage "a narrative of the Same."[85] The narrative of the "same," as feminists have convincingly noted time and again, does not tolerate gender, racial, or cultural difference.

As inheritors of the gains of suffragist activism, the young members of the *Asociación de Graduadas* prized the right to an education and to work. These women were in a position to attain what had been the goal of elite feminism from its inception. Chapter 3 examines how the pursuit of an education and a profession, as well as entrance into the male-dominated intelligentsia, was confronted by the *Asociación de Mujeres Graduadas* as a group. Their journal, *Revista de la Asociación de Mujeres Graduadas de la Universidad de Puerto Rico*, reveals the deployment of some of the strategies used by the women to empower themselves.

CHAPTER 3

Professional Women and the Refashioning of the Self

Newspapers and literary and cultural publications offered the Creole intelligentsia opportunities to disseminate its aesthetic and social concerns. Its most active sectors, intent on delineating national affirmation projects vis-à-vis American colonialist writings and the contestatory proletarian press, enlisted and organized institutions such as the University of Puerto Rico, the *Ateneo Puertorriqueño*, and the *Instituto de Literatura Puertorriqueña* as sites of cultural authority and arbitration. These organizations not only publicized *criollo* perspectives and formulations; they provided a critical discourse and interpretive guidelines to the practitioners and to their public. Given the small number of the island's intellectuals, these institutions shared members in common. For example, *The Instituto de Literatura Puertorriqueña* created and funded in 1933 by a mandate of the Creole legislature, was housed at the University. The institute awarded yearly prizes to the most meritorious works by Puerto Rican writers: Emilio S. Belaval's short stories, Julia de Burgos's and Palés Matos's poetry, Tomás Blanco's essays. In tandem with this, and of primary importance in the cultural scene of the period, was the appearance in 1935 of the *Biblioteca de Autores Puertorriqueños* (BAP), a private publishing house dedicated to encouraging works by Puerto Rican writers.[1] BAP promoted works by Tomás Blanco, Palés Matos, Clara Lair, Enrique Laguerre, Antonio S. Pedreira, and many others. Additionally, most of the writers and intellectuals of the period were *ateneístas:* Emilio S. Belaval, Margot Arce, Nilita Vientós, and Vicente Géigel Polanco to name just a few. The *Ateneo*, a private civic/cultural organization founded by the *criollo* liberal intelligentsia in the nineteenth century, but reinvigorated in the mid-1930s, became one of the principal rallying sites of this cultural formation in its resistance to North American cultural policies.

As described in Chapter 1, these cultural institutions had as their explicit mission the promotion of Puerto Rican culture as *criollo* professionals portrayed it: Spanish, white, literate, and embattled. In such a charged context the "language question" assumed principal importance. For these literati the protection of the Spanish language as well as the promotion of Puerto Rican literature took the guise of a battle; "aprecio y defensa" (appreciation and defense) became their rallying cry. The creative writing and criticism produced by these cultural nationalists was that of a class in historical retreat, a class that in a period of crisis and marginalization looked to the Spanish colonial past in a major recuperative effort.[2] Conservation was a first step. Reinterpretation and continued production were a second stage of this process. This chapter analyzes the journal of the *Asociación de Mujeres Graduadas de la Universidad de Puerto Rico* at the level of content and as an expression of the multiple voices and aspirations of professional women intellectuals-in-training. The goal is to survey the gender-based concerns present in their *Revista*, and to shed light on the extent to which this publication articulated the cultural nationalism of the *Generación del Treinta.* Is cultural nationalism present in a different way than in the journals dominated by the male intelligentsia?

I must clarify that even as I designate the *Generación del Treinta* group by their common nomenclature, I see them as a cultural formation more than simply a literary generation. By exploring the socio-cultural location of this enterprise I hope to avoid seeing these intellectuals in terms of mere generational conflict, successive "movements," "isms," and "style" as the explanation of their literary/discursive production. Following Raymond Williams's lead I endeavor to map out, "the *internal organization* of a particular formation; and its *proposed or actual relations to other organizations* in the same field and to society more generally."[3] The British theorist's conceptual framework suggests that power relations within a cultural field, as well as pressures exerted by society, may provide a more coherent explanation of the emergence of styles and "isms." In this light the study of literary journals is of preeminent importance since they function as organizers and bearers of the multiplicity of voices within an ideological cohort. The more successful journals restructure the literary system and act as arbiters of the aesthetics of a cultural formation.

Like Williams, literary critic Francis Mulhern provides useful starting points for the analysis of a literary journal within a cultural context. Mulhern's momentous study of the British periodical *Scrutiny* furnishes useful insights for the study of literary journals in their "material specificity." We should try to understand a literary journal as the dynamic organizer of competing and complementary voices in a cultural formation. A journal is not, as Mulhern understands it, "a serially published 'big book,'" but rather "a practice that unfolds in time, constituting a history that was specific to itself and at the same time bound to the other histories that made up (. . .) history as a whole."[4] Leaving aside cults of personality, he views the figures who labored in journals, in his case a journal dedicated to English intellectual life, "not as an expression of a master-subject (Leavis) but as a play of many voices, within the ideological formation of which *Scrutiny* was the organizer and bearer."[5]

Mulhern's definition of the literary journal alerts us to a number of questions regarding the nature and purpose of this practice. A journal is, of necessity, a collaborative enterprise. It provides a space where different shades of opinion within a formation are compiled and presented to the reading public. Argentine critics Carlos Altamirano and Beatriz Sarlo suggest that a key function of the literary journal is to generate ideological, literary, or aesthetic opinions within the cultural field. Generally limited to readers of literary works, the journal strives to organize its readership around polemical issues inside the cultural territory: "Ethic or aesthetic, theoretical or political, the circle drawn by a journal in order to define the place it occupies, or aspires to occupy, also determines the level of polemical distance taken vis à vis other positions included in the literary field."[6] It is in this dynamic and plural relationship that the importance of literary journals for a given cultural collective becomes paramount.

This chapter first examines the role of small literary and cultural publications as the voice of the professional middle-class intelligentsia. I propose that the influential cultural journal *Índice* had an androcentric understanding of culture and national identity. In its pages there was precious little space for women to debate and explore their concerns and their particular situation in the cultural field. *Índice*, as the masculine voice of cultural nationalism, silenced women and the debates over their rights. Was this effacement perhaps one of the reasons that prompted the *Asociación de Mujeres Graduadas* to publish a journal of their own? The second part of this chapter, dedicated to the thematic and cultural analysis of the *Revista de la Asociación de Mujeres Graduadas de la Universidad de Puerto Rico*, seeks to answer this question.

Pointing the Way: *Índice*'s Mapping of the Cultural Terrain

With *Insularismo*, university professor and critic Antonio Pedreira provided the intellectuals of his generation with a point of view on Puerto Rican culture and with a program for intellectual endeavor. But we should remember that it was in the pages of the monthly *Índice: Mensuario de historia, literatura, arte y ciencia*, published from 1929 to 1931, with Samuel R. Quiñones, Vicente Géigel Polanco, and Antonio Collado Martel as co-editors, that *Insularismo* was born. Distinguished readers of this journal were invited to send in their answers to the "¿Qué somos? ¿Cómo somos?" opinion survey. The journal's initial aim was pragmatic, according to Géigel Polanco. In his words:

> It was in April of 1929 that four young writers of the batch that in the national annals has come to be called "the 30s Generation" came up with the idea of bestowing on the Puerto Rican school system a modest monthly dedicated to History, Literature, Art, and Science, that could provide supplementary readings for the Spanish classes at the University and in the public and private High Schools.[7] (Fue en abril de 1929 que cuatro jóvenes escritores de la hornada que en los anales patrios se llama 'Generación del 30' concebimos la idea de dotar al sistema escolar de Puerto Rico de un modesto Mensuario de Historia, Literatura, Arte y Ciencia, que sirviera de lectura suplementaria a las clases de Español de la Universidad y en las Escuelas Superiores públicas y privadas.)

Índice's influence expanded beyond the editors' intended audience. The journal was widely read by writers and intellectuals outside the university, and a limited number of issues also circulated abroad in other Latin American countries including Cuba.[8]

The journal's editorial choices tell us much about its ideological project. *Índice* dedicated various issues to the works of nineteenth- and early twentieth-century Puerto Rican writers: Ruiz Belvis, the abolitionist; Tapia, one of the most progressive writers of his time; Francisco Oller, the painter. In an effort to present the roots of a *criollo* identity, situated by the editors in the nineteenth century, a number of historical figures were presented as exemplary, that is, as the founding fathers of a *criollo* Puerto Rico. The journal's hero worship also included José de Diego, known as *el caballero de la raza*, one of the most vocal early twentieth-century advocates of independence, yet a staunch opponent of the vote for women as well as of worker's rights.[9] By presenting male historical figures as the true embodiment of Puerto Rican values, *Índice* was contesting the United States's program of acculturation that insisted on disseminating, through the public school system, the mythology of the North American "founding fathers," and other symbols of American patriotism. *Índice*'s expressed aim (salutary from many perspectives) was to curtail the ever-active neocolonial propaganda machine. Yet the journal had additional ideological effects that cannot be disregarded. The cult of personality and glorification of the *criollo* past that it meant to generalize could not be readily accepted by all Puerto Ricans, especially those who had suffered at the hands of the Creole hegemony. For example, patrician poet José de Diego was notoriously antiblack and antiartisan. He had opposed the appointment of Afro-Puerto Rican physician José Celso Barbosa to the colonial government because he could not abide that the Americans had chosen a man he considered a social inferior. A lawyer for one of the sugar corporations and a legislator, de Diego repeatedly opposed progressive labor legislation. As far as the organized working class was concerned, he was one of the oppressors.

The unabashed glorification of the *criollo*/Spanish colonial past in the pages of *Índice* goes as far as justifying the institution of slavery, as well as explaining away the white slave holders' unwillingness to give up their racist privileges. Rafael W. Ramírez's essay on the repressive black code issued by the notorious governor general Juan Prim ultimately comes out in defense of the slave holders and plantation owners. "The need to keep peace on the island," Ramírez writes, " . . . to defend the rights of white people—*the minority of the country's inhabitants*—and to keep away forever the unhealthy influences of the neighboring islands, explains the existence of this law that was, like many 'bad things' from Spain, a child of the times and of the circumstances of the historical moment."[10] ("La necesidad de mantener la tranquilidad de la isla . . . de defender los derechos de la gente blanca—*minoría de los habitantes del país*—y de alejar para siempre las malsanas influencias procedentes de las islas vecinas, explican el porqué de este bando que fue como muchas 'cosas malas' de España, hijo de la época y de las circunstancias del momento histórico.") Ramírez eagerly overlooks the cruelty and injustice done to the enslaved and to free blacks. In fact, the historian portrays the rebellions of the enslaved all over the Caribbean as "unhealthy influences" over enslaved Puerto Ricans, casting the slave owners as the victims, not the oppressors. He is, moreover, unable to mask his desire to exonerate the Spanish colonial government from any real responsibility for the torture and murder of black Puerto Ricans and Africans. It is one of the very conditions of privilege, be it racial, class-bound, or gender-bound, to mask its workings and advantages. The descendants of the Creoles like Ramírez are beneficiaries of the system of white prerogatives inherited from Spanish colonial rule. His discursive strategy is to explain away the "many bad things from Spain" as one of those things that cannot be helped, thus naturalizing the inherited system of privilege.

Not only is *Índice* an advocate of a certain historical discourse, the journal also promoted the *Generación*'s position on the language question by publishing various articles authored by Puerto Rican and Spanish scholars, such as the aforementioned Rubén del Rosario, Tomás Navarro Tomás, Pedreira, Margot Arce, Géigel Polanco, and E. Fernández Vanga. Navarro Tomás's research on Puerto Rican Spanish was of immense importance for the polemic over the "language question." His work was used, and sometimes abused, to reinforce the linguistic demands made by the opponents of bilingualism. Language, as we saw earlier, is a favored issue of nationalist affirmation. In this view language must remain pure, for it cannot suffer contamination without changing and becoming something other. *Índice* takes a strong stance against the use of English in the public school system. Its writers had a vested professional interest in stopping the spread of bilingualism. When

Margot Arce returned from Spain in 1930, after completing her doctoral degree, she briefly joined *Índice*'s editorial board.[11] In her article about Spanish pronunciation in Puerto Rico, "Sobre la enseñanza de la pronunciación española en Puerto Rico," she underlines the evils menacing the Spanish vernacular of the island: *dialectismo*, *vulgarismo*, and *extrangerismo.* Arce proposes as a solution that " . . . we should adjust our pronunciation to the model offered by the proper speech of Castile—in this case undeniably the rule—which is what has been exalted by the written tradition and the artistic manifestations of our language"[12] (" . . . conviene que se ajuste nuestra pronunciación al modelo que nos ofrece el habla culta de Castilla—en este caso 'meridiano' indiscutible—que es la consagrada por la tradición ortográfica y por las manifestaciones artísticas del lenguaje"). By this, she advocates one form of colonialism over another. Puerto Ricans have to speak cultivated Castilian and rid themselves of their dialect. Arce's call for linguistic conformity illustrates the complexity of the language question in the politically charged environment of the 1930s. From her class perspective, and from the standpoint of a language professional, she calls for the use of the Castilian norm. We cannot forget, however, that, while most people opposed the exclusive use of English as the language of instruction, not everyone opposed the teaching of English in public school systems.

A close look at the contents of *Índice* reveals a desire to open a space for modern Puerto Rican literature. But this modern literature is a manly pursuit, as we see in the roster of the avant-garde poets present in the journal's pages. Ribera Chevremont, Palés Matos, Juan Antonio Corretjer, Manrique Cabrera, Graciany Miranda Archilla, and Clemente Soto Vélez all shared in a desire to renew Puerto Rican poetry. With the understanding that writers were privileged seers into the culture's "soul," these young poets were a testimony to the existence and viability of a Puerto Rican culture and, consequently, the right of nationhood. *Índice* likewise enlisted the prestige of writers from the older generation such as Luis Lloréns Torres, a practitioner of *jibarismo literario* and a recognized master of the *décima.* His literary usage of this popular poetic form was highly praised as an exemplary contribution to the advancement of the Puerto Rican "cultural personality."[13]

Índice expressed the cultural aspirations of the young men of the *Generación del Treinta.* Personal and professional relationships nurtured early on would continue in its pages and beyond. Many of its young contributors went on to occupy important positions in Puerto Rican culture and politics. For example, of the four young founding editors of *Índice*, two, Samuel R. Quiñones and Vicente Géigel Polanco, belonged to the avant-garde poetry group "Grupo No," active in San Juan in 1925. Among the young *noistas* gathered around the *Ateneo* and the University, we can also count Juan Antonio Corretjer (who became a militant and leader of the Nationalist Party), Cesáreo Rosa Nieves (who became a University professor and literary critic), Antonio Paniagua Picazo, Emilio R. Delgado, and Vicente Palés Matos (brother of Luis). The *noista* group started to wane in 1926 as many of the members graduated from the University and moved to the professions.[14] A decade later, when the *Partido Popular Democrático* was organized in 1938, Samuel R. Quiñones and Géigel Polanco went on to hold important positions in the party's hierarchy.

Women do not appear often in the pages of *Índice.* Their absence is especially noteworthy in the area of creative literature. Critic Concha Meléndez contributed more often than any other woman, with articles such as "Static and Dynamic Elements of Greek Art," and her germinal essay "Tres novelas de la naturaleza americana," on the Latin American novel. But not a single woman's opinion in the survey on Puerto Rican nationhood "¿Qué somos? ¿Cómo somos?" was ever printed. The journal did not specifically invite women to respond, nor were views on this matter, if sent, ever made public. As far as *Índice* was concerned, women had nothing to offer on Puerto Rican national identity or current affairs. It is surprising also that the volatile question of women's suffrage was never openly discussed in the journal. I suggest that this never-acknowledged gender bias had important implications for aspiring women intellectuals of the *Generación.*

The editors of *Índice,* however, were careful to present themselves as dispassionate observers of the Puerto Rican socio-cultural situation. They adopted the stance of the moderate voice of reason and learned inquiry, thereby adding to their credibility as intellectuals. This rhetorical strategy was immensely successful and did much to cement the journal's critical reputation. Yet at times its tone could not help being influenced by the rhetoric of the local and international avant-garde literary movements. The first editorial, or "Aterrizaje" (landing), reads like an avant-garde manifesto, in spite of the editors' protestations that they are objective observers.[15] I quote from the first paragraph of their inaugural issue:

> It arrives without the boastful intention of shaking up the mostly calm rhythm of our literary scene in a rough, innovative jolt, or of dislocating with bold, defiant arrogance the prevailing direction of our thinking. . . . Ours *is not an avant-garde journal* in the sense of those that so immoderately tire the century are proclaimed to be. . . . In its pages the reader will have few opportunities to form his lips into a surprised "O." Although perhaps he will have many to purse them with a puzzled curiosity. . . . We will give priority to ? over ![16] (Llega sin alardoso empeño de violentar en brusco sacudimiento innovador el ritmo más bien sosegado de nuestra vida literaria, o de dislocar, con audaz arrogancia retadora, el vigente sentido de nuestro pensamiento. . . . La nuestra *no es revista de vanguardia* en cuanto tal se predica de las que fatigan inmoderadamente al siglo. . . . En sus páginas, pocas oportunidades tendrá el lector de redondear, admirado, la boca en forma de O. Aunque acaso muchas de contraerla en curiosidad interrogante. . . . Concedemos superioridad a ¿ ? sobre ¡ !)

Índice set the standard for many of the little magazines that were to follow. In fact, comparisons became inevitable. "*Índice* summarizes the best qualities that characterize later journals," says literary critic Martínez Capó, "its central theme and that of all its contemporaries: the Puerto Rican personality."[17] Martínez Capó is right in his assessment that the literary journals that followed would in many respects be very similar to it. A number of topics appear time and again in the literary journals that range from *Índice* to *Asomante*. These themes are presented by the journals as part of a necessary cultural work; cultural work that fomented, illustrated, demonstrated, and preserved a Puerto Rican "character" or "la personalidad puertorriqueña." Some of them are: Puerto Rico's Hispanic heritage under siege; the conflict between Anglo-Saxon culture and Hispanic culture; the question of Spanish vernacular and the problems of bilingualism; the university. These questions are related to the larger theme of the need to resolve Puerto Rico's political status. They permeate the critical discourse on literature as well as the literature itself.

The project was so successful in developing critical discourses and setting the agenda for the "legitimate" parameters of Puerto Rican literature that their disciples would, with the notable exception of José Luis González, follow their directives into the sixties. Writing in 1955, for example, Martínez Capó says: "*Índice,* faithful to the word it preached, went in search of our past and honored in its pages our patriots and writers of yore."[18] Martínez Capó is indeed right. He praises *Índice* for fulfilling its program—to provide its readers with a glorious past and national heroes. His critical discourse, nevertheless, does not go beyond the laudatory. On the level of possibilities for a cultural critique, his style of analysis has more serious implications. It enthusiastically participates in *Índice*'s prescriptions decades after the journal's publication. Martínez Capó's acceptance of *Índice*'s project at face value—the journal does what it says it does—is part and parcel of the defensive style of criticism practiced by the Generation of 1930 and perpetuated by its disciples. For years to come criticism indulged in tautology as an explicative strategy for Puerto Rican literary and artistic production.[19]

Índice ceased publication in 1931. Other journals followed: *Ámbito* and *Brújula* in 1934, *Ateneo Puertorriqueño* in 1935. *Ámbito,* "La revista que difunde el pensamiento actual," was an independent University of Puerto Rico student publication that, contrary to the official university press, welcomed politically controversial subjects. Of *Ámbito* and other similar student periodicals Isabel Picó de Hernández says: " . . . they were yet another expression of the penetrating consciousness that was developing in the university student body as a result of its collective experiences. . . . Due to their clear identification with the anticolonial struggles and their open criticism of the university authorities, these publications became catalytic agents of the student movement, and the reflection of their general condition."[20] The journal also included contributions by well-known university professors and intellectuals, many of whom were also listed as editorial consultants, welcoming a mentoring relationship between the students and their *Generación del Treinta* teachers. Some of the contributions of well-known figures include an essay by María Cadilla de Martínez on the poetry of Virgilio Dávila, Pedreira's "El deporte hípico y la cultura" (the sport of horse-racing and culture), and novelist Enrique Laguerre on contemporary Puerto Rican literature. *Ámbito* also featured poems and short stories as well as editorials and articles on the language question. Jaime Benítez, who would later become chancellor of the university, contributed a series of articles on university reform. The journal reproduced some pieces by nineteenth-century intellectual Alejandro Tapia, "El loco de Sanjuanópolis" and "Universidad para Puerto Rico." *Ámbito*, it should be stressed, was not a literary journal per se. It reflected the concerns of an important sector of the student body, students who discussed the question of Puerto Rico's independence and social justice. And, as far as university reform was concerned, the journal demanded the democratization of the university.

Brújula (1934–1937) was the quarterly of the Circle of Spanish Teachers *(Círculo de Maestros de Español)*. Edited by Cesáreo Rosa Nieves and J. Asencio Álvarez Torres, this quarterly circulated primarily among Spanish teachers. Its main purpose was to provide a space for Puerto Rican letters by cultivating what it called "boricuismo."[21] *Brújula*, the compass, intended to guide Puerto Rican literature toward "Puerto Rican landscapes and color." ("paisajes y color puertorriqueño.") The Hispanic Studies and Pedagogy Departments of the University of Puerto Rico are listed as coeditors. Contributors to this journal included: Margot Arce, historian Lidio Cruz Monclova, pedagogy professor Carmen Gómez Tejera, secretary of education José Padín, historian Rafael W. Ramírez, and many others. Literary and musical criticism, poetry, and the language question were among its themes. Concha Meléndez wrote on José de Diego; Margot Arce wrote on Carmen Alicia Cadilla's poetry; and Cesáreo Rosa Nieves wrote on the *criollo* and patriotic aspects of Puerto Rican poetry in "Dos ángulos de la poesía en Puerto Rico."[22]

In 1935 Samuel R. Quiñones, Géigel Polanco, Emilio S. Belaval, Margot Arce, Nilita Vientós, Miguel Meléndez Muñoz, and Ramón Lavandero, all members of the *Ateneo*, published *Ateneo Puertorriqueño*, which was to come out until 1936 and then again from 1938 to 1940. Emilio S. Belaval's "Los Problemas de la cultura puertorriqueña," his answer to *Insularismo*, was first published here, as was Paniagua Serracante's "Meditaciones interpretativas de nuestra cultura." At the time of this journal's publication Géigel Polanco was both president of the *Ateneo* and secretary of the *Instituto de Literatura Puertorriqueña*.

As we have seen, the intellectual field in which the *Generación del Treinta* was active favored an employment of the Creole-identified nationalist discourse at the level of institutions such as the *Ateneo*, the University, and literary and cultural journals. The crossover from institutions to journals was intense. As the demands for greater university autonomy prove, the university was not totally in the hands of the professional elite. This is why the *Ateneo,* as an independent institution, became so important.[23] It served as a catalyst and safe haven for political and cultural discussions and projects. Active membership in this institution was vital to the women intellectuals of this group. Members of *Asociación de Mujeres Graduadas* hosted conferences and participated in the Ateneo's forums and publications. The *Ateneo* welcomed their participation with the tacit understanding that the task at hand was to promote the high national culture of Puerto Rico. But the members of the *Asociación de Mujeres Graduadas* must not have been totally satisfied with the types of institutional access open to women professionals in general. As we have seen, a journal as important as *Índice* showed no interest in the opinions and contributions of women, or even in the ways in which women participated in the journal's project. From reading this journal one would never suspect that the "woman question" was such a burning issue at the time, or that as citizens women had ideas about Puerto Rican culture and society. The journal of the *Asociación de Mujeres Graduadas,* which I examine in the section that follows, will provide clues not only to the projects of the association itself, but to the silences of male-dominated institutions in relation to women intellectuals.

Revista de la Asociación de Mujeres Graduadas de la Universidad de Puerto Rico: A Journal of Their Own?

The first issue of the *Revista de la Asociación de Mujeres Graduadas de la Universidad de Puerto Rico* came out in October, 1938.[24] The *Revista,* according to its editor Margot Arce, was not directed solely to the members of the association, nor would it be a feminist journal "in the political sense of the word." As Arce explains:

> It is not the intention of this journal to limit its activities to the group of women composing the Asociación de Mujeres Graduadas of the University of Puerto Rico. . . . Nor do we intend to create a feminist journal, in the political sense that is often given to that adjective. *We are not going to defend the exclusive and excluding interests of only one group,* nor are we going to reduce our activity to merely demanding rights.[25](No es el propósito de esta revista limitar su acción al grupo de mujeres que forman la Asociación de Mujeres Graduadas de la Universidad de Puerto Rico. . . . Tampoco intentamos hacer una revista feminista, en el sentido político que suele dársele a este adjetivo. *No vamos a defender los intereses exclusivos ni excluyentes de un grupo,* ni a reducir nuestra actividad a la mera exigencia de derechos.)

The vehemence of Arce's voice is striking. Negations and protestations open the first two paragraphs. She defines the aims of the journal in the negative, and insists that the journal not be labeled feminist or active in feminist politics. The *Asociación de Mujeres Graduadas* seems to be eager to protect itself against accusations of elitism, on one side, and to avoid alienation of their male peers on the other. The association, after all, was in part an offshoot of the conservative feminism of the previous decade. Such feminism, as I discussed, had insisted on defending its class privileges, "los derechos exclusivos y excluyentes de un grupo." Elite feminism had lost that round of the class battle when universal suffrage was adopted.

The journal, the reader is told, will be the voice of professional Puerto Rican women in the public arena. At the same time, the stated intention cautiously aligns the journal with some of the most important goals of the influential male intellectuals of the time. The *Asociación de Mujeres Graduadas* announces its resolve to participate in Puerto Rico's social and political debates "and contribute in some way to the spiritual life of our people"[26] ("y contribuir de algún modo a la vida espiritual de nuestro pueblo"). As was the case during suffragist struggles, Arce points out that professional women can help Puerto Rico by addressing questions that traditionally have been the domain of women: "As women, we are inclined with loving preference to moral and pedagogical issues, to that which concerns education, health and the well-being of children and women, to the passing of necessary and prudent laws, and the amendment of faulty laws."[27] ("Como mujeres, nos inclinaremos con preferencia amorosa hacia las cuestiones morales y pedagógicas, hacia lo relativo a la educación, salud y bienestar del niño y de la mujer, hacia la aprobación de leyes necesarias y prudentes, y la enmienda de leyes erradas.") The journal implicitly promises not to threaten the socially instituted gender division of labor and to give preferential treatment to questions that have to do with the role of women as guarantors of morality, educators of children, and caretakers of others.

In a strategic move the first editorial tries to strike a balance, however precarious, between woman and nation. It vows to accomplish a dual mission: to address problems that have to do with Puerto Rican women and with Puerto Rico as a nation. The women take great pains not to be labeled as politically irresponsible. They assure the reader that the *mujeres graduadas* can be trusted with important questions such as the present and future of the nation. The editorial states: "The destiny of Puerto Rico is important to us; we also consider it important that Puerto Rican women totally accept the dignity of their sex and be capable of finding an efficient solution to the problems that concern them as women in particular and as Puerto Ricans in general."[28] ("Nos importa la suerte de Puerto Rico; también nos importa que la mujer puertorriqueña acepte plenamente la dignidad de su sexo y sea capaz de ejercer una acción eficaz en la solución de los problemas que le atañen como mujer en particular y como puertorriqueña en general.") These professional women have something to say about Puerto Rican cultural, social, and political matters. The editorial carefully casts women's participation in the affairs of the nation as a fulfilling of commitments, not as an unwarranted intrusion. Arce writes, "First and foremost it is our unavoidable obligation to attend to the duties that correspond to our triple condition as women, university graduates and Puerto Ricans."[29] ("Atenderemos primero, y por obligación ineludible, al ejercicio de los deberes que nos impone la triple condición de mujeres, de graduadas de la Universidad y de puertorriqueñas.") They want recognition as women, as professionals, and as Puerto Ricans. The editorial can be read as a response to Antonio Pedreira's call in *Insularismo* to the *criollo* youth of the nation. He had omitted women but, nonetheless, they want to come forward and be counted.

A detailed analysis of the contents of the journal reveals the new ethos and mission, as well as the limitations, of the professional women educated by the University of Puerto Rico. These women provided models for new modes of being and behaving that became especially important to the industrialization projects of the late forties, fifties, and sixties. Their journal explores new possibilities in the public sphere for privileged, educated, middle-class women. During the next three decades many of the contributors to the pages of the *Revista* became authorities in their fields and trained the next generation of professional educators and social workers.

My examination of the *Revista* will discover what issues are most prevalent and pressing for the group. Even though this is not a purely literary journal, enough importance is given to literature that we may discern a literary canon favored by the editorial staff. To explore this question I will determine the frequency with which Puerto Rican, Spanish, and Latin American authors and subjects appear, and also consider the related question of the presence of exemplary figures to whom an issue, in part or in whole, is dedicated. I will also ascertain what other subjects besides literature appear in the journal and what weight they carry. In addition, the frequency and significance of debate over "the language question" and the related area of how cultural nationalism is represented in the journal must also be determined. Lastly, I will examine the extent to which political and world events inform the contents and perspective of the *Revista*.

The first article of the inaugural issue (1, 1 [1938]) is a transcription of the educator Carmen Gómez Tejera's keynote speech at a soirée hosted by the Circle of Spanish Teachers in homage to Alejandro Casona, the Spanish dramatist.[30] Tejera praises Casona's didactic theater, his children's stories, and the revival of Spanish classic theater.[31] Her stance is laudatory, as befits an homage, and proposes Casona as a model for Puerto Rican teachers and the public in general. He represents Spanish tradition and culture (Golden Age and Modern). Set within the scenario of colonial cultural politics, the homage is emblematic of the effort of Puerto Rican intellectuals to encourage ties with a larger Hispanic community abroad.

Tejera's speech is followed by Herminia Acevedo's article on children and learning, "Como aprende el niño." Acevedo displays her knowledge of the new pedagogic methods in vogue during the 1930s, and shows her enthusiasm for what the pedagogy professor sees as the promises of a New Deal in the field of education: "These schools have discarded the old Socratic, Spencerian, and Herbartian methods and, ignoring harsh protests by the defenders of mental discipline, they have established the New Deal in education."[32] ("Estas escuelas han descartado los viejos moldes socráticos, spencerianos y herbartianos y a pesar de la crítica severa de los defensores de la disciplina mental, han establecido el Nuevo Trato en la educación.") Roosevelt's New Deal was a symbol of hope in the desperate economic situation of 1930s Puerto Rico and a source of ideas on how to remedy it. New Deal policies would be enthusiastically received, and would play an important part in the populist politics of the emerging *Partido Popular Democrático*.[33]

The next article, written by Isabel Andreu de Aguilar, the association's president, "La educación de adultos como movimiento cultural de estos últimos tiempos," is a transcription of the conference delivered at the Association for Adult Education. The school, for Andreu de Aguilar, is a way to ensure democracy. According to the veteran educator, there is an urgent need to combat illiteracy in order to ensure economic prosperity and political stability. Her talk is directed at the professional women educators responsible for the schooling of adults who, most likely, were economically disadvantaged. In the island's social context of the 1930s this is a politically charged endeavor. At stake was the continuing issue of who would be in charge of educating Puerto Ricans of the different social classes, and to what ends. Indeed, the practices and experiences of working-class cultural institutions in the 1910s and 1920s had shown that politically active workers wanted and needed to be in charge of the contents as well as of the institutions that would shape and inform their consciousness.[34] Would an education that perpetuated the social—gender, class, racial—hierarchies benefit poor people? For its part, the professional elite was intent on controlling curricula and the availability of education in Puerto Rico. As discussed earlier, the type of expertise they possessed allowed professionals to perform indispensable functions in the administration of commerce and government.[35] Furthermore, in an agricultural society like Puerto Rico during the first half of the twentieth century, professional and technical expertise was at a premium.[36] No doubt, Andreu de Aguilar's desire to combat illiteracy is sincere. Other countries had done it, and she proposed that Puerto Ricans can succeed at this task too. Yet, the author does not face the problem from the perspective of those who are to be educated. As we will see later in this chapter, education is implicated in the question of competing class interests.

An article by Berta Cabanillas on the economic problems of the housewife, "Problemas económicos del ama de casa," addresses the issue from the perspective of the upper middle-class Puerto Rican consumer, a small group in 1938. According to the author, "The responsibility of satisfying all of our population's needs falls upon more than three hundred thousand women, housewives, in their multiple obligations as directors, administrators, and providers of the home."[37] ("La responsabilidad de satisfacer todas las necesidades de nuestra población recae sobre más de trescientas mil mujeres, amas de casa, en sus múltiples obligaciones como directoras, administradoras y proveedoras del hogar.") This well-intentioned article is typical of the impulse in so-called women's magazines to "educate the housewife" in her new role as consumer. Dispersed throughout the journal are advertisements for women's clothing, pianos, and cars. The ads, no doubt, were a way of defraying the production costs of the journal, but they also point to the availability and marketability of new consumer goods for an elite sector of the population. They appeal to professional women who worked and for whom there existed a whole new array of consumer goods "al alcance de casi todos los bolsillos." Research on the transformation of the United States into a consumer culture and on women as consuming housewives suggests that during the first decade of the twentieth century, as Carol Asher writes, "Along with the ideal of the single family home came the new housing style which lessened the housework but opened the way to commodities to enter the home."[38] The availability of new consumer goods and the changing role of women as consumers was, though not widespread, an increasing possibility for privileged sectors of the Puerto Rican population.

A quick glance at one of the 1930 issues of *Puerto Rico Ilustrado*—the major photo-illustrated weekly of the time—reveals to what extent American consumer goods had penetrated the Puerto Rican market.[39] Cabanillas's article is very much in the vein of magazines such as the *Ladies' Home Journal,* which saw fit to outline the duties and responsibilities of the housewife. She justly laments that the new Puerto Rican consumer has no real say in the types of products that are available on the market. But her pseudo-economic analysis does little more than laud the nuclear patriarchal family structure: "The family is the basic unit of our economic system"[40] and the women are charged with a moral obligation to "invest" the paycheck of their husbands wisely. ("La familia constituye la unidad básica de nuestro sistema económico.") Cabanillas ends her article proposing that housewives could form clubs and associations of conscientious and informed consumers in search of a "New Deal" that would ease some of the difficulties endemic to housekeeping and home economics.

In the section dedicated to creative writing there are two poems by the Chilean poet Gabriela Mistral, "Recado a Victoria Ocampo en la Argentina" and "Recado a Lolita Arriaga en México." The association will support her candidacy for the Nobel prize in literature some years later. She had been a visiting professor at the University of Puerto Rico, and was a close friend of many within the group, especially Margot Arce. Mistral was a consul in Madrid when Margot Arce met her in 1928 at the *Casa Internacional de Señoritas*, a residence for foreign students of the *Universidad Central*. Arce was instrumental in bringing the poet to teach at the University of Puerto Rico in 1933. Moreover, Mistral acted as a mentor and a model of the woman intellectual to the members of the association. She chose to live and work in close community with other women and could be considered, in the parlance of today, a woman-identified woman.[41]

Generally, the last section of the journal reviewed the cultural activities sponsored or attended by the members and included a page of news dedicated to the members' professional and personal lives. These last pages recorded the various activities and concerns of the group's board of directors' most prominent members: Andreu de Aguilar, Nilita Vientós, Margot Arce. The association had 368 members in 1940 and was making active efforts to increase recruits. The *Revista* meticulously reprinted the resolutions, budget, election of the board of trustees, and news pertinent to its functioning. The association also held social events at clubs and restaurants. When a book review section was included as part of an issue, works preferably by international and local women were reviewed.

The association's journal came out for six years, from 1938 to 1944, with Margot Arce as its editor. Arce was affiliated with the *Departamento de Estudios Hispánicos* for the duration of the *Revista*'s publication and beyond. The journal provided the members who were also university professors with a space to publish their criticism and essays. The *Revista* fulfilled an important role in the intellectual project of the members of the Association, and, as Arce reminded them, the journal added to the prestige of the association. On several occasions, Margot Arce warned the members that the lack of funds should at all costs be remedied in order to sustain the publication. The nature of the ties between the journal and the university is personal, professional, and institutional. Besides Arce, many of the women who contributed to the *Revista*'s pages were University of Puerto Rico professors or instructors.

The second issue of the journal (1, 2 [1938]) is dedicated to Eugenio María de Hostos, the liberal nineteenth-century Puerto Rican thinker and educator. Antonio Pedreira and three members of the association write on de Hostos: Andreu de Aguilar on Hostos and women's rights, Margot Arce on "Hostos anecdótico," and Antonia Sáez on the children's theater written by Hostos.[42] The editorial by Margot Arce stresses the exemplary nature of the patriotic values embodied by de Hostos. She writes: "Fortunately, in every country there are always half a dozen privileged men in whom the virtues that are its essence and patrimony have been incarnated and in whom they come to life and become singularly fertile. These men become and are recognized as examples, as paradigms and stimuli for the action of others."[43] ("En toda patria hay siempre, por fortuna, media docena de hombres privilegiados en quienes las virtudes que son esencia y patrimonio suyo encarnan y se hacen vivas y singularmente fecundas. Esos hombres se convierten y son reconocidos como ejemplos, como paradigmas y estímulos para la acción de los demás.") In the same editorial Arce reminds the readers that countries rely on exemplary figures, as well as ideals to guide the present and the future. Arce writes, "The fatherland is much more than the piece of land where one is born; it is also, and above all, the sum total of our memories, traditions, experience, and the customs that we share as a human group."[44] ("La patria es mucho más que el pedazo de tierra en donde se nace; es también y sobre todo, el conjunto de recuerdos, tradiciones, experiencia y costumbres comunes de un grupo humano.") The association, Arce continues, offers de Hostos as one of the symbols of the best virtues of the patriot: "It is up to us today to offer Eugenio María de Hostos as one of these symbols."[45] ("Nos corresponde a nosotras hoy ofrecer a Eugenio María de Hostos como uno de estos símbolos.") This issue was published in cooperation with and distributed by the Comisión pro-centenario de Hostos. The journal participates in the centenario festivities, giving full credence to the promotion of a virile nation created by a chosen few men whose patriotism should be emulated. The nation's trajectory, according to Arce, can already be mapped in its past, and projected into the future. Hostos provides much needed inspiration to face the nations's degraded neocolonial present.

We should not forget that Hostos was one of the first Puerto Rican thinkers of the nineteenth century to advocate for women's education. A perennial critic of Spanish despotism, he wrote his voluminous works outside the island, and is claimed by the Dominican Republic as one of its heroes. His liberal ideas and cosmopolitan thinking were the object of Pedreira's 1932 doctoral thesis "Hostos: Ciudadano de América" (Citizen of America). Of course, this commemorative issue puts forth no explicit vision of the nation that might originate from the experiences of women, but the choice of Hostos helps to position the role of women as central to the education of the nation. Moreover, the centennial provides Margot Arce with the opportunity to expound freely on the meaning of patriotism and on the duties of every patriot.

In the third issue of that first year (1, 3 [1939]) the journal published a long essay by the Spanish scholar Fernando de los Ríos on the "Problemas de la universidad moderna." Of the lecture by de Los Ríos, Arce says, "And as university women we want the University of Puerto Rico to respond vigorously to the mentioned ideal and *to contribute in that way to the formation of the leading class of the country*, capable of carrying out the only real reason for the State, which is justice."[46] ("Y como universitarias querríamos que la

Universidad de Puerto Rico respondiera vivamente al ideal señalado y *contribuyera así a la formación de una clase directora del país*, capacitada para ejercer la verdadera y única razón de Estado, que es la justicia.") The talk, delivered previously in Cuba, assumes a male student body, but Arce envisions elite women as the implied readers of the text too. Arce's strategy of implicating professional women in discourses that are explicitly directed to a male audience becomes possible because no great compromises or shifts in power relations are at stake in her resemanticizations.

A note on the death of Spanish poet Antonio Machado as well as one of his poems, and an essay by Juan de Mairena are featured in this issue. The section dedicated to Puerto Rico includes a piece by the poet Clara Lair and an essay on the theater of nineteenth-century social thinker and historian Salvador Brau, written by Antonia Sáez. Additionally, Herminia Acevedo writes on the role of the social sciences in the modern primary school curriculum.

The fourth and last issue of the inaugural year (1, 4 [1939]) included more on the mission and functioning of the modern school by Herminia Acevedo. We also find an interesting article by sociologist Justina Carrión on the new woman of 1939.[47] This article, because of its explicit discussion of "model feminine behavior," is worthy of special attention. The new woman is, according to Carrión:

> Svelte, agile, worried about her weight, this lass with painted fingernails who during the day alternates the tennis racquet or the pool with readings dealing with government, sciences or language arts, and at night shows off gracefully grandmother's curls and heavy skirts, worn over bare legs at a dance with no chaperones; this girl who lights her cigarette as she comments on the President's latest speech.[48] (Esbelta, ágil, preocupada de su peso, esta chiquilla de uñas teñidas que durante el día alterna la raqueta o la piscina con el texto de gobierno, ciencias o idiomas; y por la noche luce con gracia los rizos y la falda abultada de la abuela, sobre unas piernas desnudas en un baile sin chaperonas; esta niña que enciende un cigarrillo mientras comenta el último discurso del Presidente.)

Puerto Ricans have been alarmed by this new woman who came with the social and economic changes of the past decade. But Carrión assures the reader that these changes must not be feared. The fact that there may be higher divorce rates due to the greater economic independence of women is preferable to an unhappy home. Carrión also dismisses the idea that the new independent women will lose the "feminine" attribute of passivity. This will not happen if, as part of their college education, they are taught that the home comes first, "su misión como mujeres está por encima de su misión como profesionales."[49] Nonetheless, Carrión, as if in passing, advocates that maternity should be voluntary. With an education the benefits to themselves and their families far outweigh the problems. They will be better wives and mothers, just as Belaval yearned for in his *Los cuentos de la Universidad* three years earlier, and as Mercedes Solá promised at her *Feminismo* lecture in the

Ateneo eighteen years before Carrión. The educated middle-class women can have it all within the bounds of capitalist patriarchy. Carrión writes:

> The daughter understands, the wife tolerates, the mother models, not intuitively as our altruistic and self-sacrificing mothers did, but rather according to convictions springing from the study of human conduct. And all of this while at the same time being excellent teachers, lawyers, pharmacists, in a word, good professionals. These will be the multi-faceted girls, fragile of body and vigorous of spirit, who will leave the University next May.[50] (Hija que comprende, esposa tolerante, madre que modela, no por intuición como lo hicieron nuestras madres, tan altruistas y tan sacrificadas, sino por el convencimiento que les otorga el estudio de la conducta humana. Y todo esto, siendo excelentes maestras, licenciadas, farmacéuticas, en una palabra buenas profesionales. Así serán esas chicas polifacéticas, frágiles de cuerpo y vigorosas de espíritu que abandonan la Universidad en mayo próximo.)

Puerto Ricans should not worry about the new generation of young women because underneath the facade of the new woman lurks the old *criolla*. The new woman has been, so to speak, only silver plated on the older model. Carrión stresses at the end of her article that "if we gently scrape off the glaze of modernism that covers her, we will find a sentimental, romantic and conservative woman who is the living image of ourselves"[51] ("si les raspamos delicadamente el baño de modernismo que las cubre, encontraremos la mujer sentimental, romántica y conservadora vivo retrato de nosotras mismas").

Also in this issue, Isabel Andreu de Aguilar writes on the significance of the Mexican Revolution, and Margot Arce explicates a poem by Antonio Machado. The Puerto Rican poet Evaristo Ribera Chevremont contributes a poem. We also find an excerpt from the *Comentarios reales* by Garcilaso de la Vega, el Inca. The biographical notes on Chevremont and those on Garcilaso are found on the same page, visually suggesting a canonical approximation between the two authors. This number includes a report on a trip to Argentina taken by the members of the association on behalf of the group. Finally, we find an article on the legality of providing contraceptive information to women. The discussion is directed more toward control of the poor and disabled population than to middle-class women as potential users of this kind of service.[52]

What can be concluded from the previous examination of the contents of the inaugural year of the *Revista*'s publication? During the first year nine contributions were of a purely literary nature. Spanish authors and themes are treated four times and two Latin-American authors are featured. Another Latin-American theme is featured, but it is non-literary—the Mexican Revolution. Puerto Rican authors on Puerto Rican themes appear eight times. Of these, three are of a literary nature and five of an exemplary founding-father category. Education as an article theme or focus is featured five times.

The debate on language and bilingualism is not addressed during the first year. Questions relating to women are the focus of three articles during the first year. Of the total, sixteen articles or literary pieces were written by women while six were by men.

The first year was a good indication of the pattern the *Revista* would follow in the years to come. What idea of culture did the journal operate on? The type of cultural capital that circulated in the journal responded to the needs of a minority of Puerto Ricans, whose familiarity with the literate culture of Spain and Latin America would better equip them to affirm a difference vis-à-vis the American colonial presence. This cultural and class difference concurrently separated the *criollo* professional minority from the rest of the population. The critical discourse imparted with the reading of those literary and philosophical texts could not contribute to an objective critique of the history that had favored the literate minority. Nor did the texts encourage any radical redistribution of cultural capital other than through the very channels that were set up to establish the differences.

Absent from the literate discourse that circulated in the journal (and at the University) were systems of thought that would question the class division, the racial division, and the cultural divisions that make up the history of Puerto Rico's Spanish colonial past and its present. History as the result of the actions of a few great men, who incarnate "the virtues that are the essence and patrimony of a people," exempts the people from the responsibility, and from the benefits, of conscious historical agency. This is why the founding-fathers cult—of de Hostos in the case of the journal—is in reality detrimental to the empowerment of the underprivileged classes. For it is never the case that a founding father does not belong to the privileged elite, or that a radical (or Jacobin) founding father is presented as a "model." The underprivileged are invited to conceive of historical changes as the results of the actions of people who are neither of their same social class, nor of their same racial background or gender.

Let us look now at the contents of the second year, 1939–1940. The first issue of that year (2, 1 [1939]) contains a speech by Ana María O'Neill, professor of psychology, to the graduating class of an all-girl school, and an essay by Julio B. Ortiz, dean of the business school at the University of Puerto Rico, on population control and the standard of living. Herminia Acevedo writes on the type of preparation that the schoolteacher needs in order to excel; Julia Córdova Infante, Spanish teacher at the renowned Central High School, contributes an essay on the Mexican novelist Jaime Torres Bodet, followed by an excerpt from one of his novels. The poet Carmen Alicia Cadilla writes an introduction to poems and a short story ("El negrito Chelo") by Carmelina Vizcarrondo, specialist in children's stories and folklore. Nilita Vientós participates with an essay on Daumier's painting *El Quijote,* and Berta Cabanillas writes on manners and proper behavior in the home. The issue additionally features a short piece in memory of American social worker Grace Abbott, a role model for the social workers of the association. As a reformer, Abbott had started her career at Hull House and at her death she was on the University of Chicago faculty. Commissioner of the public schools, José Gallardo, ends this issue with a short piece on the objectives of the public school system.

The second issue (2, 2 [1940]) is dedicated to the memory of Antonio S. Pedreira, who unexpectedly passed away in 1939. Biographical notes on Pedreira are included, as well as personal recollections by those who knew him: "Valor puertorriqueño de la obra de Pedreira," "Don Antonio, maestro de la juventud," "Mi amigo y maestro," "Ausencia del maestro." These pieces are followed by more personal messages to Pedreira taken from letters written to him throughout his career. Nilita Vientós writes on the meaning of *Insularismo* as an introduction to an excerpt from Pedreira's essay. At the end of the issue there is a fairly large section dedicated to the annual meeting of the association.

The third issue, of 1939–1940 (2, 3 [1940]) opens with the campaign to submit Gabriela Mistral's candidacy for the 1940 Nobel Prize for Literature. Arce's editorial explains the association's reasons for supporting Mistral:

> First of all, we recognize the high value of Gabriela Mistral's poetic work and its significance for Hispanic America. Secondly, we are pleased that the extraordinary merit of a woman of our race, who sings and speaks in our own language, may be recognized so honorably. Thirdly, we feel obliged to recompense, albeit in a small way, the admirable pedagogic labor that Gabriela Mistral has carried out at the University of Puerto Rico, and the tenderness with which the poet has sung, repeatedly, in verse and prose, the beauty of our landscape and *the peaceful charm of our moral environment*.[53] (En primer lugar, reconoce el alto valor de la obra poética de Gabriela Mistral y su significación para la América Hispana. En segundo lugar, se satisface de que el mérito extraordinario de una mujer de nuestra raza, que canta y habla en nuestra propia lengua, sea reconocido tan justamente. En tercer lugar, se obliga a corresponder, siquiera sea en pobre medida, a la admirable labor pedagógica realizada por Gabriela Mistral en la Universidad de Puerto Rico, y a la ternura con que el poeta ha cantado reiteradamente, en verso y prosa, las bellezas de nuestro paisaje *y el encanto apacible de nuestro ambiente moral.*)

The issue is dedicated in its entirety to Mistral. There are short notes by notable Spanish and Latin-American as well as Puerto Rican writers on Mistral, an anthology of her poems and prose, plus critical essays on the Chilean poet's works by Margot Arce, the Argentine Eduardo González Lanuza, the Spaniard Guillermo de Torres, and the Peruvian José Álvaro Sánchez. A separate section is dedicated to Mistral and Puerto Rico: here the *Revista* offers the personal testimony of Mistral's impact on a number of her Puerto Rican friends and students.

In the last issue of this second year (2, 4 [1940]) Arce comments on the war and what it means to her. Arce says in her editorial observations: "Those of us who call ourselves Christians, those of us who love the old Europe for what it has given us in matters of art, thought, and the science of life, are full of anguish at this time as we wait for a miracle to take place so that Christ's promise to Peter might be carried out."[54] ("Los que nos llamamos cristianos, los que amamos la vieja Europa, por lo que nos ha dado en arte, en pensamiento, en ciencia de vida, vivimos estos instantes llenos de angustia, esperando que se haga un milagro y que la promesa de Cristo a Pedro se cumpla.") At the rhetorical level Arce constructs a good Christian "we" who side with the old, true Europe, and an evil fallen Fascist and Communist Europe as a "they" who are responsible for the war. Note that she will not let die the idea of "Europe," which for her is synonymous with art, thought, civility. It is not European culture as a whole that is on trial, but the fascist aberration. She has no real explanation for the causes of the war—just a Manichean good Europe versus a bad Europe formulation.

More than a sum of articles, a journal is a semiotic object whereby meaning is produced and circulated in a way very specific to its genre. In the case of the *Revista,* a juxtaposition of Margot Arce's editorials with the actual contents of the journal clarifies the *Asociación de Mujeres Graduadas*'s cultural undertaking. Her commentaries at the beginning of each issue of the journal touch on a variety of political and cultural issues (Puerto Rico's political situation, the World War, etc.). In this case, for example, Arce proceeds to introduce the Spanish scholar María Zambrano, Ortega y Gasset's disciple and former collaborator in the *Revista de Occidente.* Zambrano's presence in this issue, if we read the journal syntactically, is an illustration of the thinkers of the "good Europe." Zambrano was invited to the island as a visiting Professor. For Arce, Zambrano represents "lo español esencial," and she praises her as one of the most legitimate exponents of young Spanish thought. Zambrano also acts in this issue of the *Revista* as a model for the balanced woman intellectual. Arce writes that

> it's surprising to find in a woman such logic and clarity of doctrine, so much intellectual richness, such order and system in the explanation of her ideas, because these qualities seem to be more specific to the masculine intellect. But in the case of María Zambrano we find them *side by side* with the delicate intuitions, the gift of poetry, the grace of sensitivity and of gestures befitting the purest and most enchanting femininity.[55] (sorprende hallar en una mujer, tal lógica y claridad de doctrina, tanta riqueza intelectual, tal orden y sistema en la exposición de sus ideas, porque estas cualidades parecen ser más propias del intelecto varonil. Pero en María Zambrano se nos presentan, *lado a lado,* con las delicadas intuiciones, el don de la poesía, la gracia de sensibilidad y de gesto propios de la más pura y encantadora feminidad.)

The passage sheds further light on the models for the woman intellectual favored by the editor of the journal. But it simultaneously points to the ambivalence a woman of letters might feel concerning her status as thinker and as social agent. As mentioned earlier in this chapter, even women intellectuals accepted the dualistic formulation that casts women as the negative element in a binary of opposition: woman as potentially unruly body and emotion that had to be contained, and man, as intellect and reason. This puts men in the awkward position of not having bodily appetites. Contradictions aside, Arce compliments Zambrano's intelligence by presenting her as a woman with the intellectual powers of a man and the *accoutrements* of true and pure femininity (see Illustration 5).

Arce's introduction is followed by two of Zambrano's essays, "El conocimiento poético" and "Estoicismo culto español: Jorge Manrique." Zambrano was invited to lecture several times at the *Ateneo*, as was customary with guests of the association. In addition, the association presented a motion to the University Board of Trustees to hire her as philosophy chair. Arce, we should remember, was at this time also Vice-President of the Ateneo. Zambrano would in the future contribute a number of articles to *Asomante*, the association's second journal. Many who collaborated with the *Revista* would also contribute to *Asomante*. In other words, the contacts made during the time of the *Revista* were lasting academic relationships. Such is the case with other Spanish writers, Juan Ramón Jiménez, Pedro Salinas, Gustavo Pittaluga, Vicente Llorens, and Luis Santullano, all of whom contributed to both journals.[56]

This issue includes other examples of European achievements by the "good Europe," an essay in homage of Sigmund Freud, and a poem and a letter to the journal by poet Juan Ramón Jiménez. Milagros Arce de Raffucci explicates the *beatus ille* theme in the poetry of three Spanish masters, Garcilaso, Fray Luis, and Góngora. Their poems are included as illustrations of the theme. Psychologist Gustavo Pittaluga writes on *courtoisie*, "Climaterio de la cortesía," from a historical and psychological point of view. This is a reprint of an article that originally appeared in *Revista de Occidente.*

Only two articles on Latin-American thematics are included in this issue. Isabel Andreu de Aguilar publishes a piece on the hero of Spanish-American independence, general Antonio José Sucre. Carmen Gómez Tejera writes on adult education in Puerto Rico; Antonia Sáez writes on the teaching of the Spanish vernacular, while objecting to bilingual education as practiced on the island. Teresa Amadeo writes on bilingualism in Mexico, offering readers a point of comparison with the Puerto Rican situation.

What does an examination of the thematics of the second year of the *Revista* tell us? Spanish authors and/or themes are treated eight times. European themes other than Spanish make their first appearance: they are featured twice. Latin-American authors or themes are treated fifteen times, an increase due to the Mistral homage. Puerto Rican themes occur eleven times. Education as a theme or focus of an article is featured six times. The debate on language and bilingualism appears twice during the second year. Questions relating to women are handled in two articles during that year. Of the total that year, twenty-seven articles and/or literary pieces were written by women and twelve by men.

The education of the Puerto Rican population, especially that of children, is of great importance in the pages of the *Revista.* The teaching of Puerto Rican school children in the vernacular is understood by the members of the association as the keystone of the educational process. But what about the aims and the components of this education directed toward children? The women did not seem to have a critique of the contents of the curricula that went beyond the glorification of middle-class cultural necessities and expectations. More importantly, the pedagogical methods in vogue at the University at the time did nothing to include community involvement or consultation in the educational processes. The owners of industry and commerce had an interest in educating the masses in this period, especially when it came to inculcating discipline and habits of proper behavior such as orderliness, punctuality, and respect for authority, all to be learned at school.

Among the electoral promises made to Puerto Ricans at the time, education had a stellar role. As Isabel Picó de Hernández tells us: "Featured prominently were those of freeing the university from the influence of party politics, guaranteeing the total autonomy of the university, and extending to all the social classes the benefits of higher education."[57] With the rise of the *Partido Popular Democrático* to power in 1940, the party instituted a number of changes in the government structure that favored the professional sector of the petite bourgeoisie and provided them with new opportunities. "In the early years of the Popular government," according to Picó de Hernández, "certain needs became apparent within the productive apparatus that obliged the PPD to consider the problem of the social function of higher education and the need to create the conditions that would allow it to satisfy the enormous demand for professionals, technicians, and administrators that the new economic order would require."[58] University students and the more democratic members of the petite bourgeoisie spearheaded the demands for reforms in a coalition that pressured the *populares* to make good their electoral promises. Demands, promises, and needs coalesce accordingly, as she points out, " . . . education is one of the significant dimensions of the so-called social policy employed by the Popular leadership, especially as an instrument for consolidating the diverse sectors of the people."[59] We should not be surprised, then, to find that schooling—elementary, adult education, and higher education—is one of the foremost issues discussed by the association. With the large expansion of the professional middle class in governmental bureaucracy and business, the members of the association took an active part in the debate over who would be in charge of grooming this population for its leading role in the transformation of Puerto Rico's economy.

The *Revista*'s third year, 1940–1941, starts with an issue (3, 1 [1940]) dedicated in its entirety to social work, specifically to "Problemas de la niñez en Puerto Rico." Recall that social workers comprised a large part of the membership of the association. All the articles in this particular issue of the journal have to do with children's education and development, as well as mental retardation and physical handicaps. But current international events markedly affected the tone and the contents of the *Revista*'s next issues: the impending second World War, North America's participation in the war, and the hopes that a new post-colonial "world order" would follow the Allied victory. The journal issue dedicated to Spanish-American solidarity is an example of the influence of world events on the *Revista* (3, 2 [1941]). As a result of the war, Arce writes, "Our timid hope today turns in anguish toward the Americas. . . . In the danger, the fruit of continental solidarity has ripened."[60] ("Nuestra tímida esperanza se vuelve hoy, angustiada, hacia la América. . . . En el peligro, ha madurado el fruto de la solidaridad continental.") Toward continental solidarity Concha Meléndez writes on the Cuban patriot and poet José Martí, "La ruta hispanoamericana de Martí," Emilio de Toro Cuevas, on the importance of Pan-American conferences; Antonio Rivera, a history professor, analyzes the significance of *bolivarismo* in the 1826 congress of Panamá, and Adolfo de Hostos offers "El americanismo de Hostos." Included as part of the issue is a translation of Theodore Roosevelt's speech on the fiftieth anniversary of the Pan-American Union. This is followed by "Los aproches del puente," Tomás Blanco's rebuttal to the well-publicized slogan "Puerto Rico, a bridge between cultures," in which he decries the blind optimism of the concept and its role in the panorama of U.S. imperialism. The last section of the issue consists of a report on the yearly convention of the *Asociación de Mujeres Graduadas*, and the association's recommendation of Concha Meléndez for director of the Hispanic Studies Department.[61]

For the third issue (3, 3 [1941]) Arce's editorial reflects on the need for university reform and the nefarious effects of U.S. colonialism in Puerto Rico. Arce writes:

> The sickness is deeper: the spiritual crisis of our youth is the same crisis that the whole Western world is experiencing at this moment; in our case made worse by forty-three years of colonized life without hope, forty-three years of a defective and inadequate primary and secondary educational system, by forty-three years of the systematic intent to supplant our vernacular language with English, by forty-three years of materialist philosophy in adoration of success, by forty-three years of a lack of leaders, of live examples, that might stimulate the generous enthusiasm and emulation of the youth.[62] (El mal es más hondo: la crisis espiritual de los jóvenes es la misma crisis por que atraviesa todo el mundo occidental en estos momentos; agravada en nuestro caso, por cuarentitrés años de vida

> colonial sin esperanza, por cuarentitrés años de un deficiente e inadecuado sistema de enseñanza primaria y secundaria, por cuarentitrés años de intento sistemático de suplantación de nuestra lengua vernácula por el inglés, por cuarentitrés años de filosofía materialista adoradora del éxito, por cuarentitrés años de ausencia de líderes, de ejemplos vivos, que estimulen el generoso entusiasmo y emulación de los jóvenes.)

Also in this issue is a reprint of an essay by Max Scheler, "Saber culto y categorías del saber." María Cadilla de Martínez writes on the poetry of Juan Ramón Jiménez; Luis Palés Matos and Margot Arce introduce a poem and short story by Carmen Marrero; Josefina Rodríguez López analyses the poetry of Jorge Guillén; and Antonia Sáez contributes an excerpt from her new book *Las artes del lenguaje en la enseñanza primaria.* The last essay of the issue, "La educación de adultos, problema de nuestra cultura," is a reprint of a talk by Isabel Andreu de Aguilar delivered at the *Ateneo* as part of the important 1940 symposium *Foro del Ateneo.* That forum was a turning point that signaled the alliance of Creole politicians and intellectuals as leaders of the populist coalition.[63]

The last issue of the third year (3, 4 [1941]) was dedicated to the *Congreso Interamericano de Escritores* held and sponsored by the University of Puerto Rico in April of 1941. Among the presenters were: Concha Meléndez, Ciro Alegría, Jorge Mañach, Mariano Picón Salas, Ernesto Montenegro, Nilita Vientós Gastón, and William Carlos Williams. The focus of this conference was literature and literary criticism. Male presenters dominated. Judging from the table of contents of the journal, it seems that the only two women who participated were from Puerto Rico.

During the third year of the *Revista*'s publication Spanish authors and themes are treated only once; European themes four times; American authors make their first appearance with two essays. Latin-American authors or themes are treated seven times. Puerto Rican themes appear seven times. Education is featured twice. Social work carries the day with thirteen essays. This year prominence is given to issues in Puerto Rican society. The debate on language and bilingualism is not featured, neither are questions relating to women. Of the total, twenty-two articles and/or literary pieces are written by women and sixteen by men (four more then the previous year).

After looking at the contents of the first three years, we have yet to find in the pages of the *Revista* any critical engagement with the culture of the underprivileged classes. Does the journal conceive of the poor as having a culture? Absent from the journal is any type of article that would entertain even the theoretical possibility that the underprivileged classes have a culture that is not derivative—just a passing on of customs and behaviors brought to the island by the Spanish colonizers. The *mujeres graduadas* seem to labor under the presumption that through education the poor would ultimately desire the same kind of cultural practices and icons that the middle and upper classes favor. A "cultured person" is one who, according to the operative discourses on culture, is in possession of a certain "high" culture. Access—at the structural level—to this type of culture is so limited that perforce only a few will ever be able to possess it. The professional women's endeavors underscore their ownership of a valuable and scarce resource—cultural capital.

The fourth year, 1941–1942, *Revista* (4, 1 [1941]) starts with an issue dedicated to the memory of Puerto Rican feminist Ana Roqué de Duprey on the nineteenth anniversary of her death. Arce's editorial has high words of praise for Roqué de Duprey the scholar, educator, and feminist. She highlights the fact that the kind of feminism that Roqué de Duprey espoused was not the undignified street type: "Her feminism *shuns street disorder,* limiting itself to demanding what is just and advocating for women's civil and legal dignity."[64] ("Su feminismo *rehuye la alharaca callejera;* se limita a demandar lo justo y a exigir para la mujer dignidad civil y jurídica.") Arce is critical of the suffragist leader nonetheless. According to her, Roqué de Duprey believed too fervently in the promises of freedom that the North Americans made to Puerto Ricans at the onset of the occupation. The deceased feminist leader had been a close friend and associate of many of the older members of the association—journalist Angela Negrón Muñoz, folklorist María Cadilla de Martínez, and feminist leader Andreu de Aguilar, and the more junior Concha Meléndez, all of whom pay tribute to the memory of their friend and mentor. Additionally, Andreu de Aguilar's 1935 essay on the history of the suffragist movement is reprinted in its entirety. All things considered, the homage to the deceased *sufragista* and educator is a faint reflection of the suffragist origins of many professional women, some of whom were still active in the association.

The second issue of that year (4, 2 [1942]) announces the willingness of the members of the association as a whole to aid in the war effort. They extend their solidarity to the people fighting fascism. Arce writes, "We defend the principle of individual freedom, of laws, of free choice, of just reciprocity between nations; we oppose force and paganism with a Christian and spiritual conception of man; an aspiration to civilized and equitable life."[65] ("Defendemos el principio de la libertad individual, el del derecho, el de la libre determinación, el de la justa reciprocidad entre las naciones; oponemos a la fuerza y al paganismo una concepción cristiana y espriritual del hombre; una aspiración de convivencia civilizada y equitativa.") Arce stresses that this duty is very much in accordance with the responsibilities of womanhood. In this vein the journal published a telegram of support sent to the colonial governor of the island. And in their annual conference held at the year's end one of the themes discussed was the state of war and the importance of an organization such as theirs.

Antonia Sáez, with Margot Arce and Secretary of Public Education Pedro Cebollero, chime in on "El niño y la lengua," about the negative influence of bilingualism on the primary school student. However, most of the space is dedicated to assessing the association's accomplishments, goals, and projects during the previous five years. At one of the association's meetings Ana María O'Neill spoke of women's work in defense of democracy—an urgent subject in light of world events. The keynote speech given on that occasion by Isabel Andreu de Aguilar proudly recounts the achievements of the association—publications, conferences and seminars, financial aid for the members, social gatherings in honor of outstanding members, and concrete proposals for the betterment of the University. In the roster of their publications we find Antonia Sáez's book *Dirigiendo al niño* (a whole issue of the journal was dedicated to problems of children in Puerto Rico [3, 3 (1941)]) book-length essays by Dominican intellectuals Juan Bosch and Jiménez Grullón; works by Puerto Ricans poets Matos Paoli and José Antonio Dávila. We also find an announcement about folklorist María Cadilla de Martínez's forthcoming book. Additionally, Julita Córdova Infante, undersecretary of the group, offers personal testimony on the meaning of the association in the cultural life of Puerto Rico. According to Córdova Infante the association is an inspiration for young Puerto Ricans: "We have contributed to awakening and nourishing the artistic and literary sensibility of our people through exhibitions, conferences, and publications."[66] ("Contribuímos a despertar y nutrir la sensibilidad de nuestro pueblo divulgando los valores artísticos y literarios a través de exposiciones, conferencias y publicaciones.")

Educational reform at all levels is the topic of the third issue of this fourth year (4, 3 [1942]). The members report on their intervention as part of the university faculty in public debates regarding *reforma universitaria.* As mentioned earlier, the overhaul of the educational system was a fundamental part of the reformist demands of the intelligentsia, as well as a way of rallying support for the populist alliance. Included here are the series of documents relating to the association's project for reform submitted to the legislature. Bolstering their bid are articles by Ortega y Gasset, José Lázaro, and Pedro Cebollero on the university. Even Alfonso X, el Sabio's regulations for the good functioning of the university are reprinted here, to illustrate, perhaps, the superiority and longevity of the Spanish model of education over the imposed U.S. colonial one.

The last issue of 1942 (4, 4 [1942]) included the project for a new philosophy of education in elementary schools, comments by the association on the project, an article by Justina Carrión on modern women and marriage, Marcel Weinrich on polylinguism in Puerto Rico, and Andreu de Aguilar and Carmen Gómez Tejera on reconstruction after the war; Margot Arce writes on poet Antonio Machado; Herminia Acevedo on the Eighth Pan-American Congress on Childhood; and Angela R. de Tudo on Simón Bolivar.

Of the total, the fourth year of the *Revista*'s publication features twenty-one articles/literary pieces written by women and seven by men. This is a dramatic decrease in the number of male contributors from the previous two years. Questions relating to women are the focus of twelve articles during the fourth year—the highest number ever. This is due to the homage in memory of feminist pioneer Roqué de Duprey. Education and the bilingual question also feature prominently: five articles on education and four on the language and bilingual debate. Literature occupies a minimal space this year: two poems by Puerto Rican authors, a critical essay on Antonio Machado, and an essay by Ortega y Gasset comprise the whole literary content of this year. Only one article has as its theme a Latin-American figure.

As the examination of its contents shows, the many voices that comprised the journal helped to formulate a particular critique of imperialism by offering a Spanish, *criollo* Latin-American, and *criollo* Puerto Rican exemplification of high culture, much as *Índice* had done a decade earlier. This critique of imperialism echoes that of the men of the *Generación del Treinta*, but enlarges the number of voices and interrupts the masculine monopoly on the question. The *Revista* makes space for the incorporation of its members as discussants in the debate: on one hand, by presenting an active agenda of conferences, publication projects, and public activities; on the other, by enacting a dialogue—on paper—about these topics.

The fifth year of publication starts out with a three-part editorial by Margot Arce (5, 1 [1943]). First she discusses the association's position on the Atlantic Charter and the right of Puerto Ricans to determine their future once the war is over. The editorial reads:

> Once again our members have demonstrated their profound and conscious interest in the questions that directly affect our country; once again, with their clear vision and decisive responsibility, they have been the first to reflect the spirit of the moment. Our duty as Puerto Rican women and as professionals was to demand an inalienable right, the right of all peoples to self-determination.[67] (Una vez más nuestras asociadas han demostrado su profundo y consciente interés por las cuestiones que afectan directamente a nuestra patria; una vez más se han anticipado con clara visión y decidida responsabilidad a recoger el espíritu del momento. Nuestro deber como puertorriqueñas y como profesionales era demandar un derecho inalienable: el derecho que todo pueblo tiene a la libre determinación.)

Arce points out that four months later the Puerto Rican legislature followed the association's lead and made similar pronouncements. The second part of the editorial announces the association's leading role in the organization of a committee composed of sixteen women's associations, *Comité de Emergencia de Asociaciones Femeninas de Puerto Rico.* This committee was formed in order to face the problems brought about by the state of war—shortages, rise in unemployment, and the need to lower maritime tariffs. Arce stresses that the actions of the committee can be very efficacious because it goes beyond partisan politics and is "a beautiful example of civic solidarity." ("un bello ejemplo de solidaridad cívica.") Lastly, Arce discusses the visit of the Congressional Chávez Committee to the island. Here the editor tackles the question of bilingual education and politics.

That bilingual education was a failure is a deeply held conviction in the works of Arce, Nilita Vientós, and other educators close to them. In their view, politics and education should be separate. English, as the colonial language, implied a disastrous intrusion in matters of education. Arce argued that expert opinion had proven that the Spanish vernacular, not English, should be used exclusively to teach Puerto Rican school children. Moreover, children had not learned either of the two languages properly, and worst of all, this erroneous educational practice had damaged the students mentally and emotionally. Arce writes:

> The consequences of the disgraceful years of primary school instruction in English are so grave that they go beyond all exaggeration. This is not the place to discuss them; let it suffice to say that they have hopelessly mutilated the mentality and sensitivity of thousands of Puerto Rican children. Besides the fact that they learned neither Spanish nor English correctly.[68] (Las consecuencias de los desgraciados años de enseñanza en inglés desde los primeros grados son tales que rebasan toda exageración. No es éste el lugar para discutirlas; basta decir que han mutilado irremediablemente la mentalidad y la sensibilidad de miles de niños puertorriqueños. Aparte de que, ni el español ni el inglés se aprendieron correctamente.)

Let us consider some of the questions raised by Arce's formulation of the role of education as a vehicle of colonialism. While she decries the evils of mixing politics with pedagogy and recriminates the colonial government for doing this, she also insists on the role that education has in forging and preserving the Puerto Rican personality. Such preservation is a political task, aided primarily by the kind of educational system envisioned and desired by Arce and her group. She asserts that a broader system of education should prevail, not the exaggerated emphasis on English-language education currently in vogue. Arce writes:

> To teach a people in a language that is not its own is a pedagogical error so crass that to demonstrate it would be like rediscovering the Mediterranean. To give the primary place to language instruction in an educational system is an even graver error. But to ask a people to shed its own culture and traditions as if they were changing clothes is something that comes close to the absurd.[69] (Enseñar a un pueblo en una lengua que no es la suya propia es un error de metodología pedagógica tan craso que demostrarlo aquí sería como volver a descubrir el Mediterráneo. Conceder a la enseñanza de lenguas la primacía en un sistema educativo es todavía errar más gravemente. Pero pretender que un pueblo se despoje de su cultura y de su tradición como quien se quita un traje es algo que raya en el absurdo.)

Arce advocates what she calls "the true education of the Puerto Rican people." Any democratic state has the right to legislate on matters that pertain to the education of its citizens. She concludes that "It is time for Puerto Ricans to enjoy this right. They have earned it with their loyalty and their adhesion to the cause of the Democracies."[70] ("Ya es tiempo de que Puerto Rico goce de ese derecho. Se lo ha ganado con su lealtad y su adhesión a la causa de las Democracias.")

As these passages illustrate, Arce's position on the evils of bilingual education in the Puerto Rican context forcefully indicts the colonial school system. Nonetheless, she is not advocating some sort of pedagogy of the oppressed, nor can we read in her statements a stand against a system that promotes the colonized mentality in general. It is true that in the majority of instances anti-colonial discourses and decolonization movements, for example in Africa, have been forged in the shadow of colonial school systems, and even there the question is far from simple. But in the case of Puerto Rico this anti-colonial discourse, because of its class origins, promoted the superiority of white racism and of classism. Historically, when Puerto Rican workers organized their own educational programs, they stressed a progressive international curriculum, directly in keeping with political, philosophical, and aesthetic philosophies that could sustain their political empowerment projects. This was very clear in the workers' theater movement and in the choice of readings among tobacco workers, for example. As Rubén Dávila Santiago explains, already in 1902 tobacco artisans had organized in the town of Caguas a "Social Studies Center" that would nurture other such organizations and trade unionist leaders. The most favored writers among workers were Victor Hugo, Alexandre Dumas, Emile Zola, and Karl Marx. Bakunin and Kropotkin were widely discussed. Education for these workers had to be, according to Dávila Santiago, integral, rational, coeducational, liberating.[71] Workers organized libraries, as well as small publishing and bookselling venues such as the *Germinal* agency in Caguas. Dávila Santiago reports on some of the titles they carried: "*Evolution and Revolution* by Reclus, *The Problems of Life* by Laugel, *Historical Sketches from the French Revolution* by Champard, *Determinism and Responsibility* by Hamon, *Capital* by Marx, *The Revolution in Russia* by Tolstoy, *Religion* by Harreta, and *On Germany* by Heine. Among their pamphlets we can mention *Science and Religion* by P. Gori, *Where is God?* by M. Rey, *Among Peasants* by Malatesta, *Modern Slavery* by Alarcón, *To the People* by J. de Médico, *Religious Pestilence* by Most, *God's Crimes* by de Faure, *Liberation Criterion* by Bonafullia, *Education and Paternal Authority* by Girard."[72]

During the most expansive years of the workers' movement, their internationalist and anticlerical curriculum was in direct opposition to the Creole class. When Puerto Rican workers looked to Spain, they embraced the ideals and institutions of Peninsular *anarcho-syndicalists.* This was a Spain that

Creoles absolutely disavowed, regardless of the admiration that many Creoles felt for the Republic. The *jibarista* and *criollista* educational projects that the populists espoused did not and could not incorporate the liberationist pedagogy that workers had developed in the first two decades of the century. Education, freedom, and democracy held radically different meanings for the two groups.

At this point in 1943 the *Revista* published a lengthy essay by Carmen Gómez Tejera on Puerto Rican music and the visual arts, plus Margot Arce's reaffirmation of Pedreira's classic, "Reflexiones en torno a *Insularismo.*" The rest of the (5, 1 [1943]) issue is dedicated entirely to the association's business. Gómez Tejera read her article on Puerto Rican art to three high-school groups and broadcasted it over the radio on December 13, 1942. Tejera circumscribes herself solely to elite music and visual arts as historically cultivated on the island.[73] Of greater interest is Margot Arce's re-evaluation of the legacy of Pedreira's canonical essay, *Insularismo.* Given that Puerto Rico's destiny was being played out, in part, in the theater of the World War, she wished to raise the consciousness of readers and rally them toward political action.

Conjuncturally, according to Arce's "Reflexiones," Puerto Ricans have a unique chance to demand more political rights from the colonial establishment, but alarmingly, "We do nothing and time is of the essence. And even if this is a time of action, of action that we can only qualify as revolutionary, we should not fail to season our action with reflection."[74] ("Nada hacemos y el tiempo apremia. Y aunque la hora sea de acción, de acción que sólo cabe calificar de revolucionaria, no está de más el condimentar la acción con el pensamiento.") Pedreira's essay allows her to revisit some of the questions he posed while at the same time paying homage to his powers of prevision. The university reforms that are now under way were all laid out in Pedreira's book. Pedreira's text, she stresses, is still important for the directions it pointed to and for its fundamental place in Puerto Rican thought. She laments, in passing, that the author should have dedicated more time to an explicit discussion of the first three decades of American colonialism. She also rejects his fear of democracy in general by making the distinction that it is the reigning "quantitative" (read American) type that needs to be rejected, not the Spanish or "qualitative" version. However, her most fervent objections to Pedreira's text are directed at his negative vision of women. Arce protests that:

> At this point, I would like to and should mention that the author's judgment of women reflects many of the ingenuous prejudices of the XIXth century and that he is unfair in the particular case of the Puerto Rican woman. In their majority our women are not "feminists, nor bridge-players, nor are they addicts of the society pages." Among their "tiny" ideas they are usually concerned with things of central importance and their social action has frequently been more efficient, valuable, and disinterested than that of the men. It is incomprehensible that regarding women, Pedreira would have left words that seem more like the

> boasting of a naive snob than a dispassionate and impartial judgment.[75] (En esta coyuntura, quiero y debo advertir que el juicio del autor sobre la mujer recoge muchos de los ingenuos prejuicios del siglo XIX, y que es injusto para el caso particular de la mujer puertorriqueña. En su mayor parte nuestras mujeres no son 'feministas, ni son amantes del bridge, ni se desviven por la crónica social.' Entre sus ideas 'chiquitas' suelen preocuparse por algunas de primera importancia y su acción social se ha dejado sentir muchas veces con más eficacia, valor y desinterés que la de los hombres. Resulta inexplicable que Pedreira haya dejado sobre la mujer palabras que más parecen un alarde de ingenio snob que una estimación desapasionada y ecuánime.)

Arce does not contest Pedreira's view of feminism. Like him, she casts feminism in the same negative light as playing bridge, worrying about social gossip columns, and activities that engage idle and vain women. This is surprising given her friendship with many suffragist mentors and associates throughout her early professional life. It is quite possible that what bothers Arce, even at this later date, is the perceived "pro-Americanist" baggage that the feminist struggles still carried. She shuns feminism, but recuperates "woman." Not all women are the same, she argues. Women like herself are involved in matters of primary interest for society and the nation, Arce maintains, having participated with more success, courage, and generosity in the life of the nation than men. Any *estimación desapasionada y ecuánime* would see the truth of her pronouncement. She demands credit and praise for her group of women.

Feminism, following the logic of the cited text, is for egotistical women. Generous women do not think only of themselves, their needs, problems, and rights, but work for the benefit of society at large. Arce seeks to embody this position by taking it upon herself to reflect on Puerto Rico's problems in general, and by tackling the big questions pertaining to the political destiny of the Puerto Rican people. She writes:

> And what will our destiny be? A few days ago, during a public debate, some lawyers and legal experts came to the conclusion that the Atlantic Charter is not applicable in the case of Puerto Rico. That from the legal point of view, that of written law, it might not apply to us does not bother us in the slightest. . . . At the dawn of victory and peace, neither the dead letter of the law nor the personal opinions of statesmen will decide the future of peoples. What will prevail will be living justice, the "winged seeds" that Unamuno spoke of, and divine justice speaking through the mouths of the people.[76] (Y ¿cuál ha de ser nuestro destino? Hace pocos días, en una discusión pública, unos juristas y abogados llegaron a la conclusión de que la Carta del Atlántico no es aplicable al caso de Puerto Rico. Que desde el punto de vista legal, de la ley escrita, no lo sea, nos tiene absolutamente sin cuidado. . . . En la mañana de la victoria y de la paz, no será la letra muerta de la ley, ni las opiniones personales de los estadistas, las que decidan el futuro de los pueblos. Será el derecho vivo, las 'semillas aladas' que diría Unamuno y la justicia divina, hablando por boca del pueblo, los que se impondrán.)

And in a moving appeal Arce ends her essay by warning the readers that it is not enough to have programs for economic and social security. It is important for Puerto Rico to liberate its spirit, *liberar el espíritu.*

The editorial of the second issue of that year (5, 2 [1943]) deals again with university reform and the political status of the island. Arce reiterates that university reform must be accompanied by reforms at all levels of public school education; that all teaching must be conducted in Spanish, and that more attention should be given to the study of Puerto Rican culture and problems. She also advocates admission exams for the University of Puerto Rico. The mission of the university is to form (the irony is lost on her) "cultured men, capable professionals and investigators endowed with a free spirit and the willingness to serve selflessly and efficiently."[77] ("hombres cultos, profesionales capaces e investigadores dotados de un espíritu libre y de una disposición de servicio eficaz y desinteresado.") She proposes that the university should reach out to those who will never have a university education by instituting cultural missions that "bring it closer to the people." True university reform must work to prepare Puerto Rico for "freedom and civil dignity." Arce explains the role of the university in the post-colonial world order that should follow the end of the war: "The end of the war is coming and with it we look forward to the liquidation of the colonial system in the world. It is up to the University to prepare the people of Puerto Rico for the political changes that in all justice our country should experience."[78] ("El fin de la guerra se acerca y con él esperamos la liquidación del sistema colonial en el mundo. A la Universidad corresponde preparar al pueblo de Puerto Rico para el cambio político que en justicia debe alcanzar nuestra patria.")

The second part of the editorial insists, specifically, on the necessity of a political change in the colonial status of the island. Not only does Puerto Rico have, like all nations, an inalienable right to freedom. Puerto Rico, in her view, is inherently, and by temperament, democratic because "It has generously defended a democracy that it does not know and that it has never experienced, but that it intuits in the end because it is part of its Hispanic spiritual patrimony."[79] ("Generosamente ha defendido una democracia que no conoce, que nunca ha vivido, pero que intuye finalmente porque es parte de su patrimonio espiritual hispánico.") Because of its Hispanic culture Puerto Rico partakes in the Hispanic spirit and the, purportedly, democratic Hispanic approach toward life. The economy, political and class struggles, gender interests, laws that promote democratic freedoms, racial discrimination, all disappear in favor of this idealistic mystification she calls the Hispanic spirit. She explains that: "Respect for man's dignity and moral integrity is one of the defining characteristics of the *Hispanic attitude towards the world.* No one is more deserving of a full democratic life than this people who, rather than struggling to hold on to some material possession, is struggling for an ideal that is the substance of its spirit and of its culture."[80] ("El respeto a la dignidad y a la integridad moral del hombre es uno de los caracteres definidores de la *actitud hispánica ante el mundo.* Nadie merece mejor la plenitud de una vida democrática que este pueblo que lucha no por conservar un bien que posee, sino por alcanzar un ideal que es sustancia de su espíritu y de su cultura.") Arce declares herself personally in favor of political independence for the island and decries what she considers the irresponsible attitude of most politicians regarding this matter: some are totally silent, others exclusively pragmatic. "The salvation of the spirit," writes Arce, "ideals, and rights don't count at all."[81] ("La salvaguardia del espíritu, el ideal, el derecho, para nada cuentan.") These politicians do not want to pay the price for independence, which Arce understands to be sacrifice and risk. It is the responsibility of the political and cultural elite, of which she is a part, to prepare the people for independence. "It seems to us," she warns, "that it is urgent to prepare the people so that they will not be caught without the moral character needed to face a new political and economic reality."[82] ("Nos parece que urge preparar a este pueblo para que no le sorprenda desprevenido sin la disposición moral necesaria para afrontar una realidad política y económica nueva.")

The editorial is followed by an essay on Andrés Bello's pedagogy, written by Concha Meléndez, and by the speech he delivered at the inauguration of the university in Chile in 1843. Also featured is Jaime Benítez's address to members of the University. In it the current chancellor responds to student activists who are discontented with the state of affairs, "Once again I request that which I have requested from the very first: collaboration. It is a service that can be interpreted as support, help, orientation, criticism, opposition. All within the basic framework of a shared task."[83] ("Solicito una vez más lo que he solicitado desde el primer momento: colaboración. Es un servicio que puede traducirse en apoyo, ayuda, indicaciones, crítica, oposición. Todo ello dentro del marco básico de la tarea común.") The association responds to his call for collaboration with its own position paper delivered to the council for higher education, "Ponencia de la Asociación de Mujeres Graduadas ante el Consejo Superior de Educación." The issue closes with Nilita Vientós on language legislation, "La legislatura y el problema de la lengua."

The editorial of the third issue (5, 3 [1944]) is written by Nilita Vientós. This signals a change of guard and of direction in the aims and program of the *Revista.* The issue is dedicated to the memory of Lloréns Torres. Vientos writes of the poet:

> He has been the Puerto Rican writer who has had the most profound and adequate vision of the invisible Puerto Rico, which is the real one, the one that is buried beneath our indifference, saddened by our lack of understanding, humiliated by our cowardliness, confused by our leaders, deflated by our lack of faith, cast into the shadows by those who only have eyes for the external and

the obvious.[84] (Ha sido el escritor puertorriquenõ que más profunda y adecuada visión tuvo del Puerto Rico invisible, que es el real, el que yace sepultado bajo nuestra indiferencia, lleno de tristeza por nuestra incomprensión, humillado por nuestras cobardías, confundido por nuestros dirigentes, falto de ánimo por nuestra carencia de fe, arrojado en la sombra por los que sólo tienen ojos para lo externo y obvio.)

Arce appears as a contributor with "La realidad puertorriqueña en la poesía de Lloréns Torres," and Luis Palés Matos dedicates a poem to Lloréns. This is followed by an anthology of Lloréns's poems and a reprint of an essay on the poet by Concha Meléndez and Antonio Pedreira.

The last issue I have been able to locate is dated March and July, 1944. Edited by Nilita Vientós, it does not have an editorial note and consists of only four items: an essay by Francisco Matos Paoli on Unamuno, an article on social work in Puerto Rico, an essay by Jorge Luis Porrás Cruz on Calderón de la Barca's "La vida es sueño," and lastly, a report on the teaching of religion in the public school system—a measure on which the association would not pronounce itself due to the small number of associates available to respond to the question.[85]

In sum, the fifth year of the *Revista*'s publication features Puerto Rican themes nine times. Education as a theme or focus of an article is featured three times. The debate on language and bilingualism is featured once. It should be noted that the preponderance of the Puerto Rican theme is at an all time high since education and the language and bilingual debate are part and parcel of the Puerto Rican theme. Spanish authors or themes are featured twice, and Latin American authors or themes are treated once. Questions relating to women are the focus of only one article during this final year of the journal's publication. The number of articles written by women, ten, is higher than those written by men, six—as was the case during the entire history of the journal.

From my examination of the thematic contents, contributors, and editorial stance under the direction of Margot Arce, we can see that though significant, the Spanish and Latin-American literary component of the journal—around thirty-four contributions—is not the most important. To this we may add the thirty-some pieces on Puerto Rican literature. The sections dedicated to pedagogy, which include methodology, research on children and education, university and school reform, and the language question, consist of more than thirty articles. If we choose to put the pieces on Puerto Rican literature and culture together with the section on pedagogy, which could include the language question and university and school reform, this section would constitute by far the most important pursuit of the *Revista*. Of much less weight in the journal is the space dedicated specifically to women's issues not related to the association—seventeen articles.

Untimately the *Revista* pulls in two different directions: toward literature and literary criticism, and toward issues more strictly related to pedagogy and social work. This rift responds to the makeup of the membership of the *Asociación de Graduadas* and to the members' professional interests. This might explain why publication of the *Revista* stops, and a new journal—dedicated in its entirety to literature and issues of high culture—takes its place.[86] Nilita Vientós Gastón had gained valuable editorial know-how while assisting with the *Revista.* Though a close and dedicated collaborator on the first journal, she would impart a new character to the *Asociación de Mujeres Graduadas*'s second editorial venture, *Asomante.* The association would finance the new journal, but the editorial decisions would be left to Vientós Gastón and a group that sided with her more internationalist cultural vision.[87] A lawyer by profession, but an editor and critic by calling, Vientós Gastón and those who joined efforts with her initiated in 1945 the literary journal that would become synonymous with literary culture in Puerto Rico for the next three decades.

Illustration 1. From left to right: Concha Meléndez, Antonio S. Pedreira, Manuel García Díaz, Margot Arce, circa 1927. *(Courtesy of Seminario de Estudios Hispánicos Federico de Onís, UPR.)*

Illustration 2. *Los cuentos de la Universidad,* book jacket cover by Carmelo Filardi, 1935. *(Courtesy of Carlos Filardi, son of Carmelo Filardi.)*

Illustration 3. Emilio S. Belaval by Carmelo Filardi, 1935. *(Courtesy of Carlos Filardi, son of Carmelo Filardi.)*

Illustration 4. *Tuntún de pasa y grifería,* book jacket cover by Carmelo Filardi, 1937. *(Courtesy of Carlos Filardi, son of Carmelo Filardi.)*

Illustration 5. Isabel Andreu de Aguilar (left), María Zambrano (second from left), Margot Arce (center), unidentified member of the AMGUPR, and Herminia Acevedo (right), 1940. *(Courtesy of Proyecto de Digitalización de la Coleccíon de Fotos del Periodico El Mundo, Universidad de Puerto Rico, Recinto de Río Piedras.)*

Illustration 6. Ramón Lavandero, Conrado Asenjo, Margot Arce, Spanish painter José Vela Zanetti, Nilita Vientós Gastón and Jaime Benítez. Ateneo Puertorriqueño, 1940. *(Courtesy of Proyecto de Digitalización de la Coleccíon de Fotos del Periodico El Mundo, Universidad de Puerto Rico, Recinto de Río Piedras.)*

Illustration 7. Margot Arce, doctoral graduation photograph, 1930. *(Courtesy of Dr. Carmen Vázquez Arce.)*

Illustration 8. Margot Arce and Luis Palés Matos at the Ateneo homage to the poet, May 20, 1938. *(Courtesy of Proyecto de Digitalización de la Coleccíon de Fotos del Periodico El Mundo, Universidad de Puerto Rico, Recinto de Río Piedras.)*

CHAPTER 4

The New Creolism: Three Responses to Pedreira

Just as none of us is outside or beyond geography, none of us is completely free from the struggle over geography. That struggle is complex and interesting because it is not only about soldiers and cannons but also about ideas, about forms, about images and imaginings.
—Edward W. Said, 1993

Readers who peruse the inaugural issues of the journal *Ateneo Puertorriqueño* (1935) will find in its pages some of the most important writers active in the intellectual field of the time. The opening "Cartel" (placard) states the editor's intention to forge links with the past generations of *ateneístas*, explore the artistic manifestations of the Spanish "spirit," and join other Hispanic cultures in a fraternal dialogue. After a thirty-year hiatus the publication is back, and editors and contributors signal its readiness to influence the present cultural scene. Eager to usher in Keyserling's new vitalist era, the young writers grouped around the *Ateneo* are quite enthused by what they see as the "generous possibilities of militant Hispanicism."[1] ("generosas posibilidades del hispanismo militante.") Of course, their combativeness sought to exclude explicitly the new colonizer and his culture, but the editors are careful to clarify that theirs is neither a regressive attitude nor an adherence to racial determinism. Rather, they seek the lessons of the past to understand the future. This reincarnation of the journal intends to be modern and inclusive of diverse points of view, and their avant-garde rhetoric, however subdued, seeks to underscore this point playfully. The new journal is a radio receptor that "will tune the sensibility of its antenna to pick up all the vibrations that make our contemporaries feel and think"[2] ("afinará la sensibilidad de su antena para recoger todas las vibraciones que hagan pensar y sentir a la contemporaneidad"). And as the editors conclude their introduction, they mischievously adopt staged masculine pugilism as their metaphor for intellectual debate. In the spirit of sportsmanship "we approach the edge of the ring in which we live to salute, with friendly gesture, the press and the intellectuals of the Spanish-speaking world"[3] ("nos acercamos a la orilla del cuadrilátero en que vivimos para saludar, con ademán amigo, a la prensa y a los intelectuales del mundo hispanoparlante"). Much has changed in Puerto Rican society since 1898, and the young editorialists epitomize these transformations.[4]

Two of the essays discussed in this chapter—Belaval's and Blanco's—were first published in this inaugural issue of *Ateneo Puertorriqueño.* Also featured is Margot Arce's "Los poemas negros de Luis Palés Matos," an essay analyzed in Chapter 7. Other contributors that first year include *Índice* alumni Samuel R. Quiñones, who expounds on the works of acclaimed novelist Zeno Gandía in "El novelista de Puerto Rico: Manuel Zeno Gandía," and Latin Americanist Concha Meléndez who explicates Mexican visual arts. Cultural analysis is represented by Emilio S. Belaval, "Los problemas de la cultura puertorriqueña," Tomás Blanco, "Elogio de *la plena,*" and Miguel Meléndez Muñoz, "Artesanía, industrialismo y maquinismo." Poetry and fiction are showcased with the inclusion of the *negrista* poetry of Luis Palés Matos, neo-romantic poems by Clara Lair, and a short story by Belaval. Finally, Nilita Vientós Gastón provides dance and music criticism with her "El resurgimiento de la danza" and a piece on the romantic aesthetics of German composer Richard Wagner. This first year of the journal of the *Ateneo Puertorriqueño* illustrates the diverse interests of these major participants in the debates over Puerto Rican culture. Pedreira's *Insularismo* had been published the year before, and young Creole intellectuals organized to "broadcast" their responses throughout the pugnacious arena of the intellectual field.

This chapter discusses three works that dialogue with Pedreira's *Insularismo:* Tomás Blanco's "Elogio de *la plena,*" Emilio S. Belaval's "Los problemas de la cultura puertorriqueña," and Margot Arce's "El paisaje de Puerto Rico" (1939), a text that appeared in the journal *Horizontes.* Each in its own way addresses the causes of the ongoing crisis of legitimacy faced by the Puerto Rican elite. Blanco's brief yet rich essay tries to grapple with the concept of popular culture and its place within a national project. Belaval's much longer piece is a historical meditation on the past and future of a *criollo*-led nation. Arce, for her part, provides a testimony of the difficulties inherent in the discursive reappropriation of the land, a vital component of the recuperative nationalist projects that occupy us in this book.

Courting the Mulatto Nation: Tomás Blanco's "Elogio de *la plena*"

By the 1920s the destruction of the world of the *hacienda* was almost complete. Coastal sugar fields and urban centers like San Juan, Mayagüez, and Ponce were overwhelmed with displaced laborers. The vertiginous downward mobility that characterized the 1920s brought together sectors of the Puerto Rican population that previously had lived somewhat separate existences. Workers from the mountainous coffee- and tobacco-growing areas joined those who toiled in the sugar cane fields and needlepoint factories of the coastal regions. It is at this time that the spirited music known as *plena* spread like wildfire among the laboring classes all over the island. The genre, originating in poor neighborhoods of the seigniorial city of Ponce, reflects the Afro-Caribbean aesthetic sensibilities of its composers, musicians, and the people who first enjoyed it. The early period of the *plena*, as critic Juan Flores explains, corresponds with the first twenty-five years of the century, ending in the mid 1920s with the first *plena* recording.[5] Its master composer and performer, Joselino "Bumbúm" Oppenheimer, was an agricultural worker by day and musician by night. The *plena*, first identified with the poor neighborhood of "La Joya del Castillo," owes part of its origins to the amalgam of styles and rhythm brought to Puerto Rico by migrant workers from the British islands—St. Kitts, Barbados, Jamaica—who settled in the region of Ponce.[6] Its Puerto Rican roots are in the *bomba.* Flores clarifies: "all of the early *pleneros*, including Bumbúm, were originally *bomberos*."[7] To this are added elements of other genres such as *seis* and *danza.* Historian Ruth Glasser, for her part, has shown that the second stage of the genre's success is closely related to Puerto Rican immigration to the city of New York. During this second phase of expansion, she places the *plena* in the context of the island emigrant community's constant contact with diverse groups of African-American, Cuban, and other Caribbean musicians, and in the midst of the early "race" record industry. The emigration of the plena coincides with the Latin-American tropical and tango music boom. Mulatto musician Rafael Hernández, who composed *plenas*, *boleros*, and many other genres, lived, performed, and was beloved in New York, Cuba, the Dominican Republic, and Mexico.[8] While the elites of these countries were busy theorizing about national culture, common folk were dancing to music styles they had no trouble inventing, modifying, or adopting as their own.

Plenas cover a multitude of themes. Among the most well-known we find one lamenting the murder of Bumbúm, the famed *plena* virtuoso killed at a dance: "Matan a Bumbúm. Matan a Bumbúm. Matan a Bumbúm en un baile de plena, señores." Another tells of the departure of a lover who wants to return to her hometown: "Helena, Helena. Helena, Helena. Helena, Helena me dijo a mí: yo me voy Papito santo al pueblo de Manatí, donde tengo la casita donde yo te conocí." Some have social meaning such as this one expressing solidarity with the needleworkers' strike: "Dicen las bordadoras que si no hay plata no van pa'lla." There is also an interesting *plena* that gleefully anticipates the troubles of patrician politician Antonio R. Barceló with the newly appointed colonial governor Theodore Roosevelt Jr., "Yo quiero ver los leones. Yo quiero ver los leones, cuando llegue el cazador." We find philosophical *plenas* reminding the listener of the uselessness of vanity: "Tanta vanidad, tanta hipocresía, si tu cuerpo después de muerto pertenece a la tumba fría." There are jocular ones, sometimes making fun of the awful quality of chewing tobacco that will not be sold on credit: "¡Qué tabaco malo! ¡Qué tabaco malo! ¡Qué tabaco malo, mi negra! ¡Qué tabaco malo!" Smuggling and police surveillance are the themes of a *plena* bemoaning the fact that the government has a new patrol boat: "Los muchachos de Cataño no pueden contrabandear porque el gobierno tiene una lancha que juega con los golfos del mar." Lastly, we have some that celebrate the joy of community and the pleasure that dancing and singing bring: "Uno ve como goza María cuando escucha cantando a José una plena que es todo pimienta y que baile la negra Mercé."

When in 1934 Tomás Blanco wrote his encomium, "Elogio de *la plena:* variaciones boricuas," the debate over the blackness of Puerto Rican culture was in full swing. Luis Palés Matos's *negrista* poetry had caused a stir among the reading public. Blanco's "Elogio" represents an intellectual's attempt to reconcile Puerto Rico's racial heterogeneity with white Creoles' sense of identity as a ruling-class-in-the-making. He assures his readers that the *plena* as a symbol of Puerto Rican culture need not be rejected by white Puerto Ricans. In fact the author chides his fellow intellectuals for not appreciating this rich music, especially María Cadilla de Martínez, Pedreira, and others. Blanco reasons that racial prejudice is responsible for the music's rejection among the educated elite, and proceeds to analyze the nature of racial prejudice on the island. His arguments rest on the premise that racism in Puerto Rico is of such a mild form that it does not qualify as white supremacy. Unlike the legal segregation of the southern United States with its Jim Crow laws, what operates in Puerto Rico is a type of silly social prejudice. In fact, even this mild racism is, according to him, an echo of North American influences.

Nonetheless, Blanco does not entirely excuse the elite, asserting instead that their fears are unfounded: "One cannot explain these puerile manifestations of prejudice except as an unthinking protest at the possibility of being considered savage Negroes."[9] ("No se explican estas pueriles manifestaciones del prejuicio sino como protesta irreflexiva de que se nos pueda considerar negros salvajes.") This is a sophisticated insight on his part. Only the cultural compulsion to pass for white can explain the angry outburst of those who are in danger of being found out as not white enough. They would be excluded from the many privileges afforded those marked as white in a white supremacist system. Therein lies the pitfall of the *blanqueamiento* (whitening) ideology; it structurally must exclude those aspiring to whiteness from the advantages reserved for those marked as truly white. Yet, without being critical of the ideology of whitening, the author nonetheless understands the anxieties it produces, especially for a Creole elite that adheres to the tenets of white supremacy in order to construct its identity. At this juncture, Creoles fear being mistaken for a mulatto elite in charge of a mulatto people, especially in the eyes of the white American colonial power. As the author puts it, "And this seems to happen not only in individual cases, but above all, and because of wrongheaded patriotism, when this refers to our people taken as a whole."[10] ("Y esto parece ocurrir no sólo en cada caso individual, sino sobre todo, y por mal entendido patriotismo, cuando se trata del conjunto de nuestro pueblo.") While Blanco forcefully insists that being black and being a savage are two completely different things, he is quick to take issue with the most recent census that found too many "pure" blacks in Puerto Rico for his liking, and offers the reader a comparison that in his view contests the census: "To verify this suffice it to compare our darkest blacks with some *cocolos* from the Windward Islands, with certain jazz band musicians from North America, or with those Frenchified Senegalese who saunter around Europe."[11] ("Para cerciorarse de esto basta comparar nuestros pardos más prietos con algunos cocolos barloventeños, con determinados jazzbandistas de Norteamérica, o con los afrancesados senegaleses que se pasean por Europa.") The author's observation is quite telling in that dark-skinned blacks from the Lesser Antilles were common enough in the coastal regions of Puerto Rico. These migrant workers and sailors were a known reference point throughout the island's history. Nonetheless, he forgets that not all dark-skinned Puerto Ricans are foreigners. Interestingly, in his effort to nationalize the *plena* for the elite, Blanco wants to de-couple it from its Afro-Caribbeanness, the very element in its genealogy that modern scholars stress as a fundamental building block of the style.[12] Yet it is precisely his point that there is no basis for an Afro-Puerto Rican, let alone a Caribbean, affirmation or presence of any importance in *plena*. The jazz band reference is of interest too, in light of its suggestions of seductive American "otherness." Additionally, Blanco is apparently unaware that he mocks the very French Senegalese immigrants and students responsible for nurturing the *Négritude* movement, an irony lost on him as he makes his point about who belongs where.

At times the author waivers between courageous anti-racist vindication and anxiousness to sever ties with any and everything African. Blanco bravely advances the idea that Puerto Ricans are a mixed-race people: "The fact makes us neither cold nor hot, for I do not think it a special honor or dishonor to be *mestizo*, white, black, yellow or red."[13] ("Aceptamos el hecho sin frío ni calor, pues no creo que sea honra o deshonra especial ser mestizo, blanco, negro, amarillo o rojo.") He also recognizes that the populace, for its part, affirms its racial mixture in universally known sayings like, "when the bomba *calls*, he who doesn't shake an ear, shakes his backside"[14] ("cuando la bomba *ñama*, el que no menea oreja, menea una nalga"[15]). On the more serious political side he clearly repudiates Nazism and the racism of the southern United States, adding that "to maintain the essential inferiority of certain races is a mere imperialist pretext"[16] ("mantener la inferioridad esencial de ciertas razas es un mero pretexto imperialista"). Finally, shunning essentialism, the author sides with anthropological and economic theories to account for differences among countries and peoples. All this being said, however, Blanco proceeds to put in place his own version of the "racial democracy" theory of hierarchical inclusion so popular among white Latin Americans throughout most of the twentieth century.

The author's problematic defense of *plena* rests on the assumption that to elevate this musical form he has to "whiten" it, stressing the Spanishness of many of its aspects: its octosyllabic verses reminiscent of the *romance*, and its Peninsular melodies. Only in the rhythmic patterns does the genre exhibit a diluted relationship to an earlier, undeniably Afro-Puerto Rican *bomba*. Blanco explains:

> The barbaric *bomba*—a black dance, a slave dance—bestowed upon its great-grandchild, the *plena*, her best attributes: natural vigor, percussive and rhythmic effects. Rhythm, par excellence, is black. The *plena* partakes of this excellence with extraordinary wealth: trepidant sonorous rhythms, syncopated, repeated, monotonous, which are combined with others that are changing, long, elastic, fleeting and full of insinuation. This Negroid element underlines the singing and plays with it. Beyond that the *plena* is—plainly—white.[17] (La bomba barbara—danza negra, baile de esclavos—dotó a su biznieta, la *plena*, con lo mejor que ella tenía: vigor natural, efectos de percusión y ritmos. El ritmo es excelencia negra. De esa excelencia participa la *plena* con extraordinaria riqueza: sonoros ritmos trepidantes, sincopados, repetidos, monótonos, que se combinan con otros variables, alargados, elásticos, fugaces y llenos de insinuación. Este elemento negroide subraya el canto y juguetea con él. Por todo lo demás la *plena* es—plenamente—blanca.)

The author's poetic description of the rhythmic aspects of the *plena* is quite accurate. Yet his assertion that, rhythm aside, the *plena* is fully white or more in keeping with European musical idioms fails to take into account aspects fundamental to the understanding of this musical genre. We must remember that the *plena* functions in an oral and aural culture. Ray Pratt's study of the blues reminds us that "the oral tradition encourages a greater degree of emotional, and perhaps even physical, involvement in the environment, which in turn allows for a more developed sense of community as well as a heightened collective awareness and even 'collective consciousness.'"[18] Spontaneous and improvised activity as well as nonverbal, often unconscious communication, becomes possible in a form that effectively bypasses the

"European tradition rooted in a pattern of structure and regularity."[19] Blanco is correct in seeing the *plena* as a product of transculturation, which he denominates with the term "mulatto." But his paternalistic discourse depoliticizes the *plena* and wrenches it from its popular contestatory anchoring. Juan Flores reminds us that *plenas* "give voice, usually in sharp ironic tones and imagery, to the experience of working-class people in all its aspects."[20] He stresses that a "shared social world and perspective" not only gives the genre meaning, but is accountable for its aesthetic structure, "its boisterous syncopated rhythms, improvised instrumentation and vigorous call-and-response vocal cadences."[21]

Blanco's essay is a courageous broadening of horizons in the narrow racial environment of his intellectual circle, and it is not my intention to dismiss its importance. The essay argues for a modernization of perspectives by making merciless fun of those who privilege the *danza* as a national symbol, mistakenly believing it to be more acceptable because it is less black. Ángel Quintero Rivera has argued that what many intellectuals of the *Generación del Treinta* obstinately construed to be "white" peasant music were in effect hybrid musical forms that had managed to mask their African ancestry through what the author calls the "melody-zation of the rhythm."[22] Moreover, when in the 1930s Creole intellectuals recuperate the *danza* as their hallowed exemplar of untainted Creoleness, they are able to do so only after disregarding the profound hybridity of this musical form and the black and mulatto artisan social stratum from whence it came. This willful myopia was not shared by the nineteenth-century Creole elite, who understood very well that it was mulatto and black musicians who composed the music and played it to entertain artisans and patricians alike. Formally, the dance genre that became the *danza* stemmed from the much-transformed and reworked contredance, with Afro-Puerto Rican *bomba*, and other Afro-Caribbean styles, camouflaged to garner elite patronage and attest to artisan dignity and respectability.[23] As Quintero Rivera very pointedly argues, the *danza* is a metaphor for the strictures endured and small triumphs achieved by the artisan class in its effort to incorporate itself into the *hacendado*-led "great Puerto Rican family." That the economically weak Creole elite needed the support of the artisans is evident in the elite's willingness to include them, albeit as underlings, in their reformist projects. In that context, music, as a skilled occupation, allowed a number of artisans access to gainful and respectable employment in municipal and other bands. The mixed-race, nineteenth-century urban population that developed its own clubs and newspapers, like *El Artesano, El Heraldo del Trabajo, El Obrero, Revista Obrera,* had in the *danza* one of its vehicles of social mobility.[24]

"Elogio de *la plena*" was written against the grain of those arguments that rejected the music precisely because of its humble origins, its perceived "vulgarity," and its blackness. We must not overlook the great importance of music as a means to claim social space.[25] The nature of music as an event is to enter the body and elicit a response from those who experience it. To have the affluent population dancing to the music of the working class does effect—up to a point—a temporary lowering of social barriers. It is interesting that Blanco penned this essay from Madrid, and its moving dedication hints at his desire for a rapprochement:

> To the folk of the shores and plains of the littoral who gave us the plena; to the city of Ponce, that claims her as her own; to the black folk of Cangrejos, Sunoco, and Loíza who never tire of adoring her; to Canario and his Group who caught her on records; to Germán the Caguas Musician who exalts her between the strings of his bordonúa; to Ramón Lavandero who finds ecstasy in her; to Luis Palés Matos who owes her a poem; to all those who sing, dance, and perform her [Spanish feminine]; to those who create her, and to those who find enjoyment in her: cheers![26] (A ese pueblo costero de las playas y sabanas del litoral que nos inventó la plena; a la ciudad de Ponce, que la reclama como suya propia; a los morenos de Cangrejos, de Sunoco y de Loíza que no se cansan de rendirle culto; a Canario y su Grupo que la aprisionaron en discos; a Germán el Músico de Caguas que la exalta entre las cuerdas de su bordonúa; a Ramón Lavandero que se extasía con ella; a Luis Palés Matos que le debe un poema; a todos los que la cantan, la bailan y la tocan; a los que la crean y a los que con ella se recrean: ¡salud!)

This touching dedication, colored perhaps by the nostalgia of one far from his homeland, evinces an immense desire to unite the popular mass culture with literate culture; to bring together in a moment of celebration black and mulatto folks with sympathetic Creoles willing to reach out. "Elogio de *la plena*" is the site of a social utopia where racial antagonism has been superseded by a truce. Yet it is a coming together in which "white" culture determines the terms of the peace. Glossing over real class and racial struggles, Blanco wants the *plena* to be a symbol of *convivencia*—harmonious living. Its perfect form flows above uneasy social reality. "The *plena*," Blanco explains,

> goes beyond local hodgepodge. Without denying the medium, it selects and measures its materials. From heterogeneity it creates a homogeneous typical diversity. Just as it collates and harmonizes in a fiery popular orchestra those instruments and voices that serve as its vehicle despite their different lineage, so too it composes and harmonizes the dissimilar racial influences that lend support and background to its originality.[27] (La plena supera la burundanga ambiente. Sin renegar del medio, selecciona, dosifica y coordina sus materiales. De lo heterogéneo crea una homogénea diversidad típica. Según compagina y concierta en una brava orquesta popular y característica los instrumentos y las voces que le sirven de vehículo, a pesar de sus distintos abolengos, así también compone y armoniza las influencias raciales disímiles que prestan base y antecedentes a su originalidad.)

The author is careful to clarify that the *plena* is the music that best expresses the times; it is, in his view, a metaphor for society. *Plena* constructs a spatiotemporal dimension where people of dissimilar class and racial origin need not fight each other. Instead of the class struggle, he imagines cooperation. Disruption is avoided, and those instruments—and peoples—of low lineage find their place in a society where *criollo* hegemony is shaken but maintained. *Elogio de la plena* symbolically provides a—subordinate—space for the working-class, racially-mixed population to join in the populist alliance that the professional middle-class spearheaded from 1938 on. Yet, and this must be stressed, the essay attempts to contain and redirect popular participation. Blanco achieves this containment rhetorically when he subordinates the *plena* by sexualizing it: "Nubile mulatta of aged-rum hue," he writes,

> of straight hair and mischievous eyes that could be taken for Andalusian; of slightly archaic Spanish tongue, and of agile feet like a jungle beast. . . . Rarely vulgar, though she might on occasion be coarse, but of primitive shamelessness that is more naïveté than insolence. And even so, she need only refrain just a bit to make you proud in polite society—dancings, beaches, salons—without losing face among her peers.[28] (Mulatica de tez dorada como ron añejo; de pelo lacio y ojos pícaros que pueden pasar por andaluces; de parla castellana, un poco arcaica; y, de ágil paso sensitivo, como bestezuela selvática. . . . Rara vez chabacana, se muestra en ocasiones chocarrera, pero con desvergüenza primitiva que tiene más de ingenuidad que de descoco. Y aún así, le basta con refrenarse un punto para hacer buen papel en sociedad—*dancings*, playas, salones—sin desmerecer entre sus congéneres.)

The peers he humorously mentions are musical genres: "the somewhat disheveled Seis, the gentrified Danza, the exotic Fox, the ceremonious Waltz, her cousin the unbridled Rumba, and the greased-up Tango." Yet Blanco is at the same time describing the favored fantasy sex object of the *criollo:* the mulatta—socially subservient, sexually uninhibited, or rather, available, yet innocent, who nonetheless knows how to behave in public. The *plena* can "pass," like many Puerto Ricans who favor this strategy as a means of social mobility.

Ultimately, we can read the essay as a strategy of containment and as a commentary on the possibilities and the limitations of the populist alliance poised to take form three years later.[29] At the time of the publication of "Elogio de *la plena*," intellectuals such as Luis Palés Matos and Tomás Blanco found some of the racism inherent in Pedreira's *Insularismo* to be too obstinate and overt. In an effort to countervail some of that essay's divisiveness and shortcomings, Tomás Blanco responded with two book-length works that offered important modifications to Pedreira: *Prontuario histórico* (1935) and *El prejuicio racial en Puerto Rico* (1942).[30] In *El prejuicio racial,* Blanco returns to the nineteenth-century metaphor of the great Puerto Rican family, "la gran familia puertorriqueña," to present a vision of racial and cultural unity in the face of the growing social crisis of the 1930s. The author found it imperative to show that racial prejudice in Puerto Rico was not as brutal and nefarious as the North American brand. According to *El prejuicio racial*, Puerto Rico had never experienced "true" racism, only a benign form of racial prejudice. He puts forth a history of slavery where Christian principles inherent in Spanish culture always mitigated the abuses of the system. Blanco's revisionist history of racial relations in Puerto Rico goes plainly against the truth. As Arcadio Díaz Quiñones shows, a reading of nineteenth-century abolitionist texts will prove that Blanco advances some of the same arguments put in place by the very supporters of slavery. *El prejuicio racial*, in its blind defense of the felicity of the Spanish colonial past, insists on a vision of a "whitened" Puerto Rican culture whose overwhelming superiority "diluted" the Africans, their descendents, and their cultural presence. Furthermore, he forgets that North American abolitionists provided an inspiration for Puerto Rican abolitionists, black and white. As Díaz Quiñones points out,

> Blanco's "conciliatory" proposal, which projected itself paradoxically into the past, was almost able to erase all traces of the violent, arbitrary acts perpetrated by Spanish colonialism, as well as both the resistance and the resentment of *Creoles* and Spaniards, whites and blacks, freethinkers, masons, and "Americanized" Protestants, who struggled against the old Catholic order and its racist mythologies.[31]

Additionally, for Díaz Quiñones *El prejuicio racial* presents a harmonious vision of "the altruistic supremacy of Hispanism, a version of history that erases all conflict and postulates pacific coexistence, while at the same time erasing the very history of the people subordinated."[32] In sum, Blanco's historical revisionism strives to present the history of slavery as if it were the history of abolition. Ultimately, his response to Pedreira could not entirely divest itself of elitism and Hispanophilia.

Noted critic Mercedes López-Baralt's edition of *Insularismo* details how carefully Blanco had read Pedreira's essay, including copious and candid margin notes that would be the genesis of "Elogio de *la plena*" and *Prontuario histórico*. For her, Blanco's *Prontuario histórico*'s more explicitly anti-imperialist discourse accounts for its lesser place in the canon of island letters and its sparse diffusion by the school system.[33] This debate on the nature and character of Puerto Rican culture involved a third element, Luis Palés Matos's "black poetry," of which Blanco was a staunch defender. Some have seen in Palés Matos's poetry a parody and refutation of *Insularismo*.[34] His controversial poetry polarized the intellectual field and forced its members to take sides. Chapter 7 examines Margot Arce's influential vindication of Palés Matos's poetry. Paradoxically, Arce exemplifies a "positive response" to his verses while holding steadfastly to the theory of the "Spanishness" of Puerto Rican culture. Other writers would add their voices to the debate with essays of historical interpretations as well as works of fiction. Such is the case of Emilio S. Belaval whose *criollista* proposal is analyzed next.

Criollismo as Generational Challenge: Emilio S. Belaval

Lawyer, essayist, fiction writer, and dramatist, Emilio S. Belaval asserts in "Los problemas de la cultura puertorriqueña" that the most urgent problem facing Puerto Ricans is the need to explore the true contours of their national culture. This is part of the new generation's polemical and iconoclastic mandate. As a member of the group heading the *Ateneo,* he takes this task to heart. As he will argue, Creole intellectual leadership can no longer be postponed. Belaval's essay intends to further vivify the discussion of cultural nationalism by casting it as a renewed form of *criollismo.*

In general, the meaning of *criollo* as "Spanish-descended" signals a distancing from European origins. The roots of *criollo,* according to Dieter Woll, situate it as a word used by Spanish masters to refer to the slave born in the master's house, as distinguished from one born in Africa, a *bozal.* The first African slaves were brought to work in the mines of the island of Hispaniola as early as 1505, followed by a much greater importation in 1510. Woll argues for a Spanish precedence of the term over a previously accepted Portuguese one, since slavery was widespread in the Spanish colonies before it became so in Brazil.[35] The first Portuguese recorded usage of *crioulo* is found in Frei Luís de Sousa in 1632. Seventy years *earlier* Mexico gives us the first recorded use of it in a 1562 Spanish document from Puebla: "a black of mine . . . of fourteen years of age . . . *criollo* of the said province of Yucatán"[36] ("un negro mío . . . de hedad de catorze años . . . *criollo* de la dicha provincia de Yucatán"). We also have news of the term being used in Havana in 1578: "black slave, *criolla* of this village"[37] ("esclava negra, *criolla* de esta villa"). Once the word spread widely to designate black slaves born in the colonies, it was adopted to refer to the children of Spaniards born outside Spain. Inca Garcilaso reports both uses in Perú in 1602, and locates its origins among the black population.[38]

Cuban scholar José Juan Arrom argues for a cultural rather than racial meaning for *criollo,* which he defines as anyone born in the Indies. In 1788 we have the first known record of the word in the Puerto Rican context by visiting cleric Fray Iñigo Abbad who writes, "they give the name criollo indistinctly to all those born on the island, be they of any caste or mixture"[39] ("dan el nombre de criollos indistintamente a todos los nacidos en la isla, de cualquiera casta o mezcla que sean"). Arrom advances the idea that the end of the slave trade in the nineteenth century did away with the distinction between Africans born overseas and those in the Americas. European immigration continued, however, and, in his estimation, this led to the use of the term for whites, or very light-skinned mulattos, or *mestizos* who lived as whites. Arrom underscores that, "If all those born in America, of European origin, are *criollos,* not all *criollos* are, necessarily, of pure European origin."[40] After the wars of independence, as national identification grew more pronounced, *criollo* came to mean national and autochthonous to a country, and in the literature of the 1930s "what is essentially of the Americas"[41] ("lo esencial americano").

Significantly, the term *criollo* is used in Belaval's text to mean both the white descendents of the old *hacendado* elite and the hybrid people and culture that has evolved since the inception of the Spanish colonial project—in other words, that which has become common and native to the place. Careful not to leave out any of the uses of the term, Belaval wants to create a semantic rapprochement among all the usages of *criollo.* It is no mere accident that a member of the Spanish-descended elite would put in place a discourse that asked his cohorts to assume their role at the head of a would-be coalition of diverse social classes and races. Elite Spanish Creoles are trying to fathom how to lead racially mixed subaltern Creoles into a modern hegemonic project vis-à-vis the new colonial power.

Reading against the backdrop of contemporary social and political events we can better grasp the urgency of "Los problemas." Just a year earlier, in 1934, sugar cane workers had organized an island-wide strike, disrupting production and adding to the generalized atmosphere of uncertainty and crisis. The workers, for their part, had called upon the charismatic leader of the Puerto Rican nationalist party, Pedro Albizu Campos, to act as a mediator in the dispute, in clear repudiation of their own labor leaders. Though this coming together of workers and the petty bourgeois *Partido Nacionalista* could not be sustained, the *Nacionalista*'s intrepid militancy, and the rhetoric that it popularized, was on everyone's mind. Albizu Campos's fiery oratory was heard in person and on the radio around the island, and the press kept readers informed about the Nationalist Party's pronouncements and activities.[42]

Belaval's search for a new discourse regarding North American culture seeks to pursue the question of Puerto Rican racial heterogeneity to a much further extent than Pedreira ever did. The lawyer/essayist proposes that the very different attitudes toward race mixing upheld by the two colonial powers are key to understanding the present, as well as the possibility of a future relationship with the United States. Belaval himself, though he never mentions Albizu Campos, inserts him in the change that had been taking place in the past five years. We should also keep in mind that neither Belaval nor other intellectuals of his group discounted the economic roots of Puerto Rico's problems. Yet rather than embracing an overtly anti-colonial resolution to the crisis, his social sector was far more inclined to privilege cultural explanations and to propose cultural answers. Faced with the Spanish past, racial mixing, and colonial modernity, Belaval asserts that it is imperative to proceed with cultural analysis, even as we await the ultimate clarification of the island's political status. Addressing a clearly male audience, he invites them to adopt a "virile" and "courageous" reflection and plan of action. As Belaval puts it, "the only way to vigorously counteract our bewilderment is to project a cultural nationalism where we can all agree on a consistent vision of what is Puerto Rican."[43] ("La única forma de contrarrestar vigorosamente nuestro desconcierto es mediante la proyección de un nacionalismo cultural donde podamos coincidir todos en una consistente visión de lo puertorriqueño.") This reinvigorated and true *criollismo* would cast aside "our puerile concept of Creolism"[44] ("nuestro ñoño concepto de la criollicidad"). The crisis demands the most urgent response. Like Pedreira, he views democracy with great apprehension, believing that the working classes misunderstand its true meaning. Unlike Pedreira, however, Belaval is less fearful of Afro-Puerto Ricans. He embraces race mixing as a reality and a pragmatic solution to racial antagonism, while allowing white Puerto Ricans to preserve their racial hegemony. As explored later, his call for racial "reconciliation" is quite in keeping with Tomás Blanco's appeal for "convivencia" or peaceable relationships among Puerto Ricans of all racial and class backgrounds. But the author is asking his *male* addressees to accept the fact that they are leaders. Throughout the essay's historical narrative the emphasis is on the conqueror and *his* projects, the landowner and *his* culture, the intellectual and *his* mission. Indians, blacks, women of all races, the peasantry and working classes are spoken about, not dialogued with. They are construed as part of the problem that must be dealt with urgently.[45]

In the introduction to "Los problemas" the author invokes the monstrous image of a fetus with two umbilical cords to dramatize the predicament of Puerto Rican culture in its linkage to two colonial "mothers." The first sections of the essay explore the question of Puerto Rican colonial history and the legacies of that history. In his brief consideration of the issue of the island's indigenous past, Belaval concludes that given the early decimation of the Indians we cannot count that heritage as part of the national make-up, as does Mexico for example. While he laments the forced servitude and demise of the Indians as the result of Spanish conquest, the author paradoxically blames the Tainos for not leaving a permanent legacy to Puerto Rico's national culture. The indigenous population is seen here as part of the sediment of the national edifice, a reified presence euphemistically constructed as place.[46] Explaining that the Indians' very submissiveness made their conquest easy, he concludes that their importance to the development of the nation is negligible. In the author's words, "To our culture they left very little: a few *areytos*, some ceramic, an incipient mythology, a romance, the love of the cacica Loaiza and the mulatto Pedro López, and a melancholy: the knowledge of being orphaned of the human element of the land where we were born."[47] ("Para nuestra cultura dejaron muy poco: unos areytos, un poco de cerámica, una mitología incipiente, un romance de amor, el de la cacica Loaiza y el mulato Pedro López y una melancolía: la de sabernos huérfanos del elemento humano de la tierra en que nacimos.") At this point in the essay, no mention is made of the slaves brought from Africa, of early race mixing among the three groups, or of the painful and ingenious adaptations that a conquered and devastated people are compelled to make.

The present state of affairs was due in part to the loss of Puerto Rico's indigenous population, in his view an anomaly among colonized countries, depriving the island of a vital element of resistance that could have served it well in its four-hundred-year development. Without this indigenous "layer," Puerto Ricans look to distant lands, and sometimes to other races, for solutions to their problems. In his words, "Our culture was not a problem of assimilation or grafting. It was a culture of total conquest, transplanted to our ground from a distant military, Catholic, and monarchical land."[48] ("Nuestra cultura no fue un problema de asimilación, ni de injerto. Fue una cultura de conquista total, transplantada a nuestro suelo, desde un lar distante, militar, católico y monárquico.") By presenting the history of the genocidal conquest of the Tainos as a legacy of "failure" on the part of the Indians to future generations, Belaval sets the stage for the assertion that Puerto Rican culture is in its fundamental aspects "vitally Spanish." This clever rhetorical strategy allows him to advance the thesis of the profound Spanishness of the culture. As the author puts it, "The Indian failed us in the task of creating for us the plasma of combat against the foreigner."[49] ("Nos falló lo indio para crearnos el plasma de combate contra el estranjero.") Plasma—blood or vital fluid of life—is a word used a number of times in the essay in lieu of a more complex formulation of how power differences affect cultural conflicts and cultural production.

The author asserts early on that Puerto Rico is the most Spanish of all the former colonies for two different but interrelated reasons. On one hand, he chastises the intelligentsia for their excessive attachment to Spanish culture, an attachment that makes them reticent to take their place as a Puerto Rican ruling class. On the other hand, he is not able to give up his own investments in the idea of Spanishness and the superiority he ascribes to it. As he puts it, "To the work of constructing Puerto Ricanness, we only added the land. The spirit was provided by Spain."[50] ("A la obra de construcción de lo puertorriqueño, sólo pusimos la tierra. El espíritu lo puso España.") It would be interesting to ascertain who the "we" is who added the land. The question of land, however, is of crucial significance. The author minimizes the importance of land when the Spanish take it from the Indians; yet land and a servile labor force attached to it becomes the very basis of *hacendado* power. His meager mention of Indian resistance is explained by his interest in telling the story that really matters to him, how Creole nationhood flourished under Spain and

Spanish immigrants in the nineteenth century. This is the reason for his schematic account of the first three hundred years of the colonial enterprise. Most historians agree that during these three centuries black and mixed-race Puerto Ricans comprised the vast majority of the population. Belaval glosses over the founding of the first colonial settlements by Andalusians and Basques, the early importation of enslaved Africans, the role of piracy and contraband carried out with the British, French, and Dutch, and the construction of walls and fortresses around the capital. By characterizing the colonial venture as a foundational epic journey, the author signals his lack of interest in delving deeper into the genocidal Spanish conquest and subsequent race and cultural mixing with Tainos and Africans. Rather, he underscores the periodic immigrations of Spaniards from diverse regions as a seamless process of incorporation. For him, Spanish cultural influences are sine qua non. As he puts it: "Asturians, Andalusians, Castilians, and Basques people our land and take possession of the contours; folk songs, sayings, popular music, musical instruments, Christmas traditions, saints' feasts, religious legend, architecture, agrarian customs, family structure, social delineation. People and legacy are absorbed."[51] ("Astures, andaluces, castellanos y vascos pueblan nuestra tierra y se apoderan de la expresión del contorno; romancero, refranero, canto popular, instrumental músico, tradiciones natividales, hagiografía festiva, leyenda religiosa, trazo arquitectónico, costumbres agrarias, constitución familiar, delineación social. Se absorben la heredad y las gentes.") Spaniards of diverse regional origins come to mix and contribute to all areas of life. Contrary to historical reality, he whitens the first three centuries of Spanish colonial rule effacing the racial and cultural realities that characterized the era.

What Belaval calls "our Europeanizing nineteenth-century" starts with the *Real Cédula de Gracias* of 1815, discussed in Chapter 1. The author writes in detail—and with a degree of admiration—about the Creole culture that developed during that century, but he is critical of the dependency on Spain that this fostered, then and now, among the descendents of the immigrants. He believes that his contemporaries suffer from an anxiety of affiliation most detrimental to the very ones called upon to lead the nation's destiny. This critique notwithstanding, "Los problemas" portrays the *hacendado* as the paradigmatic figure of Puerto Rican national culture. As Belaval would have it, the landowner is the only real historical protagonist of his narrative. At the dawn of Puerto Rico's national history, the conquistador is a morose personality, a lonesome civilized man left in the hot tropics: "He stuffs himself with tobacco, a drug formerly unknown to him, he couples with the Indian woman, whose skin reminds him of the Moorish girl of his Alhambra, and gets drunk on melancholy and distance."[52] ("Se atiborra de tabaco, droga que el no conocía, se ayunta con la india, cuya piel le recuerda la morisca de su Alhambra y se emborracha de melancolía y de distancia.") The colonization of the territory institutionalized the subordination of native and black women seen as poor substitutes for the genuine article—the Moorish girl. Curiously, the author looks upon the defeated Amerindian people and Africans who were coerced into providing free or cheap labor, as the enemies of the white man, not the other way around. Here and in other writings part of the "mission" of the Spanish man is to dilute—by means of sexual intercourse—this enemy blood. The role of the European-descended woman, when she finally makes an appearance, is to provide him with a legitimate family. Nonetheless, the *hacendado* "does not abandon his exotic sexual commerce, a compensation for living in an uncivilized area in the hope that in the years to come the 'free mulatto' would be his ally"[53] ("pero no abandona su comercio sexual exótico, que es la compensación del área no civilizada y la seguridad de que en el mañana, el 'pardo libre' será su aliado"). Yet, as we will see in *Los cuentos de la Universidad*, Belaval's treatment of black and mulatto men discloses a great ambivalence about the possibility of such an alliance. In "Los problemas," some *hacendado* violence is present, but portrayed as inevitable. And while Indians and blacks provide labor and sexual gratification, they do little else. The author does not entertain the notion that processes of transculturation could account for subaltern practices of resistance and dissemblance. Nonetheless, Belaval will try to face the question of *mestizaje* in the latter part of the essay. Blacks and mulattos will reappear when he discusses what to do about democracy, militant workers, and a populace that has been irrevocably changed by the new socioeconomic conditions of the past thirty-seven years.

Belaval's description of the nineteenth-century *hacendado* created by the new immigration is both sympathetic and admiring. He is a heroic figure, vigorous, economically solvent, and in control. On this account, Belaval conforms to historical reality. The new European immigrants had indeed replaced the poorer, less-educated and mixed-race small landowners of the first centuries. For his part, Belaval describes him in this essay as an authoritarian but benign patriarch, one who sets the tone for Puerto Rico's rural culture: "who will as soon hunt down his steer as his black, will crucify his slave with lashes, yet will open his barrels of wine to the whole village for a hat dance. Toward him converge in search of their subsistence Indians, blacks and *criollos*, mulattos and *mestizos* whom he forces to live in a disorderly mass"[54] ("lo mismo caza su res que su negro, que lo mismo crucifica a cintarazos un esclavo que abre las espitas de su vino a todo el caserío para un baile de sombrero. A él converge en busca de sustento el indio, el negro, el criollo, el mulato y el mestizo que hace vivir en un abigarrado montón"). Individualistic, authoritarian, yet civil and honorable, he both acquiesces with and at times mildly resists public and church authority. His sons study in Europe, most probably medicine, Belaval says. Indeed there is no question of daughters studying in Europe in that period. In the nineteenth century Creoles did not spend money on costly educations for their daughters.

In "Los problemas" peasants will be dealt with in much less flattering terms. They are depicted as deferential to the landowner as long as their needs are reasonably met, accustomed to the vagaries of seasonal work and to protection when calamities strike. Neither do country folk mind if the *hacendado* robs them of their daughters or overtaxes them, because they also count on his largess on holidays in the form of dance, rum, fritters, and stew. Even today this centuries-old culture of deference and paternalism once linked to the *hacienda* persists, according to Belaval: "Examine the rural psychology of our land and you will find this institution of our life profoundly rooted"[55] ("Examínese la psicología rural de nuestra tierra y se encontrará profundamente enraizada en esta institución de nuestra vida"). The author explains that peasants (invariably portrayed as males) retain a longstanding sense of dependency and making do, a mistrust of authority figures, be they priests, the police, health or social workers, or anyone who comes to trouble their sense of justice, life, or gender relations.

Some of the contradictions we see in this piece have to do with the author's efforts to account for cultural change while also wanting to give a sense of permanence to the culture he describes. His genealogy of the *hacendado* and the peasantry responds to a desire to show how these two groups interact in the present. The permanence the author seeks to trace, however, is often more a wish than an actuality. As mentioned earlier, by 1935 when this essay was published, the world of the *hacienda* was no more. The working classes had gone from sharecroppers to proletarians working for huge agro-businesses, needle industries, and tobacco factories. The author understands this phenomenon well, as we see in his account of the U.S. stranglehold on the country's economy and the creation of mammoth absentee sugar monopolies. He feels for the ruined small landowners who, having sold their land at exorbitant prices, now only find high prices in consumer goods plus the vicissitudes of an impoverished life. Nonetheless, Belaval is also forced to admit that the common people have marginally profited from the restructuring of the economy, even in its colonial capitalist form. Changing material conditions have affected popular culture in ways that the author accepts with some bitterness, interpreting working-class aspirations through the prism of his social class. He begrudgingly concedes that the poor have more participation in politics, while also deriding subaltern access to political rights. Accordingly, his claim is that the common folk are in a state of confusion regarding the true meaning of democracy and citizenship rights. As Belaval sardonically puts it, "Furthermore, wherever there was a soapbox, the people were told that dew from heaven called 'free speech' was guaranteed; that the people of Puerto Rico had acquired the right to call any living being an idiot, at the top of one's voice, if one so chose, even if that any living being was the President of the United States."[56] (Además donde quiere que existía una tribuna pública, se hizo saber al pueblo que un rocío del cielo llamado 'libertad de palabra' estaba garantizado; que el pueblo de Puerto Rico había adquirido el derecho de decirle idiota a todo ser viviente, a voz en cuello, aunque el ser viviente fuera el Presidente de los Estados Unidos.) Belaval laments that rural workers have become intractable due to the importation of some aspects of democracy to the island. The author grants that workers' salaries have gone up to a certain extent, and that modernization has refashioned previously oppressive relationships. Additionally, the Catholic church now had competition from Methodist pastors who had a more direct contact with the faithful, wore pants instead of cassocks, and gave practical advice regarding the benefits of having fewer children. In his words, "The worker's fear of the Catholic [hierarchy] was in part dissolved with this new concept of a religion that had a more civic character, just as fear of the military had waned when the people saw a general without a mustache."[57] ("El temor a lo católico se disolvió un tanto con esta nueva tesis de la religión que tenía más bien un carácter cívico, como antes se había disuelto el temor a lo militar, cuando el pueblo contempló a un general sin bigotes.")

Belaval's mocking interpretation of the social changes taking place contrasts with the more disillusioned positions of Pedreira and Arce, and with the rigid and desperate view held by nationalist leader Albizu Campos. The author of "Los problemas" is a pragmatist who reminds his *ateneísta* readers that popular enthusiasm toward the modernization of social relations was inevitable and that the poor had acted out of self-interests that did not correspond to those of the elite. He rightfully observes that in the service of American capitalism schools were built, phonographs were installed in neighborhood bars, and the Red Cross was organized. Additionally, schoolteachers engaged in social work, sanitation workers delivered quinine to peasants, schools had basketball teams and free dentistry, and Protestant pastors set up Christmas trees for children. Thus, the world built by the *hacienda* was not only gone, but irrevocably destroyed as *jíbaros* and urban laborers squarely rejected its hierarchical premises to take advantage of the new conditions. Belaval points out that as new mythologies were replacing old ones, former social distinctions of race and class were threatened. The necessities of wages had given workers from the interior the possibility of selling their labor elsewhere, and a new money economy could now account for social prestige. As the author puts it,

> In this state of affairs, more humane, more accessible, with the legend of the generous Abe, with free schools, a walkabout peon in perpetual leisure, with overseers without bullwhips, with a goodly amount of children learning to read in confusing proximity, without social distinctions of caste and color, with no aristocratic sense other than money, the incipient sense of Puerto Rican nationhood was filled with unwholesome dissociations.[58] (En este estado de cosas, más humano, más accesible, con la leyenda del buen Abe, con escuela sin paga, con un peón caminero en perpetuo ocio, con capataces sin

traílla, con una buena cantidad de chicos aprendiendo a leer en abigarrado montón, sin diferenciación social por casta o color, sin más sentido de lo aristocrático que el dinero, el sentido incipiente de la nacionalidad puertorriqueña se llenó de miasmas disociadoras.)

In sum, Belaval acknowledges that the Creole social hegemony backed by Spain had been oppressive to most poor people in some ways that American colonial hegemony was not, and that democracy had dealt a fatal blow to the Creole political project and ethos enthroned by 1897. He understands that the old Creole autonomy project was undergirded by a rigid authoritarianism masked by a paternalistic rhetoric that many among the newly formed proletariat squarely rejected. He urges Creoles to concede power to some degree, in order to reposition themselves as a hegemonic class. Resigned to this state of affairs, Belaval calls on others like himself to do the same. Consequently, the author's task in the second part of the essay will be to argue for a consensus among the educated elite that would allow them to speak with one voice. Recognizing that this is not easy, he calls for Creoles to embrace a change of consciousness that will help them to be reconciled with their true selves and with their new historical mission.

The question of Puerto Rico's racial composition is one of the dominant themes of the second part of the essay. Here Belaval's project becomes explicit as he exhorts other Creoles of his class to lead this racially heterogeneous nation without fear. While the first years of the twentieth century had been "years of stupor where our solution for historic continuity is broken,"[59] this need not be the case now ("años de estupor donde se rompe nuestra solución de continuidad histórica"). Indeed, Belaval reproaches Creoles for what he sees as too weak an attachment to Puerto Rico and its realities, and for their now chimerical projects of affiliation to Spain, Latin America, or the United States. To regain their former ascendancy Creoles must formulate a stronger, more inclusive brand of *criollismo* that can be attractive to enough people. In the author's view Puerto Ricans of all social classes lack a truly coherent idea of the possibilities of this new *criollismo.* The poor, because they were oppressed under Spain and are now confused by the promises of democracy. The well-to-do, because they were comfortably ensconced within the Spanish colonial system and are now demoralized due to their lack of power. Belaval emphatically rejects the American idea of Puerto Rico as a bridge between North America and South America: "the immediate future of Puerto Rico is the projection of a cultural nationalism"[60] ("el futuro inmediato de Puerto Rico es la proyección de un nacionalismo cultural . . ."). Puerto Ricans need to look to each other in order to change their situation.

The author confesses that he has been discouraged by what he sees as a lack of interest in Puerto Rican culture reflected in the educated classes' literature: "I have looked anxiously for the theme of my land and I have not found it. . . ."[61] ("Yo he buscado ansiosamente el tema de mi tierra y no lo he encontrado. . . .") It behooves Puerto Rican writers to search for the fundamental themes of Puerto Rican life, which Belaval enumerates for the reader: Indian, conquest, *hacienda*, sugar mill, smuggling, slavery, *mestizaje*, Catholicism, Spanish political repression, masonry, agrarianism, hagiography, polygamy, religious celebrations. Attention to these and the many other factors that have shaped Puerto Ricans as a people will perhaps allow the elite to leave behind "our burden as whites, our terror of blacks, and create a profound nationalism within which our thinking feels perfectly comfortable"[62] ("nuestro ritornelo de blancos, nuestro pavor al negro y crear un profundo nacionalismo dentro del cual nuestro pensamiento se sienta perfectamente cómodo"). Creoles need not fear discussion of Puerto Rico's racial heterogeneity because they should understand that they still have the upper hand. The Spanish colonizers, Belaval explains, had come to stay, to make this land their home, to take root in the land, "to conquer the region and the soul of the region"[63] ("a conquistar la región y el alma de la región"). Belaval's language here is quite euphemistic. The author does not explain that the practice of *blanqueamiento*—so well-entrenched—assures Creole hegemony, but this point is crucial in my view. The Spanish conquest of the Americas was not as simple and benevolent as he makes it out to be. Like all colonial enterprises it was an economic and geopolitical venture. But the rape and the cohabitation with the Indian and African woman was an additional means of establishing their hegemony. In the process of subjugating the native peoples of the Americas and of acculturating them under Spanish laws and to Catholicism, race mixing was an added weapon in the Spanish arsenal and was not meant to occur without rules and sanctions. Belaval glosses over these fine points to make the more contemporaneous argument that the United States's intervention established a new racial hierarchy on the island—one predicated on the desirability of racial segregation. But the older racial hierarchies that validate *blanqueamiento* are still firmly rooted in Puerto Rican life.

Belaval warns his audience about the fundamental and glaring difference between the Spanish colonizer's attitude toward race mixing and the American phobia regarding it. After thirty-six years of occupation, Belaval explains, it is clear that the American colonizers have no interest in mixing with Puerto Ricans racially. Crucially, this lack of interest in forming family and affective bonds with Puerto Ricans facilitates Creole control over blacks and mulattos. As the author states, "our *criollo* will never have more than two bloods: the Spanish one and the African one"[64] ("nuestro criollo nunca tendrá nada más que dos sangres: la española y la africana"). Here, *criollo* means Puerto Ricans in general. The new colonialism of the North Americans was a purely economic and political enterprise, contrary to the Spanish colonial attitude that gave rise to a *mestizo* America. As Belaval explains it, the United States wants a mere union with Puerto Rican but not a fusion, which would entail race mixing and a more positive attitude toward racial difference.

Rejecting Pedreira's ideas of race mixing as confusion, Belaval sees it as a salutary practice in Latin America and Puerto Rico. Provided that Spanish *cultural* supremacy was maintained, and that white phenotypical traits remained very visible, race mixing redounds to the benefit of Creoles. In Puerto Rico, Euro-Latins have never given up their *blanchitude*—whiteness is a valuable commodity that non-whites lack.[65] Ultimately, Creole men control whiteness because of their control over white women. This allows the author to wax poetic about the need to reaffirm and reconnect "with our old politic of fusion, with our free sexual transit that hitherto had created the best degree of harmony and consistency in Boricua ethnology"[66] ("a nuestra vieja política de fusión, a nuestro libre tránsito sexual que hasta ahora creó el mejor grado de armonía y de consistencia en la etnología boricua"). In reality such sexual transit was neither free nor harmonious. Well-to-do white men controlled—and still control—a system that in effect reaffirmed white male privileges. That his cultured readers understood this is patent in their acceptance of the idea that whiteness absorbs and diffuses blackness. Virtually all Creole intellectuals had stated time and again that Puerto Rico was the whitest island of the Caribbean, that blacks had left no trace of African cultures in Puerto Rico. This insistence can only be explained as a tremendous anxiety over the fact that to Americans, most Puerto Ricans were too racially ambiguous to be of European descent exclusively. Belaval, and nearly all his readers, were most likely of provincial Spanish or Corsican descent, an identification that previously had afforded their parents and grandparents economic opportunity and prestige under Spain.[67] That this was no longer true under American colonialism frustrated and angered Creoles.

For Belaval there can be no real understanding between Creoles and Americans because they see Creoles, and the rest of the Puerto Rican people, as racially inferior. The elite is, at best, quaintly Latin. Most Americans "maintain a courtesy learned in commercial textbooks, to approach the clients and sell things *(approaching the clients)*, until they close their doors. Later they retire to their houses to listen to the stories of *Amos and Andy* and to speak ill of black people"[68] ("sostienen una cortesía aprendida en textos comerciales, para acercarse al cliente a vender *[approaching the clients]*, hasta que cierran las puertas. Después se retiran al fondo de sus casas a escuchar las historietas de *Amos y Andy* y a hablar mal de los negros"). On this point he was quite right. Few Americans living on the island had an interest in befriending Puerto Ricans or understanding their culture and values. On the other hand, only the most "Americanized" Puerto Ricans, the author insists, have any friendship with North Americans. He points to inane lifestyle influences such as the adoption of a picturesque bilingual vocabulary, of which he gives as examples "parquear" to park the car, "aló" hello, "all rai" all right. He also mentions women's sexual emancipation as a purported importation, but claims that the impetus in this case really came from Europe, not from the United States. As discussed earlier, Belaval is wrong on this count. The question of women's suffrage was very much embroiled in the colonial and class politics of the day. Elite Puerto Rican women actively looked to the United States for allies in their cause, to the consternation of many elite men.

Belaval argues, in line with Pedreira, that only the members of his generation are equipped to face the cultural, economic, and social problems that colonialism has engendered. They have been educated under its ambivalent educational system for thirty years, and were raised in the new context. Young men must accept the limits imposed by geography, understanding the pull of the past, and the reality "that we are mestizos and that we are willing to follow, whatever its course, the destiny of our people"[69] ("que somos mestizos, y que estamos dispuestos a correr, cualquiera que sea su rumbo, el destino de nuestro pueblo"). This generation's bitterness must give way to reconciliation, a call that is made a number of times in this essay. Belaval is heartened by the fact that the cultured *men* of his own generation are willing to abandon the illusion of everlasting ties with a Spanish past. This new immersion in "our Creoleness" is the means the author insists by which Puerto Ricans will have access to the future. There are signs of an incipient "belligerent Creolism" in the new studies on Puerto Rican literature, history, medicine, sociology. These previously overlooked areas are finally the object of attention of the intelligentsia. Faced with new colonial and social realities, a cultured minority linked to the *Ateneo* and the university must be ready to influence the future. Cultural nationalism, for Belaval, is not a task for politicians, but for a young cultured elite. The previous generation of intellectuals has done nothing to shed light on or remedy the dilemma of what to do regarding North American culture on the island. Now the struggle over the nation-state has become disastrously complicated by the present world situation, the advent of democracy, the opportunism of politicians, and antagonistic Anglo-Saxon values.

The author does not hesitate to condemn the concession of U.S. citizenship to Puerto Ricans and the public school system as utter failures. Yet, as I discussed earlier, this was not an idea equally shared by all sectors of the population. He questions the meaning of a nationality that, rather than being a well-thought-out and desired union of two peoples, was a unilateral imposition sold to the people in the guise of an advantage. This gave a veneer of respectability to "the most encompassing, and least human form, of economic colonialism, something previously unknown in Puerto Rico"[70] ("la forma más absorbente, más poco humana, de coloniaje económico, cosa que Puerto Rico no conocía"). Belaval is right that, as actualized in Puerto Rico, U.S. citizenship was meant mainly as a cover for American policies and their interests. Puerto Ricans have used it and have been subject to it in ways that are still being debated today. What few contest is that the new vertically integrated form of economic production and exploitation imposed after 1898 radically changed the lives and destinies of Puerto Ricans in ways not imagined during the Spanish domination.

Like the imposition of U.S. citizenship, the failures or advantages of the coeducational public school system were hotly debated issues among educators and intellectuals at the time, due to the tremendous impact that increases in literacy could have on the island. Belaval sees the public school system as another ill-fitting foreign affliction. His censure of the educational system, moreover, is in keeping with the *ateneístas'* general condemnation of bilingual education. For Belaval the current system fails to prepare men to participate seriously in the deliberations concerning the future of Puerto Rico. As the author sees it, the graduating students find themselves in the midst of confusing ideals—quixotic Latin values in conflict with North American pragmatic utilitarianism. His critique underscores that a colonial school system disconcerts and disempowers those formed within it. Even though students may be fascinated by politics, the author explains, their interest is superficial and reflects the perplexity that exists in their larger environment. Yet schooling has also elevated working-class leaders, a fact Belaval comments on with some alarm: "our populace in the thickets is enthroning its chiefs."[71] ("Nuestra manigua popular está entronizando sus caudillos.") This restless and contestatory populace in the thickets had ideas of its own that cannot be allowed to carry the day. The referent is to black Cuban revolutionaries and runaway slaves who famously found in the "manigua" cover from which to launch their attacks at those in power. The analogy would certainly make sense to his intended audience. The rise of popular leaders outside official control would not bode well for the *criollista* project.

Readers of "Los problemas" would be hard-pressed to find any overt political solutions to the problems the author outlines. What we find is a reformist agenda with muted political overtones. Belaval calls on the new generation to be active in the civic and legal arena, and to bring with them higher standards than those practiced so far. This is an argument for more effective legislative power in the hands of Puerto Ricans as well as judicial reforms and protectionist legislation. The author poignantly wants to "create a resounding cry that would echo in the consciousness" of those Puerto Ricans who have participated in the despoliation of the island and its people.[72] ("crear un hondo clamor que retumbe en la conciencia") His program nevertheless is somewhat vague. To face the "utilitarian" philosophy of American culture, Puerto Ricans must counter with "an absolute reintegration of our former spiritualist philosophy"[73] ("una reintegración absoluta a nuestra anterior filosofía espiritualista"). But we must ask if a cultural nationalist agenda can turn back the clock of capitalist penetration. If Puerto Ricans must take a "decisive step toward moral healing of all our dissociative miasmas," what is, more concretely, that step?[74] ("paso decisivo para el saneamiento moral de todas nuestras miasmas disociadoras.") The author stresses that Puerto Ricans must be vigilant not to fall into "the extremist attitude of a weepy independentism" that holds on to the old-fashioned values of the past[75] ("la actitud extremista de un independentismo plañidero"). This could well be a critique of the militant and conservative independentism of the Nationalist Party. This never becomes clear since throughout the essay the author chooses to portray positions rather than to name names. A year later, in May of 1936, Belaval was one of the signatories of a manifesto by *Frente Unido Pro Constitución de la República de Puerto Rico*, a broad united front seeking independence. The document condemned the colonial system, and asked all Puerto Ricans to unite in the demand to form the Republic of Puerto Rico.[76]

Another aspect of Puerto Rican life that has undergone surprising change according to the author is religion. Under the aegis of the new colonial power, Belaval concedes, Puerto Ricans have modified their extreme Catholicism by joining churches that put more emphasis on ethical discipline and on cultural practices that develop civic action as a desirable value. And while he praises the advent of freedom of speech and "the right to a virile and frank polemic," ("el derecho a la polémica franca y viril,") the author warns that those lacking in culture have felt overly empowered.[77] All these freedoms have helped to embolden common people and fostered in them new aspirations, a situation that Belaval sees as unreasonable: "We frankly have to tell the Puerto Rican worker not to dream of being able to earn five dollars a day, of having a car, a radio, state insurance, savings account, money for a vaudeville show, and participation in the stock market."[78] ("Hay que decirle francamente al obrero puertorriqueño que no sueñe con poder ganar cinco pesos diarios, tener automóvil, radio, seguro del estado, cuenta de ahorro, asistencia a un vodevil y jugar a la bolsa.") And he adds that government programs must not go beyond their means. We should remember that Belaval writes this in the midst of the Depression and that desperate workers had organized waves of protests throughout 1933 and1934. There were disruptions in public transportation and trucking, strikes against gasoline companies that practically paralyzed the country, and stoppages in the cane, garment, and tobacco industries. Violent repression against militants of the Nationalist Party was the order of the day. In this context of generalized anxiety his counsels to his readers include "sobriety, consistency, cordial rhythm"[79] ("sobriedad, consistencia, ritmo cordial").

The last section of "Los problemas" is dedicated to the theme of reconciliation. The first step toward national self-knowledge requires that his readers accept that they are a people of the Spanish Caribbean, not a part of the United States. Creoles must return to their Latin worldview or *latinidad*, but they must also stop looking to Spain for their identity, and face the question of race in Puerto Rico. He reiterates here the themes discussed before: rejection of overt and crude forms of white supremacy; a belligerent Creolism that is accepting of race and cultural mixing in the time-honored way. Puerto Rico is a small island, he reminds his readers, "a naive tropic, a place of peace where our vital Spanishness is conserved and transformed into a Creoleness with a good mulatto percentage, but where the white man has imposed his spiritual regime and the black man does not allow others to forget him in the structure of this regime"[80] ("un trópico ingenuo, un sitio de paz donde se conserva y se transforma nuestro españolismo vital hacia una criollicidad, de buen porcentaje mulato, pero donde el hombre blanco ha impuesto su régimen espiritual y el hombre negro no permite que se le olvide en el esquema de ese régimen"). In the face of monopoly capitalism, or as he puts it the contrary philosophy of life imposed by the United States, Puerto Ricans should promote a more traditional way of life. The author suggests that some of the institutions that modernization has demolished need reviving, especially the land tenure patterns of the *hacienda*, for example. Other things need to be controlled. This is very clear when it comes to the education of the masses. Nostalgically, he praises the old order of the cultured artisan who did not aspire to the social mobility that capitalist modernity—contradictions notwithstanding—promises.

As social critique, the richness of "Los problemas de la cultura puertorriqueña" should not be underestimated. The text is full of pointed observations that give a nuanced glimpse at an embattled society in the midst of conflicted change. Genteel Creole that he is, Belaval detests the ways in which the new colonial gaze captures Puerto Ricans. His assessment of North American tourism is a case in point. As mainlanders and their *Kodaks* descend on the island, he interprets their gaze as an aggression, because they exoticize the island's culture and its people. He forgets that Creoles—in more covert ways—had always been guilty of appraising and policing blacks and mulattos, and of training a colonizer's eye on them. As an elite man he resents being the object of this ocular insult. Taking Cuba as a point of comparison, he bitterly criticizes the developing tourism industry's promotion of a "crude tropicalism." Afraid that Puerto Ricans will act like Cubans who noisily project the mulatto as spectacle for the benefit of the tourists, he warns that, "While Cubans were spending their time dancing the rumba for tourists, one of the fiercest oligarchies of the Americas was allowed to take hold."[81] ("Mientras el cubano se dedicaba a 'rumbear' delante del turista se estaba creando una de las más fieras oligarquías de América.") This assessment of the Cuban situation is unfair and does little justice to the history of anticolonial and antiracist struggle on that island; neither does it take into account the history of class alliances between Cuban and American sugar interests. Moreover, the question of Afro-Cuban self-representation and the role that Creole elites played in constructing an ideology of *negrismo* is far more complex than his offhand remarks allow for. Yet his caustic critiques of the compulsion to present tourists with "*local color* based on jungle, voudou, and of hotels with an American plan" is not unwarranted.[82] ("*local color*, a base de jungla, de ñañiguismo y de hoteles con plan americano.") Tourism as commonly practiced all around the world promotes a host of distortions and contradictions in the host country. And like Margot Arce in her essay "Las raíces," he prefers the type of tourism he fancies is possible in Europe—a sort of pilgrimage Creoles have traditionally embarked on to acquire the kind of exposure that brings prestige and does not dislocate the order of things. But *jíbaros*, the author explains, are no match for the picturesque characters one can find elsewhere. Shunning the sensationalistic imperial eye, Belaval exclaims, "We have neither black, nor gaucho, nor bandit, nor Indian."[83] ("No tenemos ni negro, ni gaucho, ni bandolero, ni indio.") He means this in the sense of a marketable folkloric national type. On the other hand, he urges his readers to rediscover their island. Puerto Ricans should get to know their island better in order to reflect on the effects of modernity on its towns and on the people.

"Los problemas de la cultura puertorriqueña" is a text written by one of Puerto Rico's most mordant writers. In a tone that is both playful and pained, the young Belaval makes very trenchant remarks on the state of Puerto Rican literature from its nineteenth-century beginnings to the first three decades of the twentieth. His sobering review humorously chides Puerto Rican readers and writers for their corny aesthetic tastes and excessive acceptance of bad literature: "When the literary study of our nineteenth century takes place, there will be a toppling of idols that will be frightful."[84] ("Cuando se haga el estudio literario de nuestro siglo diecinueve, va a haber un derrumbamiento de ídolos que meterá miedo.") He especially deplores the "poetic consulate" and "lyrical passports" of visiting Spanish and Latin-American poets who write sappy occasional poetry on local themes in deference to their Puerto Rican public, even taking aim at Gabriela Mistral's visit to the island. His most severe judgments however are reserved for current Puerto Rican writers. The topic has been treated with the same seriousness afforded a meal of pork on the spit. As Belaval laments, "This explains the air of small-town and hammock nostalgia, the reticent peasant, of colorful rooster, of sugar cane alley."[85] ("Por eso tiene ese aire de inocencia añorante, pueblerina, de hamaca, el jibarito recunquero, de gallito coloreado, de batey.") He is merciless toward what he calls the tepid Creolism that passes for serious writing.

Creole women and black and mulatto intellectuals are belatedly addressed in the essay as potential helpers in the nation-building task. Women are called upon as wives. And while Belaval wants companionate marriages, he desires a woman "valiant, long-suffering, proud who keeps the rules of Puerto Rican sentimentality and makes of her home that chosen place of tradition, of national culture"[86] ("valiente, sufrida y altiva vela por los fueros de la sentimentalidad puertorriqueña y por hacer de su hogar sitio predilecto de la tradición, de la cultura patria"). She must not have such modern desires as would impede her functioning as a proper wife. Interestingly, his return to tradition also includes restoring *tertulias* (gatherings) in pharmacies, plazas, casinos, cafés, and corner stores, social spaces where men of various social strata could socialize and discuss issues of the day. Leaving social hierarchies in place, his dream is that Puerto Ricans may find solutions to their own problems. He includes mulatto and black intellectuals in his plea: "let our cultured whites, mulattos, and blacks help us find common cause in the same desire for culture, and let us examine our origins once again so that we may place ourselves in the meridian of reality"[87] ("que nos ayuden nuestros blancos, mulatos y negros cultos a poner el punto de conciliación en un mismo afán de cultura y mirar una vez más a nuestros orígenes y empezar a colocarnos en el meridiano de la realidad").

The author concludes "Los problemas de la cultura puertorriqueña" with an emotionally charged vision of Puerto Rican life under a renewed Creole hegemony. In summation, the problem of Puerto Rican culture is that young elite men have lacked the courage to lead intellectually, because of a now passé and misguided attachment to Spain. They have allowed themselves to be used by the United States, and as whites they have postponed the now urgent reconciliation with a racially mixed popular majority. The role of the writers is to use their *criollista* cultural capital to invest in this nationalist project. Mindful of the class and racial struggles that underpin Puerto Rican life, Belaval dreams of a society where no *man* feels dominated or feels the need to dominate others, where cultured men will find solutions to the nation's problems, where leaders are not self-interested. His hope for the future is that Puerto Ricans can create for themselves a "life that is sober, virile, spiritual, and consistent"[88] ("una vida sobria, viril, espiritual y consistente"). The optimistic combativeness of his vision projects itself into that future: "Until then, I will keep insisting."[89] (Hasta entonces, yo seguiré insistiendo.")

The Pull of the Land: Margot Arce's "El Paisaje de Puerto Rico"

In 1939, five years after Antonio S. Pedreira published his agenda-setting *Insularismo*, young university professor and up-and-coming intellectual Margot Arce responded to *Insularismo*'s call for reflection and action with "El paisaje de Puerto Rico"[90] ("Puerto Rico's Landscape"). Her text, less remembered by intellectual historians than the two more-celebrated rejoinders by Emilio S. Belaval and Tomás Blanco, is a clear statement of her desire to participate in a dialogue that, in the main, has been held by male intellectuals. While not as lengthy and ideologically ambitious as its model, the essay takes to heart *Insularismo*'s urgent summons to rethink and define

Puerto Rican singularity. "El paisaje de Puerto Rico" approaches its subject by means of a lyrical tellurianism and is best described as a lyrical piece rather than a sociological essay. My analysis centers on the text as it appeared in 1939. A subsequent reprinting of it in 1950 reveals editorial changes that softened the political stances originally taken by the author. The same factors that account for the change in tone in her essay "Las raíces," the political repression and censorship of the era, could account for her more politically reserved attitude in the second printing. One of Arce's favored rhetorical strategies in "El paisaje" is to find equivalencies between the land and the people. Once the particularities of the island are mapped, they are offered as explanations for the distinctiveness of its inhabitants. "El paisaje" presents the scenery, the people, and their idiosyncrasies to readers seemingly unfamiliar with the terrain as the author invites them to embark on a voyage of rediscovery.

The essay opens with an analogy in which Arce invokes the authority of Cervantes to describe the island: "Of my island of Puerto Rico one could say what Cervantes said of Salamanca: 'it bewitches the will to return to her of those who have enjoyed the peace of its ambit.'"[91] ("De mi isla de Puerto Rico se puede decir lo que decía Cervantes de Salamanca: 'que enhechiza la voluntad de volver a ella a cuantos la apacibilidad de su recinto hayan gozado.'") She segues with a statement of Puerto Rico's geopolitical and economic significance to both Spain's and the United States's colonial enterprises. The island's geography and its history as a geopolitical borderland and neocolonial factory, Arce argues following Pedreira, "has retarded its definition as a country and a people"[92] ("le ha retardado su definición como pueblo"). Puerto Rico's stagnation during Spanish colonial times, the result of the island's position as a military stronghold, has worsened today due to its strategic importance to the United States vis-à-vis the Panama Canal, its economic significance as a sugar-producing factory for corporate capital, and a captive market for American manufacturers. This political and economic garrote gravely threatens its present and future. Moreover, lucidly Arce states that attachment to Spanish culture is a defensive reaction to the United States's colonial politics, given the concerted attempts by the U.S. and Puerto Rican supporters of American colonialism who "spare no effort to diminish our Spanish patrimony"[93] ("no escatiman esfuerzo para mermar nuestro patrimonio español"). Interestingly the author seems to despair at the island's *entire* colonial history, not just at the past forty years of it: "And because Puerto Rico has not known a moment of liberty or full national life, it has been unable to create its own, distinctive character, and it is natural that it clings to things Spanish considering them to be its only real possession."[94] ("Y como Puerto Rico no ha conocido un solo momento de libertad ni de vida nacional plena, tampoco ha podido crearse carácter propio, distintivo, y es natural que se aferre a lo español como lo único que considera realmente suyo.")

Pawns in the expansionist game of North American capitalism, the younger generations find themselves in the midst of a struggle between the persistence of Spanish tradition and the ferocious pull of the novel and foreign. Nevertheless, except for some of the major cities, Puerto Rico's social values and character have stubbornly remained profoundly Spanish in spite of "North American colonial policies and pro-American Puerto Rican policies"[95] ("la política colonial norteamericana y la política puertorriqueña proamericana"). Adroitly, the author of "El Paisaje" separates herself both from the new colonialism and its Puerto Rican allies, thereby preparing the way for a third position—that of the protectors of the Puerto Rican character.

The author walks a delicate line. Her assumption, following Pedreira, is that there exists a unique Puerto Rican character and personality, Spanish at its core, which has not been allowed to develop fully and define itself. By alluding throughout the essay to the metaphor of the individual (the nation as a person), the author is able to speak of growth—possible, stunted, or natural. Ultimate definition will only occur when the island frees itself from the incompatible alien presence in its economy, politics, and values. Puerto Rico, Arce proposes, though lacking the majesty of other Latin-American regions, is a peaceful place loved by those who visit it. Puerto Rican mountains, she says, are not like the Andes: "a South American told me that compared with his Andes, our mountains of such modest height seemed to him like hills"[96] ("un americano del sur me decía que, comparadas con sus Andes, nuestras montañas de tan escasa altura le parecían colinas"). Not even the tallest trees have the stature of those found in South America. The island is characterized, rather, by its small size and child-like grace, unjustly subjected to the tyranny of a rhythm of life extraneous and harmful to it. As elsewhere in the essay, there is abundant use of possessive pronouns which lay claim to the objects described.

Arce assumes with nineteenth-century European literature on nation and race that land and man are inseparable, affecting each other both positively and negatively.[97] The well-established German concept of Volkgeister—national soul—permeates her discourse. People and land are linked in a symbiotic and indissoluble bond taking one back to the nation's very topography. The island's undulating mountain ranges, its abundance of rolling green, the climate, the changing sea, the sky, the scents, the sounds, and the vegetation, all this had influenced the people's character. Thus, "the tellurian has more pull on us than the spiritual"[98] ("lo telúrico puede más en nosotros que lo espiritual"). Along with being the product of racial mixing, its people have developed a number of attributes proper to Puerto Ricans alone, such as a particular speech, sentimentalism, and hospitality, that are now in danger of changing. The struggle is presented as a contest between two diametrically opposed antagonists, an idea common to the Latin American identity essay from José Martí's "Nuestra América" to Fernández Retamar's "Calibán." Yet

Arce also couples colonial modernity to economic instability and economic misery, in unambiguous condemnation of the North Americans: "The feverish and artificial activity registered in the cities is the result of the moral influence of the United States, of the indigence to which we have been reduced after years of capitalist economic exploitation on a grand scale."[99] ("La actividad febril y postiza que se registra en las ciudades es resultado de la influencia moral de los Estados Unidos, de la indigencia a que hemos llegado tras de años de explotación económica y capitalista a grande escala.") What the unnatural foreign influence has also unfortunately produced is the contemptible "pitiyanqui," that chimerical being, part native and part Yankee, the ignoble result of relentless Americanization. If, as Arce assumes, the true self of Puerto Rican life rests in the *hacienda* economy with its ensuing paternalistic culture, in Catholicism, and in a slow pace of change, then the new economy and social activity of the cities are counterfeit. Change in this context can only be perceived by the author as traumatic. Yet, as José Juan Beauchamp reminds us, the land as desired good is a *rhetorical construct* formulated by writers that contrasted with the population movements of the the period decidedly away from the land: "The exodus from the country to the city and not the return to the country is proof that for the ruined *hacendados*, the small landowners, and the coffee laborers, the utopia was the city, and that the aspiration of the return to the land was not a part of their vision of the world, even though nostalgia affectionately reared its head at times, but not as an aspiration to return as presented or aspired to by the writers who treated the theme."[100]At the ideological level environmental determinism has a legitimizing function here, allowing Arce to establish that the occupied land of Puerto Rico does have rightful owners who have been unnaturally—that is wrongfully—alienated from their land. Only the native owners of the land have the right to possess and use it. But this is not all. The author can construe some events as more natural or intrinsic than others. If the essay correctly points to colonial modernity as exploitive in many respects, it also misrepresents the Spanish colonial past as functional and germane to the land. The oppressive Spanish military rule is barely mentioned, and slavery and the servitude of the peasantry are totally omitted. What is represented here is a nostalgic desire to return to a period when *criollo* power was a historical possibility. As Beauchamp has said of the tellurian literature of the period, "the myth of the land is associated with the land in the hands of Puerto Rican proprietors, not to the lands in the possession of the sugar bourgeoisie."[101] Or of impoverished peasants, for that matter.

Arce's essay partakes of the "negative vision" often inherent in nationalist logic, which assumes that certain characteristics of the nation are fixed, and that to alter them would mean the destruction of the nation. "The 'positive vision' of national affirmation," Richard Handler explains, "is invariably accompanied by a 'negative vision' of assimilation and death."[102]

Imprecision, mixture, and hazy boundaries are a threat to the nation, as is cultural, political, and linguistic assimilation. Many authors present cultural transformation and race mixing as a problem for the race/nation. This would explain, in the case of Puerto Rican nationalist discourse, the lament of Pedreira and others who see these processes as pollution and the reason for the paralysis of the Puerto Rican "soul." Arce attributes to bilingualism the noxious effects that Pedreira saw in race mixing. In the nationalist logic, identity is a fixed entity that cannot be in flux; neither an individual nor a collective can be two things at once or, heaven forbid, bilingual.

Contradictorily, "El Paisaje" argues for the uniqueness or, at least, the differentiation of Puerto Ricans from other cultures and countries, by representing the people of the island as residually Spanish. Again, a vitalist metaphor, in this case a plant, best conveys her meaning. The island's particular geography has acted upon this core identity, has modified the people's moral character, and, among other things, "has made us sensual and restless; has forced us to cling to the land in search of equilibrium, and to sink long and avid roots into the ground."[103] ("nos ha hecho sensuales e inquietos; nos ha forzado a agarrarnos a la tierra en busca de equilibrio y a hundir largas y ávidas raíces en el suelo.") On the other hand, Puerto Rico's limited size, its climate, and topography, so different from the Castilian mesa or the Argentine *pampa*, have produced a different kind of person. If Castile's and Argentina's geography are places where "man *[sic]* knows a longing for the infinite," in Puerto Rico, "mysticism and philosophy are all but impossible . . ."[104] ("el hombre conoce ansias de lo absoluto," "La mística y la filosofía son casi imposibles . . ."). Puerto Ricans are impoverished even in this respect.

This textual strategy allows her to claim a filial relationship with an established culture, Spain, as well as tellurian uniqueness for Puerto Rico, in fundamental opposition to the aggressor, the United States. Yet the apparent downside inherent in this connection, that the perpetual children of Spain cannot but be lesser transplanted Spaniards, paradoxically allows her to explain why Puerto Ricans fell prey to North American intervention. Climate, historical accident, and race mixing are the culprits that have conspired to make us weak: "Thus can be explained that a materialistic and utilitarian culture has supplanted in such a short time the disinterested and quixotic idealism we inherited from our forefathers."[105] ("Así se explica que una cultura materialista y utilitaria haya suplantado en tan breve tiempo al idealismo desinteresado y quijotesco que heredamos de nuestros antepasados.") Environmental determinism provides an explanation for Puerto Ricans' unfortunate attraction to the new materialism.

"El Paisaje" describes the Puerto Rican as a type or "species" by his weaknesses. Absence of initiative, of daring, of commercial sagacity has made him gullible, "allowing himself to be easily won over by outside currents"[106] ("se deja ganar fácilmente por los aires de fuera"). The author uses the generic masculine throughout. In addition to being guileless, "the Puerto Rican man *[sic]* is a sentimentalist; the senses and the emotions rule his life more than the spirit. There is in him a mixture of Spanish pride, side by side with the tenderness of the black man."[107] ("El hombre de Puerto Rico es un sentimental; los sentidos y las emociones rigen su vida más que su espíritu. Hay en él una mezcla de la soberbia española, lado a lado con la ternura del negro.") A certain romantic racialism here, which allows the author to blend these disparate elements into a synthesis of the "primordial" and the "refined," is cause for hope, "the promise of an original culture"[108] ("la promesa de una cultura original"). However, these elements are united hierarchically where the supposed racial trait of Spanish pride, often a shorthand for the colonial enterprise, is superior to black tenderness. The oft-wished-for black tenderness, moreover, willfully misrepresents the relationships of subordination and exploitation of blacks by whites that resulted from slavery and its aftermath. If Puerto Ricans as a group are lacking and contradictory in character, there is still reason for hope. The assumption remains that the superior Spanish will win over the inferior black, allowing only the desirable qualities of Africans and their descendents to surface. As we can remember, Pedreira had not been shy about expressing his ideas on this issue either.

The gender politics expressed in the essay merit further attention. The use of the generic male commonly employed to refer to both men and women gives Arce, as a female ennunciator, room to use a somewhat accusatory tone, sparing women the imputation of lack of manliness leveled at Puerto Rican men. We must remember that in cultural nationalist essays, manhood, adulthood, and independence are often synonymous, and imply a recognition of the nation's international rights. Pedreira's *Insularismo*, as we have seen, had consecrated the thesis of the lack of vigor of the Puerto Rican character, paving the way for what later would be known as the "docility thesis." His appeal to action was to the young male intellectuals, not to women. Pedreira despaired, blaming "native" men for Puerto Rico's feminine character that had made them nervous and susceptible, incapable of making firm decisions. Arnaldo Cruz Malavé has very perceptively studied the convergence of heterosexist and nationalist discourses in Pedreira's text.[109] Arce, of course, does not address the fear of homosexuality. In her essay, however, she rejects Pedreira's accusation that women are to blame for the nation's problems. As the guarantor of the essay's authority, she wants to clarify her position on the issue. Some passages of the essay directly point to political and economic exploitation as the evil culprits that beset the island, not at feminity.

Tellurianism, in the literature of the period, has its stylistic implications. As José Juan Beauchamp clarifies, "To the mythicized land are attributed moral and spiritual, and of course, aesthetic qualities."[110] Arce at times transforms the femininity of the landscape into a loving description of her island—the greater part of the text. Her characterization of Puerto Rico's landscape is quite lyrical, more reminiscent of poetry than of an analytical genre such as the essay. The purported "virility" of the essay as a genre allows for a transgressive reading of the feminine narrator praising feminine sensuality in a language customarily used by men regarding a female beloved. The narrative persona takes obvious pleasure in the profusion of "undulating" greens and the description of the island's sensuality. The land's scents are "humid," with "dense orange blossoms" and "disturbing acacias" by day, and by night they become "indefinable," "inebriating." The enchanting land, warm and welcoming, "girdled by that virile sea, and under that voluptuous sky, has all the charms of the feminine"[111] ("ceñida por ese mar viril, y bajo ese cielo voluptuoso, tiene todos los encantos de lo femenino"). Its very soil, soft, humid, and fresh is ductile to the touch of the rural pottery maker. The female enunciator does not shy away from occupying such a masculine subject position. Another aspect of the essay worthy of note is that the vulnerability of the island is expressed a number of times by modifiers such as small and childlike: "Childishness is often a trait of our landscape."[112] ("Lo infantil es a menudo un rasgo de nuestro paisaje.") Both the characterization of the island's landscape as feminine, and references to its childlike vulnerability, allow the author to enlist with subtlety the metaphor of the island as vulnerable woman/child, as she argues against the evils of an aggressive colonialism.

Interspersed throughout the essay are quotations from Puerto Rican poets called upon to illustrate certain aspects of the Puerto Rican climate, scenery, or mood. The voices of established poets José Gautier Benítez, Luis Lloréns Torres, and the young and controversial Luis Palés Matos, simultaneously lend authority to the piece and buttress the author's assertions, allowing her to showcase her knowledge as a literary critic. The essay ends with the authoritative voice of Chilean poet and long-time friend Gabriela Mistral. Her poem dedicated to Puerto Rico, "Phrase in the Caribbean Sea, On the Day of the Liberation of the Philippines," ("Frase en el mar Caribe, en el día de la liberación de Filipinas,") implores the archangels to save the island soon: "Before the end / of my step and eyes; / before my flesh / becomes fable; / before my knees / fly in the gusts."[113] ("Antes que en mí se acaben/ marcha y mirada;/ antes que carne mía;/ ya sea fábula;/ antes que mis rodillas/ vuelen en ráfagas.") The title of the poem alludes to the fact that while the Philippines have achieved their independence, Puerto Rico has not.[114] The inclusion of Mistral's poem is not accidental. The poem is an international act of solidarity by an extremely well-respected figure whose words, at least among Latin Americans, carried enormous weight and prestige, adding a geopolitical dimension to her claims. Arce's intention is to underscore this celebrated intellectual's recognition of the justice of independence for the island. This essay, ostensibly a meditation on Puerto Rico's landscape, allows the author to voice opinions on the dangers of vertiginous change, the felicity of the Spanish past, the ravages wrought by the sugar monopolies, the shortcomings of Puerto Ricans as a people, and the rightfulness of political self-determination.

CHAPTER 5

The Nation as Male Fantasy: Emilio S. Belaval's *Los cuentos de la Universidad*

Responding to culture—clarifying, explicating, valorizing, translating, transforming, criticizing—is what artists everywhere do, especially writers involved in the founding of a new nation.
—Toni Morrison, *Playing in the Dark*, 1990

Women intellectuals made important challenges and contributions to a public sphere that sought to diminish them in theory, as well as in practice. This problematic relationship is exemplified in the life and works of women who endeavored to create a space for themselves in an intellectual field virtually dominated by men. To conceive the nation in terms of (white) male adulthood and virility leaves out women and men who do not fit the classification and are therefore excluded from *criollo* spheres of power.[1] We should remember that even while under attack by North American colonial institutions, Creole men wielded power on the social and, to a certain extent, the economic fronts.

This chapter further interrogates nationalism by addressing its interpellation and positioning of women (black and white) and black Puerto Ricans (men and women) in a number of short stories by Emilio S. Belaval. We will look to narrative fiction for clues regarding male reaction to women's challenge of the gender system, because fictional texts often allow us to explore levels of the imaginary directly related to desire and wish fulfillment. Belaval's *Los cuentos de la Universidad* (*University Stories*, 1935) are of special interest because they are set in one of the most hotly contested terrains in colonized Puerto Rico.[2] In this academic setting our author explores, albeit tentatively, Creole apprehensions over racial conflicts. While not his best known literary work, Belaval's sardonic collection of short stories is nonetheless exciting reading. The stories allow us to appraise the *criollo* reaction to the upheaval in the gender system in the 1920s, at least as represented by one of its most sardonic writers. In addition, in a number of the stories gender meets race, laying bare the connections between these categories. We will see that not only were women students not welcomed in this would-be utopian space of the university, neither, with very few exceptions, were blacks and mulattos. As I will show, gender and race dynamics endeavor to keep the subaltern subjects of Belaval's text at bay. Written at a time of great ideological flux, this early collection of stories lends itself to a pointed analysis of gender and racial politics. Given the serious tone of the intellectual discourse of the time intent on rallying political support for cultural nationalist projects, Belaval is among a handful of Puerto Rican fiction writers to experiment with humor, irony, and pleasure. The final section of this chapter interrogates the politics of irony and humor employed in these stories and comments on the implications of the use of irony directed at subordinate social/textual subjects.

Los cuentos de la Universidad has been published four times: 1935, 1945, 1967, and 1977.[3] A comparative look at the various editions shows that Belaval revised some of his stories substantially. We can assume that the author wished to leave the amended version as the definitive edition, but for purposes of literary and cultural history we need to interrogate the nature of these profound textual revisions. The first edition was reprinted without changes in 1945. The revisions I allude to were made for the 1967 edition, also reprinted in 1977. The two versions differ in that virtually all references made to race are excised in the later volume. The original stories, first written between 1923 and 1929, unabashedly present a Creole vision of race relations and racial politics that later becomes untenable in the decades following World War II. As first written, the stories show great ambivalence toward the oppressive racial divisions and hierarchies prevalent during the early decades of the twentieth century. In spite of the ironic viewpoint presented in the stories, Belaval—together with most intellectuals of his formation—assumes and propagates discourses of black racial and cultural inferiority.

This chapter's analysis is centered on the 1935 edition of these stories, for it is here that Belaval most clearly addresses Creole uneasiness with Puerto Rico's multi-racial history. It is here that "the problem that no one wants for this innocent land," that is, racial strife, appears as an anxiety that pervades many of the short stories. Most importantly, two stories disappear from the later version: "Un craneo chato se arrima a la luna" ("A Flat Cranium Leans on the Moon") and "La estatua de marfil se rompe" ("The Ivory Statue Is

Shattered"). The first story, which this chapter explicates in detail, is a sustained exploration of the "tragic mulatto" theme. The second story, not analyzed here, deals specifically with a young man's attainment of sexual maturity. The author's deletion of "La estatua de marfil se rompe" in subsequent editions is not due to racial content, but to its very obvious sexual theme and language. This story unabashedly mentions masturbation, "la pasión solitaria," the brothel, "la casa que tiembla," and the pleasure of sexual arousal, "aquella chica que le engolosinaba su virilidad exaltada." There are also allusions to sexual fetishism: "He lived with his fetish things that would have made the most conspicuous lovers at the café blush with shame." ("Vivía con su fetiche cosas que hubieran hecho enrojecer de vergüenza a los más conspicuos amadores de la peña.") And while another of his piquant stories, "Lohengrin ha perdido su cisne," does not suffer the same fate, a mention of the male sex organ is deleted in the revision: "I was afraid they would measure my penis." ("Tenía miedo que me fueran a medir hasta el pipí.") Nonetheless, expunging one of the risqué stories or censuring the sexual content of a number of them, though lamentable, does not have the same impact on the book as do the excisions of racial themes and conflicts.

The University as National Territory

Los cuentos de la Universidad follows the exploits of a group of male students at the newly created University of Puerto Rico.[4] Belaval gives us a humorous, and at times ironic, account of political awakening among future professional men. We can read their political and sexual coming-of-age along gender, racial, and class lines. These stories, set in the 1920s, offer some insights into the thoughts and desires of a privileged sector of the population scarcely a decade after the United States's occupation of the island in 1898. Belaval's young men have been sent off to the university in the hope of acquiring a profession. Alfredo Guillén, a recurring character in many of the short stories, surveys the campus with other recently arrived students only to find that its very architecture is somewhat foreign: "Alfredo Guillén had to agree with the outraged cad, that all those classical structures lacked propriety, maybe even sense . . ."[5] ("Alfredo Guillén tuvo que convenir con el indignado chusco, que a todas aquellas estructuras clasiconas les faltaba un poco de propiedad, tal vez de sentido . . ."). His life in a small rural town had not prepared him for the state of things in this urban environment: "he also noted that his new world was touched by even greater contradictions—gymnastics, military fanfare in such an innocent land!, Protestant music, men whose trousers were too wide, women whose skirts were too tight, a picturesque speech in two misused languages . . ."[6] ("además notó que su nuevo mundo estaba tocado aún de mayores contrasentidos—gimnasia, fanfarria militarista ¡en una tierra tan inocente!, música protestante, hombres con pantalones demasiado anchos y mujeres con faldas demasiado estrechas, una fabla pintoresca, en dos lenguas mal sabidas . . ."). Disharmony with his Creole ethos includes Protestant music in a Catholic country, an emphasis on physical fitness, and linguistic pollution. All this modernity clashes with Alfredo Guillén's genteel, old-style upbringing, producing "a divorce with so many harmonious things that remained there in his fragrant manor, so nineteenth century, where even the tropical sun penetrated with the discreet grace of a guest who does not want to disturb"[7] ("un divorcio con tantas cosas armónicas que quedaban allá en su aromosa casona, tan siglo diecinueve, donde hasta el sol del trópico penetraba con la discreta gracia de un huésped que no quiere molestar").

Out of the students' disenchantment with the colonial higher education system, a new comradeship and political solidarity is born. Their malaise with the foreign intrusions in their lives will grow into the political revolt depicted in the last stories of the collection, "La termópila en la plaza del mercado" ("Battle in the Market Square") and "El decálogo para una tierra inocente" ("Ten Commandments for an Innocent Land"). At that later point the students' political awakening plays itself out in attempts to take over the university. Their revolutionary fervor takes the form of fiery demands for *criollo* cultural autonomy. As one of them puts it, "Fellow citizens, this university must be our republic, a republic governed our way, *that would resemble us all!* If we allow others to usurp the *biological right* to our own interpretation, to a philosophy of place, we are lost."[8] ("¡Ciudadanos, esta universidad debe ser nuestra república, una república regida a nuestro modo, *que se parezca a todos nosotros!* Si permitimos que se nos usurpe nuestro *derecho biológico* a una interpretación, a una filosofía de sitio, estamos perdidos.") In *Los cuentos* the contested territory of nationalist struggle is decidedly cultural. The student links the university and the nation's culture as he harangues his comrades: "Culture must be profoundly *Indigenist* if it is to have physiognomy. Therefore, I propose that we let it be known to the regime that we are not willing to tolerate any other interpretation of our life than that imposed by our territorial decorum."[9] ("La cultura ha de ser profundamente *indigenista* si quiere tener fisionomía. Por lo tanto, yo propongo que se le haga saber al régimen que no estamos dispuestos a tolerar ninguna otra interpretación de nuestra vida que no sea la que imponga nuestro decoro territorial.")

The male students see the university as a land that must be liberated. It is the site of a political utopia where an indigenous culture (understood as white, Spanish, Catholic, of seigniorial values) "que se parezca a todos nosotros" is to flourish. This combination of race and biologism, "nuestro derecho biológico a una interpretación," is seen as a natural right by Belaval's young student. Social hierarchy is interpreted here as biologically preordained. The callow white *criollo* purports to speak from the position of the "indigenous" subject, in defense of his "indigenous" culture. What is fascinating is that Belaval's rendition of the student's perspective is historically accurate, and semi-autobiographical.[10] The writer fictionalizes the political radicalization of a growing professional elite, his own class.[11] Throughout the short story collection it becomes clear that the "nosotros"—those who are demanding the right to determine the course the indigenous culture will take—is a homogeneous, Creole sector of the island's white elite. Belaval relies on racial and biological theories of culture in order to legitimate the claims of his characters vis-à-vis colonial power.[12] As discussed in Chapter 1, the university provided the children of Creole elite with the means of remaining at the top of the island's social pyramid. At the same time, the creation of the university had the effect—unintended by U.S. colonial powers—of fostering an *esprit de corps* among many of these fledgling professionals. The colonial university became one of the sites of ideological contestation. In these stories, however, the university is represented as *the* privileged locus of the rise of nationalist sentiment.[13] Yet, Belaval's portrayal stops short of depicting these *criollo* interests as overtly class-based. As is typical of cultural nationalism, there are definite connections between culture, nationalism, and gender politics that make this elite group's particular struggle for hegemony synonymous with the struggle for national identity and nationhood. The university's vital role in the production of knowledge and of trained professionals such as managers, lawyers, bureaucrats, and agronomists cannot be underestimated, especially in an agricultural society where so few had access to higher education.

A look at the jacket of the first edition of *Los cuentos* can give us further perspective. It features a drawing of a young woman reclining on an ottoman as she smokes (see Illustration 2).[14] She is only wearing a pair of high-heeled slippers, a cap, and a graduation gown, unbuttoned. In this scene of frontal nudity, the woman's eyes are closed and her knees are bent as if in coitus. The implied reader/viewer of these stories is invited to gaze at the nakedness of this woman from a voyeur's perspective; she looks into the distance unaware of being gazed at. Is this image meant to entice the reader to read the stories? The drawing suggests that underneath this university gown is a female body that reveals its true identity: not the student who has achieved the credentials signified by the robe, but a sexualized body ready to be enjoyed.

A number of meanings are conflated when this image is juxtaposed with the stories. The nation is like the body of a woman. The students allude to this system of metaphors a number of times: this woman—the feminized university—belongs to us, and we cannot allow her to be penetrated and tainted by foreign men, *extranjería discordante*, or *el régimen*. Consequently, Puerto Rican men have to defend the honor of the woman/university/nation. In one of the stories, "Lohengrin ha perdido su cisne," Belaval writes: "None doubted that Alfredo Guillén was capable of taking possession of the university, not even *the university itself who, maiden after all,* regarded her student with the respect women feel toward the male who decorously performs the duties of manhood."[15] ("Ninguno tampoco dudó que Alfredo Guillén no fuera capaz de apoderarse de la universidad, ni siquiera *la propia universidad que doncella al fin,* guardaba por su estudiantón el respeto que siempre infunde a las mujeres, el varón que cumple decorosamente con ellas, los menesteres de la varonía.") The imagery is overtly sexual. The university is a maiden who respects her champion, adept at performing his manly duties. Casting the university/nation as female and its citizens as male, in the compulsory heterosexual *criollo* gender dynamics of the 1920s, leaves little symbolic space for women as patriots. But there is yet another meaning attached to this caricature of the woman student. It should be read against the grain of the great changes taking place during the 1920s in the lives of scores of women of all social classes, due to the social and political changes brought about by the advent of dependent capitalism. Belaval refers to historical changes regarding sexual mores, occurring as a result of the U.S. influence in Puerto Rican life. Confusion reigns regarding new sexual roles, and young men can no longer appeal to *la erótica nacional,* the old rules of sexual behavior, when dealing with members of their own social class. However, when it comes to subaltern women, the men have free reign. The old rules of sexual behavior seem not to have been equally disturbed. As discussed later, there are a number of references to the sexual encounters *criollos* have with *mulatitas sentimentales,* needlepoint workers with few options for social mobility.

Two of the stories deal specifically with the changes in sexual conduct and gender roles for *criollas.* Women students, one of the stories tells us, are in part responsible for the ridiculous changes in men's behaviors and attires. They force *criollos* to adopt U.S. fashions and attitudes. In "Tony Pérez es un niño flan" ("Tony Pérez Is a Dandy"), Beti Mendoza takes the newly arrived Antonio Pérez out on the town only to give him advice on how to treat women and how to become popular at the university. Beti tells Antonio after her fourth cocktail:

> —Listen, Antonio, don't be fooled by those poor devils at the university who still believe that an educated woman has as much sense as a chicken. Today we women demand to be regarded with respect!
>
> —It's only natural—murmured Antonio, who was already a bit drunk.
>
> —Take care of your health, exercise, and learn to be nice. We must be given a chance; never feel you have rights. Why don't you change your name to Tony?[16]
>
> (—Mira, Antonio, no te dejes embaucar por esos chicos famélicos de la universidad, que se creen todavía que una mujer de colegio es lo mismo que una gallina. ¡Hoy las mujeres demandamos una idea más respetable de nosotras!
>
> —Es natural—murmuró Antonio, quien ya estaba un poco ebrio.

—Cuida de tu salud, haz ejercicio y aprende a ser agradable. Hay que darnos una oportunidad a nosotras; no sentirse nunca con derecho a nada. ¿Por qué no haces que te llamen Tony?)

This exchange implies that the men must have felt that they had "rights" over women which Beti, a modern woman, sees as inappropriate. Even while Tony the protagonist is infatuated with this exciting new type of woman, the narrator's tone ridicules Beti's protests. Furthermore, the suffragist movement, it is hinted, has negatively changed *criollas:* Beti drinks, wears tight clothing, loves jazz, and has a more "relaxed" attitude toward sex than *criollo* decorum would allow. Beti even indulges in the sin of visual pleasure, lustfully gazing at the scantily dressed males at the pool or tennis court. She impinges on an area of male erotic activity, and is ultimately chastised by the characters and the narrator. Belaval's indictment is clear: "For his activities at the court, Tony Pérez had shorts of such a red color that they would make the loincloth of any authentic Carib Indian envious, and for the pool an outfit that allowed Beti Mendoza to make the most delicious reflections concerning the corporeal panorama of her comrade in saxophonic follies."[17] ("Para sus faenas del court, Tony Pérez tenía unas bragas de un color rojo, que hubiera hecho morir de envidia al taparrabos de cualquier caribe auténtico y para la piscina de nadar otros arreos que le permitían a Beti Mendoza hacer las más sabrosas reflexiones sobre el panorama corpóreo de su compañero de locuras saxofónicas.") The saxophone is a veritable symbol of U.S. cultural encroachment. Yet Belaval admiringly makes many humorous references to its effect on Beti and Tony and on everyone else. Who can resist its sexual lure? The saxophone (fox-trot, jazz) is too great a rival for the autochthonous dances. As the narrator blissfully agrees, "Gentlemen, this jazz is serious stuff! . . . Behind every saxophone whining in the night, there is a conspirator against the bauble of our complicated modesty."[18] ("¡Caballeros, esto del jazz es una cosa muy seria! . . . Detrás de cada saxófono que gimotea en la alta noche, hay un conspirador contra el miriñaque de nuestro pudor alambicado.") In another story, "Exaltación de Bebé Pacheco" ("In Praise of Bebé Pacheco"), Belaval deals more explicitly with the contrasts between a modernized/Americanized woman and the ideal *criolla* who would make a good wife and mother for the patriotic/professional *criollo.* New to the university environment, Bebé Pacheco decides to explore which behaviors and possibilities are open to her as a young woman. Bebé, says the narrator, is a keen observer. She does not want to be left out like the conservative girls: "She saw the lonely soirées, almost old-maidenly!, of the girls who were faithful to the tradition of their innocent land. . . ."[19] ("Vió las peñas solitarias, ¡cuasi solteronas!, de las chicas que habían conservado su apego a la tradición de su tierra inocente. . . .") Yet, as the omniscient narrator tells us, Bebé is also suspicious of the frivolity of the overly Americanized girls, "who thought they were obliged to rid themselves of their Creole sentimentality in order to copy the fashion models in *Vogue*, the gropings on the boat ride and at the moonlit party, teasing desire, and repressing their feminine decorum to play trivially with the most forbidden things"[20] ("que se creían en la obligación de despojarse de su criollicidad sentimental para copiar las figurillas del *Vogue*, las andanzas cinegéticas de la canoa y del parti a la luz de la luna, domeñando anhelos, reprimiendo su leyenda femenina para juguetear con un sentido trivial de las cosas más prohibidas"). What Belaval bemoans is the change in "criollicidad sentimental." A Creole structure of feeling has been exchanged for a subjectivity modeled by foreign commodities: fashion magazines, the film industry, jazz music, and a new permissiveness in the courtship rituals. He is critical of women's desire to experience previously unexplored feelings, sights, and ways of relating. He is also somewhat playfully disdainful of their physical mobility and autonomy. Perhaps Belaval is decrying the havoc that ideas of "free love" could bring to the gender privileges enjoyed by the males. Women had to respect the legal and emotional strictures that traditional courtship and marriage imposed on them. They would not be suffered to "juguetear" or play with forbidden things, "las cosas más prohibidas." These most forbidden things are a male privilege.

Bebé, the young woman of this story, at first waivers between the two types of men available to her at the university. Would she choose the ridiculous boys dressed in wide pants and sporting servile imitations of foreign fashions, or would she choose those fiery Don Juans, interested in more serious things than sports and movies? "As a woman," Belaval writes,

> she was attracted to the native type of her innocent land, to that don Alfredo of the romantic serenades and clashes with the regime, in whose resonant body still lived a chivalrous concept of things, but her *silly*, small town *cinema dreams* dragged her toward that new puppet in the erotic costume-jewelry box of her land, who had a jovial concept of life, and *a more ample sexual scheme for women.*[21] (Como mujer sentíase atraída por el tipo nato de su tierra inocente, por aquel don Alfredo de las serenatas románticas y de los encontronazos con el régimen, en cuyo cuerpo fragoroso aún vivía un concepto señorito de las cosas, pero *sus bobos sueños* de la *cinema* pueblerina la arrastraban hacia aquel monigote nuevo en la bisutería erótica de su tierra, que traía un concepto jovial de la vida, *un más amplio esquema sexual para la mujer.*)

After a controversy over her bust line, Bebé (compared in the story to a tasty dish) will finally end up in the camp of the *criollos* "of a more discriminating palate," ("de paladar más displicente,") a more difficult conquest than the Americanized *extrangerizantes.* Her protruding breasts—more in keeping with the traditional fashion than the flattened flapper bust line in vogue at the time—had inspired a group of young men to write a poem in their honor. Her very body is the site of controversy. The men in both camps feel they have the right to use her anatomy for their own purposes. But as the story would have it, these events—and the verses they inspired—would endear her to the *criollos inconformes*, the nonconformists who invited her to be a part of their group. As the narrator tells us: "When she least expected it, Bebé Pacheco found herself living the same life as the rebel circle, with a desire for a higher femininity, a new femininity agreeing to root itself in the soul of the land, landscape, ideas, sentiments, types, and masculinist philosophy."[22] ("Cuando menos se lo esperaba, Bebé Pacheco se encontró viviendo la misma vida de la peña inconforme, dentro de un anhelo superior de femenidad *[sic]*, una nueva femenidad que aceptaba el enraizamiento con el alma de la tierra, paisaje, ideas, sentimientos, tipos, ideario masculinista.") The new femininity acceptable to the men has to take into account their nativist ideology and make space for male privileges. We do not see the male idiosyncrasies changing to accommodate women's subjectivity. It is Bebé who ultimately gives up the pleasures associated with modernization: "Lost to her cultured soul were the attraction to the boat rides, to jazz, to the foolish boy of wide trousers, to puerile capers, and she gave herself more to the amorous reserve of true love, to the nativist philosophy of those pale youths of noble manly prejudices . . ."[23] ("Perdió para su ánima culta atracción, la canoa, el jazz, el niño fatuo de anchos calzones, aquel retozo pueril y se dió más al amoroso recato de los amores enteros, a la filosofía indiana de aquellos chicos paliduchos, con excelsos prejuicios de varonía . . .") This woman belongs in the house, not in the public sphere. The narrator sides with this vision of Creole women who would always and forever be emotionally available to their husbands, "who demanded of women a more profound sensibility, the old theological anguish between good and evil, the waiting, the surrender, the cordial vision of the well-loved woman, willing to live patiently and birth abundantly, who always made her home her emotional horizon. She was the most ideal, the most loyal of friends."[24] ("que exigían de la mujer una sensibilidad más profunda, la vieja angustia teológica entre el bien y el mal, la espera, la entrega, la visión cordial de la hembra bien amada, dispuesta al paciente vivir y al abundante parir, que hizo siempre de su casona, su horizonte emocional. Fué la más ideal, la más leal de las amigas.") There is, perhaps, a reference here to the use of birth control. "Abundant birthing" not under women's control was a target of feminist critique within the international feminist movement. Voluntary motherhood was not a value held by Creole men and by Catholicism. At the rhetorical level, it should be noted, Belaval identifies *criollo* values as indigenous ("la filosofía indiana") to those pallid youths. The reader is told what it is that men desire of women. The women, it seems, have no right to demands of their own. In a misogynist language Belaval lists the requirements that the traditional Creole male seeks in a woman. She must be wife, mother, and mistress of the house, well acculturated in Catholic values, patient and forgiving of her husband's whims, pliable to his authority and guidance, fertile, and loyal. Her horizon of self-fulfillment should be reduced to the home.

The new gender relations, or *la nueva erótica criolla*, are a lot like the old ones. The new *criolla* is college-educated, which should lend her greater sensibility, *una sensibilidad más profunda*. Nevertheless, she is not expected to benefit materially from her college education except to exploit it as a kind of dowry when she marries. She is still virginal and elevated on a pedestal that is nonetheless a sexist trap. Bebé Pacheco, we are told, takes it upon herself to mend the wounded values of her country and countrymen: "Her generous soul felt the resolve to make noble reparation."[25] ("Por su alma generosa pasaron propósitos de reparación hidalga.") She would be the supporting woman suited for this impoverished and degraded land. The new *criolla* had to lead an exemplary life, Belaval tells us: "In an impoverished land one had *to wait* for the man with a loyal smile; one had *to erase* all the bitterness of conflict with a sensitive passion; *be a clean shadow* among the dirty shadows of humble living, where solace was found in licentiousness, in a pig roast, a cock fight, and a swig of rum."[26] ("En tierra pobre había que *esperar* al hombre con una sonrisa leal, había que *borrar* todas las amarguras del desconcierto con una pasión sensitiva, *ser sombra limpia* entre las sombras sucias de aquél vivir humilde en el cual la compensación estaba en la mancebía, en la lechonadita, en el redondel del gallo y del trago de ron.") Forbearance, cheerfulness, self-effacement—these are the qualities Belaval prescribes for women in Puerto Rico. The story ends with the beatification of Bebé. One of her new admirers says: "You're admirable Bebé! You're much better than us. When you return to your hometown we'll have to canonize you. Saint Bebé Pacheco of the Immaculate Soul! Revered sister of the new Creole *ars amandi*."[27] ("¡Eres admirable, Bebé! Mucho mejor que nosotros. Cuando vuelvas a tu pueblo habrá que canonizarte. ¡Santa Bebé Pacheco, la del alma limpia!, hermanita ché de la nueva erótica criolla.") The new *criolla*, the stories seem to imply, should act as facilitator of men's self-actualization.

Belaval's masculinist fantasy leaves little room for a female subjectivity that is not male-identified. Modernization of gender relations is ridiculed and scorned as are the models for it that appear in the nascent cultural industry (films and women's magazines). Underneath Belaval's "modest proposal" that *criollas* keep intact the norms of *criollo* decorum lie the assumptions that these women may not have choices or desires of their own. College-educated and relatively privileged women are asked not to make waves and to fall in line with the projects of men. Chancellor Benner's survey on university students' attitudes reveals some striking similarities with Emilio Belaval's rendition of the gender and racial expectations of a large sector of the student and professional intelligentsia taking shape during the late twenties. Shifting definitions of gender and gender expectations threatened the homogeneity and stability of the masculinist national identity discourse. How else can one explain the alarm—cloaked as mockery—expressed in Belaval's stories?

Moreover, there is an unmistakable connection between the more sexually liberated women, island-men-as-Americanized-dandies, and the colonial regime. In a previous story the narrator lamented Tony Pérez's political naïveté:

> Of course the young man is not worried about the pained grimace of the land. Neither is he concerned with the fierce rancor of the *criollos* who want to wring his bloomers. Women adore him, the regime watches him with glee, and life awaits him, like a ball of fascinating colors, where he will continue his childish banter with the dictates of manhood.[28] (Al chico, desde luego, no le preocupa el mohín doloroso de la tierra. Como no le preocupa tampoco el fiero rencor de los criollos que lo miran con ganas de estrujarle las pantaletas. La mujer lo adora, el régimen lo mira complacido y ahí lo está esperando la vida, como una pelota de fascinantes colores, donde él podrá seguir su pueril retozo con todos los fueros de la varonía.)

Belaval seems to be issuing a warning that in the war of the sexes the colonial regime wins. Ready acceptance of foreign customs and culture is a distraction from serious political work. Is Belaval saying that Creole cultural mores need not be modernized? His response is ambiguous, not unlike that of many within the social group he represented.

Sentimental Mulattas and the Ungrateful Ex-Slave

As we have seen, the rules regarding gender relations were in flux when it came to Creole women and men. Clearly, courtship and marriage were to occur only among members of one's own race. But not so sexual escapades. White women enjoyed the luxury of a genteel courtship, while mulattas would provide sexual dalliance for the young students. Men's sexual experience was thus acquired with the socially subaltern women. One of our protagonists, Arturo Montes, follows this socially sanctioned libidinal economy to the letter: "Arturo Montes had a multitude of girlfriends, especially among the gracious craftswomen of a handkerchief factory at one of the university crossroads, around the hill of the Franciscans, where our hero found, in the slender *mulatta* needlepoint workers, lips as red as the dittany flower."[29] ("Novias tuvo Arturo Montes a granel, sobre todo entre las gentiles oficialas de un taller de pañuelos que había en una de las encrucijadas de la universidad, en los alrededores de la cuesta de los franciscanos, donde nuestro héroe, encontrara en las juncales *mulaticas* del pespunteo, bocas con tanto rojo como el del ítamo real.") The student's preferred haunt is the needlepoint factory where mulattas work for a miserly sum.[30] Like well-off men before him, Arturo trains for the day when he will have both a white wife and a mulatto mistress: "Even in his erotic life that rascal had followed the municipal system. He had a girlfriend, with the hair and waist of a consort, whom he promenaded in the evenings at the university or around the elegant gathering of the plaza . . ."[31] ("Hasta en su erótica aquel barbián había seguido el sistema municipaloide. Tenía una novia, con cabellos y cintura de consorte, que paseaba por el atardecer de la universidad o por la ronda clásica de la plaza elegantona . . .") In this sexual division of labor the mulatta allows the white woman to be virtuous,

> but having returned the official girlfriend to her honest boarding house, he went after *loves of a spicier skin*, displaying his bachelor's urge to delve among that other, more colorful, tenderness—sighs of *colored girls careless of their virtue!*—where he was at times accompanied one night or another by Alfredo Guillén, Isidro Montalvo, or Luciano Aldavín, depending on the spiritual tide amongst them.[32] (pero, depositado el noviazgo oficial en su honesto pensionado, iba en pos de otros *amorcillos de más especiada dermis*, luciendo espuela de barragán, a recoger los dobleces de aquella otra ternura, más abigarrada—¡suspiros de *mozas trigueñas que no cuidaban mucho de su doncellez!*,—a donde le acompañaban alguna que otra noche Alfredo Guillén, Isidro Montalvo o Luciano Aldavín, según estuviera la marea espiritual de uno u otro.)

This is one of the benefits of being a Creole man with prospects. The language is tongue-in-cheek, and the custom is somewhat criticized here. As the young men revel in their sexual escapades, there is little doubt that they see the sexually uninhibited mulattas—who look, taste, and smell delicious—as one of the bonuses that come with power:

> —In my town, the shapeliest mulatta is one of the lilies that adorn the Mayor's staff [the symbol of his power].[33] I will follow suit just in case I ever occupy the municipal seat.
>
> —Undoubtedly,—assented the shameless Luciano Aldavín, son of another mayor.
>
> —Indeed, those mulattas have such savor—
>
> —And color!—interrupted someone.
>
> —And scent!—added another.[34]
>
> (—En mi pueblo, la mulatica mejor formada forma parte de las azucenas de
>
> la vara. Yo debo hacer lo mismo por si alguna vez llego a la poltrona.
>
> —Indudablemente,—assentía el sinvergüenza de Luciano Aldavín, quien era hijo de otro alcalde.
>
> —¡Luego estas mulaticas tienen un sabor!—
>
> —¡Y un color!—interrumpía alguien.
>
> —¡Y un olor!—añadía otro.)

If it is socially sanctioned for these young bohemian (white) Creoles to pursue the socially subservient mulattas, no such privilege is bestowed on the young mulatto. Where does he stand in the *criollo* libidinal economy? His fate is quite different.

The dilemma of the social position of the mulatto is the subject of the story "Un cráneo chato se arrima a la luna" ("A Flat Cranium Leans on the Moon"), a story the author deleted in the revised edition. Belaval portrays the young student Baldomero Santana as a self-loathing mulatto who envies his white comrades' social privileges. The narrator faults Baldomero for his own unhappiness, and for not staying in his assigned social place. At the beginning of the story we encounter the tortured young student. He suffers in silence the terrible conflict of his "dual blood." He is, the narrator tells us, a black man with a white soul and sensibility. This duality is reflected in his appearance. "He is a figure of brusque lines" ("Es una figura de trazos bruscos"), whom the narrator describes as having

> crinkled hair, of an oily blackness; flat forehead; the eyes sunken in the feverish burrows formed by two aggressive cheekbones. There is a ferocious whiteness in his teeth, and his skin, tamarind color, fears neither sun nor shadow. Bronze muscles make of his frame a column of proud virility. Yet, it is irritatingly marred by the haughty cephalic index.[35] (el cabello crespo, de una negrura aceitosa; la frente plana; los ojos escondidos en la madriguera calenturienta que forman dos pómulos agresivos. En sus dientes hay una blancura feroz y su piel, color tamarindo, no teme al sol ni a la sombra. Músculos de bronce hacen de su contextura una columna de bien hecha masculinidad. No obstante, en ella se ha detenido con torva desazón, el soberbio índice cefálico.)

Note that where the mulattas in the stories are beautiful and desirable, the mulatto's features are jarring and threatening. His physical description is marked by disharmony. Baldomero, for his own part, is uneasy about his looks: "He fears his flat cranium, his angleless nose, and his eyes clouded with rancor. He is also unhappy."[36] ("Teme a su cráneo chato, a su nariz sin ángulo, a sus ojos empañados de rencor. El también se siente infeliz.") Baldomero takes no pleasure in his body, for his very body betrays his mixed ancestry:

> He is disturbed by his white soul in perpetual dialogue with his tamarind colored skin, his guilty soul who wants to hide behind his abrupt brow, but a soul who also inflames his nights, nights that explode in dreams, making him cringe at the sight of a milky silhouette whom he has to put away, as one would a mad woman, in the satchel of mulatto agony, so as not to lose his reason.[37] (Le molesta su alma de blanco en perpetuo diálogo con su piel de tamarindo, su alma inconfesa que quiere vivir oculta tras de su ceño abrupto, pero que le inflama la noche, se la estalla en sueños, lo hace crujir al paso de una silueta láctea y a la cual tiene que encerrar, como a una loca, en el saco de una agonía mulata, para no perder él también el juicio.)

As the narrator would have it, Baldomero's morbid obsession with "whiteness" is solely his fault. Furthermore, the narrative voice suggests that Baldomero suffers because he voluntarily segregates himself from others. His self-inflicted neurosis is a product of his misbegotten body and his wayward soul.

By portraying the mulatto's resentment as unwarranted, the narrator exonerates the patronizing white power structure of all blame for the history of slavery and, consequently, for the socially subservient position the character is forced to occupy. Belaval writes: "Why then that *hatred toward the manumitive hand?* . . . That rancor of his was a betrayal of his circle of friends, of his rooming house buddy, of the whites at the university who had trusted him to mend a problem that no one wanted for his innocent land."[38] ("¿Por qué pues aquel *odio contra la mano manumitiva?* . . . Aquel rencor suyo era una traición para su tertulia, para su compañero de hospedería, para los blancos de la universidad que habían confiado en él, que contaban con su lealtad para soldar un problema que ninguno quería para su tierra inocente.")

Belaval and his narrator somehow fail to understand the true reasons for Baldomero's bitterness. He is expected to feel gratitude toward the Creoles who believe they have generously granted him his liberty. In this scheme, slavery is understood as an attribute, not as a circumstance. Even a modern mulatto is conceived of as a former slave who should be grateful to the *mano manumitiva* for his freedom. At the rhetorical level the metonymy works to the advantage of the Creole *liberators* whose actions and historical responsibility are made less visible by the author's generous use of the disembodied hand that grants freedom. Moreover, the mulatto appears as a betrayer of the trust whites have placed in him—to keep race relations cordial in the face of tacit segregation and white supremacy. Belaval's story taps into the old theme of the "mulatto as overseer" called to mediate between the white master and the black slave. Belaval does not want a revolt in his "innocent land," as he calls Puerto Rico. A racial revolt would no doubt endanger the racist privileges of the Creoles in the midst of the menacing downward mobility that characterized the first three decades of the twentieth century.

For his part, Baldomero specifically rejects black and mulatto women as objects of desire. This rejection of the black woman in favor of the white norm is a sign of the in-group tensions that, as St. Clair Drake explains, "[reinforce] the subordination and the exploitation of the more Negroid portion of any collectivity defined as 'black' with a wide skin-color range."[39] Baldomero dismisses his mulatto girlfriend and lets her know that she is not desirable the way a white woman would be. The shunned girl, in turn, confesses that she also prefers a white man to the dark Baldomero: "Yeah! The truth is that you only like white women. Oh, don't protest! What for? It's the same with me! I have never been able to love one of us. With you I wanted to make an exception; you were so like me! So attuned to my problem!"[40] ("¡Bah! La verdad es que a ti sólo te gustan las blancas. ¡Oh, no protestes! ¿Para qué? ¡Si a mí también me pasa! Nunca he podido amar a uno de los nuestros. Contigo quise hacer una excepción; eras tan igual a mí! ¡Tan dentro de mi problema!") The narrator laments Baldomero's situation as tragic and tries to get at the root of mulatto self-loathing, but is not willing to examine white supremacy structurally.

An accurate insight of the narration, nonetheless, is the mention of the role of white women within this system. The young Baldomero realizes that, as things stand, white women are the symbol of social achievement and respectability denied him. The "preferred" solution to the racial oppression experienced by the mulatto character is race mixing and dilution, not open defiance. But one of the dead ends of this process is that whiteness can never be truly achieved. The other more serious problem is that this process of *blanqueamiento*, or "whitening," has the effect of keeping the racial division of society intact, with whites at the top and dark-skinned blacks at the very bottom. When we take a closer look at the status of Baldomero's "preference," we must ask if this predilection is a free choice, or if it is indicative of the profound racial stratification of Puerto Rican society. Belaval does not question any of the very practical reasons that would impel the characters to desire a white partner, nor does he ever portray black self-love. In this society whitening is an elusive ideal blacks are urged to desire and are faulted for all at once. Again, when Belaval casts the mulatto as pathetic and resentful, he exculpates the white power structure of all blame.

At one point in the story Baldomero's socially induced obsession leads him to dream about his own death, in a reverie that has definite necrophilic undertones: "At night he dreamed that Lolita, a milky form of frightened breasts, was emptying his veins, that they both observed the blood as it flowed in his miserable room, his lowly, illegitimate blood, and that his face was becoming white, very white, and his cranium began to take an illustrious shape, through the miracle of love."[41] ("Por la noche soñó que Lolita, una forma láctea que tenía los senos asustadizos, le estaba vaciando las venas, que ambos veían correr la sangre por su cuartucho, su sangre de pueblo, de barraganía y que su rostro se iba quedando blanco, muy blanco, mientras su cráneo iba espigándose en línea prócer, por milagro de amor.") His tainted blood is flushed out of his body by a white beloved, cleansing him, making him white. The beast becomes a beauty, the prince is awakened by a kiss: "Suddenly an avid little nose, a voluptuous nose posed near his lips a kiss, a kiss that was like a liberation from all his rancor, his longing to be a beau fulfilled, a reaffirmation by the ideal type."[42] ("De pronto una naricilla ávida, voluptuosa, husmeó cerca de su boca un beso, el beso que era como una liberación de todo su rencor, su ansia de galán redenta, el espaldarazo al tipo ideal.")

While Baldomero dreams, white women consciously understand their role in the preservation of white privilege. When a professor at the university lectures on the inferiority of blacks and the dangers of race mixing, the white women agree wholeheartedly:

> How cruelly the girls protested against the sexual expansionism of [white] man, who at the moment of sentimental upheaval, had questioned the sensual prestige of the bourgeois eroticism of the [white] woman! One could not hope for mercy from that female, *who knew she was the guardian of an ancestral order, who would never agree to descend from the severe rank of white, Catholic woman, champion of the century.*[43] (¡Qué crueles las protestas de las chicas contra el expansionismo sexual del hombre [blanco], quien al momento de la revuelta sentimental, había puesto en entredicho, el prestigio sensual de la burguesa eroticidad de la mujer [blanca]! No había que esperar misericordia de aquella fémina, *quien se sabía guardadora de un orden ancestral, quien nunca estaría dispuesta a descender de su severo rango de hembra blanca, católica, dueña del siglo.*)

For a white woman to marry a mulatto would be to relinquish her social privileges: racial prestige, religious prestige, and even her newly acquired rights. The quintessential *dueña del siglo* would lose it all. In this racist sexual hierarchy Creole men and women have different, but complementary, roles. White men could have sexual encounters with mulattas, who were seen as rivals by white women. While the language used by Belaval to convey this is obscure and euphemistic, the story reveals that white men have the historically important role of conquering the black race by diluting it. White men could descend where white women could not, "to the spiritual trafficking of the man, who had trusted his victory over hostile elements, in the powerful dilution of sex."[44] ("hasta el tráfico espiritual del varón, que había cifrado en la poderosa dilución del sexo, su victoria sobre todos los elementos hostiles.") In this scheme, is the body of the mulatta—and by extension the black race—conquered hostile territory?

One thing is clear, the production of a "cosmic race" does not elicit the same enthusiasm from white women as it does from white men. And even as the Creole men see extreme racism as silly, they are more than happy to practice the familiar inclusive type long sanctioned by those in power. To the dogma of racial purity preached by an obstinate visiting professor in our story, the men respond with a belligerent Creole affirmation that includes the ideology of *mestizaje.* This "criollismo beligerante" was in part inspired by the campus visit, days earlier, of a South American Indigenist thinker.[45] The men are eager to applaud the idea of race mixing as they themselves traditionally practiced it: "Someone, still suffering from his first sexual setback, pined for a mulatta—blue-eyed, gentlemen!—whose sweet love had the boisterous frolic of a mulatto jungle."[46] ("Alguien, sufriendo aún los primeros descalabros del sexo, plañía por una mulata—¡de ojos azules, caballeros!—cuyo dulce amor tuviera el amplio jolgorio de una selva mulata.")

Belaval's message about *mestizaje* is fraught with ambiguity, not unlike that of his fellow writer Tomás Blanco, who had also tackled the question of Puerto Rico's racial heritage.[47] After all, Baldomero is the product of a long-term relationship between a mulatta and a white man, but these ties are marked by illegitimacy. Though it may be customary for young *criollos* to form attachments with mulattas, these affairs produce chaos and tragedy in the long run. Such is the case of Baldomero and his parents. He feels sad and guilty as he

> remembered the shadowy page from his childhood; his father's visit, once or twice a week, to the house in the slum, where a lowborn concubine aged as he [Baldomero] grew up. He remembered that father who had in his most intimate self the sadness of the white man who knows he has been touched by the devil's tail, and whose sadness reappeared occasionally amongst the silver threads of the adulterous gentleman's beard.[48] (rememoró la página turbia de su niñez; la visita de su padre, una o dos veces por semana, hasta la casa del arrabal, donde envejecía la barragana de pueblo y crecía él, aquel padre que tenía en su cuero íntimo la tristeza del blanco que se sabe tocado por el rabo del demonio, cuya tristeza se veía aparecer, de cuando en cuando, por las hilas de plata de la barba del señorito barraganero.)

The mother—no longer a young girl—is, as the author puts it, a *barragana*, or kept woman. The father—ipso facto *barraganero* because he consorts with her—feels guilty. He is uneasy about the arrogance of the illegitimate son, who is the product of "the compensatory happiness that a lowborn woman, clay vessel, had brought to his sexual unhappiness"[49] ("la compensadora felicidad que una mujer de pueblo, vasija de barro, le había brindado a su infelicidad sexual"). Furthermore, Belaval gives the race-mixing question an interesting twist. It is not black people who have been vanquished and subjugated; it is the white man who unfortunately has had to yield to an inferior race. Belaval gives voice to the racist fantasy of the irrevocable genetic antagonism of the races. According to the narrator, the white man "had had to bear the invasion of the inferior type, his suspicion of not having been the victor, that one day that human penchant toward absorption would become the instrument of his defeat, and that he would find himself with the macabre reality of seeing his type, his regime, his animism lost forever"[50] ("había tenido que soportar la invasión del tipo inferior, la sospecha de no ser él el vencedor, de que algún día aquel sentido humano de la absorción, pudiera convertirse en cuervo para sus ojos ilusos y pudiera encontrarse con la realidad macabra, de ver su tipo, su régimen, su animismo perdido para siempre"). Yet *criollos*, whether fictional or factual, are still socially hegemonic in the early years of the century and to this day. How could they have lost when they are still the masters of polite *criollo* society and of its subaltern subjects? The *barragana* lives in a slum; her son will not be a full *señorito;* he will not enter the (albeit apprehensive) elite that remains virtually white.

What is surprising is Belaval's insistence that whites have had to suffer blacks, and not the other way around.

When Baldomero, in his despair to shed light on his situation, studied the history of race relations, and "read all the important texts he could find on the elusive subject" ("leyó todos los textos señeros que encontró sobre el tema evadido"), he comes to the conclusion that whites—not the enslaved, and socially segregated blacks—are the victims of history.[51] The history texts he reads show him that blacks and mulattos care nothing for the nation. They are happy to let themselves be used by the forces of colonialism: "he learned that foreigners sought out rebellious mulattos like himself, willing to be publicly displayed, in order to exploit the new republic that had surged out of the effervescence of a few picturesque revolutions"[52] ("supo como el extranjero buscaba al mulato, inconforme como él, con ansias de vitrina mundanal, para explotar la naciente república surgida en el hervor de unas cuantas revoluciones pintorescas"). The language is very obscure here. It suggests that in the young republics, mulattos are the willing instruments of foreign manipulation. One wonders if this is a reference to Cuba and its wars of independence or to Puerto Rico and its thwarted movements for self-determination. Mulattos, illegitimate and traitorous sons of the nation, bring pain to their countries. As the author puts it, "The variegated nation suffered from this grafting, a rootless graft that was accustomed to a wandering freedom, to the crowded slums, a graft dressed with ostentatious elegance, who offered ladies yellow carnations; a hunter of white meat, against which he exercised a fierce carnal vengeance."[53] ("La nacionalidad veteada se dolía de aquel injerto, que no hacía tierra, acostumbrada *[sic]* a la libertad andariega, al hacinamiento de los arrabales, que vestía con desaforada elegancia y regalaba a las damas ramos de claveles amarillos; cazador de carne blanca, contra la cual ejercitaba una fiera venganza genésica.") True nationalists—Creoles—lament the presence of this "grafting" of the mulatto on the national tree. The mulatto, almost by definition, is not rooted in the land; he is overly superficial; and he preys vengefully on the white race, according to the story. This despicable social type welcomes foreigners in order to hurt *criollos.* "The type was contemptible, dark invader, who neither lived nor died graciously, but who was capable of opening the door to any discordant import, if that would help him gain a foothold in the spiritual regime of the white man."[54] ("El tipo era deleznable, invasor oscuro, que no tenía gracia para vivir, ni aún para morir, pero que era capaz de abrirle la puerta a toda extranjería discorde, con tal que le ayudara a aupar su planta hacia el régimen espiritual del blanco.") There is a life and death struggle in the soil of the nation where true patriotism battles the "black peril." Native white men are martyrs for the motherland. White men's torments at the hands of black people are endless, it seems. As the young mulatto studies history he realizes that, "In all these pages Baldomero Santana found that his tragedy was matched by another tragedy, his unhappiness by another unhappiness, his bitterness by another bitterness; *he understood that the other* [the white man] *had suffered as much as he had.*"[55] ("En todas aquellas páginas, Baldomero Santana encontró que junto a su tragedia, había otra tragedia, frente a su infelicidad otra infelicidad, ante su amargura otra amargura; *comprendió que el otro había sufrido tanto como él.*") What we have here is a Creole rendition of Rudyard Kipling's colonialist propaganda.[56]

The stereotypes reiterated in the story are classics of racist defamatory literature against people of African descent: the black man ludicrously mimics the institutions and manners of white men and European culture. Ironically, whites force their victims to acculturate and then mock them for doing so. Never mind that whites themselves in their colonial metropoles are also swept up in the modernizing capitalist forces that have potent effects on people's habits of being in Europe and North America too. Never mind either, that the surplus value cruelly extracted from the oppressed made possible the splendors of the capitalist/colonialist classes. The discourse of "the white man's burden" eschews dialectical explanations, proposing glibly, instead, that those in power produce culture and the powerless mimic mindlessly for the sake of imitation. In this oft-repeated racist delusion, all this mimicry causes prolonged suffering to whites, who, try as they may, cannot escape their "carnal enemy's" noxious smell:

> [Baldomero] saw him [the white man] surrounded by simian Calabar athletes who robbed him of sports trophies; by discursive darkies, of horrible green, blue cashmeres; by loud high-toned blacks; by mulattos armed with democratic top hats. [Baldomero saw the white man] feeling the tremendous anguish of proximity, battered by the sun, the brow bronzed by a toxic heat, the enemy smell always at the reach of his nostrils, which at times he felt came from shapes he [the white man] had thought to be white.[57] (Lo vio envuelto [al blanco] por atletas carabalíes, simiescos, que le robaban el troféo de la planta desnuda; por negritos discursivos, con horribles casimires verdes, azules; por grifos estentóreos; por mulatos armados de chisteras democráticas; con una tremenda angustia de vecindad, agobiado de sol, bruñida la frente por un calor tóxico; al alcance de su nariz siempre, un olor enemigo, que a veces sentía surgir de formas que él creyó blancas.)

Black people's struggle for athletic and intellectual achievement, self-determination, and respect in the face of colonialism and racial oppression is horribly ridiculed here.[58] The author's dreadful caricature of people of African descent reveals his own fears and an unwillingness to reject racist propaganda, or to relinquish racist privileges. Race mixing, in this scheme, allows white men to fight the black menace by spreading their white seed and their white culture. They mercifully impregnate dark women in order to dilute the advancing black tide, but they are not rewarded for their efforts. The reader is asked to believe that white martyrs of this battle for civilization are fighting a thankless war: "hoping to find in sexual concord, in the laws of culture, a solution to that shadow that had grown within him, that even had the secret key of his soul with which to vanquish him in the future. Perhaps the other [the white man] had suffered more than he [Baldomero]!"[59] ("buscando en la concordia sexual, en los fueros de la cultura, solución para aquella sombra que había crecido dentro de sí mismo, que incluso tenía la llave secreta de su alma para vencerlo en el mañana. ¡Tal vez el otro había sufrido más!")

In this brazen misrepresentation of the history of black people in the Caribbean and elsewhere, the mulatto Baldomero ends up pitying the good master for the travails of civilizing others. The very title of the story, "Un cráneo chato se arrima a la luna," with its reference to the flat shape of the character's head, gives credence to phrenologic fantasies—the racist notion that the varieties of the human cranium's shape determine one's level of humanity. This rhetoric of white-European racial supremacy has as a constant the positioning of Africans at the lowest end of the chain of evolution. The ladder of human racial evolution is a well-established trope of European racist thought. According to J. A. de Gobineau, a paladin of white supremacy, "The black variety is the lowest and lies at the bottom of the ladder. The animal character lent to its basic form imposes its destiny from the moment of conception. It never leaves the most restricted intellectual zones . . . If its faculties for thinking are mediocre or even nonexistent, it possesses in its desire and as a consequence in its will an intensity that is often terrible."[60]

At the end of Belaval's story the young mulatto student disappears, unable to endure the social stigma systematically attached to his race, and his frustrated desires for a white woman—the obligatory object of desire for all those who aspire to upward social mobility or stability. The narrator hints that Baldomero migrated to another country where he could descend to the realm ascribed to the lower classes. Both the narrator and Baldomero agree on this: "It was better to emigrate, to a great metropolitan slum, where there were many races, many people of sordid hair, perhaps a port tavern or an obscure smoking den!"[61] (¡Era mejor emigrar, hasta un gran arrabal metropolítico, donde hubiera muchas razas, muchas greñas sórdidas, tal vez una taberna de puerto o un fumadero oscuro!) The white students, it should be noted, do not see themselves as racists, nor do they ever wish to question their racial privileges. They are willing to open the doors of opportunity for this particular mulatto whom they expect to act as a grateful token.

The narrator makes his presence visible at the very end of the story. He becomes a character of sorts. His appearance, though, adds a problematic ending, for he reveals his complicity in this racial drama. The narrator asserts, "I know where he is, but I tell no one. He is fine where he is. I know where he is, but I will never tell!"[62] ("Yo sé donde está, pero no lo digo. Está bien donde está. Yo sé donde está, ¡pero no lo diré nunca!") The narrator is Baldomero's confidant, but he remains aloof. His passivity does nothing to change or, at the very least, denounce the terrible conditions that caused Baldomero's annihilation as a social agent. The *criollo* confidant chooses to remain silent on the question of racism.

Irony and Its Discontents

Belaval experiments with caricature, irony, and humor throughout *Los cuentos de la Universidad.* His criticism, directed at colonialism and mindless assimilation of U.S. cultural objects and mores, pointedly chastises the frivolous men of his class who were the willing instruments of this assimilation. The character of Tony Pérez is a case in point. Belaval's satirical intentions have led some critics to comment on the writer's pessimism. As Luis Rafael Sánchez views it, "The humor that tinges with irony, sarcasm, and uncomfortable hilarity a good part of the book, acts as a thick envelope for the bitterness at its core."[63] ("El humor, que tiñe de ironía y burla y risa destemplada buena parte del libro, es un revestimiento espeso para la amargura que constituye su meollo.") Yet, as we have seen, Belaval's caricature of female students is double-edged in that it greatly trivializes women's aspirations; the writer sees no merit in the advantages that modernization might bring to women.

Throughout the collection readers are invited to approach the stories from the perspective of the "mirón furtivo" or the optic of the voyeur, as Luis Rafael Sánchez notes and I concur.[64] In the first part of this chapter, I examined this lens as a *gendered* perspective present even on the jacket of the first edition of the stories. This voyeuristic point of view allows the "male" reader to experience a greater degree of closeness with the characters. Yet it also has another effect. It prompts me to question my uneasiness regarding the author's complicity with the gendered and racist ordering of Puerto Rican society in the first part of the twentieth century. For me and for others who interrogate discourses of white and male supremacy it is difficult to read simple humor and irony in the short stories examined here.

Irony is present, as critic Linda Hutcheon proposes, "in the space *between* (and including) the said and the unsaid; it needs both to happen."[65] Ironic communication differs from ambiguity in that it has an affective charge or edge. According to Hutcheon, irony is always polemical and "weighted" in favor of what is not said, for it "involves the attribution of an evaluative, even judgmental attitude, and this is where the emotive or affective dimension also enters."[66] Irony functions, then, as part of a tonal and emotive continuum, which Hutcheon organizes from minimal to maximal affective charge.

Undeniably, humorous ironies play an important part in many of the stories. For example, in "El verano de Hortensita se complica" ("Hortensita's Summer Gets Complicated") a serious-minded American naturalist is unable to find love. He loses the girl, blinded as he is by his single-minded research of the peripatus, a kind of tropical worm. As an acute scientific observer, Mr. Tim detects the worm, but is unable to see that Hortensita loves him. This is one of the ludic functions of irony where a benevolent teasing or playfulness dominates.[67] In another story, "La pasión rural de Tintagiles Bermúdez" ("The Rural Passion of Tintagiles Bermúdez"), irony is ludic, and more importantly, self-deprecating. This story was the object of extensive revisions for the 1967 edition. The author chose not to include a number of passages that have to do more explicitly with sexual humor. The young protagonist's search for the perfect woman of the land—the nubile, simple, pure, fertile, *jíbara*—is thwarted by his own overly romantic expectations. When Tintagiles takes what he believes to be his perfect "earthy" woman to a party, he discovers that she has a huge louse dangling from one of her braids. Tintagiles's vision of an erotic paradise is shattered by a little louse who grows ever larger in his imagination. The object of the author's humor is not the peasant girl, but the overly romantic young man:

> What was that? A playful little night insect in love with his beloved's face? . . . With hypnotized eyes Tintagiles Bermúdez understood that the intruding explorer of her ear was the most absurd, the most vulgar, the most tragicomic visitor to occupy a decent head of hair: his rustic sweetheart had an indiscreet louse descending on her locks, a louse fascinated by the party lights, a Cinderella of a louse who wanted to spy on the triumph of its feeder.[68] (¿Qué era aquello? ¿Un insectillo juguetón de la noche enamorado del rostro de su amada? . . . Con los ojos hipnotizados Tintagiles Bermúdez comprendió que el intruso husmeador de la oreja era el más absurdo, el más vulgar, el más tragicómico visitador de una cabellera bien: su rústica beldad tenía descendiendo un indiscreto piojo de su cabellera, un piojo fascinado por las luces de la fiesta, un piojo ceniciento que había querido curiosear el triunfo de su alimentadora.)

The character is responsible for his own defeat. His fantasy of the perfect "peasant" woman is his undoing, and the head louse is the instrument of his downfall. The narrator distances himself from the character and includes the reader in the joke: "The devilish louse was relentless in its curiosity. It was a cynical louse, a humorist. The moment came in which Tintagiles Bermúdez in his anguish saw it as the size of a kernel of corn, then that of a coin, growing ominously, almost hiding the ear, the face, the pompous breasts, the powerful body of his beloved."[69] ("El endiablado piojo, no cejaba en su curiosidad. Era un piojo cínico, humorista. Llegó un momento en que en su angustia Tintagiles Bermúdez lo vió del tamaño de un grano de maíz, más tarde de una moneda, creciendo fatídicamente, casi ocultando la oreja, el rostro, los senos pomposos, el cuerpo poderoso de la bien amada.")

As exemplified here, many of the stories are irreverent and frank when it comes to sexual allusions and the depiction of pleasure, an exception in the fiction published at the time in Puerto Rico. When Tintagiles Bermúdez declares his love to the agriculture student—his perfect *jíbara*—he is quite forward, and the sensual charge between them is quite evident:

> The girl forgot her agriculture class. With the volatile words of Tintagiles Bermúdez she felt happy, as open as a furrow, fertile, erotic mother, capable of living a devilish incest with the babe in question [Tintagiles].
>
> —If only I could see you naked! now, with that smell of earth that covers you—the incorrigible nephew of Juan Teodoro murmured in her country-girl ear.
>
> —Fool!—laughed the woman, in order to free herself of the tremendous weight of incest.
>
> —You had to be like this! It's your color, your smell, those teeth, the roundness of your shoulder, of your elbow, of your breast.[70]
>
> (A la chica se le olvidó la clase de agricultura. Bajo la palabra volátil de Tintagiles Bermúdez se sentía contenta, tan abierta como el surco, ubérrima, madre erótica, capaz de vivir un diabólico incesto con el bebé de marras.
>
> —¡Si pudiera verte desnuda!, ahora, con ese olor de siembra que tienes encimamurmuraba en su oreja campesina el incorregible sobrino de Juan Teodoro.
>
> —¡Loco!—reía la mujer para aliviarse del tremendo peso del incesto.
>
> —¡Así tenías que ser! Es tu color, tu olor, esos dientes, esa cosa redonda en el hombro, en el codo, en el seno.—)

In Belaval's stories, the young men admire women's breasts and talk about their sexual desires with audacity. Here even women gaze at men's bodies lustfully.

Critic María Rodríguez Castro has suggested that the targets of Belaval's critique are the children of the "old families," that is, the elite that has had to reorganize itself as the result of the United States's colonial presence. She points to the urban setting of the stories as an exception in a literature that insisted on the idealization of the *jíbaro.* She writes, "Far from invoking the placid and harmonious image that was insistently adjudicated to rural society, these objects are the preview of the disorder and the vertiginous urban rhythm that imposes its dynamics on these small town remains."[71] The targets of Belaval's irony are multiple, as the story of Tintagiles's rural passion suggests. As a writer who had taken to heart the irreverence of the avant-garde, Belaval critiques the abuses of the literary *jibarismo* (one-sided romanticizing of the peasant) that was in vogue in poetry, essays, and fiction. His irony is fired at a dual mark. He addresses other writers and those who idealize the peasantry without belonging to the group themselves. Belaval's audience, or discursive community, is essential to the successful production of ironic meaning in his works. Discursive communities, as Linda Hutcheon argues, are fundamental to ironic communication given that they precede and enable the comprehension of irony.[72] Yet it is the very context and the power relations evoked by irony's evaluative edge that become problematic, if not inappropriate, when Belaval's objects of ridicule are socially subaltern subjects. His critique simply does not go high enough.

Bohemian Dreams and Creole Prophecies

Taken as a whole, Belaval's treatment of the mulatto characters is overly ambiguous. He explores racial hierarchies without truly questioning them. The stories deploy a paternalism practiced by many Creoles who viewed the "racial question" as, first and foremost, the fault of black people. The narrator obliquely refers to "the problem that no one wanted for this innocent land," that is, a social confrontation along racial lines. In "Un cráneo chato se arrima a la luna" the paternalistic "sympathy" that the narrative voice feels toward Baldomero as a social outcast is nullified when he is made to disappear as a social agent at the end of the tale. Is the mulatto's disappearance from the (educated) social scene a secret *criollo* desire? The narrative begs the question.

The last story discussed here, "Se enciende la lámpara de Aladino" ("Aladin's Lamp Lights Up"), seems to support this conclusion. The scene takes place in a brothel managed by a mulatto where students out for a good time demand a woman from the mulatto pimp. The brothel also doubles as a marijuana den where the young men smoke at their leisure.[73] The mulatto presents them with a black woman whom they reject: "When will you bring us a *white* woman, you smuggler?"[74] ("¿Cuándo vas a traernos una *blanca*, tú que eres contrabandista?") To spite the young gentlemen Antoñón, the mulatto, taunts them with a pale, nubile *jíbara* afflicted with tuberculosis, but tells them that he will not sell her. After a melee the students leave the mulatto for dead and burn down the brothel: "Let's torch it! It will be a pleasure to send Antoñón to hell on a skewer."[75] ("¡Incendiemos! Será un gusto encaramar a Antoñón hasta el infierno asado al palo.") One of the prostitutes, a mulatta, saves him from the flames just in time. The students merrily depart from the scene in possession of the white peasant girl, "Give the girl your arm; she is our loot, even with her broken nose."[76] ("Dale el brazo a la chica; es nuestro botín, aunque se le haya estropeado la nariz.")

The symbolism of this story is almost transparent: the colony is a degraded brothel; the urban mulatto must be neutralized; and the Creole students will "save" (and then use) the white peasant—the favored symbol of the nation. The *jíbara* in turn is mute, and her desires are interpreted for her. With prophetic accuracy the metaphors of this story play out the power relations and racial alliances that would come into fruition in the populist movement of the 1940s, the movement spearheaded by the professional elite to which Belaval belonged.

In the end, *Los cuentos de la Universidad* underscores the subordinate position of people of African descent in the Creole scheme of things. Furthermore, when their resistance to the descendants of the slave owners is shown, those who resist are struck down; Baldomero, the mulatto student, disappears; Antoñón, the mulatto brothel owner, is cruelly left to die a fiery death. Yet it can be argued that all the characters who interact in the brothel act in the most sordid of ways. Under the influence of narcotics the young men shed all pretense of civility, and the bloody struggle for power ends in a conflagration. The irony in this story lies perhaps in the fact that the politically idealistic students are willing to kill a man in order to satisfy their lust. At the very end of these university short stories we reencounter Alfredo Guillén surveying a university now in shambles, not toppled as the result of a heroic overthrow of the foreign colonial power, but destroyed by the force of a terrible hurricane.

If, in the end, the students' takeover of the nation/university is not achieved, we must wonder who bears responsibility. Rapid Americanization? The destruction of the old gender system? Puerto Ricans of African descent? A Creole nostalgia that insists on recuperating the earlier structures of domination? Perhaps all of these things combine to frustrate the students' nationalist dreams. By using caricature and irony Belaval's stories expose the aspirations and the foibles of an important faction of the Puerto Rican elite at a vital moment in the conceptualization of national identity. Also revealed, unwittingly, are the gender and racial divisions stubbornly entrenched in the Puerto Rican elite. The nation's subaltern subjects would not be able to look to these Creole fabulations for a dependable portrayal of a nation "that would resemble us all."

CHAPTER 6

A Brave New (Discursive) World: María Cadilla de Martínez's *Milestones of the Race*

For the master's tools will never dismantle the master's house.
They may allow us temporarily to beat him at his own game,
but they will never enable us to bring about genuine change.
And this fact is only threatening to those women who still
define the master's house as their only source of support.
—Audre Lorde, 1984

In her highly original essay, "Beyond Miranda's Meanings: Un/silencing the 'Demonic Ground' of Caliban's 'Woman,'" noted Jamaican scholar Sylvia Wynter suggests that to make sense of the subjectivity of Afro-Caribbean women, we should look beyond the meanings of womanhood as constructed in Western feminist as well as in masculinist discourses.[1] Yet as we saw earlier, even as Creole women's contribution to cultural nationalist dialogues helped to expand notions of participation and authority within the Puerto Rican intellectual field, the particularities of the literary milieu made it difficult for other voices to be heard. While race and racialist discourses featured prominently in Creole discourses of identity and nationhood, neither Afro-Puerto Rican women and men, nor working-class participants overtly entered Creole-sanctioned cultural institutions. This chapter examines a work of fiction by noted suffragist, folklorist, historian, and teacher María Cadilla de Martínez where gender, race, and nation are interwoven, allowing us further perspective on the representation of the popular within the *criollo* conceived nation. Cadilla de Martínez's *Hitos de la raza: cuentos tradicionales y folklóricos (Milestones of the Race: Traditional and Folkloric Stories)* (1945), a collection of neo-romantic vignettes about folklore and history, aims at educating the reader about Puerto Rico's past. Two of the tales discussed portray the theme of slavery and servitude from the point of view of a woman writer, a rare occurrence in Puerto Rican literature. "Tate" narrates the story of a manumitted slave who, decades after the abolition of slavery, remains at the service of the family who had freed her. "Relieve indígena," for its part, recounts the captivity of the Indian woman Iviahoca at the time of the Spanish conquest. *Hitos de la raza* dramatizes the racial hierarchies most vital to the Creole discourse about nationality. Intertwined in "Tate" and "Relieve indígena" we find the author's valuation of the proper relationship between race and nationality. Tellingly, "Palomas afectivas," the last piece to appear in the book, allows the reader to glimpse a revealing portrayal of the Creole woman intellectual that completes the social and racial panoramas of *Hitos de la raza.*

As a promoter of women's suffrage and an advocate of women's education, Cadilla de Martínez helped to create a space for the women of her generation and for the young women writers of the *Generación del Treinta.* Their vision concerning national culture was in concord in many respects with hers. Born in 1886, Cadilla de Martínez belonged to the feminist group who forged a path for the young Margot Arce and Nilita Vientós. She was one of the young women who responded to Ana Roqué de Duprey's call to form the *Liga Femínea* in 1917, and was among the first to face the question of authority for Creole women intellectuals in all its complexities. Moreover, we can view the male-orientated formulations of the cultural nationalism of the *Generación del Treinta*, heavily invested in a rhetoric of male adulthood and virility, as a response to the suffragist debates that culminated in universal suffrage at the beginning of the 1930s. In her lengthy career she published fourteen works in a variety of genres and had an ongoing interest in painting and music. Cadilla de Martínez initiated her labors as a school teacher in 1903 and retired in 1936 from the University of Puerto Rico's Department of Pedagogy. Before elucidating the author's contribution to the socio-racial imagery of Creole nationalist discourse, however, we will briefly consider the problem of the relationship of gender and colonialist representation in the broader Caribbean context.

Woman, Native, and Miranda's Other

The early establishment of the category of "native" as exploitable labor went hand in hand with the appropriation of the vast expanses of land on the American continents by European colonizers. This categorization was soon extended to various populations of Africa, facilitating the subjugation of millions of Africans who could complement or supplant the coerced labor of indigenous American populations. Recall that even as early as Columbus's letter to the Spanish Crown announcing the first contact with the indigenous people of the Americas, we can find the foundations of a colonialist discourse that would be with us for centuries. Sylvia Wynter proposes that, read through a post-colonial lens, we can detect even in a work such as Shakespeare's *The Tempest* the dramatic rendering of the inauguration of a new ontological system in the West.

Shakespeare's highly allegorical work reflects the drama of the implantation of European hegemony in the Atlantic world after 1492. We meet the magician Prospero, the main character, an aristocrat in exile who has taken possession of Caliban's island with the help of his magic and that of his servant, the "dainty" spirit of the winds, Ariel. Prospero enslaves the native Caliban after the latter has welcomed him and taught him how to survive on the island. Miranda, daughter of Prospero, accompanies her father in his exile. Prospero's stated ambition is to return victorious to Milan where he would seal his restoration to power with the nuptials of his daughter and the heir to the Neapolitan throne.

Scholars from diverse colonial and anticolonial perspectives have aptly charted the complex careers of Caliban, Prospero, and Ariel, paradigmatic masculine figures of *The Tempest*.[2] In the case of Latin American thought we should recall the Arielist propositions of José Enrique Rodó in response to the expansionist designs of the United States; Aimé Césaire's reformulations of Caliban as the symbol of the exploited and rebellious black man confronting racial and colonial injustice; and Manuel Fernández Retamar's Caliban, who summons the solidarity of the people of Latin America confronting the recrudescence of neo-colonialism.[3] What has been neglected in many of these studies is a more attentive study of Sycorax and Miranda, the feminine characters of the play. Nonetheless, these female figures are central to this drama of usurpation and mystification. Sycorax, mother of Caliban, never appears on stage. Yet, as the progenitrix of the "monster" Caliban, she lurks as a demonic presence who, years before, had transformed Ariel into a pine tree. When Prospero mentions her, it is to insult Caliban and to threaten and coerce Ariel. It is from Sycorax that Caliban inherits the island. Sycorax, the indigenous (or black) woman, is identified with the natural elements of the island and possesses a power that is antagonistic to the colonizer Prospero. Miranda, returning to Wynter's formulation, functions within two ambits. As the daughter of Prospero the colonizer, she symbolizes sexual difference and the maintenance of European racial supremacy. She is the trophy that Caliban covets in his conflict with Prospero. And if she does not emerge wholly as a presence in her own right, capable of constructing an autonomous subjectivity, this possibility nevertheless exists. We know—because Miranda herself tells us—that she has the knowledge that makes her superior to Caliban. She is the one who teaches him the language of the colonizer and feels that she has enough authority to reproach her slave

Caliban for his ingratitude: " . . . I pitied thee, / Took pains to make thee speak, taught thee each hour / One thing or other: when thou didst not, savage, / Know thine own meaning . . . I endow'd thy purposes / With words that made them known."[4] Moreover, by accusing Caliban of being in truth a "villain," she is fully conscious that as the daughter of Prospero, who also happens to be the duke of Milan, she enjoys the protection afforded by her social rank.[5]

Shakespeare's drama inscribes colonial power relations in such a manner as to dispense with indigenous (and black) women, given that Caliban's women folk are not provided with embodiment in this symbolic universe. As Wynter aptly puts it, "What is the systemic function of her own silencing, both as women, and more totally as 'native' women? Of what mode of speech is that absence of speech both as women (masculinist discourse) and as native women (feminist discourse) an imperative function?"[6] The power relations personified by Shakespeare's mise en scène are still valid in the cultural and symbolic universes of Caribbean people, Puerto Ricans included, where dramas of colonization and class struggle are still unfolding. In the case of early twentieth-century Puerto Rico, we see how affluent white women, daughters and inheritors of hegemonic privileges, steadily forge a space for themselves as producers of knowledge. Much is at stake, given the correlation between subjectivity and ontological presence with civic stature and citizenship rights. In this context it becomes critical to ponder the meanings and the effects of the effacement of the multiple subjectivities of black women, for they are necessary to the maintenance of the system of domination.[7] Women of African descent, relegated in discourses of the national to the status of inconsequent subjects, of usable labor force without recognized agency, have barely begun to speak in our literature and in our historiography.[8] If, from the perspectives of power, blackness in Puerto Rico has been represented as nonexistent, antinational, domesticated, or highly sexualized, from feminist Afrocentric perspectives the realities still to be explored tell a very different story. Afro-Caribbean women writers write against the grain of demonizing master narratives such as *The Tempest*.

Cadilla de Martínez participated in the projects that promoted and produced a national literary culture with her many works, including this particular retelling of the "milestones of the race." She used her authorial standing to weigh in on the question of the nature of Puerto Rican culture for a modern audience. In her stories Indians, Spaniards, blacks, mulattos, and Creoles represent some aspect of the nation *outside* and away from the troublesome North American presence. It is only in the last story of *Hitos de la raza* that the modern crisis of legitimacy is obliquely mentioned. Fittingly, the figure of the woman intellectual comes to give closure to the narration. Yet closer scrutiny reveals a feminine narrative persona as a perdurable presence throughout the text.

Cadilla de Martínez was a mentor and teacher for scores of women intellectuals and professionals, and a founding member of various professional and cultural associations.[9] She published both scholarly and fictional works, including a collection of short stories entitled *Cuentos a Lilian* (1925), a doctoral dissertation on folk poetry, *La poesía popular en Puerto Rico* (1933), a study of customs and popular traditions, *Costumbres y tradicionalismos de mi tierra,* (1938), and a compilation of popular tales and traditions, *Raíces de la tierra* (1941). She also would add her voice to essays about the *jíbaro* with "La campesina de Puerto Rico" (1937). Her work established a model for the study of folk tales and popular poetry that remained unchallenged until very recently. As an educator and a compiler, Cadilla de Martínez set out to document and popularize customs, historical events, and traditional stories and folkways that she feared were fast disappearing with the modernization of Puerto Rican society.

Before Cadilla de Martínez a number of writers in the regionalist or *costumbrista* vein had also inquired into the popular roots of Puerto Rican culture. Indeed, one of the founding texts of Puerto Rican literature, Manuel Alonso's *El gíbaro [sic]*, published in 1845, describes scenes of peasant life and culture, and propounds a description of the Puerto Rican that excludes black Puerto Ricans from Puerto Rico's national identity.[10] Our author was very well aware of the genre as previously practiced in Spain as well as in Puerto Rico and the rest of Spanish America.[11] Her most immediate referent in Puerto Rico is the oeuvre of her former mentor, historian and writer Cayetano Coll y Toste. His *Tradiciones y leyendas puertorriqueñas* (1926), was a model for her own work.

Chapter 5 explored how the treatment of gender and race in Belaval's short stories reflected the elite's apprehension over the black and mulatto population perceived as alien to the island's culture.[12] To present black people as a problem or as festive characters masks the domination and the exploitation to which blacks have been subjected throughout the course of Puerto Rican history. Recent scholarship on politician and physician José Celso Barbosa, for example, contests these derogatory myths by positing, instead, the existence of an ongoing critical consciousness regarding racism among Afro-Puerto Ricans at the beginning of the twentieth century. In his writings, Barbosa passionately dialogued with other black thinkers who were fighting for racial justice in Cuba and in the United States.[13] At the popular level there was also a response, at times diffused, at times organized, to racial and class oppression among the working classes, as we discussed earlier.[14]

Like Family: Servitude, Subaltern Maternity, and Historical Memory

Hitos de la raza was published in 1945, scarcely a decade after the heated debates generated by Luis Palés Matos over the role of blackness in Puerto Rican popular culture and national identity. Nonetheless, there are many indications that the writing of *Hitos de la raza* coincides with the polemic. Cadilla de Martínez's literary and erudite production is an implicit contribution to the discussions of that moment.

Tate, the character that gives title to the first of Cadilla de Martínez's stories considered here, is presented as the classic mammy of pro-slavery literature. Soot black, glassy-eyed, happy, she is the versatile and indefatigable maid who adores her masters and is eternally grateful to them for her manumission. The servile and entertaining Tate is the surrogate mother of all the white children of the house. Note that it is they who narrate the story in the first person plural:

> Tar black and jolly, she was almost a tradition in our family. She was all-knowing and could do it all to perfection: sewing, cooking, sweeping, washing, etc. She had been a slave, or rather the *manumitted* servant of our grandfather, and in gratitude to him, she had served as nanny to all of our mother's children. With eyes of moving porcelain, mischievous, her pupils seeming to dance against a white background that contrasted with her skin, she regarded us at all times of the day, and many nights we saw them above our heads. She liked to please and entertained us with her talk and her ways. We all loved her immensely.[15] (Retinta y alegre, era casi una tradición en la familia. Todo lo sabía y todo lo podía hacer con perfección: costura, cocina, barrido, fregado, etc. Había sido esclava o mejor dicho, servidora *manumisa* de nuestro abuelo y por agradecimiento a él, se quedó sirviendo a nuestra madre como niñera de todos sus hijos. Con sus ojos de porcelana movibles, traviesos, cuyas pupilas parecían bailar en un fondo blanco que contrastaba con su tez, nos enfocaba a todas horas del día y en no pocas noches los vimos sobre nuestras cabezas. Era complaciente y divertía con su charla y sus modales. Todos la queríamos muchísimo.)

Tate's *raison d'être* is her lifelong dedication to her masters. As a domestic her work does not belong to her but to her "family." Moreover, her productive and affective labor on their behalf required that familiarity coexist with subordination, a fundamental requisite of this type of social relation. As scholars of domestic labor have repeatedly pointed out, domestic service, before and after emancipation, did not presume that the domestic worker should have a private life distinct from that of her masters or employers.[16] In that way her energies would be transmitted without impediments to the family that hired her. In many instances her masters made it very difficult for the enslaved woman to maintain her own family bonds. Even after slavery the absence of a family life could be a condition for employment and patronage.

In Cadilla de Martínez's tale, the children of the house coax Tate into telling them one of her tales: "We wanted her to talk to us, to entertain us. . . . Her accented *bozal* pronunciation amused us so much that it made us laugh."[17] ("Queríamos que ella nos hablara, que nos entretuviera. . . . Su acentuada pronunciación de negra bozal nos divertía tanto, que nos hacía reír.") Tate assents to their wishes and tells them that they named her Monserrate when she was baptized, that her first master was a certain Don Andrés, and that she had been sold by the hacienda Montegrande to another landowner.[18] Tate also reveals that her father had been a "coartado," a name used to designate slaves who worked, often for many years, to buy their own freedom. Additionally, we learn that she would secretly meet her loved one, Dámaso, at the *candungué* and *guateque* dances in honor of the patron saint of the town.

Tate narrates this in the ironing room, architectonic *locus* of domestic work and workers, to which the children of the house have access as a site of adventure. Initially, when the children importune her, the mammy wants to be left alone. Tate tells them that she is busy, "Toy ocupá, niños," or threatens them with her finger and chastises them when they all speak at once, "¡*Arrechucen* una sola, pol la bía!" Neither does she hesitate to correct their mistaken notions, "¡quía ser, niño!" Her annoyance hints at her agency and volition. Yet, Tate is not at complete liberty to talk. Her silences hide what she does not want to or cannot tell the children about her past: "Without answering, she began to fill a pipe, one she used to smoke whenever she could . . . She merely said that they let her have a smoke. And soon after, large tears made her cheeks shine."[19] ("Sin contestar, Tate se puso a *liar* un *jumazo*, el que acostumbraba fumarse cuando podía . . . Dijo solamente que la dejaran *jipiar*. Y poco después gruesas lágrimas le lustraban sus mejillas.") As Tate intones a popular slave song to amuse the children, she falls into a trance that ends in her collapse, and her employers have to send for the family doctor to see to her. The terrified and confused children are admonished by their mother never to ask the former slave about her past. She then proceeds to recount the most tragic episode of Tate's life. At fourteen Tate had been raped by the white overseer of the *hacienda* who forced her to be his concubine, though not before her parents had died trying to protect her. Months later the twins, "dos zambitos," born of the rape also die. Deranged by these traumatic events, she became useless as a worker and was sold to the family of her current masters. Tate, grateful for the good treatment she received from her new masters, generous to the point of manumitting the traumatized slave, had remained in their service ever since.

It is of interest here that the mother warns the children not to ask Tate about her past. The former slave should not be made to remember. When music mnemonically penetrates Tate's self-censure, the mammy suffers a collapse as she remembers the ballads of her youth and the horrors of enslavement. The narration, however, does not permit the former slave to recollect fully, let alone to express herself about her situation. She does not have the social power to utter the words that might be heard regarding the pain of slavery. Yet because both exploitation and resistance marked the experiences of the enslaved, when Tate suppresses the memory of exploitation, and when the mother further silences it, the memory of resistance is also in danger of disappearing. The version that remains, then, is a truncated account of the traumatic experiences of a life of servitude. The mother admonishes the children that they all should make an effort "to make her forget, if possible, this oppressing and bitter slavery she experienced in her youth. From now on, children, never remind her of her past."[20] ("hacerla olvidar, si es posible, aquella esclavitud opresora y dolorosa que experimentó en su juventud. Desde hoy, hijos, nunca le recuerden su pasado.") In this story it is the *criolla* who interprets the mammy's narrative. The mistress of the house—ultimately the Creole woman of means and education—speaks for and about the subaltern woman.

True to the norms of early ethnographic writing, Cadilla de Martínez translates the mammy's "black Spanish" by providing the reader with footnotes in standard Spanish with which to interpret Tate's speech. When Tate tells the children that "In the hacienda they called me Tate, but in church I was baptized with the name Monserrate, like the Virgin," the reader is provided with a "translation" in a footnote.[21] ("Nel jabeque de la chimbá me dieron el Tate. Ma la Iglesia ar cristianá, me aproprió Monsirriate, com'me tocaya la Visne.") The voice of the socially subordinate requires a translator that can render it intelligible to the reader not accustomed to that kind of speech. Slavery, here and in virtually all the works of this period, exists in the realm of the unspeakable. As a rule, the literature of the *Generación del Treinta* implicitly or explicitly ends up silencing the subject. If Tate's narrative were allowed to articulate the ultimate ontological and social consequences of the true cost of slavery for slaves and their descendants, Creole responsibility for the history of slavery in Puerto Rico would be exposed to the wide world. The self-censure of the mammy reflects her lack of power, but not a lack of consciousness. And if she stays as a servant for life in the house of these masters, it is because she had precious few options in a country where landlessness meant misery and hunger, and where the "vagrancy" of the poor was officially punished by the government.[22]

In short, the real hero of Tate's story is *criollo kindness*, a kindness that eschews the slave master's accountability, and that requires that the slave know her place and how to behave. When the mammy manages to tell the children that her father was a manumitted slave, though her sobs do not allow her to go any further, the children become perplexed and frightened by her pain. Realizing that they are upset, Tate is careful to restrain her emotions. As the narrator says, "When she finally noticed our alarm, our emotion, she tried to erase this impression and feigning mirth she said, 'Well, let me tell you a love story! Don't you want to hear it children?'"[23] ("Cuando por fin se dio cuenta de nuestro sobresalto, de nuestra emoción, trató de deshacer la impresión y aparentando alegría dijo, '¡Bamó! ¡Parrar de nobios! ¿Queré, niñoj?'") She offers to entertain them with a love story to dispel the consternation produced by her sorrow, for she does not have the luxury of upsetting the master's children. The slave's narrative is thus transformed into a *love* story, "¡Parrar de nobios!"

The vignette ends with the voice of the mother who gives the children/readers an acceptable *criollo* interpretation of Tate's life. As a loyal "member" of the Creole family, Tate is awarded the right to forget. However, this ostensibly generous reward works to the advantage of the masters. They remain in control of Tate's narrative, and thus in control of the discourse about slavery. In this racist paternalistic scheme the mammy is regarded as having a noble soul, "nobleza del alma," a highly problematic and almost meaningless reward for her troubles. Try as it might, this revisionist discourse could not completely achieve its goal of policing collective memory. For subaltern populations, as well as for those who assume in their reading a subaltern and Afro-centric perspective, the possibility of reclaiming suppressed discourses always remains open.

As we have seen, reclaiming memory is fraught with dangers, but not only for Tate. If on one hand it is significant that the author rescues slavery as an integral part of the historical past, on the other hand, it is important to examine the conditions under which this inclusion takes place. We need to interrogate the portrayal of Tate's subjectivity and the ways in which she is allowed to speak to us. Can we or can we not hear her voice? Granted, the text does not conceal Tate's reality as a slave. After all, it narrates episodes in the life of a woman who endured the exploitation and other horrors of the slave system. The story does give some conditional presence to the mammy. However, by remaining frozen in a moment of speechlessness, Tate's silence regarding her station as a domestic for life and the social subordination that this represents are never allowed to be questioned. Her past oppression receives no real vindication and her lifelong servitude remains unchallenged.

Until quite recently, hegemonic discourses have conceded very limited intelligibility to the black Puerto Rican woman. She has been, above all, the dancer, the "mulata danzarina," object of desire of Creole men, and "the black woman who raised me," her emotional and manual labor appropriated by others. Such positioning has been virtually static in our cultural symbolic system.[24] But as historical agents black women have an existence *for* themselves, outside and beyond the assigned socially subaltern position. It would be fitting to meditate on the ways women of African descent have been understood, represented, addressed socially and culturally in Puerto Rico. Contrary to what has happened in other Caribbean contexts, critics have scarcely begun to concern themselves with the complex multidisciplinary work that the study of black Puerto Ricans demands.[25]

Cadilla de Martínez published *Hitos de la raza* with a didactic purpose in mind. She wanted to tap into an emotive memory that could help to foster "norms regarding our customs and the development of a binding ethics"[26] ("normas costumbristas y para el desarrollo de una ética vinculadora"). Her task was to look for values that would nurture the bonds among Puerto Ricans and between them and their past. She seemed to have hit her mark, given that this book was awarded an *Instituto de Literatura Puertorriqueña* prize in 1945, the year of its publication. In six of her vignettes she makes a point of mentioning the historical sources that support her narratives: Fernández de Oviedo's chronicles of the Spanish conquest, *Historia general y natural de las Indias;* nineteenth-century intellectual Alejandro Tapia y Rivera's *Biblioteca Histórica de Puerto Rico* (collection of historical documents); Coll y Toste's journal, *Boletín Histórico de Puerto Rico;* documents of the Spanish Archivo de Indias; and Salvador Brau's history, *Historia de Puerto Rico.* The remaining vignettes are based on popular stories handed down orally. Only the closing piece of *Hitos de la raza,* told from the first person point of view and set in the present, eschews obvious historical or folkloric guarantors. Its narrator is a young woman who speaks to her mentor, a somewhat older man, about the proper symbols for the Puerto Rican nation. I will discuss later the implications of this dialogue. For now, I address the author's concept of cultural transmission.

Cadilla de Martínez's understanding of culture in general and the island's popular cultural legacy leads her to view cultural transmission in a simplified manner. Her insistence on direct ties with Spain allows her to gloss over the diverse cultural practices that evolved in the struggle for domination, survival, and resistance that always marked the relationship between Spaniards, Creoles, and people of African and indigenous descent. In another one of her books, *Raíces de la tierra* (1941), she gathers testimonies that are related by rural informants that illustrate, according to her introductory essay to that book, "the virtues and defects of the race"[27] ("las virtudes y los defectos de la raza"). Accordingly, one of these permanent virtues passed down by the Spaniards to their Puerto Rican descendants is a "natural" stoicism vis-à-vis adversity, "The stoic, Senechist suffering of the caste"[28] ("el sufrimiento estoico, senequista de la casta"). Conforming to the usage of the day, the author uses "casta" and race interchangeably to mean lineage. More importantly, her belief in national types stems from a static understanding of culture as a set of fixed qualities rather than practices and processes linked to a particular history. And even though a number of her informants are black, she does not consider that Afro-Puerto Ricans might have a distinct perspective due to the social relations put in place by the slave system, and later by racial discrimination and subordination.[29] Neither does she consider that modified practices of the numerous West African cultural groups brought to the island in shackles might be a part of the ongoing process of transculturation taking place within the heterogeneous population from which Puerto Ricans are descended. To name a few of these forcibly transplanted groups: the Wolof (Jefofe) and Serer (Berbesi) were Muslims from Senegal. From what is today's Guinea-Bissau we have the Biafada (Biáfara), Banyun (Bañol), Biocho (Biojo), Cacanga, Bram (Brama, Gola or Burama). The Nalu, Terranova were possibly from the eastern Guinea coast. The Zape

(Landuma, Baga, and Tenme peoples) originated from today's coastal Sierra Leone and Liberia. We also have the Mandinga (Malinke or Mande-speaking people) anywhere from Gambia eastward to present-day northern Ghana and western Upper Volta. Finally, we can place the Bakongo (Manicongo) as coming from the lower Congo Valley.[30] This willful blindness to the cultural heterogeneity of the island is also present in her other works. For example, while the author reports having attended a celebration on Loíza Street in the black neighborhood Barriada las Palomas of Santurce, in her 1933 book *La poesía popular en Puerto Rico*, her assessment of what she witnessed does not hint at even a pretense of cultural sensitivity. After describing the small barrel drum used as accompaniment by the singers, she explains that the dance was "a kind of primitivist vertigo in which the dancers gesticulate and sing strange songs, some of them unintelligible"[31] ("una especie de vértigo primitivista en el cual los danzantes gesticulan y cantan canciones extrañas, algunas de ellas ininteligibles"). What she describes from the perspective of an uncomprehending outsider is the participatory call and response *bomba* dance in which highly skilled dancers duel with the drum, at times following and at times leading the particular beat played at the moment. Moreover, in this type of dance, the dancer is never a mere follower, but will be assessed by her or his inventiveness, physical prowess, and the beauty of the figures performed. Cadilla de Martínez records some of the verses she heard on that occasion, together with others gathered by a student of hers. She herself attests that there were enough Afro-Puerto Ricans who saw these celebrations as part of the fabric of their lives: "According to what I have been able to find out, these dances by blacks usually are celebrated on Saturday nights and at times during the day. Daytime dances are very rare and only occur in the event of a commemorative feast."[32] ("Según averigüé y pude observar, esos bailes de negros se llevan a cabo los sábados por la noche y algunas veces durante el día. Los de día son muy raros y sólo cuando se trata de celebrar fiestas conmemorativas.") Of course the verses she finds "unintelligible" are not so for the singers and dancers of that neighborhood. Begging the question of how many working people could afford to dance during the daytime on weekdays, it is also important to remember that oppressed people have not always been anxious to reveal their lives to the prying eyes of outsiders. The same woman who might be a cook or maid in the houses of the white middle-class university professor by day, might be dancing the *bomba* with friends and family on Saturday night. The author is not ready to present as "typical" of the national character the practices of cultural resistance and innovation she finds in this dance. Rather this becomes noise, "the song and chorus are of a monotonous and strident intonation."[33] ("La canción y el coro son de entonación monótona y chillona.")

Likewise, Cadilla de Martínez's portrayal of the indigenous Taino resistance to the domination and brutality of the Spanish colonization relies on a number of racial fantasies shared by most Creole intellectuals of the time. Her story "Relieve indígena" is the rewriting of an episode from the conquest of the island of Borikén. The author draws her inspiration from the chronicler Fernández de Oviedo, who greatly praised the services that Becerrillo, a particularly savage attack dog tremendously feared by its Indian victims, rendered the conquistadors. According to the Spanish chronicler, the deeds of this assault dog during the conquest of the indigenous peoples of the Antilles deserved the payment of "a share and a half for his master, just like a crossbowman, in all the raids in which the dog took part"[34] ("parte y media para su amo como se daba à un ballestero en todas las entradas que el perro se hallaba").

It is interesting to note that the story of Becerrillo appears as part of a discussion about courage where the chronicler affirms there are animals that surpass many men in their intelligence and virtues. This is a partly veiled criticism of some Spaniards who, according to Fernández de Oviedo, lacked courage and good judgment. He reports that after a hard and bloody fight during which many Indians were captured, "Captain Diego de Salazar decided to throw to the dog an old Indian woman from among the prisoners he had taken there"[35] ("acordó el capitán Diego de Salaçar de echar al perro una india vieja de las prisioneras que allí se avian tomado"). As it turns out, this was a way of feeding the dog. The captain gives the woman what she believes to be a missive and asks her to take it to the governor at a short distance from there, "and he said this so that as soon as the old woman left and was no longer among the people he could release the dog after her"[36] ("é deçíale aquesto para que assí como la vieja se partiesse y fuesse salida de entre la gente, soltassen el perro tras ella"). The dog is let loose and very soon catches up with her. The woman, terrorized, kneels down to speak to the dog, imploring it not to harm her. Fernández de Oviedo's narrative retrieves the words of the old woman to the dog: "'Dog, Mr. Dog, I am going to take this letter to the governor,' and she showed him the letter or paper she was holding, and said to him, 'Don't hurt me, Mr. Dog.'"[37] ("'Perro, señor perro, yo voy á llevar esta carta al señor gobernador' é mostrábale la carta ó papel cogido, é deçíale, 'no me hagas mal, perro señor.'") Fernández de Oviedo relates that all the people present were astonished when they saw that the dog did not attack the Indian woman: "And the dog stopped at once when he heard her speak, and very gently came up to her and raised a leg and pissed on her, as dogs are wont to do at a corner, or when they wish to urinate, without doing her any harm."[38] ("Y de hecho el perro se paró como la oyó hablar, é muy manso se llegó á ella é alço una pierna é la meó, como los perros lo suelen haçer en una esquina, ó quando quieren orinar, sin le haçer ningún mal.") The Christians marveled at this incident, and when the governor Juan Ponce de León hears of this, he allows the woman to go free because, as the chronicler relates, "he did not wish to be less merciful to the Indian woman than the dog had been, and he ordered her released, free to go wherever she wished, and she did so"[39] ("no quiso ser menos piadosso con la india de lo que avia sido el perro y mandóla dexar libremente y que se fuesse donde quissiese, é assí lo fixo").

It would be fitting to ask if this episode of canine and soldierly generosity is not a repression and mystification of a terrible reality. Attack dogs like Becerrillo were part of the conquest of the Antilles and the rest of the Americas. Fernández de Oviedo wants to underline this fact, as he also gives us news of a cub of Becerrillo named Leonçico (little lion) that was brought on terra firma by Vasco Nuñez de Balboa as part of his troops. While Fernández de Oviedo tells us that he himself did not witness these particular actions of Becerrillo, he claims to have it on good authority that this actually took place. What is obvious is that he admires the dog's abilities and the great help that it afforded the conquistadors in their assaults and in the persecution of the Tainos. We should ask ourselves why Fernández de Oviedo includes such a story. This curious episode of what the Spanish called the "pacification" of the Indies, perhaps gives us a glimpse into the soldiers' uneasiness with the wanton violence of the period of conquest. This said, I want to put aside the question of invention that might be at work in this primary historical document, and examine the rendition of this event proposed by Cadilla de Martínez four centuries later. The author radically changes key aspects of the story of Becerrillo. In her version, we follow the fortunes of Iviahoca, a name the author gives to the Indian woman of Fernández de Oviedo's chronicle. She comes of her own accord to the Spanish camp where her son, called here Ocoro, was taken prisoner among a host of other Tainos. To save her son from a lifetime of slavery, Iviahoca bargains for her son's life by pleading with Captain Diego de Salazar to take her instead. Curiously, while the narrator tells us that the Spaniards used "lenguas," or translators, in their dealing with the Indians, there are moments when this recourse proves to be superfluous, and communication is achieved effortlessly. The Indian woman simply "seemed to realize that the Spanish Chief had an understanding and generous heart"[40] ("parecía darse cuenta del corazón comprensivo y bondadoso del Jefe español"). Incongruously, the Spanish usurpers are characterized as kindhearted. Captain Salazar is moved by the sorrow of the Indian mother and, accordingly, decides to make her his courier. In this rewriting Salazar does not throw her to the dogs, as Fernández de Oviedo tells us. The captain simply orders that she be watched by some soldiers sent after her, with the dog in pursuit, to ensure that Iviahoca will complete her mission. When Becerrillo corrals her, the old woman falls on her knees and begs the dog not to harm her.

Quite possibly the author found the original version, as narrated by Fernández de Oviedo, to be too truculent. For this reason the Becerrillo of our author's narrative is not as fierce: "As if understanding her words, or out of the miraculous and intuitive respect that old age inspires, the dog looked at the woman without harming her."[41] ("Como si comprendiera las palabras de ella, o por el milagroso e intuitivo respeto que inspira la ancianidad, el perro miraba sin hacer daño a la mujer.") Cadilla de Martínez also omits another detail present in the original chronicle. In her version the dog does not mark Iviahoca with urine. We are told that out of deference for motherhood Becerrillo urinates somewhere near her and allows her to complete her mission successfully. As a reward for Iviahoca's fidelity, both Ponce de León and Salazar free her son, but decide to keep her hostage. The son refuses to leave without his mother, declaring that he would rather be executed than have either his mother or himself enslaved: "I thank you, Christian, for your generosity, but I cannot accept it. . . . I prefer to be executed to purchasing my freedom at such a hard price, or be reduced to the harsh slavery your soldiers visit on us."[42] ("Agradezco, cristiano, tu generosidad para conmigo, pero no puedo aceptarla. . . . Prefiero que me den la muerte a tener libertad a tan duro precio y también a quedar reducido a una esclavitud bajo el duro trato que tus soldados dan a los nuestros.") Here again the author reorients Oviedo's text, eliminating the crudeness of the original by adding certain romantic elements. Ponce de León and Salazar are gentlemen who let the captives go, under the condition that they show gratitude and loyalty to the conquistadors. Mother and son are transformed into good savages capable of engaging in courteous exchange with the Spanish nobles. On closer inspection, however, only these two particular captives are singled out for liberation. The other Indians are quickly forgotten by the narrative. A magnanimous Ponce de León tells mother and son, "The nobility of soul that both of you have demonstrated with deeds and words assures us of your gratitude and that we can count on your loyalty."[43] ("La nobleza del alma que en vosotros dos ha quedado demostrada con hechos y palabras, nos asegura que seréis agradecidos y que podemos contar con vuestra fidelidad.")

Indian claims to freedom are rather ambivalently represented in this text. The author is careful not to make the Spaniards appear as usurpers of lands and of indigenous lives. In the disputes between Spaniards and Tainos both are described as valiant fighters for noble causes. Indian enslavement is mentioned without any indictment of the Spaniards for their bloody deeds. While the author refers in her footnotes to the mass suicides of Indians who, facing the destruction of their way of life, opted to poison themselves, the narrative sides with the conquistadors. Indigenous suffering is represented, yet it is also mystified by means of a neo-romantic and melodramatic discourse that conceals the true meaning of the conquest. In its mention of Indians who rebelled against the invaders and against the *encomienda* system, the text vacillates between admiration for the resistance of the Indians and an unabashed glorification of the conquest. When Iviahoca intercedes to liberate her son from what the author characterizes as a "shameful" slavery, it is not clear that such enslavement shames the conquistadors. The dishonor of slavery falls on the enslaved, reiterating a discourse that blames slaves for their victimization. This discursive strategy is often used to great effect by colonizers, slave masters, and those in power. Instead of being conceived as the exploitation and theft of the slave's life, bondage is represented as a moral condition of the enslaved, exonerating thus the master who reaps all manner of benefits from the system. In addition to this ideological reversal, the Indians of this fiction are represented as impossibly noble savages. The history behind the European fantasy of the noble savage is a long one. Suffice it to say here that the simplistic dichotomy of barbarian/noble savage was already present in Christopher Columbus's letters to the Spanish crown, a master text of Spanish colonial literature. From the first colonial encounters, Caribs, or rebellious savage Indians, are portrayed as the obverse of the peaceful Taino Indians. According to recent anthropology, however, the barbarism of the Carib Indian is a colonial invention.[44] It is more likely that the purported Caribs were displaced Tainos from the Lesser Antilles. The so-called Caribs possibly belonged to other Arawak groups who were unfriendly to Europeans. In short, savages happen to be all Indians who rebelled against colonial rule. After the "pacification" of the indigenous populations and the radical disruption of their cultures, the colonizers would import African slaves who ontologically and physically came to fill the vacancy left by the alarming decimation of the Amerindians.

While Iviahoca and her son run to the mountains to lead a *cimarrón* life free of the conquistador, the Spaniards keep their booty and are left firmly in control. They become the ones responsible for narrating this story of maternal love to their Creole descendants. They are implicitly designated as perpetual storytellers of this narrative of their origins as rulers. The Spaniards are positioned as bards and keepers of the oral tradition: "they rejoiced in telling their children the wondrous events of this dignified indigenous sketch."[45] ("se complacían en contar a sus hijos la singular maravilla de aquel dignificado relieve indígena.") It is appropriate nevertheless to ask what kind of story the children of the Spaniards pass on to future generations. In the end we are left with an apologia for the conquest in which the voice of indigenous resistance is muted in favor of the tale of how Creoles came to inherit the land and their means of maintaining social ascendancy. When read from this perspective, the story shows how lettered discourse allows the ideological heirs of the "discoverers" to maintain the power achieved by military force, intimidation, cruelty, and blackmail.

There is yet another aspect of this story that needs to be examined in the light of the *Generación del Treinta's* ideologies of gender. Cadilla de Martínez proposes that feminine forces or, rather, maternal abnegation has an important role to play in the history of the nation. She interprets the history of Taino defeat as the triumph of the maternal nation-building power of devotion. The first section of the story is dedicated to setting up the narrator's premise. We are told in the opening paragraph that "The love of mothers was always a source that fecundated with blood the fields of the homeland."[46] ("El amor de las madres fue siempre un manantial que fecundó con sangre a los huertos de la patria.") The power of this love has shaped the land and the people, giving them their unmistakable character. It "[a]imed towards the future; with sure foresight it has shortened distances . . . It was a magic feat that in our midst erased the word *impossible.* Overcoming all other feelings it has been a true aegis."[47] ("Flechando al porvenir, con acierto previsor, acortó distancias . . . fue brazo mágico que en nuestro paisaje borró la palabra *imposible.* Superando a todo otro sentir ha constituido una verdadera égida.") The author wants to infuse the cultural nationalist project with a feminine dimension. To do this she uses Amerindian women as symbols. On one side, the text proposes that maternal virtues are the true defense of the nation, not the deeds of the conquistadors. On the other side, her intention to describe women as eternal builders of the nation, well intentioned though it might be, ends up distorting the history of indigenous women, the victims of rape, forced labor, cultural dislocation, and other atrocities of the conquest. Historically, the colonial enterprise consumed the lives of these Indian women, as it did black women. Any discussion about transculturations in the Americas should take into account the violence and the multiple strategies of resistance that accompany these processes. Moreover, the maltreatment of Indians facilitated the enslavement of Africans and their descendants. Transculturations were effected on the very bodies of the transculturated subjects, with distinct results depending on the different access to power amongst the Spaniards, and the women and men of the subaltern groups.

Cadilla de Martínez reinscribes women as founders of the nation, while simultaneously retrieving a nationalist discourse where race and nation are practically synonymous. If *Hitos de la raza* is an illustration of those aspects that have somehow marked the development of the "race" and bestowed its distinctiveness, what are we to understand by race? Iviahoca and her son flee to the mountains—to become *cimarrones,* we can presume—so we have to ask when and how they become part of the race. This is never answered clearly. The discourse of Puerto Rican *mestizaje* (and the ideology of "racial democracy" devoid of conflict) that would be so enshrined by the 1950s is still being formulated in the 1930s. "Race" mixture is not dramatized in the story. Are we talking about a Puerto Rican "race," about a "homo portoricensis," a separate human group, literally the product of race mixing? The author does not answer this question here, but her other writings indicate that the purported homo portoricensis is a "pure" descendant of Spaniards, who could have a slight mixture of Indian and African ancestry.

Cadilla de Martínez relies heavily on a number of metaphors proper to nationalist discourse in order to fabricate her Puerto Rican race. Here we have again the nation as a collection of individuals who form a species or biological type, and the nation as a biological being. Such typologies presuppose the existence of distinctive national essences that distinguish a particular nation from other similar entities. As with other writers, the metaphor of "national type" or race allows Martínez to construct a genealogy of the homogeneous nation. In place of class conflicts she proposes a history of natural evolution.[48]

Puerto Rican's *casta, raza,* or race was Spanish, as understood by Cadilla de Martínez and most of her colleagues at the time. Never mind that "Spanishness" has always been a highly contested and unstable concept in Spain itself, as mentioned in Chapter 1. The Spanish Civil War (1936–1939) made it painfully clear that not all Spaniards shared the same vision for their country's social and political destiny, and that they too developed their own mythologies about race and regional identities. But, according to the author, as descendants of people of Spanish "blood," Puerto Ricans supposedly shared the worldview of their Peninsular ancestors. Yet, contradictorily, her story of Tate belies her racialist discourse by providing a voice—however muffled, distorted, and mediated—to the history of race mixing, resistance, accommodation, and the pain of servitude.

We must take into account in our reading of this work that Cadilla de Martínez was a folklorist who wrote in the genre of *tradiciones.* The work of the folklorist—collecting and editing the experiences and stories of a subaltern group for the consumption of educated classes—is fraught with ambiguities and inconsistencies that stem from the very nature of this kind of project. Yet, as we saw in Chapter 1, the subaltern subjects of colonialism and Creole hegemony were infinitely more dynamic and complex than any typological description of "our people and their culture" could do justice to. The new political and socioeconomic conditions of peripheral modernity effected dramatic changes in the behaviors, aspirations, and self-representations of the agricultural and industrial proletariat, who flatly rejected many older habits of being and deferential social practices. These social actors are not easily defined by the limits set by folklorist discourses.

The reductionism of cultural nationalism seeks to define rather than describe social reality, as Juan Flores notes.[49] These projects to record the past often edit out conflicting elements from their narratives. In most instances, as anthropologist Richard Handler points out, when folklorists, who often are part of a nationalist intelligentsia, set out to record traditions, "*they attempted to rejuvenate them,* both among the 'folk' who practiced them and among their urban compatriots."[50] Appropriation of the past often fulfills a present-day function. Of course, this does not mean that long-standing cultural practices do not exist; rather, they are always in a process of transformation and their existence implicates relations of power.

The last story of *Hitos de la raza*, "Palomas afectivas" ("Doves of Affection"), merits a short commentary because it sheds further light on the interrelations of gender, bourgeois feminism, the nation, and the role of race and class within the nation. The narrator of "Palomas afectivas" is a young woman who feels free to walk in the streets of her town and talk to whom she pleases. As she strolls through the outskirts of town toward the seaside, she meets her good friend Don Donato whose interesting conversation and vast knowledge of traditions and customs of the past instruct and inspire her. Although some of the townspeople deemed him a poet, a maniac, and a visionary, the narrator humorously tells us that "no one could deny that in his manners as well as in his behavior he always was a perfect gentleman"[51] ("nadie podía negar que tanto en sus maneras como en su trato era siempre un perfecto caballero"). In the safety that their mutual respect affords her, she is able to ponder philosophical questions, folkloric curiosities, and current events.

On this occasion the conversation centers on the deplorable state of the nation. Morally and economically the country is not what it used to be before the North American invasion. As Don Donato affirms, the flourishing native industries of yesteryear, as well as agriculture, are in decline.[52] The old man also laments that Puerto Ricans lack resolve and look to outsiders for their well-being. Politicians, for their part, lack idealism and dignity. As Don Donato sees it, only deeper national unity can heal the nation. But he assures the young woman that we should not look to "a racial, religious, or linguistic unity as was believed in the Middle Ages, and as is still believed by many Teutons."[53] ("una unidad racial, religiosa o lingüística como se creyó en el Medievo y como todavía lo creen muchos teutones.") Rather, the common experience of living on the same land and sharing similar ideals should be enough to bolster a sense of *civismo* (civic duty) and national consciousness. To achieve this, Puerto Ricans must endeavor to assess correctly the worth of what is theirs, labor to resist all conflicting influences, and rid themselves of hate and immorality.

This nationalist program, however, shuns any manifestations of militancy in the ranks of the working classes. As we see in his never-ending catalogue of the nation's ills, Don Donato adds to his list of woes the workers' misplaced idea of progress: "They misunderstand their rights, believing that they should only aspire to a good salary with minimum effort, reducing their work hours and the yield of their workdays."[54] ("entienden erróneamente su derecho: creen que solamente deben aspirar a ganar un buen jornal con el menor esfuerzo, reduciendo sus horas de trabajo y el rendimiento de sus jornadas.") The laborers' demands for better salaries and conditions are seen here as "jaibería" or uppityness and irresponsibility. Disregarding the inherent contradictions between capital and workers, Don Donato dreams of an industrial peace at the expense of workingmen and women. Nothing escapes the old man's criticism: education, the justice system, politics. Ultimately, he advocates "a new ideology if we want to be saved from decadence"[55] ("una nueva ideología si queremos salvarnos de la decadencia").

Yet even though in the first part of the story the concept of racial unity is discarded as a misguided belief that only Germans cling to, Cadilla de Martínez shrewdly recuperates it in the end. A better social organization "will produce a race perfected by its vitality and efficiency to endure"[56] ("dará una raza perfecta por su vitalidad y eficiencia para perdurar"). What is hoped is that Puerto Ricans will not imitate the murderous excesses of present day Europe. Even if "Teutonic" racial ideology is repudiated as excessive and characterized as sinful, the idea of one nation, one race, one language is maintained at the base of practically all nationalist ideologies. What Puerto Ricans need in order to respond more efficaciously to U.S. colonial exploitation, affirms "Palomas afectivas," is to reject egotistical individualism and constitute themselves into a better-organized nation. For this appeal to communalism to work, however, people of all social classes must still remain in their place. As proposed in the text, the dislocations of colonial capitalism are to be countered with notions of national identity and race, panaceas that will solve internal problems—class struggle—as well as external ones—colonial exploitation.

Even with references to the perils of the European war, the story ends on a greatly optimistic note. The young woman bids farewell to her friend and tells the reader, "With this hope both of us—my old friend and I—went assuredly to meet the new dawn."[57] ("Con esa esperanza los dos—mi viejo amigo y yo—nos fuimos tranquilos al nuevo amanecer.") The action of the narrative is set in 1913, a time when debates over woman suffrage and access to higher education and the professions for the lettered woman had already begun to take place. Ultimately, the discussions between Don Donato and the young woman are meant to demonstrate the narrator's competence as a thinker, just as suffragists were making perfectly clear that they were ready to exercise the vote and participate in the nation's affairs. Yet as enacted in the narratives we discussed throughout this chapter, this hope of a new dawn is limited, given that it is to be available to educated white women of certain means, not women of the working classes. I very much suspect that this fictional characterization could be a self-portrait of the author as a young woman.

The stories discussed here, "Tate," "Relieve Indígena," and "Palomas afectivas" illuminate a continuum of the views that women intellectuals of the time held about Puerto Rico's multiracial past. A close reading of Cadilla de Martínez's work reveals the particular position of the feminine Creole thinkers vis-à-vis the complex interaction among gendered racial discourses, class, and nation. Our author, the new Creole Miranda, speaks to impart her point of view. As I have suggested in my analysis of *Hitos de la raza*, however, this quest for national roots is limited. Women of indigenous and African descent are inscribed as minor protagonists in the national drama. Notwithstanding her desire to give voice to these women, her texts do not fully recognize the resistance and struggles that a fuller accounting for our multiracial history demands. To seek the voice of Sycorax and her sisters we will have to wait for other writers to take up the challenge.

CHAPTER 7

Negrismo, Literary Criticism, and the Discourses of White Supremacy

Racist ideology usually involves an esthetic appraisal of physical features, a mythology about traits of mind and personality correlated with physical features, and an almost mystical belief in the power of "blood" to elevate or to taint.
—St. Clair Drake, 1987

The Cultural Politics of Race

Our analysis of the *Asociación de Mujeres Graduadas de la Universidad de Puerto Rico* revealed the contradictory interests of women intellectuals who sought to reconcile their gender-based claims with the political projects of their class. Taking as our example their first journal, *Revista de la Asociación de Mujeres Graduadas de la Universidad de Puerto Rico,* I examined some of their projects and aims as well as the discursive strategies adopted by these women intellectuals as they forged a network that would support their aspirations. Attitudes regarding race, class, and the historical role of the intelligentsia as defender of the Puerto Rican personality were common to the whole generation, and the women of the *Generación del Treinta* shared a number of concerns, assumptions, and beliefs with their male counterparts. I propose that this unified outlook came at a cost—albeit not readily acknowledged—to the women who comprised this group. Women's participation in the nationalist discourse was welcomed, so long as they were willing to give up or minimize gender-based differences and agendas. Yet they also understood that there were some advantages to speaking as women, "como mujeres puertorriqueñas." This constraint was to foster, among many aspiring women intellectuals, the adoption of a rhetoric of "objectivity" and "professionalism" that the male intelligentsia in general assumed to be incompatible with women's concerns. Consequently, to ensure their authority in the public domain, they often constructed and projected a professional persona that strove to be "genderless." Opting at times not to pronounce themselves on matters that might be construed as overly feminine by their male counterparts, they tacitly but strategically accepted the discursive convention that required both addresser and addressee be thought of as male, the "universal" subject. This purportedly gender-neutral position, however, was not without contradictions.

As shown in previous chapters, Margot Arce and her group developed no oppositional analysis of the gendered power structure, but promoted instead the notion of opportunity for the skilled and educated. An ideology of professionalism, which by its middle-class nature is the purview of a few, enabled Margot Arce and the women of the *Asociación de Mujeres Graduadas* to maneuver and prosper in a tightly controlled intellectual field. Opening a space for women in the Creole intellectual field was no small accomplishment. The rhetorical position assumed by Mercedes Solá as she addressed the *Ateneo* in her 1922 "Feminismo" speech, and the one that Margot Arce takes in her lecture on the poetry of Palés Matos at the same institution in 1938, for example, are worlds apart. In Arce's discourse there is no need to apologize to the men in the audience, no false modesty, no hesitation. She delivers her lecture, "Los adjetivos en la 'Danza negra' de Palés Matos," to a willing audience that has come to listen to a scholar's explication of the poet's technical virtuosity. The photographic record of that night's conference shows a proud Arce surrounded by smiling male colleagues and Nilita Vientós, all of whom were assembled to pay homage to Luis Palés Matos[1] (see Illustration 8).

At the *Ateneo* tribute to Palés Matos, Arce is presented as an authority on his poetry, which she first analyzed in 1933. She, together with Tomás Blanco, provided what later became the canonical interpretations of Palés's black poetry. But Arce's explications, due to her institutional anchoring at the University, would more permanently enter the production of knowledge on Palés Matos's work. Moreover, her lectures and essays positioned her as a mediator in the heated controversy over the meaning of Palés's poetry. Race, racial identification, and racialist thinking were key elements of the Puerto Rican *negrista* controversy. This chapter analyzes this debate against the narrowly Hispanic interpretations of Puerto Rican culture and society. To this end, I examine Arce's *hispanismo* as it relates to the racist biases in place in the nationalist discourse of the *Generación*. By juxtaposing Margot Arce's ideas on the "Spanish race" in selected essays, and on the "Negro race" in her analysis of Palés Matos's *negrista* poetry, we see how a system of white supremacy provided the underpinnings for her critical writings. Ultimately, this racialized system informs how the *Generación* helped to shape the discourse of national identity in the three decades that followed.

Racism and the Intellectuals of the Agrarian Crisis

This chapter is divided into two parts. The first section reviews a number of assumptions at the base of the ideology expressed by leading members of the Creole intelligentsia during those years. The second section examines key texts by Margot Arce in an effort to trace the development of the orthodox interpretation of Palés Matos's "black poetry." Ultimately, even in the last reworking of her essays on Palés's *negrista* poems, people of African descent are positioned outside the realm of Puerto Rican culture. Whether the intent is inclusive or exclusionary, the alienation of Afro-Puerto Ricans from the national patrimony is a primary assumption in the writings of the "black poetry" debate.

Nationalist ideologies, as discussed in Chapter 1, have discursively deployed notions of race that declare the uniqueness of the surging nation. European nationalisms provided an opportunity for the exercise of racial doctrines that espoused the special mission of the nation and its race in the world.[2] "Racist ideology," St. Clair Drake tells us, "burgeoned during the late nineteenth century when ethnocentric evaluations made by Europeans were merged with theories of biological determinism and anthropometry."[3] The fabulous profits that the traffic in black bodies and labor provided Europeans and Euro-Americans, as well as the partition of Africa amongst a number of European nations, necessitated the propagation of the "Negro" stereotype in the press, the pulpit, and the theater (mainly as minstrelsy). The authority of scientific discourse was abused in order to propagate myths about Africans and peoples of African descent worldwide. Travel literature and evangelical campaigns were used as a basis for production of the spurious knowledge about the Continent and its peoples that accompanied the imperialist "scramble for Africa."[4] The discourses of Western nationalism and imperialism reassured Europeans that their plunder and destruction of the African continent was the logical outcome of white racial superiority, that is, ingenuity, enterprise, might, beauty, morality, kindness. Mystification abounded in these discourses whose imprecise usage of terminology could attribute inborn superiority or inferiority to ethnic groups, nations, and tribes. "Some anthropologists," St. Clair Drake tells us, "tried without success to restrict the word *race* to groups of human beings characterized by common anthropometric measurements of the cranium and the body and with certain combinations of hair type, skin-color and eye coloring."[5] In many countries, nonetheless, the popular press and politicians used "race" to mean nationality (the "British race" or the "French race"). Furthermore, St. Clair Drake explains, "The wide variation led to myths about some pure ancestral type that had once existed but had been diluted and sometimes *polluted.*"[6]

English historian Martin Bernal has explored the connections between the rise of nationalism in Germany and France, for example, and theories of racial supremacy and the mythification of "race." Bernal's first volume in his lengthy study of how the idea of "Ancient Greece" came to be fabricated by the German Romantics, proposes that Christianity, the idea of progress, racism, and romanticism combined to advance a notion of Ancient Greece as the root of Western-European-White civilization. In this view, which Bernal calls the Aryan Model of Greek history, Greeks are mistakenly understood as belonging to the "white" race. The accounts of ancient Greeks who testified to their civilization's connections to Egypt were dismissed by a nineteenth-century European scholarship that labored to discredit the Ancient Model of Greek culture. This Ancient Model maintained that the Greeks had many of their roots in Egypt.[7] The whitening of ancient Greece is but one example of European racialism and negrophobia. In addition to making Greece Aryan, some of the most renowned European intellectuals participated in the creation of a perverse racial fantasy that conceived of "races" as frozen stages of human evolution. For example the Comte de Gobineau, a paladin of this discourse of white-European racial supremacy wrote: "The black variety is the lowest and lies at the bottom of the ladder. The animal character lent to its basic form imposes its destiny from the moment of conception. It never leaves the most restricted intellectual zones . . . If its faculties for thinking are mediocre or even non-existent, it possesses in its desire and as a consequence in its will an intensity that is often terrible."[8] The idea of the overly sensual "nature" of people from the African continent appears as one of the mainstays of this defamatory literature. To cite de Gobineau again, "Many of the senses are developed with a vigour that is unknown to the two other races: principally taste and smell. It is precisely in the greed for sensations that the most striking mark of its inferiority is found."[9] But even well-meaning authors who wished to extol the virtues of this mythical exotic difference accepted the fantasy of the hypersensuality of dark-skinned people.

Aesthetic preferences assumed an almost dogmatic credence in the works of eighteenth- and nineteenth-century biologists. Notice what the French biologist Cuvier gives as an "objective" description of the characteristics of the white race. His description is blatantly subjective and self-interested. "The Caucasian (race) to which we ourselves belong," writes Cuvier, "is chiefly distinguished by the beautiful form of the head, which approximates to a perfect oval. It is also remarkable for variations in the shade of the complexion, and colour of the hair. From this variety have sprung the most civilized nations, and such as have most generally exercised dominion over the rest of mankind."[10] In the same breath Cuvier identifies the supposedly uniform shape of the head possessed by all white people with beauty, with civilization, and with the destiny to rule over all the rest of mankind. So much for science.

The history of race and racism is inseparable from that of the Atlantic World of the past five hundred years. Spanish and Portuguese colonialist expansion gave rise to the first debates over the nature of the peoples in the lands these monarchies had appropriated after 1492. While the operative concept in distinguishing the numerous Amerindian peoples they encountered had been religious—people were either Christian or pagan—as early as Columbus's letter of "discovery" to the Spanish Crown we see the notion of "cannibal" associated with some of the groups hostile to the Spanish. More would follow in the Bartolomé de las Casas and Juan Ginés de Sepúlveda debate.[11] This controversy had implications for the status of the conquered groups as usable labor force, and impacted the future of people of African descent in the centuries ahead. The concept of "cleanliness of blood" or *limpieza de sangre* had already been operative in Spain with regard to Moorish and Jewish converts before 1492.[12] It would gain added ferocity with the vast new riches and opportunities that the crown would administer in its "Golden Age," literally a period made so by the gold and silver from the colonies.

For close to two centuries now the process of interracial and intercultural mixing, known in Latin America as *mestizaje*, has troubled thinkers who labored to reconcile this reality with ideologies about nation building. In the nineteenth century, statesmen and intellectuals often saw race mixing as a national problem that deserved decisive remedies. Argentine thinker Domingo Faustino Sarmiento, for example, conceptualized the question as one of a struggle between European civilization and Indian barbarism. His proposed solution was to increase the immigration of whites from certain regions of Europe, ostensibly helping the nation to become more civilized, and to champion genocidal campaigns against Indians. In Cuba, on the other hand, abolitionist and Creole intellectuals like Jose Antonio Saco, who opposed the slave trade mainly, proposed that to counteract the massive influx of slaves during the nineteenth-century plantation boom, race mixing could be a way of augmenting a mulatto population that would act as a buffer between blacks and whites. There were by Saco's own reckoning already three million black people on the island.[13] As elsewhere in Latin America, this race mixing was to take place among white men and black and mulatto women, not between white women and black men. For his part, poet José Martí, the Creole father of Cuban independence, interested in fostering an egalitarian concept of the future nation and in surpassing racial conflict, asserted that there was or should be no such thing as black, white, or mulatto in Cuba, but that all people born on the island were Cubans regardless of race. Martí's essays and journalistic articles have done much to advance the concept of a *mestizo* America, somewhat influencing the various discourses on nationalism and modernity that flourished in the first three decades of the twentieth century.[14]

For a number of Latin American intellectuals in the early twentieth century, the figure of the *mestizo* and the *mulato*, when contained and disciplined, would come to represent the uniqueness of the nation. In response to the ever-increasing presence of the United States, Latin American intellectuals found in *mestizaje* a convenient metaphor for cultural and national difference. Mexico is a case in point. Writing in 1925 in the context of postrevolutionary Mexico, philosopher and former secretary of education José Vasconcelos formulated the novel concept of the "cosmic race," made up of a new more-perfected human being, an amalgam of all the races and herald of a better future. Yet even in his scheme Mexico's Indians were only "potentially" Mexican. For Vasconcelos race mixing had to be accompanied by acculturation into a Creole norm.[15] This idea had enormous sway among Latin American intellectuals and writers because, as we will see in my discussion, it provided a way of addressing racial and cultural heterogeneity without threatening the supremacy of Creole elites. For a century now, discourses proclaiming the *mestizo* or mulatto nature of Latin American nations have been propagated in both elite and popular culture. If at one level this is an official recognition of a historical and social reality, at another equally profound level the ideology of *mestizaje* has obscured the real social and class hierarchies that support, and in turn are supported by, light-skin privilege.

By the 1930s extreme Aryan models of the origins of European cultures were grotesquely played out by Nazis and their sympathizers. Less militant versions were accepted as "truths" by many educated and uneducated Europeans and Euro-Americans. The Puerto Rican *Generación del Treinta* was not immune to these racist currents.[16] Indeed, European discourses of hierarchical "racial evolution," together with centuries of slavery and identification with white supremacy, provided many intellectuals with an epistemological grounding for their discourse on Puerto Rican national identity.[17]

Blackness, *Blanchitude*, and the Misères of Representation

It is helpful to my analysis of the racialist underpinnings of the ideology of the Creole intelligentsia to think of racism as an unacknowledged given in the culture of the period. The Puerto Rican professional middle class, to which writers and critics belonged, was visibly white or very light-skinned. The idea of a self-identified mulatto or black intellectual was pretty much out of the question. The social structure did not foster or reward it. Instead, for reasons of class, the writers of the first half of the twentieth century assisted in the construction of a rhetoric that assigned a specific role to Puerto Ricans in the national culture and politics depending on their race, class, and gender.

Racial distinctions and identifications were always present in island society, but it took the appearance of the "black poetry" of Luis Palés Matos to initiate very public discussions of Puerto Rico's Afro-Caribbeanness. Margot Arce was the first *professional* literary critic to study Palés's "black verses," and she was credited as such by the literary press of the time. Palés's *negrista* poems were an explosive issue. Before the publication of his poetry and his press declarations and interviews, the Puerto Rican intelligentsia virtually ignored blacks as historical-cultural agents. Despite the very real presence of Afro-Puerto Ricans in the labor movement and in other areas of life, Creoles did not consider that people of African descent had anything (positive) to do with Puerto Rican life. For instance, it is not fortuitous that Afro-Puerto Rican Arturo Schomburg, after whom the great collection of black literature, thought, and art at the New York Public Library takes its name, was virtually unknown to Puerto Ricans then and now. This is not to say that all intellectuals were 100 percent "white." Racial purity (or impurity) is an illusion. But racial identification has real social effects in people's lives. Light-skinned Puerto Ricans were, and are still, in the business of "passing" for white and of denying the reality of race mixing in their families and in the larger society. Such negrophobia at the intellectual level, and at the level of everyday practices, makes it evermore difficult for darker-skinned Puerto Ricans to achieve social mobility and prestige. Historian Silvia Álvarez-Curbelo has recently explored the veritable quandary that Puerto Ricans posed to the U.S. armed forces in the first decades of the twentieth century. How to classify islanders was a problem that bedeviled the strict segregationist policies of the army. The invention of the fictional category "Puerto Rican white" was a partial solution for the abundance of light-skinned mulattos in the armed forces. In fact Álvarez-Curbelo's study shows that white upper-class Puerto Ricans supported segregation, especially at the officer level, while mulatto candidates insisted that Puerto Ricans should not be classified according to North American racial rules.[18]

The *Generación del Treinta*'s discourse on Puerto Rican culture and *nuestra personalidad como pueblo* generally put on a white face and denied the presence and action of people of African descent in the nation. It is undeniable that the projects of the intellectuals of the agrarian and cultural crisis, as José Juan Beauchamp calls the *Generación del Treinta*, stimulated and supported a national literary tradition. But to accord indiscriminately an anti-colonial status to their writings is misleading. At most, this intellectual production was only *narrowly* anti-colonial. It was critical of colonialism solely in the context of United States power over the island. At the level of its epistemological underpinnings, however, this literature owes too much to Eurocentric nationalism and discourses of white supremacy, which are always detrimental to a mixed-race people or to peoples of non-European descent.

Trend-setter Ortega y Gasset, as discussed in Chapter 1, was one of the most widely read Spanish intellectuals on the Puerto Rican literary scene. His reinterpretations of Spengler were studied and accepted by the *Generación.* Nationalist poet Juan Antonio Corretjer, a less prominent member of the group at the time, paid tribute to the memory of Spengler in a newspaper article published in San Juan in 1936, "Spengler: una proyección criolla." In this posthumous homage the Nationalist poet credits the German scholar with having inspired the island's intelligentsia. "Spengler's writings," says Corretjer,

> translated by Ortega *[sic]* and published by the *Revista de Occidente* had a profound effect on us. The news of the death of the German philosopher who awoke new interests in our young souls at the time of life in which new interests do the most good, brings some memories to mind that have always made me think of a Creole projection of Spenglerian thought that has produced a great poet (Palés Matos) and a new poetry.[19] (La obra de Spengler, traducida por Ortega *[sic]* y publicada por la *Revista de Occidente* surtió entre nosotros un efecto profundo. La noticia de la muerte del filósofo alemán que trajo a nuestras almas juveniles una inquietud nueva en la época de la vida en que mayor bien surten las inquietudes, trae a mi memoria unos recuerdos que me han hecho pensar siempre en una proyección criolla del pensamiento spengleriano que nos ha dado el fruto de un gran poeta [Palés Matos] y de una nueva poesía.)

Corretjer credits Palés Matos's readings of Spengler with providing the inspiration for the "black poetry" cycle. Furthermore, Corretjer states that Spengler is responsible for inspiring the vogue of African and black themes in the West. "There is no doubt that Spengler," asserts Corretjer, "was the intellectual apostle of the appearance of the black in the artistic hemisphere of Europe. The heyday of the black as an artistic novelty comes after the appearance of Spenglerian theories. . . . Palés read and was for a time under the spell of Spengler."[20] ("el apóstol intelectual de la aparición del negro en el hemisferio artístico de Europa no hay duda. El apogeo de lo negro como novedad artística sucede a la aparición de las teorías spenglerianas. . . . Palés leyó y estuvo algún tiempo bajo el hechizo de Spengler.") Corretjer, in his enthusiasm, credits Spengler with being the propagator of "lo negro" in the artistic and intellectual circles of Europe, a claim that cannot entirely be sustained by fact.

What is of interest here is that he addresses Pales's relationship to Spengler. Literary critic Aníbal González suggests, moreover, that Palés revised and reworked Spengler's ideas on race and culture in describing the culture of the Caribbean. According to Aníbal González, "In Palés's works, as in Vasconcelos's *La raza cósmica* and Pedreira's *Insularismo,* one sees this impulse to transcend Spengler without abandoning the conceptual apparatus of his philosophy, this intent to elaborate the theory of transculturation based on Spengler that he himself refused to formulate."[21] Philosophers like Spengler—writing for a European audience—inspired Caribbean writers like Luis Palés Matos—writing for a *criollo* audience—to rethink their concepts of race and culture. Yet the referents are quite different in the Caribbean. We should also keep in mind that slavery was a part of the island's history, and that, at the time, intellectuals of African descent in the United States, the Caribbean, and Africa were writing about race, politics, and art. Moreover, antiracist discourses produced by black people (such as slave narratives) already had an over 150-year-old history.

It would prove of little value to our discussion simply to argue over the problem of "good" versus "bad" portrayals of black people in *negrista* literature. Instead, this chapter examines in a new light the role that "race" plays in Palés's "black poetry." Why did Palés's *negrista* poetry cause such a stir at the time? Ultimately, we need to examine the ideas that have accompanied this poetry across the generations of Puerto Rican and foreign readers. We need to determine what is at stake for potential readers of *Tuntún de pasa y grifería* when questions regarding racist and dehumanizing portrayals of black people are raised in this and other *negrista* poetry.[22] Unfortunately, a number of critics have glossed over these questions without seriously considering the implications of charges of racism embedded in a poetry whose most overt themes are race and racial representation.

In 1927, nine years before Corretjer's tribute to Spengler, Palés Matos had published "El arte y la raza blanca," a short piece for the weekly literary magazine *Poliedro.* The interrelation of race and gender in this early essay by Palés reveals an apprehension over the "decline of the white race" predicated on the fear that white women were escaping the control of white men. Palés explicates some of Spengler's ideas on the causes for the decline of the "culture of the white race." As Spengler would have it, the so-called decline is due to the fact that modern white women have been derelict in their duties as procreators of the race, a real-life drama reflected in the modern artistic productions of the West. Palés quotes Spengler and adds some reflections of his own:

> 'Rather than having children,' says Oswald Spengler, 'these protagonists of Scandinavian theater have spiritual conflicts.' And, therefore, classic marriage, which is a pact of blood and consequently cosmic law, is supplanted in modern societies by a kind of contract of metaphysical affinities in which the important thing, that which is primordial and basic, is the absolute freedom of action of the two parties. In this way the mother, representing race, eternity, and nature drifts away, and the Scandinavian heroine, embodying a dry and literary progress, emerges. The matron is absorbed by the suffragist.[23] ('En lugar de tener hijos,' dice Oswaldo Spengler, 'estas protagonistas del teatro escandinavo tienen conflictos espirituales.' Y así, el matrimonio clásico que es pacto de sangre y por lo tanto ley cósmica, se ve suplantado en las sociedades modernas por una especie de contrato de afinidades metafísicas en donde lo importante, lo primordial y lo básico es la absoluta libertad de acción de los contrayentes. De este modo naufraga la madre que es raza, eternidad y naturaleza y surge la heroína escandinava que es entelequia, aridez y literatura. La matrona queda absorbida por la sufragista.)

White women, the quotation suggests, exist to keep in place the socio-racial hierarchy of a world dominated by white men. Race, gender, and culture are inextricably linked, so much so that when white women strive to assert their subjectivity, as in the case of the suffragists, the whole system of racial supremacy is threatened.[24]

Palés Matos accepts Spengler's propositions on white women's role in racial supremacy without much quarrel. Like Spengler, Palés believes the West to be in a perilous stage of over-intellectualization. This is extremely dangerous for the white race, since "science" has proven that too much cerebration drains white women of their sexual and reproductive energies. Palés further emphasizes this point by adding:

> Someone assures us that extended mental tension absorbs the ovarian hormone to the point of smelting it like a grain of energy in the furnace of the cerebral functions. Due to disturbances of a psychic nature brought on by this deviation of the ovarian functions artificially converted into suppliers of mental energy, women's sexual life becomes altered as a result of a state of insufficiency that definitively sterilizes her.[25] (Alguien asegura que la dilatada tensión mental, absorbe la hormona ovárica hasta el punto de fundirla como una gémula de energía en la hornalla de las funciones cerebrales. Amén de los trastornos de índole psíquica que trae consigo esta desviación de las funciones ováricas, convertidas artificialmente en surtidores de energía mental, la vida sexual de la mujer queda alterada sobreviniendo un estado de insuficiencia que la esteriliza definitivamente.)

The real danger and the gravest implication of this loss of fertility in the white female—mother of the white race—is that colored races will benefit from this racial decline, according to Palés's gloss of Spengler. This weakening of the white race provides a window of opportunity, as it were, for the dangerous invasion by the dark races.

One such example of this aggressive behavior, according to Palés, is the Bolshevik assault perpetrated by the "yellow" race on the "white" West. Palés unabashedly sides with the imperialist nations of the West, the bearers of Western civilization, and expresses horror at the possibility of such an "invasion." Palés is in fact rewriting history, for it is the white race that invaded and conquered much of the non-white world, as the events of the past 500 years have shown. "This voluntary process of weakening," writes Palés,

> is observed aggressively by the dark races. Add to this the constant action of Bolshevism, which is the most profound reaction registered by history of Asia against Europe, and we can observe in its pathetic contours the dreadful image of the future of the white race. The Russian actions are opening a bloody and dangerous breech in the European imperialist institutions. Once the dike of contention is broken, the Asian tidal wave, full of terrible threats, will pour out over the world. The agony of the West is visible.[26] (Este proceso de debilitamiento voluntario es observado agresivamente por las razas oscuras. Añádase a esto la acción constante del bolchevismo, que es la reacción más profunda de Asia con-

> tra Europa que registra la historia, y podremos apreciar en sus lineamientos patéticos el cuadro pavoroso del porvenir de la raza blanca. La acción rusa está abriendo una brecha sangrienta y peligrosa en las instituciones imperialistas europeas. Roto el dique de contención la marejada asiática, cargada de terribles amenazas se derramará sobre el mundo. La agonía de Occidente es visible.)

Palés, echoing Spengler, laments and warns readers that white civilization is on the wane.

The poet's adoption of Spengler's racialism elicits important questions about the colonized mentality in the Spanish Caribbean. Palés's knowledge of Europe, though considerable, is knowledge available in the so-called periphery. He left Puerto Rico for a pleasure trip to the Lesser Antilles and a short trip to New York in 1950.[27] Nonetheless, in this 1927 article he enthusiastically accepts the doctrines of racial superiority of the West. The racist theories of white supremacy concocted by European intellectuals misrepresented the history of the West as the self-generated product of a superior people forgers of all that is civilized. Palés, at this stage of his career, uncritically adopts their claims of cultural/racial supremacy. But for Palés and Spengler the stakes are not the same. Palés is writing in the Caribbean context, in a colonized country with a 375-year history of racial slavery on its own soil. Moreover, Luis Palés Matos descended from a formerly well-to-do *hacendado* family in the town of Guayama, a sugar cane growing region heavily populated by Afro-Puerto Ricans.

> *The novelty resides in the fact that the discourse on "savages" is, for the first time, a discourse in which an explicit political power presumes the authority of a scientific knowledge and vice versa. Colonialism becomes its project and can be thought as a duplication and fulfillment of the power of Western discourses on human varieties.*
> —V. Y. Mudimbe, 1988

The Shape of Cultural Nationalism in Margot Arce's Literary Criticism

That Puerto Rico's hold on whiteness was tenuous is exemplified in the stir that the publication of Luis Palés Matos's "black verses" caused in the literary and intellectual environment of the early 1930s. Palés Matos's call for the creation of an Antillean poetry that would better reflect the racially mixed character of Puerto Rican culture provoked reactions as varied as outrage, derision, fear, and applause in different sectors of the reading public.[28] Palés, in the famous November 13, 1932 interview given to Ángela Negrón Muñoz, "Hablando con Don Luis Palés Matos," had stated that the creation of a literature with an Antillean character was a necessity at this historical juncture.

"The poet who abstracts himself from his genuine element," according to Palés, "under the pretense of a universalist aspiration and of transcendentalism, is a fish out of water and will only create academic poetry of interest to intellectuals."[29] ("Poeta que se abstrae de su genuino elemento, so pretensa aspiración de universalidad y trascendentalismo, es pez fuera del agua, y sólo realizará una poesía académica para uso de los intelectuales.") Moreover, Palés saw the Spanish Caribbean's black heritage as fecundly coming into cultural and social existence with the transculturation of Spanish and African cultures into a new entity. It is because of this socio-cultural reality that a truly Caribbean poetry needs to engage the black element. In this he feels a kinship with Cuba and the Dominican Republic. According to Palés, blacks are an important racial nucleus, "that has mixed with us nobly and that due to its fertile, strong, and lively nature, has imprinted unmistakable qualities on our psychology, giving it nothing less than its true Caribbean character. I am referring to the Negro"[30] ("que con nosotros se ha mezclado noblemente y que por lo fecundo, lo fuerte y lo vivo de su naturaleza ha impreso rasgos inconfundibles en nuestra psicología, dándole precisamente su verdadero carácter antillano. Me refiero al negro"). For Palés, this new Antillean poetry is not a mere poetic "ism." It is a cultural imperative. Readers can infer that where in Europe the "black vogue" is a fashionable appropriation, in the Caribbean, for Palés, the "black vogue" has an immediate cultural significance. Puerto Rican popular culture is the product of racial mixing, as Palés underscores:

> I do not know, then, even one collective trait of our people that does not show the imprint of this delicious mixture from which the Caribbean character resounds with its true tone. To deny it would be prudish. This is our reality and upon it we should construct a native and representative culture with nobility, with pride, and with a feeling of total satisfaction with ourselves.[31] (No conozco, pues, un solo rasgo colectivo de nuestro pueblo que no ostente la huella de esa deliciosa mezcla de la cual arranca su tono verdadero el carácter antillano. Negarlo me parece gazmoñería. Esta es nuestra realidad y sobre ella, debemos edificar una cultura autóctona y representativa con nobleza, con orgullo y con plena satisfacción de nosotros mismos.)

In essence, Palés called for a recognition of an accomplished fact in Puerto Rican national culture. It is clear that he refers in this interview to the national popular subject—the culture of common folks. And where others had seen Puerto Rico's black heritage as a weakness, he saw a source of strength and vitality. Yet as critic Isabelo Zenón Cruz explains, the very terms of inclusion make impossible the poet's purported inclusiveness: "Palés has separated black people from the us; he has segregated them precisely at the moment in which he sees them 'mixed' with 'us.' He has denied blacks when he presumes that 'he lives physically and spiritually with us.'"[32] Zenón Cruz adds, "Not only does Palés fail when he denies the us (Puerto

Ricanness) to blacks, since it belongs to them as much as to whites, but also by imagining a 'primitive nature' of blacks, product of the interested imagination of white exploiters. No such primitive nature exists, given that there is no essence but a situation born of a virulent exploitation, of a shameful and systematic alienation that European and white Creoles have imposed on black people."[33] Zenón Cruz's analysis points to a fundamental ambivalence in the poet's vision of the role of Afro-Puerto Ricans within national culture. The reasons for the *partial* acceptance of blacks are not idiosyncratic but historically linked to the very real desire that the Spanish and Creoles have had to secure their supremacy. This desire to maintain *criollo* ascendancy is enacted in Palés's *Tuntún de pasa y grifería* itself.

Julio Marzán reminds us that in the 1920s Luis Palés Matos's poetry effected a stylistic and thematic revolution not only in Puerto Rican literature, but in the entire context of Latin American letters. First, the poet stressed the inclusion of the people's everyday speech, welcoming what were then "unpoetic" colloquialisms into his poetry. Marzán highlights Palés's use of "Boricua" or Puerto Ricanisms, irony, and poetic personae in preference to the lyric voice and first person favored earlier. Palés Matos announced this new attitude in "Preludio en boricua" and "Canción festiva para ser llorada," and reaffirmed it in "Plena del menéalo." Into the defensive cultural context of the time, which favored a stodgy purist use of Spanish or a simplistic adoption of "jibarismos," Palés Matos's appropriation of surrealism prefigured the later wave of Latin American "anti-poetry." Marzán places Palés's *negrista* poems within his overarching poetic renewal project that "combined 'white' poetic structures with 'black' unconventional humor, social satire, drumbeat rhythms, and most important, an unprestigious, African-derived vocabulary."[34] The critic reminds us that Palés's "Menú" should be read as a satirical *ars poetica* in which the poetic persona of the restaurateur ingeniously offers the reader a "menu" of poetic styles. As Marzán puts it, "The poem celebrates the poetic possibilities of this Caribbean treasure of images from which the host is able to whip up unheard-of creations."[35]

Here is a sample:
palm trees tossed in Antillean cyclone,
slow-flame broiled sugar cane thicket
soufflé of windblown plantain groves,
torte of flame trees in their ink, . . . [36]

(Aquí te va una muestra:
palmeras al ciclón de las Antillas,
cañaveral horneado al fuego lento,
soufflé de platanales sobre el viento,
piñón de flamboyanes en su tinta, . . .)

Palés's local talk and humor bring to the period a revolutionary stylistic liberation, a point Marzán argues about the totality of the poet's oeuvre. Marzán further proposes that Palés's *conceptismo* is intended to explore the metaphysical world in search of a "numen." "Throughout his career," according to Marzán, "Palés reiterated his obsession with the frontier where the mundane touches the spiritual or metaphysical, which he perceived as the true essence of things. His poems therefore are structured to take the reader on a passage to a metaphysical realm and ultimately to an encounter with one of a number of imagistic representations of the essential that informs the soul of the individual, the collectivity, and the physical world."[37] As early as 1927 three of Palés's poems were published in Madrid through the mediation of Federico de Onís and José Robles Pazos, who had visited the island a year earlier. Marzán suggests that the defensive hispanophilic responses from Creoles were a reaction to the poet's recognition in Spain, since many Puerto Rican intellectuals were irked by the association with blackness that is integral to the *negrista* verses.[38]

The novelty and true meaning of Palés's challenge to the intelligentsia can be pieced together by looking at the responses of his peers to his provocative criticism of the *criollo* lack of vision. The response was immediate and unequivocal. J. I. de Diego Padró's "Antillanismo, criollismo, negroidismo" was published a scarce week after the newspaper interview.[39] Palés's friend and avant-garde (diepalista) collaborator sees absolutely no need to consider Puerto Rico's black heritage since black folks have no culture that in any way approximates the sophistication of Euro-American cultural achievements. As de Diego Padró puts it, "In the confrontation and shuffling of these two cultures, one superior and the other inferior, the black culture, as is natural, began weakening and losing many of its native contents. Until the black assimilated and adopted wonderfully the culture that came to us from the West."[40] ("En la confrontación y barajamiento de estas dos culturas, una superior y otra inferior, fue debilitándose como es natural, y perdiendo contenidos autóctonos la cultura negra. Hasta que el negro asimiló y adoptó a las mil maravillas la cultura que nos llegó de Occidente.") Spanish descendants have not changed, even though the tropics might have slightly affected their liver and physical features. De Diego Padró iterates that "the quantum of population that coexists in the Caribbean, despite the diversity of color and origin, is of an eminently European psychological and cultural structure."[41] ("el quantum de población coexistente en las Antillas, pese a la diversidad de color y origen, es de estructura psicológica y de cultura eminentemente europeas.) The discussion centers mainly on uncomplicated theories of cultural transmission and survival. In short, as a *criollo* de Diego Padró champions the colonialist perspective without ever mentioning it by name. What is missing here is a discussion of colonialism's effects on culture—that of the colonized elite as well as that of the subordinate classes.

Palés responded to the attacks with the essay "Hacia una poesía antillana" in which he expanded on his earlier interview. He reaffirms that both the Spaniard and the African have changed through intermixing of race and culture. According to Palés, in the Spanish Caribbean it is the mulatto who is the true representative of the majority of the population. It is in "the new mulatto type toward which has been displaced the vital accent of the three islands"[42] ("el nuevo tipo del mulato hacia el cual se ha desplazado el acento vital de las tres islas"). Palés also rejoins that there is no such thing as the purely "universal" in art and culture: "That ineffable utopian limbo of unlimited ideal extension that we call *universal culture*," is a chimerical pursuit in and of itself according to Palés.[43] ("Ese inefable limbo utópico de extensión ideal ilimitada que llamamos *cultura universal*.") The poet adds, "And the artist who, motivated by a fallacious goal of universalism, looks down upon his genuine element and takes off flying toward those zones of mirage is irrevocably lost in a chaos of words, concepts and images that lack all human meaning."[44] ("Y el artista que acuciado por un falaz objetivo de universalismo, desdeña su genuino elemento y se dispara en vuelo hacia esas zonas de miraje, se pierde irremediablemente en un caos de palabras, de conceptos y de imágenes horros de toda significación humana.") Palés ends his essay with a repetition of his original call to the Caribbean poets of Puerto Rico: "Let us forge, then, a Caribbean poetry." ("Forjemos, pues, una poesía antillana.")

In the same issue of the newspaper another hostile reaction was printed in conjunction with Palés's response. The title of Luis Antonio Miranda's retort to the interview captures the gist of his position, "El llamado arte negro no tiene vinculación con Puerto Rico."[45] ("So-called black art does not have any relation to Puerto Rico.") Miranda was a journalist and poet who had been the editor of *Poliedro*, the organ of the avant-garde movement on the island. He absolutely negates the existence of a Spanish Caribbean culture: "there is no Caribbean type just as there is no Caribbean culture" ("no existe un tipo antillano como no existe una cultura antillana"). Instead, Miranda asserts, "the Caribbean is defined to perfection in the typical continental Iberian type"[46] ("el antillano está definido a perfección en el tipo ibérico continental"). Nothing in Puerto Rican popular culture has African (or for that matter, Indian) origins, according to his delusory ethnocentrism: "On our island there is no mix of cultures at all except for the exoticism that has come to us from the north [U.S. cultural imperialism]."[47] ("En nuestra isla no hay mezcla alguna de culturas, a excepción del exotismo que nos ha llegado del norte.") Palés's confrere is horrified by the thought that black "primitivism" might be found anywhere in Puerto Rico. Black or Antillean poetry would be a "throwback" in Puerto Rico's race toward civilization: "Such art, which is clearly a *throwback*, has no relation to our island."[48] ("Tal arte, que es un positivo *salto atrás*, no tiene vinculación con nuestra isla.") Miranda's cultural paranoia stems from the "whitening" project itself, which inevitably harbors the perpetual danger of "regression." Following this whitening logic, Puerto Rican culture, like black Puerto Ricans, would eventually rid itself of all traces of black parentage—and meticulously stamp out any lingering traces of blackness understood as savagery.

Months later Palés is defended by his brother Vicente in "Sobre una poesía antillana," to which the learned avant-garde poet Graciani Miranda Archilla responded in February of 1933 with "La broma de una poesía prieta en Puerto Rico"[49] ("The Joke of a Black Poetry in Puerto Rico"). In this retort Miranda Archilla reaffirms his belief in poetry as a purely aesthetico-philosophical endeavor beyond localisms or even ideology—an ideological stance in and of itself. The controversy is in full swing when Margot Arce enters it. She will find herself in the midst of a disagreement with Tomás Blanco after the publication of her first essay on the subject.

The questions raised by Palés's "black verses" were unsettling for the white *criollos* who had a vested interest in maintaining virtually complete racial and class segregation. European racial doctrines, which placed whites at the zenith of human evolution and blacks at the bottom, enjoyed wide acceptance among the Puerto Rican literate classes. This corresponded to the very real subservient social status of people of African descent, who were likely to occupy (with a few exceptions) the lower rungs of the job market and social hierarchy. This elite implicitly nodded approval to these racist doctrines in order to provide intellectual justifications for their race-based privileges. We should note that the poems in question were labeled "verso negro" from the very beginning of their publication, even as Palés himself argued that he was writing Antillean poetry.

Yet Palés's *negrista* project, with its stated intent of including Puerto Rico's black heritage in the debate over national culture, raises questions that still need to be addressed. And while the great poetic achievements of Palés Matos (linguistic and thematic renovation, aesthetic daring, use of humor and localisms) can in no way be overlooked, the poet's desire to engage cultural diversity is problematic given the very terms upon which this effort is predicated. "Black poetry" or *poesía negrista* in the Puerto Rican context is poetry that is only thematically "black." It is not poetry necessarily written by people of African descent. Thus, "el tema del negro y de lo negro" are equivocal signifiers whose very ambiguity is endemic to the so-called "black poetry" project. Like the white abolitionist writers of the nineteenth century, most readers and critics of this poetry firmly believed that a white author could write poetry that would "interpret and penetrate the black soul." Margot Arce's essays on this topic were no exception. From her relatively privileged position in the literary elite, she helped to validate tendentious interpretations of the experiences of black people and of black cultural production.

The following section discusses some of Arce's contributions to this particular dialogue on Puerto Rican culture. Examination of her essays on Luis Palés

Matos's *negrista* poetry allows us to delineate her role in positioning people of African descent outside the realm of *lo puertorriqueño*, the national community. My textual analysis centers on a number of Arce's well-known essays about the *negrista* poetry of Palés and her later revisions of two of these essays. The earlier 1930s versions, which appeared in the press, are compared with those in her 1950 anthology *Impresiones: notas puertorriqueñas.*

Arce's "Los poemas negros de Luis Palés Matos" must be placed in the context of a heated controversy over the meaning of these poems and over the meaning of the term "black poetry."[50] At the time of the debate the poems had only been published in journals and newspapers. The appearance of Palés's collection *Tuntún de pasa y grifería* would have to wait until 1937. Arce entered the contention as one of the defenders of Palés and remained throughout the years an important agent in the poetry's canonization. It is interesting that Arce is never explicit about her role in the affair in her famous 1970s prologue and edition of Palés's works for the Ayacucho publishing house. There, as before, she situated herself outside the controversy, as the voice of objectivity.

In her 1933 address delivered at the University of Puerto Rico, Arce explains that Palés's "black verses" represent one of the poet's greatest achievements up to that date.[51] She traces his development from his provincial Guayama origins, to his early verses and readings, to the appearance of his first proper "black poem" in 1926, "Pueblo negro."[52] The author mentions the recent polemic over the poems in the press and her conviction that Palés's originality and poetic maturity are something new on the island's literary scene. She also states her understanding of poetry as closed and autoreferential and, consequently, that her analysis is subject to controversy. "All poems are their own self-enclosed world," Arce cautions, "which justify themselves and which go beyond rhetoric and logic."[53] ("Todo poema es un mundo cerrado y suficiente que se justifica a sí mismo y que está más allá de la retórica y de la lógica.") In the 1950 *Impresiones* version her opening paragraph places Palés as the recognized figure he had become and mentions the international diffusion of his poetry as testimony to its artistic merit. She also deletes the political reference to 1898 as a "tragic and decisive year," and to Puerto Rico's limited cultural environment.

Arce's analysis addresses the complexity and technical mastery of Palés's poems. She also praises his work for having achieved "a truly universal stature" by virtue of the poet's position within the modernist discourse on blackness. For her, Palés's universal appeal stems from his association with European trends. She remarks that "Even if they were worth nothing else, Palés's black poems would be valuable for the single act of having incorporated into Puerto Rican poetry a theme of current and almost universal interest: the theme of the black man and blackness. Modern people have been concerned with African music, sculpture, and myths to the point of incorporating them into the artistic manifestations of culture."[54] ("Si no tuvieran otro valor, los poemas negros de Palés valdrían por el solo hecho de haber incorporado a la poesía puertorriqueña un tema de actualidad, de interés casi universal: el tema del negro y de lo negro. La gente moderna se ha preocupado por la música, la escultura y los mitos de los africanos hasta el extremo de incorporarlos a las manifestaciones artísticas de la cultura.") Arce includes Palés and herself among the "gente moderna," that is, among modern, civilized, white people. She further explains the appeal of this new theme: "It is probable that we are living through one of those theoretical approaches to nature in opposition to civilization."[55] ("Es probable que estemos viviendo uno de esos acercamientos teóricos a la naturaleza por oposición a lo civilizado.") Arce thus constructs a binary opposition between nature and primitivism—"lo africano"—and civilization and modernity—"lo europeo." In its rewriting for her book *Impresiones*, she removes the mention of Pablo Picasso and jazz music as expressions of the preoccupation of modern people with the culture of Africans.

Palés's black themes have—above all else—a literary genesis, according to Arce. She reminds us of the poet's familiarity with the works of Blaise Cendrars, Leo Frobenius, and Langston Hughes. She also points to the influence that the rhythms of black popular dances had on his poetry. She submits a third notion with somewhat less enthusiasm: Palés was also inspired by the island's fairly large black and mulatto population. But how did Afro-Puerto Ricans inspire the poet? As Arce sees it, while Palés specifically assimilated the rhythms of Puerto Rican black music into his poetry, he did not make use of other black Puerto Rican cultural manifestations.[56] She claims that the relationship of "black poetry" to a Puerto Rican socio-historical referent is limited: "Of the Puerto Rican black, Palés has incorporated into his poetry only the rhythm of their popular dances."[57] ("Mas del negro puertorriqueño, Palés ha incorporado a su poesía únicamente el ritmo de sus danzas populares.") Furthermore, Arce asserts that the blacks in Palés's poems are not really Puerto Rican at all. She writes, "He is an exotic black: one from the African rain forest, the Cuban voudou practitioner, or the superstitious black witch from the jungles of Haiti. He is a theoretical, hypothetical, abstract black, whom Palés has not seen and whom he has created using data of literary origin."[58] ("Es un negro exótico: el de la jungla africana, el ñáñigo de Cuba, o el negro supersticioso y hechicero de la selva de Haití. Es un negro teórico, hipotético, abstracto, que Palés no ha visto y que ha creado con datos de procedencia literaria.") This statement provoked a public rebuke by Tomás Blanco that forced Arce to modify some of her views in a second article that she titled "Más sobre los poemas de Luis Palés Matos" (or "Rectificaciones" for the 1950 edition). But even in her retraction Arce holds fast to the idea of the bookish referents in Palés's literary representations. One of her unacknowledged aims is to separate Puerto Rico from the purported backwardness and savagery associated with Afro-Caribbean religious practices, practices mentioned prominently in the poetry. In the *Impresiones* version of "Los poemas negros" she responds to the reproach over the erasure of Afro-Puertoricans by adding that the black theme in Palés has a social as well as a literary genesis. ("Tiene en parte una génesis social y otra literaria."[59]) While Arce always hesitated when it came to the representation of blackness in the case of Puerto Rico, she has no qualms about doing so in the case of the other islands—the *Antillas negras*, especially Haiti. In that case she finds a seamlessly "truthful" representation. Arce believed that Palés, in poems such as "Elegía del duque de la mermelada" ("Elegy to the Duke of Marmalade") and "Lagarto verde" ("Green Lizard") masterfully exposed the "true nature" of the Europeanized Haitian elite. As she writes in 1933, "Ancestral and primitive superstition *is more powerful* than the false refinement of the salons. The little count of the lemonade can behave as if in Versailles, but just one word would suffice to strip him of the artifices of etiquette and awaken in him the old habits of his relatives in the jungle."[60] ("La superstición ancestral y primitiva *es más poderosa* que el refinamiento postizo de los salones. El condesito de la limonada puede portarse versallescamente, mas una sola palabra bastaría para desnudarle de los artificios de la etiqueta y despertarle los viejos resabios de sus parientes de la selva.") In the later version she writes, "Ancestral and primitive superstition *appears as* more powerful than the false refinement of the salons."[61] ("La superstición ancestral y primitiva *aparece como* más poderosa que el refinamiento postizo de los salones.")

Ethnic essences were not new to Arce; the concept was fundamental to her critical approach. In 1930, before these essays on Palés Matos were published, she had written a commentary on ethnic-nationalist essences entitled "El carácter español." No doubt she followed in the footsteps of the nationalist Spanish generation of '98, whose copious literature on the Spanish "spirit and character" evinced an ambiguous approach to modernization, to the Spanish imperial past and present loss of power, and to the variegated histories of the diverse peoples who had inhabited the Peninsula. Arce accepted and proceeded to illustrate the workings of that generation's racial and cultural mythologies in the Puerto Rican environment.

Palés's poetry, as she reads it, literally captures and renders the "spirit of the black race," which his superior vantage point converts into poetic "truth." But what is the "truth" that this poetry reveals? To answer this query Arce compares the Cubans Nicolás Guillén and Emilio Ballagas with Palés Matos. Taking pains to elevate the Puerto Rican poet to the status of the baroque master Góngora, Arce distinguishes Palés's art from that of the mulatto Guillén and the white Ballagas both of whom she regards as cultivating a less refined poetry:

> Luis Palés Matos is a poet of high culture, or rather, he is a *culterano*.[62] The artifice of his poetry is manifested in the truly meticulous care—*à la* Góngora—that he dedicates to the formal and metaphoric part of his work. He distances himself from the popular poetic modes; he interprets the black as a civilized and skeptical white. He thereby differentiates himself essentially from Nicolás Guillén and Emilio Ballagas.[63] (Luis Palés Matos es un poeta culto, mejor dicho culterano. El artificio de su poesía se manifiesta en el cuidado verdaderamente gongorino que dedica a la parte formal y metafórica. Se aparta de los modos poéticos populares; interpreta lo negro como un blanco civilizado y escéptico. Se diferencia así esencialmente de Nicolás Guillén y Emilio Ballagas.)

Arce testifies that Palés's capital achievement lies in the formal aspects of his "black poetry" which remind her of the Spaniard's technical virtuosity.[64] Unfortunately she makes troublesome leaps in logic that try to link a formalist analysis of Palés's poems to valuations of their worth due to the poet's whiteness on one side, and choice of themes on the other side. I have no quarrel with her assessment of his neo-baroque aesthetic, or his brilliant use of metaphors. After all, Palés can describe a rooster and cock fight in a 1937 poem as "disparo de plumas luminosas" ("shot of luminous feathers"), the ring as "rueda de luz" ("wheel of light"), and the emotions surrounding the animal as "ron de plumas que bebe la Antilla brava y tórrida" ("rum of feathers that the fierce and torrid Antille drinks"). Palés takes a topic full of sappy *jibarista* potential and gives us images of surprising freshness and energy. His appropriation of popular speech and Puerto Ricanism goes much further than Arce envisions, however. No serious poet in his environment would have dared to use undignified words like "cuajo," "hedionda," "sofrito," and "bochinche" (curdle, fetid, stir-fried, riot, and gossip) with such gusto. Furthermore, Palés in no way saw that Puerto Rican Spanish was an imperiled or debased vehicle of communication.

"We Caribbeans are not pure Hispanics," Palés had said in the interview for *El Mundo:* "We are Spaniards with mulatto manners and a black soul; the black factor acts in Caribbean culture as an isolator or as a precipitating agent."[65] ("Los antillanos no somos hispánicos puros," "somos españoles con maneras de mulato y alma de negro; el factor negro actúa en la cultura antillana como aislador o como agente precipitante.") Note that for Palés, while Puerto Ricans are still Spanish, the "black factor" provides Puerto Ricans with a large measure of (exoticized) difference. Palés Matos believed, as did all his generation, that races had innate characteristics that race mixing could reshuffle with varied results. He also thought that culture was a quasi-biological emanation of race. About the black man Palés writes:

> His attributes, *filtered through the mulatto,* evidently influence all the manifestations of our popular life. In the field of sports . . . In music he imposes the *plena,* the *son,* and the *mariyandá* . . . In politics, he gives us his passion, his

> exuberant verbosity, his elastic attitudes and his strange magnetism, that acquire in the mulatto an overwhelming mystical strength.[66] (sus características, *tamizadas en el mulato*, influyen de modo evidente en todas las manifestaciones de nuestra vida popular. En el campo de los deportes . . . En la música impone la plena, el son y el mariyandá . . . En la política, nos da su pasión, su verbosismo exuberante, su elasticidad de actitudes y su extraño magnetismo, que adquiere en el mulato una especie de fuerza mística arrolladora.)

Palés carefully stressed that those mulatto and black characteristics are present in the *popular* culture of the island. He did not include the elite in this statement, for it is clear that they are not part of "nuestra vida popular." This puts the elite in a quandary. Any successful ruling group has to project its class interests as those of the majority of the people. And the majority has to identify—in some measure—with the interests of the elite. As discussed earlier, acceptance of Puerto Rico's mixed-race heritage was a necessary political strategy embraced by intellectuals like Tomás Blanco and the populist alliance of the *Partido Popular Democrático*. Palés's detractors within the elite were not willing to consider his ultimately mild propositions. My criticism of Palés's reduction of the black experience to a mere cultural catalyst does not occlude the significance of his nonetheless bold stance, in the racist cultural context of the 1930s, regarding Puerto Ricans' relationship to an African motherland.

By insisting that black people and their experiences are fundamental to Antillean life and poetry, Palés rejected the hispanophilia and negrophobia of the *Generación del Treinta*. Arce can commit herself only in part to Palés's project. She views Palés's well-publicized statement on the role of peoples of African descent in Caribbean culture, and especially in Puerto Rico with skepticism. In her 1933 essay the critic concedes that the black presence is a differentiating element of Caribbean culture: "Por lo menos no podemos negar que el negro es un ingrediente diferenciador."[67] But in the early version she is reluctant to envision the profound cultural implications of Palés's thesis. She cautiously calls for a more thorough study of the black presence in Puerto Rico: "Sería preciso un poco más de investigación minuciosa para asegurarlo."[68] She deletes both statements for her 1950 version. In 1933 Arce is emphatic in her denial of the idea that black culture is the culture that gives Puerto Rico its Caribbean character. She claims that "it seems a bit risky to affirm that [black influence] might be . . . distinctive"[69] ("parece un tanto arriesgado afirmar que [la influencia negra] sea . . . caracterizante"). The characterizing racial and cultural influences are Spanish in her view and the view of most members of the *Generación del Treinta.*

Interestingly, from the perspective of white privilege, racism and its social expression are euphemistically called "the race problem." Arce sees in Palés's "Canción festiva para ser llorada" a faithful rendition of the troubles of the Caribbean and of Puerto Rico, including what she calls the "problema étnico." She alludes to the question but will not explain any further. Palés gives us, as Arce puts it, "a marvelous synthesis of the problem of the Caribbean: political, economical, racial and psychological drawn with irony and finesse"[70] ("síntesis maravillosa del problema del Caribe: político, económico, racial y psicológico expuesta con ironía y finura"). This later becomes in *Impresiones*: "In an admirable synthesis he lays out the whole problem of the Caribbean in its political, economic, social and psychological aspects; the tone is tinged with bitter irony."[71] ("En admirable síntesis expone todo el problema del Caribe, en sus aspectos políticos, económicos, sociales y psicológicos; el tono se matiza de acre ironía.") She omits the mention of the "race problem." This celebrated poem was one of Palés's overtly anticolonial compositions.

One of the most important revisions made refers to the question of point of view in the poems. Where Arce wanted to see objectivity, she later sees a subjective interpretation of the themes of *Tuntún*. In 1933 she wrote:

> The themes are: descriptions of towns and of black customs, evocations of African mythology, rituals and magical superstitions, visions of black landscapes and geography, a satire of the aristocracy of Haiti, and humorous contrast between the culture of whites and blacks. In dealing with these themes, Palés takes *an objective point of view* and interprets blackness with a certain complacent and skeptical condescension typical of the white man who doubts everything, even his own culture.[72] (Los temas son: descripciones de pueblos y de costumbres negros, evocaciones de la mitología africana, ritos y supersticiones mágicas, visiones de paisaje y de geografía negra, sátira de la aristocracia de Haití y contrastes humorísticos entre la cultura del blanco y la del negro. Al tratar estos temas, Palés se coloca en *un punto de vista objetivo* e interpreta lo negro con cierta condescendencia complacida y escéptica de hombre blanco que duda de todo, hasta de su propia cultura.)

But the later version reads: "In dealing with these themes, Palés takes *a subjective point of view* and interprets blackness with a degree of the complacent, skeptical and condescending perspective of the white man who doubts everything, even his own culture."[73] ("Al tratar estos temas, Palés se coloca en *un punto de vista subjetivo* e interpreta lo negro con cierta condescendencia complacida y escéptica de hombre blanco que duda de todo, hasta de su propia cultura.") Arce also modifies her initial judgment on the rhythm of the poetry: "The effect of persistence and *monotony* is obtained through the symmetrical construction or composition of the poem." ("El efecto de insistencia y *monotonía* se obtiene por medio de la construcción o composición simétrica del poema.") Where she first saw monotony, she sees variation: "The effect of persistence and of *variation* is obtained through the symmetrical construction or composition of the poem as can be seen in *Danza negra* and *Bombo*."[74] ("El efecto de insistencia y de *variación* se obtiene por medio de la construcción o composición simétrica del poema, como se advierte en *Danza negra* y *Bombo*.") She misunderstood the richness of Afro-Caribbean rhythm, a misconception she corrects in the later version.

Arce also deleted her remarks on dance as the quintessential form of expression for primitive—she means black—people. She wrote in 1933, "The interpretation of the black soul is well-crafted because dance is, in my opinion, the most transcendental choice of expression of all primitive peoples."[75] ("La interpretación del alma negra es acabada porque la danza es a mi juicio, la más trascendental voluntad de expresión de todo pueblo primitivo.") These disparaging remarks are excised from the 1950 version. Some of the more problematic implications of how Palés's "black verses" have been used are exemplified in Arce's claim that a white, "cultured" writer is a privileged interpreter of the "black soul." For whom, we ask? For a white audience, for a black audience, or for a "universal" audience? She holds fast to her claim regarding the issue of the universality of Palés's poetry. His universal vantage point, "from above" and "in white," is for Arce superior to that of Guillén: "but his [Palés's] interpretation because it is objective and distanced, achieves a higher degree of sharpness"[76] ("pero su [Palés] interpretación por objetiva y distanciada logra mayor agudeza").

Why does Arce insist on the superiority of Palés's "objective vantage point"? What is at stake when Arce stresses that Palés *is* a white man in contrast to Nicolás Guillén, for example? Arce said, "He is not at all a popular poet; he is a civilized white man who interprets blackness *with good humor and a pinch of irony*."[77] ("No es en manera alguna un poeta popular; es un blanco civilizado que interpreta lo negro *con buen humor y una pizca de ironía*.") Guillén and somehow Ballagas "see the black from below, from within and in black"[78] ("ven al negro desde abajo, desde dentro y en negro"). Palés is able to see blacks "humorously." What is so funny about the blacks that the poet portrays? The "joke" is at the expense of black people, but who is laughing with Palés? Are readers amused by what they perceive to be the stupidity or naïveté of black people? The later somewhat softened version reads, "He sets himself apart from the popular poetic forms; he interprets blackness as a civilized and skeptical white man."[79] ("Se aparta de los modos poéticos populares; interpreta lo negro como un blanco civilizado y escéptico.") But even in this later version, the author persists in keeping the slanderous remarks about blacks as uncivilized and overly credulous. Arce concludes her essay with a profession of faith in the superiority of art over historical reality. Palés's poetic renditions of the black character are deemed superior to the reality of the historical black experience. With Palés's creation, as Arce would have it, "the axiom that *poetic reality is always superior to historical daily reality* comes true"[80] ("se cumple el axioma de que *la realidad poética supera siempre a la histórica realidad cotidiana*"). Arce inflates the role of literature and proposes that it can act as a substitute for history.

On "Rectificaciones," Or, From the Lips of the Old Black Maid

Arce's essay, "Los poemas negros de Luis Palés Matos" in its 1933 version, was the object of pointed criticism by Tomás Blanco.[81] Blanco's "Refutación y glosa" disagreed with some of her critical judgments regarding the verisimilitude of Palés's portrayal of black people. In an ironic reference to democratic openness Blanco commends Arce for taking part in the public debate, and the fact that she "would leave the cloister and come out onto the street where the democratic slogan 'One man, one vote' is law; but where common sense, and democracy itself, have always recognized voices and opinions with more or less authority, more or less deserving of respect."[82] ("Saliera del claustro a la calle, donde el lema democrático 'Un hombre, un voto' es ley; pero donde el sentido común, y la democracia misma, han reconocido siempre voces y opiniones con mayor o menor autoridad, más o menos dignas de estima.") While Blanco admits that everyone has a right to his or her own opinions, he chastises Arce for her timid, if not reluctant, remarks regarding Palés's usage of local black culture as a context for his poetry.[83] He is disappointed that Arce had not put enough stress on the originality of the poems, as well as their regional and extra-regional importance. According to Blanco, Palés's genius was to link the blacks of the Caribbean to those of Africa. Blanco writes that there are no pure blacks in Puerto Rico, but that Palés is justified in his portrayal of them in his Caribbean poetry because "it is a symbol of what the poet sees in the atavistic sub-soil, in the psychological suburbs of our less sophisticated colored population"[84] ("es símbolo de lo que ve el poeta en el subsuelo atávico, en los suburbios psicológicos, de nuestra población de color menos sofisticada"). That Palés creates a composite portrayal of blacks via his anthropological and literary readings imaginatively fused with his experiences with Afro-Puerto Ricans is a testament to his genius, affirms the author of "Refutación y glosa."

Tomás Blanco's role as a propagator of Palés's poetry merits a study of its own. He wrote about Palés in the press and published two well-known essays on his poetry in a collection entitled *Sobre Palés Matos.*[85] As discussed earlier, Blanco belongs to a group of *criollo* intellectuals who have been lauded by some critics for their ostensibly liberal views, and indeed Blanco's racism is less overt than most of the writers of the *Generación del Treinta.* In his response to Arce he takes pains to underscore that Palés has, by means of a sophisticated *criollismo,* given readers works of cosmopolitan importance. Putting the finger on one of the main anxieties of the recent debate, Blanco exposes the fear among the reading public and among critics that, because the poems are quite ingenious, foreigners will identify Puerto Rico with "a narrow African localism."[86] ("un mezquino localismo africano.") He affirms to the contrary that these poems have for the first time put the island on the map, having been read by cultivated audiences in Madrid, Havana, Mexico, and New York. These views are quite consistent with those expressed in his "Elogio de *la plena*," where he had asked his *ateneísta* readers not to be so anxious about the large mulatto presence on the island, even as that essay displayed a certain level of white supremacist thinking. But, for all the good intentions of "Refutación y glosa," Blanco is again unable to get away from a certain stereotyping and usage of derogatory language toward people of African descent whom he insists on calling "darkies" or "negritos."

Margot Arce's "Más sobre los poemas de Luis Palés Matos," or "Rectificaciones" as it was renamed for the *Impresiones* collection, is an attempt to evaluate her former judgments in the light of the specific objections made to her essay by Tomás Blanco.[87] Margot Arce follows some of Blanco's critical judgments on Palés's *negrista* poems, but as their polemic shows, she is less accepting of Palés on the contributions of blacks to the culture of the Caribbean.

The issue of the representation of blackness in these poems is a complex one that needs to be discussed in detail. Tomás Blanco's criticisms centered on two questions: Whom does Palés portray in his *negrista* verses? Is his poetry an accurate representation of Afro-Puerto Ricans? The more recalcitrant critics of Palés insisted that his poems referred exclusively to Africans and Africa. Arce herself avows that she erred when she stated that Palés's black subjects were "negros teóricos." Arce writes: "Because there are Negroes and mulattos in Puerto Rico, it is impossible and ridiculous to think that Palés would not have seen them, that he would not have known them."[88] ("Como en Puerto Rico hay negros y mulatos, es imposible y ridículo pensar que Palés no los haya visto, que no los conozca.") The poet, then, has observed blacks closely in his native sugar-producing region of Guayama and in Santurce, both places with traditionally numerous black populations. Whereas in her first essay Arce talked about Palés's distant, superior, and ironic vantage point, she now sees "first-hand and cordial observation, looking at them with sympathy and familiarity"[89] ("observación cercana y cordial, mirándolo con simpatía y familiaridad"). The poet must have had the customary relationship that well-to-do whites have with blacks. Arce adds, as proof of the goodwill of whites toward blacks, that whites love their black servants. "One should not forget the close living arrangement," Arce writes, "generally loving and intimate, between the white man and his *black servants*, a custom that is quite frequent in our homes."[90] ("No se olvide, por otra parte, la convivencia, generalmente *estrecha y cariñosa*, entre el blanco y sus *criados negros*, costumbre bien frecuente y generalizada en nuestros hogares.") We would have to ask in whose homes and how cordial can the relationship of servant and employer be? The blinders of social privilege do not allow Arce to conceptualize the relationship between black and white people as anything other than one of black subservience.[91]

Arce concedes in both versions of "Más sobre los poemas de Luis Palés Matos" that in his native Guayama the poet must have heard folk songs, stories, and anecdotes handed down from slavery times. Incidentally, this is the first time slavery is ever mentioned in this whole "black poetry" debate, but the mention is in no way critical of the role that white slave owners—who listened to those stories and songs—played in the subjection of black people. She proceeds to name a number of spheres in Puerto Rican society where *anyone* could find black people or come in contact with black musical forms. Arce asks: "Who among us has never heard of the *maryandá*, the *baquiní*, the *bomba* and the *plena* dances? Who, as a child, never heard ghost and witch stories *from the lips of the old black maid?* Doesn't the interested and discerning researcher find a treasure of revealing suggestions in the all too familiar superstitions and spells?"[92] ("¿Quién no conoce entre nosotros el maryandá, el baquiní, el baile de bomba y de plena? ¿Quién no ha escuchado, cuando niño, *de los labios de la vieja criada negra*, los cuentos de brujos y de aparecidos? En las bien conocidas supersticiones y hechizos ¿no encuentra el buscador interesado y perspicaz un caudal de sugestiones reveladoras?") This passage is revealing in a number of ways. At the level of culture as the practices of everyday life, we see a certain recognition of a much more fluid relationship between social groups. People of African descent enter in and out of the lives of white Creoles. Cordial relationships among the races are portrayed as ones where the whites either have power over the labor of black people or where their cultural practices have some entertainment value that whites too can enjoy. The social imaginary of her essay is limited and stereotypical. As if this were not enough, Arce reminds us that it is fairly common to see itinerant blacks from other islands, such as the "tórtolos of Saint Thomas and Curaçao, the Haitian black, and the Cuban rumba dancers who visit us periodically with their comic operas"[93] ("tórtolos de Santo Tomás y Curazao, el negro haitiano y el rumbero cubano que nos visita periódicamente con sus Bufos"). All these instances of service, subservience, domination, or the foreign belong to the social realm where blacks and whites interact. Afro-Antilleans who have come to the island generally as workers or entertainers are reduced to romanticized domination and folklore. Arce's rhetorical strategy creates an "us" and a "them" where white Puerto Ricans can identify blacks and deal with them at a safe distance.[94]

Beloved ayahs notwithstanding, Arce is able to effect both a rapprochement and a distancing of blacks from whites culturally and socially in the 1936 version of her essay. White people observe blacks and mulattos with an objectifying gaze. Moreover, white Creole fear of the purported "social aggressiveness" of the mulatto expresses disdain for mulattos socially. The author's intention is to talk about the poet's view of blacks. But she is not aware that the language used to characterize Palés reveals her own anxiety regarding the "black peril." In her words, "He observes them in real life and he also observes the real-life products of their cross-breeding with the white race—the darky, the mulatto, the high yellow, etc.—who are so numerous and so *aggressive*. By this route he comes to the abstraction of the Negroid and of the mulatto, in other words, to the general and to the characteristic."[95] ("Lo observa en vivo, y observa también los productos vivos de su cruce con la raza blanca—el moreno, el mulato, el grifo, etc.—tan abundantes y tan *agresivos*. Por aquí llega a la abstracción de lo negroide y de lo mulato, es decir, a lo general y a lo característico.") This notion of the mulatto as essentially aggressive is deleted in the 1950 version.

Arce's text is marked by a negrophobic anxiety that leads to a privileging of the master's version of the history of black enslavement. She euphemistically resorts to calling the exploitation of black labor, lives, and hopes, an instance of the superior exerting its influence over the inferior. There is no notion here that the surplus value extracted from the exploited labor of blacks had anything to do with making the "far reaching and superior" *criollo* material culture possible.[96] As Arce defensively states,

> Neither is it accurate to deny the influence of the black in our life and customs. This influence is very clear and it cannot be scorned, *just as one cannot scorn the influence—of a greater volume and scope, of course—of the white upon the black*. The products of the crossbreeding of the two races are also very well defined types with their own distinct psychology, and they play an evident role in our world that lends a certain tone and *color* to our collective and social expressions.[97] (Tampoco es exacto negar la influencia del negro en nuestra vida y costumbres. Esa influencia es bien visible y no se puede desdeñar; *como no se podría desdeñar la influencia—mayor en volumen y en alcances, desde luego—del blanco sobre el negro*. Los productos del cruce de las dos razas son también tipos bien definidos, con su psicología distintiva y que desempeñan en nuestro medio un papel evidente que presta cierto tono y colorido a nuestras expresiones colectivas y sociales.)

The later version reads, "an influence that is very clear and beneficial in the majority of the cases"[98] ("influencia bien visible y benéfica en la mayor parte de los casos").

Even in the 1950 version the mulatto is still portrayed in a language that refers to the propagation of animals—the results of crossbreeding between the two races. This colorful mulatto is the other side of "the tragic mulatto" of Emilio S. Belaval's story analyzed earlier. In Arce's case, he is the marker of an exoticized difference that adds local color to the life of white Puerto Ricans. Yet in the end, black people are not fully Puerto Rican. The author accepts that *in the poems* people of African descent express something

Puerto Rican, but stressed, in the earlier version of the essay, that the cultural importance on the island of the *jíbaro*—coded as white—greatly surpassed that of blacks—coded as forever exotic. The black poems may express a valuable aspect of Puerto Rican culture, but "the *importance of the jíbaro* [is] much greater"[99] ("la *importancia de lo jíbaro* [es] mucho mayor"). In the later version Arce corrects her assessment of the superior contribution of the *jíbaro:* "although the *importance that has been given to the jíbaro* may be much greater"[100] ("aunque la *importancia que se ha dado* a lo jíbaro sea mucho mayor").

It is crucial that we clarify what Arce means by *real* when she argues that Palés portrays "real blacks." Does she mean true-to-life, believable? As we saw in her last essay, Arce privileges art and literature as cognitive categories. The poet can know truths that are hidden from the non-gifted, a common presupposition in her intellectual milieu. She writes about the results of Palés's poetic virtuosity: "They are live Negroes, recreated and stylized on the poetic level."[101] ("Son negros vivos, recreados y estilizados en el plano poético.") This poetic alchemy denies socio-cultural power relations in favor of stereotyping in order to keep black Puerto Ricans in the metaphorical (thus ahistorical) position of the "primitive." In picturing these "true Negroes," both Palés and Arce appeal to the racist misrepresentations to which Africans and people of African descent have been subjected by most white writers. To different degrees, Palés, Blanco, and Arce share the same negrophobic language. In Palés's poetry, according to Arce,

> There are little Negroes who are partially civilized like the little Count of Lemonade and the Duke of Marmalade, in whom the varnish of culture has not erased completely the essential and differentiating characteristics of the race. There are also, finally, the little authentic Puerto Rican Negroes, unmistakably written and evoked in verses of admirable synthesis.[102] (Andan negritos parcialmente civilizados como el Condesito de la Limonada y el Duque de la Mermelada, en quienes el barniz de cultura no ha borrado totalmente los rasgos esenciales y diferenciadores de la raza. Andan por último, los negritos puertorriqueños auténticos, inconfundibles escritos y evocados en versos de síntesis admirables.)

For Palés, Blanco, and Arce, the Haiti evoked in Palés's poetry is a symbol of the barbarous, the primitive. Nothing can hope to change this since blacks can only imitate "white" culture. This gratuitous defaming of the Haitian people is not new. It started immediately after the Haitian Revolution (1804). Palés and Arce prove the extent of the success of this opprobrious campaign, launched a century earlier by the French and the slaveholding Spaniards and *criollos.*[103] These writers not only insult a whole people, but they also show the level of ignorance and cultural alienation of the Puerto Rican intellectual elite.

Contrary to the racist practices of the Puerto Rican intelligentsia during the 1930s, a number of Cuban intellectuals befriended and welcomed black Haitian and North American writers to Cuba. Nicolás Guillén, for example, hosted both Jacques Roumain's and Langston Hughes's visits to Cuba. It would be unimaginable for Guillén to refer to his Haitian colleague as a "darky" or *negrito.* But, following the mandates of her social group, Arce's paternalistic use of the term *negritos* is meant to be polite. Puerto Rican racial politics dictated its use by the Euro-Latins who allegedly felt sympathetic to blacks and did not want to affront them with the "insult" *negro.* (One of the meanings of the word *negro,* in the Puerto Rican context, is equivalent to the slur *nigger* in English.[104]) Thus, opaque and complex discursive practices allowed Creoles to disguise racism and to believe themselves sympathetic to blacks.

As one of the champions of Palés's poetry, Margot Arce was called on to interact in a public capacity with the black Cuban performer Eusebia Cosme in 1936. Cosme recited poems by Guillén and Ballagas, as well as by Palés, to full houses of enthralled Puerto Rican theatergoers. During her sojourn in Puerto Rico, she acted as a personal emissary for Nicolás Guillén by delivering one of his letters and a book with a personal dedication to Palés Matos. Margot Arce wrote about Cosme's recitals in a short article that was published in the Cuban magazine *Carteles.* She was very complimentary of the artistry of Cosme and thankful to have been exposed to a Cuban interpreter of poems by Guillén and Ballagas, as well as by Palés Matos. Arce praised the performer's command of the stage and adds, "But the supreme accomplishment of Eusebia Cosme is to have voluntarily become the interpreter of Antillean verse. She, better than anyone else, by her race, by her birth, can penetrate into the marrow of that poetry, because that poetry moves the most secret fibers of her heart."[105] ("Pero el acierto supremo de Eusebia Cosme es haberse convertido voluntariamente en el intérprete del verso antillano. Ella, mejor que nadie, por su raza, y por su cuna, puede penetrar en la entraña de esa poesía, porque esa poesía remueve las fibras más secretas de su corazón.") Cosme had been promoted by Fernando Ortiz at the Havana Lyceum, a fact that Arce said vouched for her abilities.

Other commentators echoed Arce to some degree, but also added divergent opinions. Nilita Vientós found Cosme to have a refreshing naïveté, while Antonio J. Colorado's review of her first recital was critical of the material Cosme presented: popular verses, sayings, rumbas, boleros, poems from Ballagas's anthology, and by Nicolás Guillén. He chided her for only presenting one of Palés's poems, "Danza negra," the recitation of which he found lacking: "This profoundly cultured poetry of Palés, is not in our view *felt,* grasped by Eusebia Cosme with the same force and profundity and even poetic comprehension bestowed upon the others."[106] ("Esta poesía de Palés, profundamente culta, no es a nuestro ver *sentida,* captada por Eusebia Cosme con la misma fuerza y profundidad y hasta comprensión poética con que siente las otras.") He suggested that the Puerto Rican poem should be read in an epic tone and with quasi-religious dignity; instead: "In Eusebia it was a catalogue enumeration, cold and dead . . . neither the gesture, nor the voice, nor the pauses corresponded to the exigencies of the aesthetic drama contained in the poem." [107] ("En Eusebia fue una enumeración de catálogo, fría y muerta . . . ni el gesto, ni la voz, ni las pausas correspondieron a la exigencia del dramatismo estético que contiene la poesía.") Colorado contrasts this with her breathtaking performance of Guillén's "Sensemayá" or "Balada del Güije," and of an Afro-Cuban slave lullaby. We could speculate about the lack of enthusiasm for Palés's "Danza negra" that Cosme demonstrated in her first recital. If the Cuban performer had any familiarity with Afro-Caribbean religiosity, such as La Regla de Ocha or La Regla de Ifá, she may not have found Palés's poem that interesting. But there may be other reasons for her initial estrangement from "Danza negra."

Of those who reviewed Cosme's performances, only Pedro Juan Labarthe mentions the interesting fact that she became a "recitadora" because she could not find acceptance as a full-fledged actress in Cuba. "I, a darky, wanted to be an artist. But how could a black woman perform roles reserved for a white one? I could not be given the opportunity on the boards unless I were to play a servant or a *rumbera* Negress."[108] ("Yo negrita quería ser artista. Pero, ¿cómo una negra iba a tomar el papel de blanca? No se me podía dar oportunidad en las tablas a menos que no fuera el de sirvienta o negrita rumbera.") At that time in Cuba to become an actress in the serious theatre arts one had to be white. As a black woman, Cosme was the object of severe typecasting during her long life in theater and in film. She was discovered and recognized as a talent by Spanish actor González Marín in her native Santiago, she tells Labarthe. (He was a propagator of the new avant-garde poetry of Lorca , Machado, and Alberti to admiring audiences in his native land and throughout Latin America.) Cosme also reveals that she rehearses and studies four to five hours daily, "I am constantly reading and studying and it is the only way to achieve perfection. The audience does not want to see mediocrities"[109] ("Estoy constantemente leyendo y estudiando y es el único modo de lograr la perfección. El público no desea ver mediocridades.") We also learn that Cosme prizes artistic autonomy and does not suffer fools gladly. Like many performers she carried a good luck charm, which in her case was a sacred religious doll.

Palés's much-discussed newspaper article, "Hacia una poesía antillana," raised questions that were unsettling to most *criollos*. There he had explored the question of Puerto Rico's relationship to the Caribbean, and asked in which ways the Africans who were brought to the island as slaves, and later their Puerto Rican progeny, had affected the island's culture and history. Astonishingly for a Creole, Palés argued that the slaves must have resisted slavery and appropriated aspects of the culture of the masters for their own survival. The Spaniards, on the other hand, adapted less readily to the new land, and remained somewhat emotionally disconnected from their new situation. Though Palés relies on the problematic language of *Volkgeister* (national soul) nationalism, he still makes his point: "The dark powers of the black soul take advantage of the Spaniard's shaky spiritual state in order to introduce peculiar modes, traits and rhythms in the Caribbean whose reality in the Caribbean character is impossible to deny and which separate our people from the Hispanic people, forging our own personality."[110] ("De este vacilante estado espiritual del español, toman ventaja las potencias oscuras del alma negra para implantar en las Antillas modos, rasgos y ritmos peculiares, cuya realidad en el carácter antillano es imposible rebatir y que desvinculan nuestro pueblo de lo hispánico, forjándole una personalidad propia.") The proximity between the two races and the power relations between them produced a different reality founded on racial and cultural mixing. Yet, the entire *negrista* debate showed how little currency the concept of *mestizaje*, as an explanation of a cultural and racial reality, had with the *criollo* elite at the time. As problematic as the concept of *mestizaje* is, it at least tries to grapple with racial heterogeneity in the national polity.

Intertwined with Pale's racialist conception of culture is an incipient development of the concept of transculturation. He writes that this mixing of the races had produced a distinctive "accent" "due to the psychological mutation that I referred to before, the mixture of blood fusing their racial values and creating the new kind of mulatto toward which the vital accent of the three Islands [Cuba, Puerto Rico, Dominican Republic] has shifted. And this accent, translated into cultural terms, is not and can never again be either Hispanic or African"[111] ("amén de la mutación psicológica a que me referí antes, la mezcla de la sangre fundiendo sus valores de raza y creando el nuevo tipo del mulato hacia el cual se ha desplazado el acento vital de las tres Islas" [Cuba, Puerto Rico, República Dominicana]). Y ese acento, traducido a términos de cultura no es ni puede ser ya hispánico ni africano"). Transculturation and cultural strategies of resistance by subaltern and oppressed groups are concepts well established today, but in Palés's milieu they were not well-understood at all. Moreover, any acknowledgment of resistance could threaten the self-representation and projection of the white elite.

The aesthetic project of *poesía negrista/antillana*, and the intellectual debate on "objectivity" and the nature of representation it generated, is inextricably linked to the genre's socio-historical referents. In this light, it is appropriate to try to discern the genre's *sociopoetics*, to devise readings that explore its *socioaesthetics*. Broadly, the aim is to fuse an ideological and historical analysis with a formalist one. Most of the readers of Palés's poetry in the 1930s wanted to absent themselves from the social and literary implications of that poetry. As they saw it, it was not acceptable for one of their own, a "super civilizado" descendent of an *hacendado* family, to endeavor to express himself "en negro, desde adentro." Today it would seem that a number of well-intentioned scholars want to do the same, but for different reasons. For these critics the very genre that initially helped to establish Palés's international fame is off-limits when it comes to elucidating issues of race germane to the poems because of fears that some readings could be threatening to the poet's standing within the Puerto Rican and Latin-American literary traditions. I want to emphasize that in placing *negrismo* in its historical context my aim is analytical, not iconoclastic.

Chapter 8 will explicate a number of Palés's *negrista* verses to explore the idea that although Palés separated himself from the crude negrophobia of many within his circle, as a Puerto Rican author writing in a colonial Caribbean context, he was unable to radically question those fanciful representations of Otherness so entrenched in Western culture. This conceptualization of blacks as Other was reinforced by the critical discourse of Margot Arce as she endeavored to place Palés as a central figure in Puerto Rican letters. But as we will see later, if poems like "Danza negra" and "Majestad negra" depict an imaginary voyage to the roots of "Caribbeanness," this voyage rewrites the Middle Passage and its aftermath in a conciliatory mode. Is it fair to ask how the poems represent those who were forcibly abducted from Africa and whose work produced rum, riches, and social prestige for the Creole elite? Close reading of Palés's poems suggests that this voyage to the "papiamentosas islas del ron" and the "patualesas islas del volcán" is festive, and that precisely therein lies the attraction for many readers. Palés uses the image of the black dance as a way of tapping into the creative energies of black people. I propose that this representation is potentially exploitive. Can there be true celebration of blackness where, as bell hooks puts it, one "denies accountability and historical connection?"[112] Is it possible to celebrate black pleasure without an understanding of black pain? Palés's celebration of black culture—or the culture of the dark Other as conceived by whites—is meant for the consumption of whites, mainly. Palés participates in what bell hooks describes as a "romantic fantasy of the *primitive* and the concrete search for a real primitive paradise, whether that location be a country or a body, a dark continent or dark flesh, perceived as the perfect embodiment of that possibility."[113]

A Retreat to Stylistic Criticism

Margot Arce's participation in the "black poetry" debate is essential if one is to understand its history. Her next intervention, "El adjetivo en la 'Danza negra' de Luis Palés Matos," is a retreat to the safety of stylistic analysis.[114] "El adjetivo" provided her with the opportunity to showcase her talents as a rigorous stylist and to demonstrate the high level of artistry and sophistication of Palés's poetry. The essay was first delivered to a large audience as part of the 1938 homage to Palés at the *Ateneo*. When read in contrast with her previous explications of Pales's texts, we see a deliberate effort to move away from any theorizing on the ideological meaning of the poems. She warns the reader (and by the same token fends off possible criticisms of misreading) that her commentaries "ligeras observaciones" are subjective, a "personal interpretation that does not seek to coincide with the intentions of the poet"[115] ("interpretación personal que no pretende coincidir con la intención del poeta"). Her analysis has the effect of overwhelming the reader with its close attention to the chain of signifiers, with total disregard for the signified. No effort is made to integrate meaning into her analysis of the adjectives in the poems. The contexts, literary or otherwise, are not taken into account. Written after the controversy generated by the previous essays analyzed in this chapter, this work repositioned Arce as an expert in a strictly literary field. "El Adjetivo" redefined her as a scholar, and was intended to separate her from those seeking documentary, literal, or ideological meanings in works of art.

CHAPTER 8

Speaking For and Speaking With: The Limits of *Negrismo*'s Cultural Discourse

My project is an effort to avert the critical gaze from the racial object to the racial subject; from the described and imagined to the describers and imaginers; from the serving to the served.
—Toni Morrison, *Playing in the Dark*, 1992

Inscribing Racism: The *Negrista* Fantasy of Symbiotic Races and Cultures

My analysis of Margot Arce's essays on the "black poetry" of Luis Palés Matos has shown that there existed a consensus among the members of the Puerto Rican *Generación del Treinta* with regard to the definitions of "race." There was also a shared belief in the "primitive and sensual character" of black peoples. Viewing culture as emanating from biology, both detractors and apologists of Palés Matos's "black poetry" agreed that the white race was the producer of true culture and civilization. Following this scheme, it was in the nature of the white race to produce a literate, refined, imperialist, and technologically savvy way of life. The black race's function was to be an untamed wilderness, a natural resource that could be used to replenish the coffers and, later on, the "soul" of the Western world.

As discussed earlier, Palés's *negrista* verses and his pronouncements regarding Puerto Rico's Afro-Caribbean heritage were a progressive cultural stance in the negrophobic and classist environment of the 1930s. But at the same time, given that the poems in effect reinscribe and reaffirm white supremacy, we cannot simply dismiss the poetry's racial imagery by saying that Palés's poems are anticolonial and leave it at that. Charges that *negrismo* propagates racist and stereotypical representations of people of African descent will not disappear simply by pointing out that this poetry has a "pro-Caribbean and anti-imperialist stance." The question of the representation of people of African descent is not settled—despite the wishes of critics who refuse to engage this aspect of Palés's poetry.[1]

How are we to understand Luis Palés Matos's "black verses" today? It is precisely from an anti-colonial perspective that the *negrista* project is profoundly troubling, due in great part to its reliance on a fallacious racialist logic. Nigerian author Wole Soyinka, a clear-sighted critic of Afro-French *Négritude* literature, provides important clues to reading "black poetry" written by white authors. Though Soyinka's biting critique is directed at the project and legacy of the *Négritude* poets, his examination provides an important starting point for my own readings of the Spanish Caribbean *negrista* project. While *Négritude* poets were black and *negrista* literature was written by whites, Soyinka's clarifications are most pertinent here because they are directed at the philosophical underpinnings of what—in the case of both movements—are Eurocentric and Euro-supremacist discourses on race.

Soyinka points out that, while the vision of *Négritude* was laudable and that its importance should never be underestimated, from a post-colonial African perspective its project was flawed. "What went wrong with it," according to Soyinka, "is contained in what I earlier expressed as the contrivance of a creative ideology and its falsified basis of identification with the social vision. This vision itself was that of restitution and reengineering of the social psyche, the establishment of a distinct human entity and the glorification of its long-suppressed attributes."[2] Unfortunately, Césaire, Senghor, and their *Négritude* confreres, by extolling the apparent, indulging in over-simplifications, and by not making a profound effort to incorporate African systems of value, validated European stereotypes about Africans without intending to do so. The mistake of *Négritude* was, to paraphrase poet Audre Lorde, that it tried to demolish the master's house—the conceptual edifice proposed by Europe—by using the master's conceptual tools and visions.[3]

Négritude, according to Soyinka, betrayed African values in crucial ways: "In attempting to refute the evaluation to which black reality had been subjected, Négritude adopted the Manichean tradition of European thought and inflicted it on a culture which is most radically anti-Manichean. It not only accepted the dialectical structure of European ideological confrontations but borrowed from the very components of its racist syllogism."[4] As

Soyinka demonstrates, *Négritude* too eagerly accepted a certain Eurocentric chauvinist logic as the basis for its reassessment of blackness—construed as otherness. The *Négritude* poets readily embraced the notion—which Soyinka identifies as "syllogism (a)"—that analytical thought, or scientific inventiveness, or true art and creativity, is the province of Europeans, the only race that is highly developed. The second notion—or "syllogism (b)," popularized for centuries by white propaganda—states that Africans are incapable of analytic thought and, therefore, that they are not capable of higher development. What *Négritude* did was to amend the second syllogism by proposing that since Africans employed intuitive thought, or dance, or rhythm, and that since this was also a high mark of human evolution, Africans were then also highly developed. This "syllogism (c)," as Soyinka shows, in effect endorses the European fantasy of a symbiotic human culture, with separate but complementary branches.[5] This is unacceptable, for as Soyinka indignantly and aptly puts it, "How could the mistake ever have been made that the new propositions in (c) wiped away the inherent insult of (b), which was merely a development of the racist assumptions of (a)? They (the *Négritude* proponents) said, oh yes the Gobineaus of the world are right; Africans neither think nor construct, but it doesn't matter because—voilà!—they intuit. And so they moved to construct a rhythmic edifice, confident that its rhythmic echoes would drown the repugnant conclusion of proposition (b), which of course simply refused to go away."[6] *Négritude*, in what was meant as a defensive move, proceeded to accept as factual that humans of European ancestry have a capacity to reason that humans of African ancestry do not have. This is, as Soyinka reminds us, "one of the most commonplace blasphemies of racism."[7] Ultimately, *Négritude* acts in complicity with European cultural domination. It is antithetical to postcolonial African interests and an anticolonial African ethos. As Soyinka suggests, the cultures of the Continent, prior to colonial intrusion and in spite of it, do not favor "creative truncation." For Soyinka, *Négritude*—because of its root in European Manicheanism—suggested "that there are watertight categories of the creative spirit, that creativity is not one smooth-flowing source of human regeneration."[8]

Soyinka's African-centered cultural critique of *Négritude* helps us question the philosophical tenets of Palés's *negrista* poetry. I propose that this poetry is anticolonial in only a very narrow and insufficient way. Racism and colonialism are interlocking systems of domination; they are linked at their very inception. Palés's acceptance of the "symbiotic role of the races" reinscribes European colonial racism in a light favorable to the *criollo* professional elite, to the detriment of an inclusive antiracist and decolonizing vision. My inspiration in Soyinka's critique of *Négritude* intends to bring together a feminist standpoint and an antiracist reading to both movements.

Far from assuming a romanticizing "Afrocentric slant," I seek to engage *negrismo* with the help of thoughtful postcolonial and Marxist thinkers.

From the Outside Looking In: The Limits of Cultural Voyeurism

Rather than trying to discern what constitutes positive or negative imagery in the *negrista* project, I find it more useful to attend to the viewpoint *enacted* by the poems. I read Palés Matos's *Tuntún de pasa y grifería* through the perspective proposed by "Kalahari," a central poem of the collection.[9] "Kalahari" establishes the desiring subject—the poetic "I"—as having the power to act, and act upon the object of desire. Together with "Pueblo negro," "Majestad negra," and "Mulata-Antilla" (by choice the last poem in the author's final revision of *Tuntún*), this poem signals a clear presence of the desiring subject and its or, in this case, *his* standpoint.

In "Kalahari" the "I," or poetic voice, wistfully wonders why at this precise moment ("ahora") his imagination is given to muse over a single word, "Kalahari." He ponders the association of ideas produced by the *word*. There is no musing over the denotation—the proper name of a place in the southern cone of Africa. From the first verse, "Why suddenly the word Kalahari?" ("¿Por qué ahora la palabra Kalahari?") the poetic voice describes what he sees; he is inside, looking out. Through his clean glass window he sees this pleasant, amiable sight:

> The day is clear and beautiful. Dancing in the light
> with agile grace, are luminous and joyful beings:
> the bird, the blade of grass, the beetles,
> and the flies that in their circular and drunken flight
> bounce off the clean glass of my window.
>
> (El día es hermoso y claro. En la luz bailotean
> con ágil gracia, seres luminosos y alegres:
> el pájaro, la brizna de hierba, las cantáridas,
> y las moscas que en vuelo redondo y embriagado
> rebotan contra el limpio cristal de mi ventana.)

The pleasure lies in the discovering of new possibilities, in renaming what would otherwise seem ordinary. Through the poetic usage of the adjective, the feminized cloud's plump, swollen, sweet mass becomes a heavenly peacock:

> At times a white cloud permeates everything
> with its ample, swollen, sugary contours

and in the unctuous display of its puffiness
it is like a mighty peacock of the heavens.

(A veces una nube blanca lo llena todo
con su mole rolliza, hinchada, bombonosa,
y en despliegue adiposo de infladura
es como un imponente pavo real del cielo.)

This delectation in the expressive possibilities of the adjective is again interrupted by the persistence of the single verse stanza, "¿Por qué ahora la palabra Kalahari?" The verse brings again an onslaught of associations. This time the subject remembers the events of last evening when he and some friends visited a bordello:

Last night I was feasting with my friends
and we turned toward an absurd brothel
down in the shadowy wharf district . . .

(Anoche estuve de francachela con los amigos,
y derivamos hacia un lupanar absurdo
allá por el sombrío distrito de los muelles . . .)

The men drift to the docks—locus of work for the poor, but of commercial profit and sexual adventure for the well-to-do. This is an organic realm of dark, strong, and offensive sights and smells:

The murky water gave off a crude stench
of shellfish, and the wind undulated urgently
through the peculiar pungency of the port.

(El agua tenebrosa ponía un vaho crudo
de marisco, y el viento ondulaba premioso
a través de los tufos peculiares del puerto.)

Among the laughing, made-up women of the brothel there is one who catches the attention of the narrative voice because her passivity is seen as an invitation. In her drunken stupor she lets him have his way with her. The woman is addressed as a beast of burden. Relations of power between the *señorito* customers and the prostitutes are very clear in this scene:

In the brothel the lipsticked women
laughed noisily . . . However,
one, still, kept quiet; she kept quiet smiling,

and she let herself be taken smiling and quiet.
She was inebriated. Things went on far away.
I remember that someone said—Camella, a drink, a drink.

(En el burdel reían estrepitosamente
las mujeres de bocas pintadas . . . Sin embargo,
una, inmóvil, callaba; callaba sonreída,
y se dejaba hacer sonreída y callada.
Estaba ebria. Las cosas sucedían distantes.
Recuerdo que alguien dijo—Camella, un trago, un trago.)

Back in the speaker's present, the suggestive power of the word Kalahari facilitates another foray into the immediate past. Earlier this morning he indulged in a reverie prompted by a picture in a magazine. This daydream takes him to a bay of palm trees and hundreds of swaying monkeys. He has no explanation for this vision (familiar palm trees yet foreign monkeys?):

This morning, leafing through a picture magazine,
facing a little water dog with a red ribbon around its neck,
I spent a long time observing, observing . . .
I don't know why my drifting thoughts
cast anchor in a bay of transparent coconut palms,
with monkeys, hundreds of monkeys
that braided a sloppy chain of somersaults.

(Esta mañana, hojeando un magazín de cromos,
ante un perrillo de aguas con cinta roja al cuello,
estuve largo tiempo observando, observando . . .
No sé por qué mi pensamiento a la deriva
fondeó en una bahía de claros cocoteros,
con monos, centenares de monos que trenzaban
una desordenada cadena de cabriolas.)

Again, after this new reverie, the lone verse appears, prompting this time a deeper curiosity as to the origin of his obsession. Free association seems the only answer the poetic subject can come up with, since logic cannot explain this recurrence of the word and the thoughts it brings to the surface. The word Kalahari serves to stimulate the imagination of the poetic subject. It jolts his memories, which have nothing to do with the Kalahari itself.

His subconscious has collected this word as one would an insect. How this word came to his consciousness is inexplicable, yet this word flies, alive, against the background—seen as blinding light—of his memory:

Suddenly it has emerged incomprehensibly . . .
Kalahari! Kalahari! Kalahari!

Where has this word come from
Hidden like an insect in my memory
Pierced like a dissected butterfly
in the beetle case of my memory,
and is now alive, relentless, fluttering blindly
against the obfuscating light of remembrance?
Kalahari! Kalahari! Kalahari!

(Ha surgido de pronto inexplicablemente . . .
¡Kalahari! ¡Kalahari! ¡Kalahari!
¿De dónde habrá surgido esta palabra
escondida como un insecto en mi memoria;
picada como una mariposa diseca
en la caja de coleópteros de mi memoria,
y ahora viva, insistiendo, revoloteando ciega
contra la luz ofuscadora del recuerdo?
¡Kalahari! ¡Kalahari! ¡Kalahari!)

There is no answer to the query, however, and the question remains as the poem ends, "¿Por qué ahora la palabra Kalahari?"

This poem is a reflection and reenactment of some of the techniques of the avant-garde literature, especially Surrealism's formal devices. Sudden bursts of impressions, explorations of word play, and free associations are important facets of this poem. There is also an earnest tone, an attitude of sincerity that pervades the poem due to the presence of the desiring subject's intimate revelations. It is not clear what the subject desires, but we realize that his compulsion to know is not fulfilled. Left unsatisfied, the poetic subject is made vulnerable by his gesture of openness and by the lingering presence of the unexplained. The word Kalahari becomes a pretext for an exploration of the inner self, an instrument of self-discovery. Yet the emphasis here is on the attempts at self-knowledge, not on the referent that made the quest possible, the geographical region of the Kalahari.[10]

"Kalahari" is unique in that it is an instance of the sustained presence of the poetic "I" in a series of poems characterized by a pervasive voyeuristic stance. Why should we insist on this point? It is not because Palés Matos is a white *criollo* writing about blacks or the role of blacks in "our Caribbean culture" or "our Afro-Caribbean identity." It is because the perspective represented in the poems, independent of intentionality, is the point of view of the cultural outsider looking in.

Palés's poetic standpoint was seen as integral to the meaning of the poems from their very first reception in the late 1920s and early 1930s. For some, like Blanco and Arce, because Palés was a white, cultured poet, he was able to render a superior, more objective portrait of "el negro y lo negro." For others, the detractors of Palés, he was a false prophet of "poesía negrista," intent on bringing up what did not really exist: black culture in Puerto Rico. For them, no culture could be associated with black people, given their total absorption into the colonizer's ways. Conversely, critics in the 1970s, as my discussion of the essays of Arcadio Díaz Quiñones will show, understood Palés's perspective as *inclusive.* For Díaz Quiñones these "black poems" are the true bearer of an anticolonial Caribbean identity bent on opposing its "mulatto" identity against Yankee cultural intervention. However, for critics with a knowledge of the African continent and of the literature of people of African descent in the Americas, this poetry cannot truly include or speak from a viewpoint respectful of the humanity of those who comprise what is in effect the largest ethnicity of the Caribbean.[11]

The respect for the African survivals, contributions, culture, and struggles—blood, sweat, tears, hopes, and pleasure—that forms the basis for a definition of a Caribbean identity does not come just from having African ancestry. Any black or mulatto person can act out of a logic of white supremacy. Mere ancestry is not a guarantee of anything. The crux of the matter in *negrismo* resides in the misunderstanding of the terms "to speak of," "to speak for," and "to speak with." The consequences, rhetorical and historical, of each choice differ substantially. The critics of Palés's Afro-Caribbean poetry interchange and blur the differences inherent in each position and misinterpret their end results. Palés's poems speak *of* and *for,* as if blacks and black culture were unable to speak for themselves. The representation of black culture in *Tuntún* is very much mediated through the position of the onlooker. Moreover, I would also propose that the implied audience of the poems shares the presuppositions of the "poetic voice" inscribed in the poems. The historical and social referents—black people, black histories—seem to be beyond the reach of the poetry and its implied readership (white, male, educated). Let us take, as an example, the much-anthologized "Pueblo negro."

The first two verses of "Pueblo negro" establish the primacy of the scene as a desired and desirable vision. What is important here is that the subject has a fantasy: "Tonight I am obsessed by the remote / vision of a black village." ("Esta noche me obsede la remota / visión de un pueblo negro.") The verses that follow are an elaboration of this dream:

—Mussumba, Tombuctú, Farafangana—
is a village of dreams,
lying there in my internal haze
in the shadow of transparent coconut palms

(—Mussumba, Tombuctú, Farafangana—
es un pueblo de sueño,
tumbado allá en mis brumas interiores
a la sombra de claros cocoteros)

This black town—or people—takes form in his imagination or "mis brumas interiores." The following stanzas are a projection wherein the poetic "I" disappears completely as the reverie scene is described. The scene is objectified, apparently disembodied from the subject that perceives it. A tone of distance pervades the six stanzas of the vision in which the climate is imagined as harsh. The qualifiers produce a synaesthetic effect that renders a surprising vision:

The rabid light falls
in hard ochers over the expansive landscape.
The stones smoke, red from the heat,
and the humidity of the corpulent tree
evaporates vegetal freshness
in the sour crucible of the dry climate.

(La luz rabiosa cae
en duros ocres sobre el campo extenso.
Humean, rojas de calor, las piedras,
y la humedad del árbol corpulento
evapora frescuras vegetales
en el agrio crisol del clima seco.)

Suddenly in the next stanza feelings are mentioned, "pereza y laxitud," but we do not know if they are felt by someone or are meant to suggest what the reader must feel in this scenario:

Laziness and laxity. The puddles
ferment a dense stench of ammonia.
The compact hippopotamus sinks
in his broth of succulent mud
and the elephant of marble and tallow
grazes its vague dream under the baobab tree.

(Pereza y laxitud. Los aguazales
cuajan un vaho amoniacal y denso.
El compacto hipopótamo se hunde
en su caldo de lodo suculento
y el elefante de marfil y grasa
rumia bajo el baobab su vago sueño.)[12]

Who feels "Pereza y laxitud?" Is this the attitude of the one who has the initial vision? The next stanza presents the irruption of a voice, a singing voice denoted as "someone." This voice is not intelligible; no meaning can be extracted from the sounds except that it is not a familiar voice; it "lazily dissolves the chant." This chant, "swarming with ues that relax / on rafts of somnolent diphthongs/ and with elongated guttural sounds / that give a gift of distance to the verse," is described as if it is unfamiliar to the one who hears it. ("Pululado de úes que se aquietan / en balsas de diptongos soñolientos, / y de guturaciones alargadas / que dan un don de lejanía al verso.") The next stanza tells us that the chant belongs to a black woman, "la negra." The life of this black woman, in a far away place, is characterized by animality: "It is the Negress who sings / her spare life of domesticated animal; / the Negress of the sun-beaten regions / who smells of earth, of savage flesh, of sex." ("Es la negra que canta / su sobria vida de animal doméstico; / la negra de las zonas soleadas / que huele a tierra, a salvajina, a sexo.") The effects of the chant of this earthy "negra que canta" are remarkable, producing an atmosphere of bliss, of pleasure: "and her sensual song extends itself / creating a clear atmosphere of bliss / in the shade of the coconut trees." ("Y su canto sensual se va extendiendo / como una clara atmósfera de dicha / bajo la sombra de los cocoteros.")

The last stanza returns to the originator of the reverie, the poetic voice responsible for revealing the almost sexual fantasy. "Todo," the scene and the consciousness of it, is extinguished:

With the echo of her song
everything is extinguished,
and all that remains in my soul
is the profound u of the fierce diphthong,
in whose maternal curve is hidden
the prolific harmony of sex.[13]

(Al rumor de su canto
todo se va extinguiendo,
y sólo queda en mi alma
la ú profunda del diptongo fiero,
en cuya curva maternal se esconde
la armonía prolífica del sexo.)

The poetic "I" is left unsatisfied. The song evokes or excites the desire for possession. The vision is extinguished (a verb used in reference to fire or passion), but the desire remains, elusive, hidden, and, finally, magnified.

In view of my analysis of the distance of the poetic voice and his unsatisfied desire in "Kalahari" and "Pueblo negro," how are we to read the "celebratory impulse" attributed to many of the poems in this collection? This difficult question must be addressed because it is at the heart of this poetry's reception and enduring popularity. Let us take the example of "Majestad negra." First we should ask what or who is glorified in this poem:

Along the red hot Antillean street
goes Tembandumba of the Quimbamba
—rumba, macumba, candombe, bámbula—
between two lines of black faces.
Ahead of her a Congo—cowbell and maraca—
plays a conga rhythm *bomba que bamba.*

(Por la encendida calle antillana
va Tembandumba de la Quimbamba
—rumba, macumba, candombe, bámbula—
entre dos filas de negras caras.
Ante ella un congo—gongo y maraca—
ritma una conga bomba que bamba.)

"She" is seen walking down the street. Her name, which evokes tongue-in-cheek an African noble or *Mardi Gras* queen, also invokes the parenthetical reference to secular and sacred Afro-Caribbean and Afro-Brazilian rituals and dances. She is among black faces, facing a black man, "congo," playing musical instruments. He produces "conga" and "bomba" rhythms. There is an invitation to dance issued by the music.

The next stanza merges the movement of the "reina" with the workings of a sugar mill, so that she exudes or produces sugar as she walks. As her hips sway from side to side, "el caderamen, masa con masa," pressing, or extracting rhythms, she is the dark sugar mill pressing a sensual harvest. She accepts the invitation to dance.

Swinging her hips the Queen strolls on,
and sliding from her immense rump
are playful gyrations curdled by the cowbell
into rivers of sugar and molasses.
An ebony sugar mill for a sensual harvest,
the hips, flesh against flesh,
squeeze out rhythms, they sweat and bleed,
and the grinding culminates in a dance.

(Culipandeando la Reina avanza,
y de su inmensa grupa resbalan
meneos cachondos que el gongo cuaja
en ríos de azúcar y de melaza.
Prieto trapiche de sensual zafra,
el caderamen, masa con masa,
exprime ritmos, suda que sangra,
y la molienda culmina en danza.)

Motion and energy are masterfully conveyed by the poem's images and alliterations. There is an ascending sensuality in the verses; a climaxing, "culmina," into dance. As her hips sway, they squeeze out rhythms. Her sensuality is on display for the visual pleasure of a viewer—from whose perspective the poem is told—who focuses closely on her gluteal region. The mulatta is objectified, thus becoming available for visual possession.

It is important to note that her very body sublimates work into play when she is renamed *trapiche,* sugar mill, whose motion transforms the *zafra,* sugar cane harvest. The metaphor of body-as-mill suggests that blacks in the Americas do not really work, or that the work they do is pleasure-producing. Though there is mention of sweat and blood, hard work is sexualized and fancied desirable by the viewer. The point is not that the black anatomy so vilified by white supremacy is openly and frankly celebrated. The celebration is not without cost to the black body, seen—yet again—in its function as producer of profit and pleasure for the viewer who desires it. Who benefits from the body of the queenly dancer? The viewer for his part, and the implied reader too. As for the involvement of blacks, "dos filas de negras caras" and the drum and maraca player, their position is qualitatively different from the observation point where the poem is uttered. They are not the ones having the sublimated fantasy; they are part of the fantasy.

"Majestad negra" is an ambiguous praise-song. "She" is glorified as the best—the flower—of the Caribbean and Africa, "Flor de Tórtola, rosa de Uganda," in whose honor drums "crackle" or play as if on fire. Also on fire are the *Antillas,* burning for her, or for the desire of her, during carnival. She receives homage from the islands who offer different "gifts":

Haiti offers you her calabashes;
fiery rums are Jamaica's gift to you;
Cuba says: Come on mulatta!
And Puerto Rico: sugar-sweet *melamba!*

(Haití te ofrece sus calabazas;
fogosos rones te da Jamaica;
Cuba te dice: ¡dale, mulata!
Y Puerto Rico: ¡melao melamba!)

The desired woman is now alluring to the islands, portrayed as "male." They—Cuba and Puerto Rico—urge her, in the heat of passion, to keep on dancing for them.

The poem ends with a vibrant cheer to black people, "Hi ho, my dark-faced *cocolos!*" ("¡Sús, mis cocolos de negras caras!") and an exhortation to the drums and maracas to thunder and vibrate, "Sound, drums; vibrate maracas," ("Tronad, tambores; vibrad maracas,") as she strolls down "The glowing Caribbean street." ("Por la encendida calle antillana.") The fanfare is in her honor, but, if read in the light of the second stanza, it will also benefit the observer who now makes his presence known, "¡Sús, mis cocolos de negras caras!" and feels a sense of connection with the black men, *his* "cocolos." The poem hints at an integration with the black men, rather than with the people as a whole, which would also include the mulatta. There is indeed a will to "speak with." This possibility is thwarted not only by the sexual politics of the poem, but by the lack of acknowledgment and the sublimation of the real nature of black people's "work" expressed through the very body of the celebrated object.

Critics of *Tuntún de pasa y grifería* have long theorized on the meaning of the book's title. Aníbal González advances an idea supported by the dictionary definition of the word *tuntún* as used in "al tuntún," or "al buen tuntún," meaning "without thought or premeditation; without knowledge of the issue."[14] For some critiques the word tuntún (as in "al buen tuntún"), meaning jocularly or good-naturedly, reflects the spirit that permeates many of the poems.

Tuntún is an onomatopoeia that mimics the beat of a drum. It becomes, in the title of the whole collection, *Drum-beat of Nappy Heads and High Yellows*, or *Tuntún de pasa y grifería* (see Illustration 4). "Pasa" is a derogatory term for crimped hair and "grifería," from "grifo," refers to a person of black ancestry with light skin but who retains coiled hair. My understanding of the title is supported by a number of verses in the poem "Intermedios del hombre blanco." The section titled "Tambores" refers to the power of beating drums that, accordingly, can even affect the unsuspecting white man who is apt to dismiss their potent lure:

The night is a breeding ground for drums
that croak in the woods,
with crippled throats of hide
when some campfire awakens them.

In the dense mud of the shadow
blinking with little firefly eyes,
those big-bellied musical bugs
splash the rhythm with their feet.

With the sleepy gesture of the reptile
they lift their heads heavily
giving to the warm wind the slimy
grace of their *tuntunesque* energy.

The white man hears them
lost far off in the woods . . .
It's the assiduous tuntún that spills out
invisible in the immense night.[15]

(La noche es un criadero de tambores
que croan en la selva,
con rencas gargantas de pellejo
cuando alguna fogata los despierta.

En el lodo compacto de la sombra
parpadeado de ojillos de luciérnagas,
esos ventrudos bichos musicales
con sus patas de ritmo chapotean.

Con soñoliento gesto de batracios
alzan pesadamente la cabeza,
dando al cálido viento la pringosa
gracia de su energía *tuntuneca.*

Los oye el hombre blanco
perdido allá en las selvas . . .
Es un tuntún asiduo que se vierte
imponderable por la noche inmensa.)

Evocation plays a strong part in these verses. In the mysterious night—prolific hatchery—the drums have the power to overcome the outsider (the white man). The lure of the drums is such that he is admonished to "Cover your ears, / close every opening in your soul" ("Tápate las orejas / cierra toda abertura de tu alma"). There is no antidote for "its terrible sting / will forever run in your veins" ("su terrible ponzoña/correrá para siempre en tus venas"). The poem in fact mocks the white man, seeing in him the danger of "going native." On one hand, the poetic voice clearly sides with the drums and their awesome power. On the other, the ceremonies that bring the drums to life, smack of sensationalistic (colonialist) literature and film. The religious ceremonies with their propitiating drums are of an ominous, unintelligible, and alien character "in the sensual heaven of the black soul" ("por el cielo sensual del alma negra"). The poet tries to get at a sense of immanence (the indwelling presence of deity in the world), but misrepresents it. This double valence is characteristic of most of the poems in *Tuntún.*

Ghanaian critic Josaphat Kubayanda has read the *negrista* project as one that, albeit unintentionally, promotes a distorted or "reductionist" view of Africa, of its peoples and cultures.[16] More importantly, he sees this poetry as contributing to "inventing the primitive African" from the point of view of white supremacy.[17] For Kubayanda, Palés's poetic visions suffer, in spite of their "substantial descriptive power," due to his lack of dependable information about Africa and lack of "in-depth knowledge of the Afro-American values they seek to convey."[18] Moreover, Kubayanda proposes, "Ancestral

Africa, as in Palés Matos's 'Ñam-Ñam,' is occasionally embellished with a creative elegance but frequently colored with an exaggerated inaccuracy. The 'gran matriarca' is Africa, and the specific poetic jungle-world of cannibalistic cults is Tanganyika (part of modern Tanzania). Here Africans are made to thrive on foreign blood and African laws are rooted in violent forces . . . These African gods stand opposed to an intellectualizing order. . . . Animality comes through as the black ancestral essence."[19] These criticisms are important since the poems have been praised by many for their "accuracy" of depiction. The poems in *Tuntún*, which deal with Afro-Caribbean religiosity, obscure rather than clarify this religious expression. As Kubayanda puts it: "Palés Matos was handicapped by not knowing Africa firsthand. This handicap . . . is reflected in his presentation of African-Caribbean religions as flippant, colorful exhibits lacking organic spirituality."[20]

A poem such as "Náñigo al cielo" is a case in point. Here again we must read this poem while taking into account the perspective from which it is written. This is one of the poems which purportedly is constructed on humor and irony. The question that must be asked is, humor at whose expense? Arce understood that Palés, a "civilized and skeptical" white man, had a perspective that would authorize and enable him to make the "joke." In fact, Arce saw Palés's perspective as an "acierto" or as right on target. She shared the joke. This humor was celebrated by readers from the very first time the poems were published. But not everyone is laughing. As my discussion in the previous chapter showed, the poems present a problem of *point of view* that refuses to go away. In "Ñáñigo al cielo," Kubayanda rightfully points out, "What comes through more forcefully are anti-Voodoo mocking overtones and the inability to penetrate the deeply symbolic and emotional significance of alcohol, dress, music, and plants in the Afro-Caribbean religions. From the vantage point of the more knowledgeable insider, Guillén and Césaire will bring to light the religious and creative importance of these symbols."[21] Arce had taken pride in pointing to the outsider position as a plus for Palés's poems. This is the very distinction that Kubayanda sees as a minus. She too saw Guillén as the insider, but interpreted this as a weakness or flaw in the Cuban poet's perspective, which, after all, did not enjoy the benefits of the "from above" vantage point.

As Kubayanda suggests, from an Afrocentric point of view, the poems devalue "directly or by allusion" Caribbean-African ethnic life. Unfortunately, a number of critics refuse to take this charge into serious consideration. But Kubayanda stresses that Palés's work has an adverse impact on people of African descent: "This poet, it seems appropriate to add, passionately dreams about a primitive force in the form of an unconscious blackness which fails to harmonize with his conscious ('civilized') self."[22] The failure is one of lack of connection that allows for a judgmental approach to the Afro-Puerto Rican cultural reality, as the Ghanaian critic sees it. Kubayanda explains, "A good example of this attitude is found in the poem where he sees the Puerto Rican wake cult as a 'Falsa canción de Baquiné,' or a mysteriously passive force—wonderfully impressionistic and unintentionally damaging to Africanity."[23] He also suggests that even in the treatment of sexuality, when blacks are concerned, *negrismo* has a deleterious effect. As Kubayanda puts it, "the bodies of black characters are licentiously reconstructed" by poets who "transformed their black types into imposing phallic toys" since they had "no understanding of African sacred notions of sex."[24] Palés does not escape the stereotyping trap.

Kubayanda's own analysis of Nicolás Guillén and Aimé Césaire provides an important key to the question of how to read *negrista* poetry: "Indeed, Guillén's and Césaire's verses are splattered and spangled with the blood, chains, and tortures of the collective past. In them group experiences of toils and trammels are assimilated by the often marginal telling voice as his personal experiences."[25] It is important to stress that the poetic vision of Guillén or Césaire is not validated by the mere ethnicity of the writers. As representations of blackness they receive their force in part from the perspective of the poetic voice. More often than not their representation of black people tries to incorporate the history of resistance to oppression, not just a celebration of certain aspects of black culture that whites can also have access to for their own pleasure. But even *Négritude*, as my discussion of Soyinka's critique of the movement shows, was not exempt at times from a logic of European supremacy. Ultimately, we must ask what do blacks gain from Palés's poetry? Do Palés's efforts to intervene in *criollo* consciousness leave everything "in its place," or is there a change demanded of white consciousness? Is Palés's poetry advancing a vision more respectful of Africans' humanity in Puerto Rico and in the world?

Critic Jerome Branche agrees that *negrismo* is a repositioning of Creole hegemonic power with respect to the national identity and ethnicity debate.[26] Branche pointedly argues that through *negrismo* Creole poets bestow upon themselves the authority to represent blackness in a way that does not provide black people with wider representational venues, thus maintaining the status quo. For example, Emilio Ballagas, from a white middle-class background, uses the authority of Fernando Ortiz to support the assertion that "poesía negra" is a cultural and linguistic entity of which anyone can partake. As Branche cogently shows, Ballagas speaks from a position of privilege *for the other* in his anthologies and pronouncements regarding "black verse." Ballagas traces a genealogy and geography for "poesía negra" that separates it from the colonial legacy and racial tensions. Branche explains further: "The Ballaguian scheme, in sum, would take advantage of the mutism imposed on this subaltern social sector and would establish in one fell swoop the voice and the right of 'literary representation' for the middle class white writer."[27]

Moreover, *negrismo* reflects an apprehensive reaction to the claims of cultural autonomy made by the Harlem Renaissance and *Négritude*. Branche insists that the work of Creole poets should be read against the grain of the Pan-African discourse of Langston Hughes, Aimé Cesaire, René Maran, and "the prestige and audibility that this Pan-African discourse of the time had obtained."[28] To this I would add that because of the very claims that *negrismo* makes about its ability to represent the black experience, these poems should always be read in dialogue with the works of an international multigenerational black canon that would include slave narratives, autobiographies, novels, poems, and essays, and let the chips fall where they may.

Another clue to deciphering *negrismo* has to do with the issue of literary authority. Apologists of this movement often include Góngora and Lope de Vega as "precursors" of *poesía negrista*—as Margot Arce and Ballagas do. Many variables come into play in the matter of the much advertised ability that poets like Palés Matos are said to have in representing the black experience. Jerome Branche is troubled by critics like Mercedes Lopéz-Baralt who "take the formidable leap of converting [Palés's] Caribbean thematic in the foundational gesture of Négritude."[29] With all its faults, *Négritude* had an ideological and poetic impetus—identitarian and emancipatory in Léon Damas, Leopold Senghor, and Aimé Cesaire who coined the term in Paris in 1934.

Indeed, if *negrista* poetry can represent blackness "better" than poets of African descent can, what need is there of ever fomenting and supporting the poetry of black writers? As Branche points out, Ballagas "dismisses racial difference in a poetry of racial themes."[30] Additionally, he stresses that "the hermeneutic discourse about Palés's oeuvre, and a lot of *negrismo* itself, avoids in great measure a confrontation with racism, or with the contradictions of class and gender in a medium in which these contradictions stand out."[31] In fact we find ourselves in the extraordinary circumstance that would cast G. R. Coulthard, Richard L. Jackson, Lemuel Johnson, Isabelo Zenón Cruz, Claudette Williams, Roberto Márquez, Alba Lía Barrios, Jerome Branche, Gerald Guinness, and critics like myself as recalcitrant readers who are unduly sensitive to the racist stereotypes of this poetry.[32] Invariably apologists for *negrismo* see divergent or African-centered critiques as "misreadings" of this poetry.

Critic Alba Lía Barrios adroitly considers the element of "estrangement" in Palés's and other *negrista* poetry. Her reading of "Baquiné," a chapter of Palés's unfinished novel *Litoral*, claims that "the fundamental device is that of estrangement: to look from the outside with surprised eyes at a black religious ceremony. The gaze travels the surface, the rite becomes a magical curiosity."[33] Barrios recognizes that in Palés's *Tuntún* the inclusion of a Caribbean lexicon and rhythmic recourses is an innovative aesthetic device that gives the sense that blackness is present in the poems. Nonetheless, "they create at least the illusion that the talk is not *about* blacks but *from* blacks. We say illusion, because we believe that in Palés it is above all an aesthetic recourse that deftly plays with the presence that lexicon and rhythm confer on it."[34]

Barrios—like Zenón Cruz and Branche—sees the grotesque humor of this poetry not as a virtue, but as a failing. As we have seen reviewing the use of irony in the case of Emilio S. Belaval, the edge of Palés's irony is similarly reserved for those he considers social inferiors—Haitians and other people of African descent. As Barrios puts it, "Thus in the ensemble one perceives the derision that there is at times in the gaze of the superior toward the inferior, whom social distance converts into the strange, the curious, the comical, the folkloric."[35] When we take into account the totality of the poet's work, we realize that there is indeed a different treatment of black and white subjects. To paraphrase Barrios, his oeuvre has an intimist tone for themes that are deemed to deal with the introspective realities of whites, and a buffoonish packaging for things deemed black.[36] Caricature always has an aggressive intention.

These and other critics remind us that *Tuntún* is part of a literary tradition in Spanish that has attempted to treat the "black" theme; Lope de Vega, Quevedo, Cervantes all made fun of black characters.[37] Aggressive caricature and appropriation often go hand in hand, as the history of minstrelsy amply shows us. In the case of the United States, for example, was blackface a tribute, an imitation, or as some have argued a bid by recently arrived white working-class immigrants to exhibit their adherence to the American system of white supremacy?[38] In Cuba, *negrismo* was a movement that spanned many genres—dance, painting, novel, symphonic music, theater. Yet people of African descent were not the principal beneficiaries of this multi-generic *negrismo;* they were the raw material. Its promoters and main protagonists were Creoles. Branche gives as an instance the career of the classically trained musician Eliseo Grenet who appropriated the music of black and mulatto street musicians, becoming famous and flourishing during the 1930s in France, the United States, and England.[39] Another example of the commodification of the black vogue was the reinstatement of the carnival *(comparsas)* as a way to promote tourism. In fact, Fernando Ortiz, who in 1936 founded the Association of Afro-Cuban Studies, gave his blessings to the revival of the *comparsas* as Branche reminds us.[40] Though the recognition of Afro-Cuban spirituality undergirding the secular *comparsas* can be seen as a democratizing gesture, this arrogation of black culture as spectacle took place against the backdrop of the brutal racism and repression of Afro-Cuban culture scarcely a decade and a half earlier. The 1912 repression of the Independent Party of Color was a vivid part of the cultural memory of black Cubans. So too were the unfulfilled promises of the war of independence.[41] We can also recall that Esteban Montejo, who had been born a slave and who had fought as a *mambí* soldier, remarked in his autobiographical narrative that Afro-Cubans had not benefited much from their struggles for racial and social justice. The long tradition of the blackface theatre in Cuba, Teatro Bufo, accompanied the experience of exploitation, segregation, and hunger suffered by many Afro-Cubans. Branche points out that in general Afro-Cuban professionals did not welcome the *negrista* vogue; many saw it as a retrograde and divisive diversion from the real social conditions and problems that all Cubans needed to face together.[42]

The case of Afro-Puerto Rican poet Carmen María Colón Pellot affords us a better understanding of the terms under which race, gender, and sexuality informed the circulation of poetic discourse during the period in question. Though a teacher, journalist, and poet, Colón Pellot did not have unrestricted access to the prestigious institutions of the Creole intellectual field. Yet, as Gladys Jiménez Muñoz incisively argues, Colón Pellot's only known work, *Ámbar mulato* (1938), deftly engages—in order to subvert—the parameters of *negrista* poetry. Colón Pellot indirectly takes issue with the feminine personas and psychic states represented in the neo-romantic poetry of *criolla* Clara Lair (nom de plume of Mercedes Negrón Muñoz), whose *Arras de Cristal* (1937), published by the *Bilblioteca de Autores Puertorriqueños*, had attracted the praise of her contemporaries. At the same time, Colón Pellot's other interlocutor is Luis Palés Matos, whose poems exalting mulatta sexuality were on everyone's lips. Jiménez Muñoz explains that a poem like "Motivos de envidia mulata" is Colon Pellot's response to the double standard by which Afro-Puerto Rican women's sexuality was measured and misrepresented. In order to be taken seriously by those debating national identity, the poet addresses the reader through the tropes of *negrismo*, but with a twist. In her introduction she takes pains to correct misconceptions about Puerto Rican racial history and politics. In fact Colón Pellot's foreword to her book proposes that Afro-Puerto Ricans were the founders of the nation and that practically everyone has mulatto ancestry:

> Speaking of history, let us go back to the year 1530. Mother Spain ordered that a census be taken on the island of Puerto Rico. The total population of white inhabitants was 327 in contrast to 3,830 inhabitants of color (blacks and some Indians). Regarding such an interesting fact I will limit myself to the consideration of two aspects: first, that the colored race has exerted a notable influence in our insular life; and second, that the superstitious and *ñañigo* "perfect Negro" type does not exist here. Our current population is *jíbaro* intermingled with mulatto blood.[43] (Haciendo un poco de historia, retrocedamos al año 1530. Madre España ordena hacer un censo en la isla de Puerto Rico. El total de población blanca es de 327 habitantes en contraste con 3,830 habitantes de color [negros y algunos indios.] De dato tan interesante me limitaré a considerar sólo dos aspectos: primero, que la raza de color ha ejercido una influencia notable en nuestra vida insular; y segundo, que aquí no existe el tipo de "negro perfecto" supersticioso y ñañigo. Nuestra población actual es jíbara veteada de sangre mulata.)

The poet, as Jiménez Muñoz explains, adds much complexity to claims regarding national identity. Colón Pellot is able to correct the notion of the *jíbaro*'s mythic whiteness, and at the same time speak as a voice of the race enacting, as the poet puts it, "a mulatto and Puerto Rican poetry, like my own race"[44] ("poesía mulata y puertorriqueña, como mi raza misma").

Moreover, she repudiates portrayals that stress the excessive sexuality of the mulatta, emphasizing instead that her verse—while not repudiating sex—is not inspired by the sexual theme. The author states that she is more interested in emotional states, emphasizing that the mulatto has "exquisitely sensitive psychical fibers"[45] (fibras anímicas exquisitamente sensitivas).

By far the most suggestive aspect of Jiménez Muñoz's reading of *Ámbar mulato* has to do with her exegesis of the poem "Motivos de envidia mulata" as a "critique of the white *criolla*, particularly of how 'race' functions as an important element in understanding the sexual double standard directed at women in Puerto Rico."[46] The "white cloud" of the poem has freedom to flout social norms, yet still keep her honor, "and they rhyme you as chaste and beautiful." According to Jiménez Muñoz, "The white Creole woman was in an advantaged position at the sexual level, with relation to the black or mulatto woman. Mulattas needed to be more careful and to punctiliously follow social norms in a context where they were seen as hypersexual beings: 'I am enslaved by norms; / by Christian rules.' The point that Colón Pellot seems to make is that not only do white Creole women live differently, but they live by different rules."[47] These poems were written in the context of a discriminatory job market that forced many more black and mulatto women to work as servants in the houses of whites, or as cooks or nurses' aids. The most black women could aspire to was to become school teachers. "In that sense," Jiménez Muñoz affirms, "even though the body of the white woman had its own limitations, these did not carry the same significance as those of the black or mulatto woman."[48] Essentially, we may add, white women could marry into privilege where black and mulatto women could not.

Carmen Colón Pellot's work merits further studies that could elucidate a poetics of masks and dissemblance such as critic Jerome Branche has delineated regarding Afro-Cuban literature. The complexity of this and other poems in *Ámbar mulato* points to gaps in the *negrista* discourse of Luis Palés Matos, particularly in the case of what critic Mercedes López-Baralt has characterized as the pioneering eroticism of Palés. López-Baralt alerts the reader to the presence of eroticism throughout his oeuvre: "What we tend to lose sight of is that sensuality is one of the most characteristic traits of the work of the great Puerto Rican poet, from his earliest poems to the last collection about love and death, the Filí-Melé cycle."[49] López-Baralt shows that "Las voces secretas" harbors a voyeuristic perspective, a position the poet never abandons when it comes to women's eroticism. Nor does she shy away from analyzing some of the sexist male/female double standard present in Palés's erotic poetry.[50] Yet what needs to be added is that Palés's eroticism, in this poem where a young woman's autoerotic activity is celebrated, has a very intimate tone. When it comes to white women, sexuality is private, even protected by the marital chamber. It is hard to abandon the impression that the eroticism of black or mulatto women is treated with much less delicacy. As was customary at the time, erotic activities were divided by race. The rules of the Creole libidinal economy were different for white and black women.

Notes on the Fortunes of a Critical Discourse

The defense and critical appraisal of Palés's *Tuntún de pasa y grifería* favored by Margot Arce would prevail and endure until the early 1970s. Then emphasis would shift to underscore the anti-colonial perspective of the poems, as an early essay by Arcadio Díaz Quiñones attests. This "anti-colonial" reading became more popular in the context of national liberation and anti-imperialist literature that inspired many intellectuals and activists around the world. Indeed, Arcadio Díaz Quiñones's 1970 essay, entitled "La poesía negra de Luis Palés Matos: realidad y conciencia de su dimensión colectiva," presented a revitalized reading of the poems. His thesis is that Palés had a clear social vision in *Tuntún:* "It is precisely in black poetry—as we will attempt to demonstrate—where he shows himself most clearly as a committed writer, as radical and rebellious, as iconoclastic and irreverent."[51] Nonetheless, the analysis is timid as to the naming of racism. Díaz Quiñonez's essay only euphemistically refers to racial discrimination in the Puerto Rican context.[52] The critic's debt to his teacher Margot Arce leads him to repeat many of her judgments of the *negrista* project. He subscribes to many of her propositions regarding the poet's disenchantment with the political situation of the Caribbean and of the island: "Palés attacks this situation with his satires, at times pungent and virulent, and at others, mocking and jocose."[53] Díaz Quiñones does not present anything new on the question of the representation of race. In fact, he still assumes the perspective of the white critic who understands white as normative. From this approach, it is easy to see blacks but not the history of black struggle, resistance, defeat, pain, and triumph. He is only able to say that Palés's poems insist on the black "element," and to timidly suggest its possible uses or "value" to white Antilleans: "Because it is an important aspect of Caribbean culture and Palés hopes to recreate that society in his poetry and to give us a full view, a faultless image of that world. But, more importantly, because *blackness is the differentiating element in the Caribbean in relation to the Hispanic or the Nordic*, and the poet wants us to remember that, so as to insist that on that path there are possibilities for renovation and sources of energy."[54] We have to ask, however, who is to harness these possibilities of renewal and sources of energy? In the 1930s the Puerto Rican white elite needed to be shown that they could also use the "black element," instead of shunning it and of being ashamed that it would embarrass them in the eyes of white foreigners. Palés tried to rally and organize his readers to view people of African descent in a less menacing and more "benign" way. But Díaz Quiñones assures us that if there is a simplification of the black experience in this poetry, it is well-intentioned. It is a simplification necessary for poetic reasons: "an exaggeration that is justifiable however because it is part of a scheme, a simplification of reality that is necessary in order to capture it poetically. It is interesting to realize, for example, that when Palés evokes Africanness, he principally evokes the dances, the gods, the rituals, and the traditions that give the tribe mysterious defensive forces."[55] This emphasis on dances and rituals, however, promotes a "creative truncation," as Wole Soyinka said of *Négritude*. It privileges elements of interest to whites looking at "black culture." These are preferred elements by the white consumers of black difference. Here whites are practically "eating the Other," as bell hooks has said, and having a good time at it.[56]

But the self-recognition supposedly enacted in *negrista* poetry is impossible. We need to ask whose "self" we are talking about. Díaz Quiñones, for his part, insists that the poems promote society's self-recognition: "In effect, there are Caribbean ingredients of all sorts that allow him to create a poetry through which society can recognize itself."[57] But as I have argued, it is not society in general that is made to recognize itself here. It is the *criollo* elite who is offered possibilities of reimagining and representing an undesirable history of race relations in a way that makes blacks more "palatable" and makes whites more generous.

At this stage of his critical assessment of Palés "black verses" Díaz Quiñones still hastily repeats some of the most unfortunate of Arce's remarks. He quotes at length directly from her 1933 essay "Los poemas negros de Luis Palés Matos": "The vocabulary is heterogeneous . . . the *Negroes twangy speech*, and the silent consonants that accent the rhythm and give it the force of a drum beat. The abundance of words and sharp rhymes fulfills the goal of the clear rhythmic effect."[58] ("El vocabulario es heterogéneo . . . el *habla gangosa del negro*, y las oclusivas sordas, que acentúan el ritmo y le prestan fuerza de golpe de tambor. La abundancia de palabras y de rimas agudas sirve al propósito del claro efecto rítmico.") Regrettably, stereotypes—like the one of the slow, nasal speech of blacks—are passed on unexamined.

Díaz Quiñones was to modify his perspective in a 1976 essay, "Notas para el estudio del *Tuntún de pasa y grifería*." Here the critic is more direct about the racism of the Puerto Rican elite and the social context in which the poems were received than any previous Puerto Rican assessments: "Palés Matos wanted to contribute, through literature, to a better understanding of national reality, focusing on—in a society that ranges from furtively to openly racist—fundamental aspects of its Africanness that until that time had gone almost without notice in literature."[59] He rightly points out that even the collection's title—*Tuntún de pasa y grifería*—was an antidote to the *jíbaro* national myth and that it was understood as a provocation by the "alarmed partisans of Caribbean Hispanicism and Occidentalism."[60] In this particular essay Díaz Quiñones differs with Arce's views in the appraisal of the social context in which the poems appeared in the 1930s. Moreover, in yet another essay on Palés, Díaz Quinõnes would underscore that these poems were in a direct polemic with "the *jibarista* vision and with his teacher, the poet Luis Lloréns Torres,"[61] and that already by 1926 Palés himself declared that the world of the *jíbaro* was as distant to Puerto Ricans as "the Eiffel tower and Napoleon's white horse."[62]

One of the cornerstones of Díaz Quiñonez's "Notas para el estudio" was his explication of the poem "Mulata-Antilla." *Tuntún*'s first edition, we should remember, came out in 1937. But the later version that was augmented by Palés himself was comprised of poems written from 1925 to 1952. The analysis by Díaz Quiñones centers on the 1950 version of the poem, which, placed in the context of *poesía afroantillana,* the critic sees as an erotic and patriotic hymn. Díaz Quiñonez proposes that the poem be understood more as an evolving project than as a singularly coherent fact presented to the readers. It is "a complex aesthetic and ideological process that has evolved over a period of at least ten years, or even more if one takes into account the revisions and modifications of the second edition of 1950."[63] "Mulata-Antilla" is celebratory of the Antillean world through the body of the mulatta: "What in the beginning is a fundamentally erotic poem becomes, with the additions of 1950, the ethical and political vision of Palés. From the liberation of the senses he has moved toward the utopian proposal of the liberation of the Caribbean world."[64] Díaz Quiñones posits that the augmented version that closes the 1950 edition has the effect of affirming a Caribbean unity and identity, "centered first and foremost in racial and cultural *mestizaje.*"[65] Anglo-Puerto Rican critic Gerald Guinness cautions against reading too much anti-imperialist meaning in Palés, as Arcadio Díaz Quiñones does in this case. Guinness instead sees an evolution in the poet's vision between 1925 and 1953: "whereas the earlier *negrista* poetry presented the black experience as seen from without, the 'mulatto' poems of the 1940s and 50s evoke the Antillean reality as experienced from within."[66] This can be said of poems like "Menu" or "Canción del mar," yet I seek to problematize the reading of "Mulata-Antilla" in this encompassing pro-Antillean light.

An Ambiguous Search for Freedom

Examination of the status of the *mulata* as "heroine of the drama" of Caribbean identity reveals her as a paradigmatic figure that gives us a unique opportunity to analyze race and gender as interlocking systems. Here we should remember that the avant-garde strategy of liberation used women and women's bodies as a site in which male freedom would be fought out.[67] The same is true with regard to race. The black race would facilitate the psychic and sensual liberation of the white man, trapped by his own "super-civilization," with a way of accessing repressed or forgotten "primitive" energies—which blacks always and forever embody. The mulatta, in light of this, is indeed a privileged locus or medium where these two imperatives can be fulfilled—simultaneously—to the white man's satisfaction.

"Mulata-Antilla" establishes a relationship in which the mulatta is acted upon. She makes possible a connection between the male poetic voice and the Antilles. As the first verse reads, "And now in you, mulatta, / I take refuge in the warm Caribbean sea." ("En ti ahora, mulata, / me acojo al tibio mar de las Antillas.") The body of the dark woman is an ocean:

> Water slow and sensual as molasses,
> sugar port, hot bay,
> with a resting light
> gilding the clean ripple,
> and in the sleepy buzz of the hive
> shaped by the shore's comings and goings.
>
> (Agua sensual y lenta de melaza,
> puerto de azúcar, cálida bahía,
> con la luz en reposo
> dorando la onda limpia,
> y en el soñoliento zumbo de colmena
> que cuajan los trajines de la orilla.)

The idea of sugar and woman suggested in "Pueblo negro" reappears. This time she is an ocean of sweetness moving sensually. Possession will be sexual possession. "He" travels, or has access to the other islands, on the curves of her body. She is not the ultimate destination. He goes somewhere else through her: "And now in you, mulatta, / I cross the islands' sea." ("En ti ahora, mulata, / cruzo el mar de las islas.") Note that this mute woman's only sign of life are her pensive eyes, "la noche de tus ojos, pensativa."

His sexual tension mounts in the third stanza, signaled here by the ellipsis and the exclamation, "And now in you, mulatta . . . / oh how glorious to awaken in the Antilles!" ("En ti ahora, mulata . . . / ¡oh despertar glorioso en las Antillas!") She brings an effusion of colors, scents (of fruits and tobacco), happiness, and warmth. Delicious inebriation follows:

> fierce color reached by the high note,
> red fiery music of happiness,
> and hot winged aromas
> —lemon, tobacco, pineapple—

buzzing in one's ears
their drunken voices of delight.

(bravo color que el do de pecho alcanza,
música al rojo vivo de alegría,
y calientes cantáridas de aroma
—limón, tabaco, piña—
zumbando a los sentidos
sus embriagadas voces de delicia.)

After the climax her status is changed. Now she "is," but also simultaneously he "owns," the islands that now become "his": "Now, mulatta, you are / all the land and sea of my islands." ("Eres ahora, mulata / todo el mar y la tierra de mis islas.") She now makes available to him all her fruits in her sun-tempered body: " . . . All/ the fruits you offer me, oh mulatta!" (" . . . Todos/ los frutos ¡oh mulata! tú me brindas.")

The next stanza continues with the enumeration of her harvest. Her domain, that of the bananas and coconut, is a weapon to be used against the tourist interlopers. She is extolled as a dark Valkyrie of a green Valhalla singing a Creole song. The mulatta now becomes his freedom. The male speaker can possess freedom by having her. But we know nothing whatsoever of *her* freedom. Indeed, part of the project here is the simplification of *her* narrative of origin, or at least what a neo-Freudian reading would suggest. Possession is a displaced figure for slavery as the basis for the white man's freedom in the Caribbean. He tells her that, for him, she is fulfillment and effortless love: "You are a free immensity without limits, / you are love without obstacles and rushing." ("Eres inmensidad libre y sin límites, / eres amor sin trabas y sin prisas.") More importantly than this, her womb is the site of the union of the vital forces of "my" two races: "in your womb my two races are joined / their vital potencies unleashed" ("en tu vientre conjugan mis dos razas / sus vitales potencias expansivas"). Is she a mother of a new race here, or is she that new race herself? The male voice talks about "mis dos razas," opening a number of interpretive possibilities. This suggests that the poetic "I" is able to possess both races, by possessing the fruit of her womb. Perhaps the poetic voice is himself a mulatto? The mulatta's "torrid" love is extolled in verses that rewrite passages of the "Song of Songs." Like the biblical bride, however, the mulatta is not truly dark. She is darkened by the sun. She has lighter skin than a black-skinned black—which is what historically made the mulatta socially attractive. She is not a "pure" African.

The last stanza reiterates the male speaker's status as possessor of the Antilles, "my fiery and sensual lands" ("fogosas y sensuales tierras mías"). And again, "¡Antillas, mis Antillas!" A call to Caribbean unity is made at a decidedly political moment in the poem: "Upon the Caribbean sea, all united / dreaming and suffering and struggling / against plagues, cyclones and greed." ("Sobre el Caribe mar, todas unidas / soñando y padeciendo y forcejeando / contra pestes, ciclones y codicias.") The last two verses of the poem recapitulate the trope of the mulatta as freedom and as a medium through which ownership is achieved: "because you, mulatta of the tropics, are / freedom singing in my Antilles" ("porque eres tú, mulata de los trópicos, / la libertad cantando en mis Antillas").

Díaz Quiñones lauds this poem as a patriotic hymn to unity, and it can be read as such. But such a reading glosses over the way this poem inscribes a victimizing colonization based on gender and on race. Palés's song to *mestizaje*—social and racial—is the heroic song of the white male voice whose desire for ownership is here ultimately celebrated. We know very little of the object of desire, except as perceived by he who desires. We do not know whether the desire is mutual. His lover is mute and passive. Though the poignant concatenation "dreaming and suffering and struggling" proposes a moment of dynamic solidarity, it is not enough to outweigh its gender and racial politics. "Mulata-Antilla" is a seductive poem that gives Caribbean readers a new myth of origins where love, not violence and exploitation, gives the *Antillas* its identity. This poem has a decidedly intimate voice proper to love poetry. Yet the element of mutuality, as in most love poems, is absent. It is difficult to read the poetic persona without its racial markers—the white man courting the mulatto woman. This is the subjectivity that gives us access to the world constructed by the poem.

Luis Palés Matos himself was sensitive to charges of racism that the *negrista* project elicited. In a 1938 interview with Jorge Font Saldaña the notoriously reserved poet assured readers: "I have tried to incorporate the black theme, forgotten and disdained, into a serious notion of art. . . . Those who only see caricature in my artistic conception of the black man demonstrate a censurable limitation."[68] ("Yo he tratado de incorporar el tema negro, olvidado y menospreciado, a un sentido serio de arte. . . . Quien sólo vea caricatura en mi concepción artística del negro demuestra una limitación censurable.") But are we allowed to see the instances of stereotyping that are indeed present in some of the poems? It might be fair to say that *Tuntún de pasa y grifería* oscillates between homage and stereotype, and that this tension is impossible to resolve. A number of poems in this much-read and often-performed collection do make a mockery of people of African descent and contribute to the stereotyping that often provides a rationale for racial discrimination. Other poems reveal a frustrated attempt to speak from a less objectifying perspective.

Sociologist Patricia Hill Collins expands the definition of stereotypes or assumed qualities that justify oppression with the notion of "controlling images."[69] Hill Collins's study of these images in the United States helps us to reconsider the socioeconomic function of stereotypes in the Caribbean: "From the mammies, Jezebels, and breeder women of slavery to the smiling

Aunt Jemima on pancake-mix boxes, ubiquitous Black prostitutes and ever-present welfare mothers of contemporary popular culture, the nexus of negative stereotypical images applied to African American women has been fundamental to Black women's oppression. Taken together, the seamless web of economy, polity, and ideology functions as a highly effective system of social control designed to keep African American women in an assigned, subordinate place."[70] Hill Collins's work regarding racialized images of black people in the United States helps to dispel notions that representation of race in the media and in literature is generally value-neutral.

Following Arcadio Díaz Quiñones, Aníbal González has objected that certain critics saw *negrismo* as stereotyping. His reproach is directed notably at black critics of *negrismo* who protested against these controlling images or stereotypes. He is eager to dismiss political and social readings of *Tuntún* by casting them as "partial readings and tendentious interpretations," improper for objective and disinterested scholarship.[71] His reading of Palés privileges an intertextual relationship. While he is right to examine *Tuntún* as a poetic revision and illustration of Spengler's *The Decline of the West*, González skirts the question of the politics of representation of blacks and of blackness in Puerto Rican culture by exclusively privileging a reading that makes no judgments on the broader implications of the poetry. His position contrasts with that of Arcadio Díaz Quiñones who, as we saw earlier, confronted, albeit insufficiently, the question of the social significance of the poems. For Aníbal González the book intends to reconcile an ambivalence "between the nonchalant and explicitly contrived avant-garde gesture and the contrary impulse toward an increased social and philosophical relevance."[72] I have no quarrel with this conclusion. Aside from textual confrontations and revisions, what needs to be further explored, is a deeper hypothesis about the social referent, or even a consideration of the non-literary implications of this poetic experiment. Ultimately, for Aníbal González, the "black poems" problematic lies in literary and philosophical experimentation: "how to reconcile the spontaneity and frivolity of avant-garde art with a notion of literature as a transcendent activity. Basically this was the problem that concerned Palés the most as he wrote his *Antillean poetry.* Although there is no reason to doubt the sincerity with which Palés presented his concept of Caribbean culture, it seems clear that this was just a pre-text, yet another episode in the eminently literary exploration that Palés carried out in order to define the limitations and powers of poetry."[73] From the perspective of a reception theory that would take into account the circulation of his texts among diverse reading publics, however, things are not resolved.

To advance our understanding of *negrismo* in the Puerto Rican context we cannot forego theorizing about the social effects of the poems for different potential audiences. The perspective of possible black readers is silenced in the whole discussion of this Puerto Rican book written by a Puerto Rican author on Afro-Caribbean culture. What happens when black readers talk back or resist limiting or outrageous assessments or portrayals of the black experience? Such is the case of Isabelo Zenón Cruz's judgment about specific poems in *Tuntún* and of his lengthy meditation on race relations on the island. He is an example of a "resisting" reader, one of the first to attempt a socioaesthetic reading of *negrismo* not only in Palés, but in the general corpus of Puerto Rican literature. Sociologist and cultural critic Miriam Jiménez Román has very cogently analyzed the difficulties experienced by Afro-Puerto Ricans who challenge white supremacist thinking in Puerto Rican life. The pervasive myths of "racial democracy" and social and intellectual mores demand that Afro-Puerto Ricans not speak from a position of discontent even in the face of racist assault. As she puts it, "For black Puerto Ricans who have periodically dared to dispute the fictional image of the homogeneous and harmonious *gran familia* construct, that experience with racism has included further exclusion. So-called racial mixture, far from eliminating racism, has made invisible those whose faces still say 'Africa'. . . ."[74]

We should not forget that Palés, assuming a moderate *criollo* perspective, dialogues on culture with Spengler, another intellectual navigating his own crisis of legitimacy in the face of social changes in Europe. Ostensibly, the outcome of Spengler's influence on Palés is a book that meditates on the importance of Afro-Caribbean culture but that, some insist, does not really implicate racial politics. Many have noted that the poet's voracious reading habits filtered his portrayal of black people. But the obverse is also true. His experiences as a white Creole in a certain degree of proximity with Afro-Puerto Ricans guide his assessments of the island's black and mulatto working classes and their practices. In this respect, Aníbal González's essay is reminiscent of Arce's impulse to dissociate Palés's poems from a Puerto Rican social referent. But, read in the light of a Fanonian critique of racist colonialism, poems such as "Candombe," "Esta noche he pasado," "Ñam-Ñam," "Lagarto Verde," "Elegía del duque de la mermelada," perpetuate white supremacist fantasies of black erotomania, irredeemable primitivism, and lack of humanity.[75] Furthermore, as Zenón Cruz's explains, "To propose that the *Duque de la mermelada* has a monkey inside him, even if he is refined, and that the *Conde de la limonada* is a chimp (verse 5), and that the aristocrats who accompany him are macaques (verse 9), and that by returning to 'ancestral Africanness' by the utterance of a simple word (verses 24–29) he becomes an orangutan (verses 33–34), is to promote an injustice that has much of ignorance and too much of a prejudicial attitude against black Haitians and blacks around the world."[76] The question of colonial mimicry is not a "black" problem stemming from atavistic deficiencies of a "black soul." It is the result of complex processes that implicate geopolitics, forced integration into capitalist markets, and cultural and educational penetration, among other things. "Mimicry" is a fate suffered by all colonized societies around the world, most pointedly by their elites. Palés never mocks Creoles as "simian" in the face of their persistent imitation of the culture of the Spanish rulers in the nineteenth century. Nor does he mercilessly caricature their adoption of the capitalist culture imposed by North American colonialism in the twentieth century. This disparate poetic treatment must inform any discussion of stereotypes in his *negrista* cycle.

As my reading of *Tuntún de pasa y grifería* suggests, Palés was unable to formulate his vision in non-essentialist terms. He constructs images that purportedly represent racial essences in a well-intentioned desire to produce supposed "black types" and to include "lo negro" in the realm of Puerto Rican letters. The fanciful representation of black people in his poetry should not escape questioning and scrutiny. Nonetheless, Palés's ultimate desire to include the black presence in the debates on Puerto Rican national culture—however truncated—pointed to one of the fissures in the emerging discourse on national culture.[77] However co-opted and contained, his vision of a multiracial Puerto Rican culture interrupted the myopic *criollo* discourse on the Puerto Rican nation.

This chapter ends with an analysis of Margot Arce's introductory essay to the famed 1978 Ayacucho edition of Palés's works. Arce's explication of Palés's Afro-Antillean verses remains informed by a Eurocentric vision of Puerto Rican nationality. Even more than four decades after her initial assessment of the importance of his "black verses," she still places Afro-Puerto Rican culture in a subservient position in relation to the privileged Spanish presence. Her work on Palés's *Tuntún de pasa y grifería* most clearly reflects her generation's ambiguous response to the role and legacy of black and mulatto Puerto Ricans within the national culture.[78]

The Re-Inscription of a Dated Discourse

A theory of reception of Palés's *negrista* poems sheds new light on the debate over the socio-cultural significance of this poetry, and on the crucial role played by University professor Margot Arce in the acceptance, propagation, and ratification of Palés's poetry in the canon of Puerto Rican literature. Her explications of his "black poetry" provided its original and subsequent readership with an acceptable way of reading and understanding the poems. Arce's voice strengthened the chorus of voices (Tomás Blanco, Federico de Onís) that recognized, defended, and promoted this most important Puerto Rican poet. Through her critical interventions, she organized what for decades became the authorized and orthodox reception of Palés's verses. Arce is, in the main, responsible for guiding the readership of Palés's poetry from its belligerent reception in the 1930s to its formal entry into the Puerto Rican literary canon in the 1950s to its triumphant publication in Ayacucho's Latin

American canon, side-by-side with the great works of Latin American literature. By looking at the actual and imagined readers, together with Margot Arce's essays through the decades, in tandem with Palés's poetry, we can glimpse the complex processes of legitimation of this literary work. Thus we can better comprehend the dynamic relationship between work, criticism, and readership in a specific socio-cultural medium.

The analysis of the editorial changes Margot Arce made to her essays on Palés gives us a clue about the readership of "Los poemas negros de Luis Palés Matos" and "Rectificaciones" as they appear in her 1950s anthology *Impresiones: notas puertorriqueñas.*[79] As Chapter 7 showed, small but significant changes were made in the later versions of Arce's "black poetry" essays. These changes had the effect of making the essays less racially offensive to Afro-Puerto Rican readers, or to readers sympathetic to their point of view. Numerous insulting and contentious comments on black peoples and cultures were excised for the collection. The social context of the 1950s that, after all, was to incorporate "all Puerto Ricans" into the march of industrial progress, frowned on such overt racism, making it no longer acceptable to a much wider university-educated public. This larger public was not as racially and socially homogeneous as the literate elite of the 1930s to which Arce first addressed her exegesis. As a well known and respected university professor, she must have had the insight that her readership had expanded to include more racially mixed Puerto Ricans who frequented the University and had entered the growing and more diverse middle class.

The editorial changes made by Arce for the publication of her *Impresiones* anthology were mild. The revisions, as detailed textual analysis indicated, did not change the substance of the essays. The same can be said of her introductory essay to the complete poetry of Palés Matos that she edited for the Caracas-based Ayacucho publishing house. This 1978 edition had a wide diffusion in the Spanish-speaking world. It is still used today, becoming the basis for Mercedes López-Baralt's recent and augmented edition of Luis Palés Matos's poems.

Unfortunately, Margot Arce's racial presuppositions remained true to the vision she held from the beginning. For example, in her Ayacucho edition Arce separates Puerto Rico from what she calls the "Antillas negras"—Haiti, Jamaica, Martinique, Dominica, Guadeloupe. This assumes that Puerto Rico is non-black or an "Antilla no negra." She repeats the assumption that Puerto Ricans are first and foremost of Spanish descent, with allowances for climatic adaptations. She reiterates the idea that *jíbaros* are of pure Hispanic descent, "campesino de descendencia hispánica pura"—an error and misrepresentation. Her language relentlessly casts blacks as an exotic Other, "another racial nucleus that has mixed with us nobly." ("otro núcleo racial que con nosotros se ha mezclado noblemente.")[80] Again, "nosotros" ("us") means white Europeans. She repeats verbatim some of her previous ideas that express a "we" versus "they." She paraphrases, and subscribes to, Palés's well known press declarations: "the Negro lives with us physically and spiritually, and his characteristics, filtered through the mulatto, have a clear influence on all the manifestations of our popular life." ("el negro vive física y espiritualmente con nosotros, y sus características tamizadas en el mulato, influyen de modo evidente en todas las manifestaciones de nuestra vida popular.")[81] She updates her language in a number of instances, makes a valiant effort to be inclusive, and succeeds with mixed results. In sum, speaking of Palés's accomplishments Arce says: "He was among the first in our hemisphere to recognize the personal dignity of the Negro, his identity as a man and as a creator of culture, among the first to exalt the beauty of the mulatta and to make a caricature of the Negro who rejects his own identity."[82] ("Fue de los primeros en nuestro hemisferio en reconocer la dignidad personal del negro, su identidad como hombre y creador de cultura, en exaltar la hermosura de la mulata y en hacer caricatura del negro que rechaza su propia identidad.") Unquestioned here is the presupposition that Palés was in a position to determine what might be the proper identity of black people.

Margot Arce produced her edition of Palés Matos's complete verses and selected prose at the end of a long, influential, and prestigious career as teacher, critic, and commentator, providing a fitting closure to a professional endeavor that lasted over four decades. As we have seen in the course of this study, the history of her career is intertwined with the history of decades of Puerto Rican literature and literary criticism. Margot Arce's vision was undeniably instrumental in the formulation of a critical discourse on Puerto Rican literature and on the place of that literature in Puerto Rican national identity.

Conclusion: Writing in the (Intellectual) Minefields

As an important member of a fledgling female intelligentsia, Margot Arce de Vázquez is representative of a group of privileged women who were able to forge a public identity that opened a space for professional women to test the limits of acceptance and the necessity of compromise in their bid for legitimation. From a feminist vantage point it seems that too much was conceded, perhaps, in attaining an *authoritative voice* in a field dominated by men and their perspectives. Margot Arce never relinquished the "male," objective, and universalizing posture that she believed would help to guarantee the stability and recognition of her work. Nonetheless, her presence, and that of other women like Nilita Vientós Gastón and Concha Meléndez, did effect important changes in a male-dominated intellectual field. In the 1930s she and her group of university-educated women abandoned their conservative and middle-class feminism in favor of greater strides in the professional arena, and finally sought the possibility of equal participation in a class-bound cultural nationalist project. The career of Margot Arce, as she exemplified the group's choices and possibilities, demonstrates how the logic of the Puerto Rican discourse of national identity, as formulated by the *Generación del Treinta*, made few allowances for a democratic inclusion of women's interests or the interests of non-white and non-middle class Puerto Ricans.

In her essay "Las raíces" Margot Arce commented on the attitude that a traveler must have in search of knowledge: "I have made efforts to understand what is true and significant. For this, time is needed, a lot of time, peace, keen attentiveness, benevolence." Despite the limitations that our perspective on her work might have, these words from the teacher of so many generations of Puerto Ricans have been my incentive and inspiration. Her statement seems to illustrate, better than any other, the ideal attitude that the reader must adopt in approaching both her work and that of her cultural formation.

While Margot Arce and the *Generación del Treinta* formulated an anticolonial Puerto Rican discourse to respond to the United States's imperialism in the first half of the twentieth century, they were not fully capable of overcoming what Frantz Fanon called "the colonized mentality." The *Generación del Treinta*'s cultural nationalism was in many cases unable to go beyond a recuperation of the Spanish colonial past in which *hacendado* social hegemony was assured. In other instances, as with Emilio S. Belaval and Tomás Blanco, the group was able to formulate a new discourse on *criollismo* that sought to rally the elite as the putative head of the populist coalition that would come into power in the 1940s. While the example of Margot Arce's career shows that class projects and racial identification override considerations of gender interest, analysis of gender is fundamental to the study of national identity. As the case of Arce also suggests, racial identification worked as a vital reinforcement of class solidarity and even of authority to participate in the formulation of a discourse about national identity. The interlocking nature of gender, class, and race facilitated the exclusion of people of African descent as equal participants in the Puerto Rican nation-building project. In the end, Margot Arce was a woman who identified with a vision of a patriarchal culture that, in theory, excluded her full participation. Nonetheless, her racial and class affiliations safeguarded her from the banishment that people of African ancestry suffered at the hands of the nationalist discourse of the period.

These contradictions cannot help but trouble us. Many who are currently in a similar negotiation of the minefields of national projects and who seek to understand and respond to the ferocious "globalization" of the capitalist order feel their poignancy. We see that nationalism's subject has been inevitably defined against the interest of many of those who inhabit the nation. Knowing this, is it possible to willfully construct our own benign nationalism composed of multiple subjects in happy co-existence? This study of nationalism suggests that such strategic maneuvers must be ever accompanied by careful critical vigilance.

Notes

Introduction

1. Even as the intellectual field was undergoing a decisive process of modernization and differentiation, this intellectual formation included politicians with literary aspirations such as Luis Muñoz Marín, as well as writers who were political militants like Juan Antonio Corretjer. The lines of demarcation were still somewhat blurred.

2. My discussion of tradition as invention, especially in Chapter 4, draws heavily on Hobsbawm's conceptualization. See Eric Hobsbawm's introductory essay, "Inventing Traditions," in *The Invention of Tradition*, ed. Eric Hobsbawn, and Terence Ranger (Cambridge: Cambridge University Press, 1983) 1.

3. On the modernizing projects of this generation, see María Elena Rodríguez Castro, "La escritura de lo nacional y los intelectuales puertorriqueños" (Ph.D. diss., Princeton University, 1988). See also Juan G. Gelpí, *Literatura y paternalismo en Puerto Rico* (San Juan: Editorial de la Universidad de Puerto Rico, 1993) for a detailed discussion of the role of paternalism in Puerto Rican literature.

4. Ana Lydia Vega, "Sálvese quien pueda: la censura tiene auto," *Esperando a Loló y otros delirios generacionales*, ed. Ana Lydia Vega (San Juan: Editorial de la Universidad de Puerto Rico, 1994) 85–86. My translation.

5. For a further assessment of the ideology and tactics favored by the nationalist leader, see *La nación puertorriqueña: ensayos en torno a Pedro Albizu Campos*, eds. Juan Manuel Carrión, Teresa C. Gracia Ruiz and Carlos Rodríguez Fraticelli, (San Juan: Editorial de la Universidad de Puerto Rico 1997; 1966 first edition). See also Juan Angel Silén, *Nosotros solos: Pedro Albizu Campos y el nacionalismo irlandés* (San Juan: Editorial Librería Norberto González 1996).

6. Arlene Torres, Isar Godreau, Eileen Suárez Findlay, and Kelvin Santiago are some of the scholars who have addressed these questions in recent years. Arlene Torres, "Blackness, Ethnicity and Cultural Transformation in Southern Puerto Rico" (Ph.D. diss., University of Illinois at Urbana-Champaign, 1995). Eileen Suárez Findlay, *Imposing Decency: The Politics of Sexuality and Race in Puerto Rico, 1870–1920* (Durham and London: Duke University Press, 1999). Kelvin A. Santiago-Valles *"Subject People" and Colonial Discourses: Economic Transformation and Social Disorder in Puerto Rico 1898–1947* (Albany: State University of New York Press, 1994). Isar Godreau, "La semántica fugitiva: 'raza,' color y vida cotidiana en Puerto Rico," *Revista de Ciencias Sociales* 9 (2000): 52–71.

7. For a discussion of the colonial policies enforced by the public school system, see Aida Negrón de Montilla, *La americanización de Puerto Rico y el sistema de instrucción pública 1900–1930* (Río Piedras: Editorial Universitaria, 1977).

8. Studies of other intellectuals such as Nilita Vientos Gastón and Concha Meléndez still wait to be written.

9. See Gladys Jiménez Muñoz, "Literacy, Class, and Sexuality in the Debate on Women's Suffrage in Puerto Rico during the 1920s," in *Puerto Rican Women's History: New Perspectives*, ed. Félix Matos Rodríguez and Linda C. Delgado (Armonk and London: M. E. Sharpe, 1998) 143–170.

10. See the enlightening essay by Mary Louise Pratt, "'Don't Interrupt Me': The Gender Essay as Conversation and Countercanon," in *Reinterpreting the Spanish American Essay: Women Writers of the 19th and 20th Centuries*, ed. Doris Meyer (Austin: University of Texas Press, 1995) 10–26.

11. Pratt, "Don't Interrupt Me," 22. Emphasis in the original.

12. See Edward W. Said's "Yeats and Decolonization," in *Nationalism, Colonialism, and Literature*, ed. Terry Eagleton, Fredric Jameson, and Edward Said (Derry, Ireland: Field Day, 1988) 11.

13. Said, "Yeats and Decolonization," 11. Emphasis added.

Chapter 1

1. Antonio S. Pedreira, *Insularismo: ensayos de interpretación* (Río Piedras: Editorial Edil, 1992). Unless otherwise noted, all translations in this chapter are by the author.

2. Pedreira, *Insularismo*, 32.

3. Pedreira, *Insularismo*, 32.

4. Pedreira, *Insularismo*, 32. The discourse of the innate docility of subaltern or colonized races is but the other side of the coin that represents the subaltern races as brutal and savage.

5. Pedreira, *Insularismo*, 27. Emphasis in the original. Pedreira's effort to establish a nationalist racial mythology is not dissimilar to the definitions of true nationhood and rightful citizenship advanced by Sarmiento in Argentina and Vasconcelos in Mexico.

6. Lillian Guerra, *Popular Expression and National Identity in Puerto Rico: The Struggle for Self, Community, and Nation* (Gainesville: University of Florida Press, 1998).

7. This group, some of whom had worked together in the radical university publication *La escalera*, included sociologists, historians, and literary critics. Literature professor Arcadio Díaz Quiñónez was one of its early members.

8. Ángel G. Quintero Rivera, *Conflictos de clase y política en Puerto Rico* (Río Piedras: Ediciones Huracán, 1977).

9. For decades countless essays had circulated illustrating or explicating Pedreira's view of the Puerto Rican national culture. Dramatist René Marqués's *El puertorriqueño dócil*, for example, is a rewriting of *Insularismo* in the context of the 1960s.

10. Juan Flores, *Insularismo e ideología burguesa en Antonio Pedreira* (Havana: Ediciones Casa de las Américas, 1979) 87. For an English version of this essay see the chapter "The Insular Vision: Pedreira and the Puerto Rican Misère," in *Divided Borders: Essays on Puerto Rican Identity*, ed. Juan Flores (Houston: Arte Público Press, 1993).

11. Flores, *Insularismo e ideología burguesa,* 25. For a full account of his arguments please see Flores's detailed study, still the obligatory reference point to understand the many discourses that crisscross Pedreira's *Insularismo.*

12. Isabelo Zenón Cruz, *Narciso descubre su trasero: el negro en la cultura puertorriqueña,* 2 vols. (Humacao: Ediciones Furidi, 1974, 1975). This book, while widely read and discussed in intellectual circles when first published, has been with a few exceptions only timidly referenced by the new waves of scholars.

13. José Luis González, "Literatura e identidad nacional en Puerto Rico," *in Puerto Rico: identidad nacional y clases sociales (Coloquio de Princeton),* ed. Arcadio Díaz Quiñones (Río Piedras: Ediciones Huracán, 1981) 45–79. See also his influential essays, *El país de cuatro pisos y otros ensayos* (Río Piedras: Ediciones Huracán, 1980).

14. In the Caribbean, the line dividing mulattos and whites is, in many instances, a matter of perception and socio-economic standing.

15. González, *El país de cuatro pisos,* 24. For a study of the free mountain peasantry and the development of the middle-size coffee *hacienda* see Fernando Picó, *Libertad y servidumbre en el Puerto Rico del siglo XIX* (Río Piedras: Ediciones Huracán, 1979). Picó studies the pass-book regime, *la libreta,* that bounded the dispossessed peasantry to the land and the service of the *hacendado.*

16. Zenón Cruz, *Narciso descubre su trasero,* 29.

17. Miriam Jiménez Román, "Un hombre (negro) del pueblo: José Celso Barbosa and the Puerto Rican 'Race' Toward Whiteness," *Centro: Journal of the Center for Puerto Rican Studies* 8, 1–2 (1996): 26 and 11–16.

18. González, *El país de cuatro pisos,* 24. González explains that Corsicans were also regarded as foreigners or as French by poor Puerto Ricans even in the early twentieth century.

19. For a detailed analysis of the ideological differences between various sectors of the elite, see also Quintero Rivera, *Conflictos de clase* as well as his *Patricios y plebeyos: burgueses, hacendados, artesanos y obreros. Las relaciones de clase en el Puerto Rico de cambio de siglo* (Río Piedras: Ediciones Huracán, 1988).

20. About the political differences between the *hacendado* sector as a whole and the professional sector, see Quintero Rivera, *Conflictos de clase,* 30.

21. See Quintero Rivera, "Clases sociales e identidad nacional: notas sobre el desarrollo nacional puertorriqueño," in *Puerto Rico: identidad nacional y clases sociales. (Coloquio de Princeton)* (Río Piedras: Ediciones Huracán, 1979) 15.

22. Quintero Rivera, "Clases sociales e identidad nacional," 23.

23. Limiting universal male suffrage (for there was no notion then that women could also be full-fledged citizens) to literate, taxpaying voters only eroded the base of *hacendado* support made up of small farmers and agricultural workers who had been granted the vote under Spain in 1897 with the *Carta Autonómica.* See Quintero Rivera's *Conflictos de clase,* 34–49.

24. Qtd. in Quintero Rivera, *Conflictos de clase,* 11.

25. Quintero Rivera, *Conflictos de clase,* 52–53.

26. Quintero Rivera, "Clases sociales e identidad nacional," 24. For a detailed study of Protestant proselytizing in the early years of U.S. colonization, see Daniel R. Rodríguez, *La primera evangelización protestante en Puerto Rico 1898–1930* (Mexico: Ediciones Borinquen, 1986).

27. Quintero Rivera, *Conflictos de clase*, 49.

28. Quintero Rivera, "Clases sociales e identidad nacional," 28.

29. Manuel F. Rojas, *Cuatro siglos de ignorancia y servidumbre en Puerto Rico* (San Juan: Imprenta La Primavera, 1914) 61, qtd. in Quintero-Rivera, "Clases sociales e identidad nacional," 28.

30. José Luis González reminds us that working-class militants were often referred to by the white elite as *la negrada socialista* or "the black socialist hordes."

31. Quintero Rivera, "Clases sociales e identidad nacional," 34.

32. Kelvin A. Santiago-Valles, *"Subject People" and Colonial Discourses: Economic Transformation and Social Disorder in Puerto Rico, 1898–1947* (Albany: State University of New York Press, 1994).

33. Santiago-Valles, *"Subject People" and Colonial Discourses*, 41–48.

34. My account of the *Turbas* follows Mariano Negrón Portillo's incisive study, *Las turbas republicanas 1900–1904* (Río Piedras: Ediciones Huracán, 1990) 94.

35. Negrón Portillo, *Las turbas*, 97.

36. Negrón Portillo, *Las turbas*, 20–31 and 81–83. The rivalry between these two subaltern groups is better understood when we keep in mind that the *Federación* was a socialist trade unionist group, while the *Turbas* were not.

37. See Ángel G. Quintero Rivera for a detailed discussion, *Las bases sociales de la transformación ideológica del PPD* (San Juan: Centro de Estudios de la Realidad Puertorriqueña, 1975) 60–64.

38. Luis Ángel Ferrao, *Pedro Albizu Campos y el nacionalismo puertorriqueño* (Río Piedras: Editorial Cultural, 1990) 137–148.

39. Quintero Rivera, *Las bases sociales*, 75–80.

40. Quintero Rivera, *Las bases sociales*, 81–82.

41. Juan Ángel Silén, *Historia de la nación puertorriqueña* (Río Piedras: Editorial Edil, 1980) 291–310.

42. For a more complete analysis of the populist ideology of the *Partido Popular Democrático* see *Del cañaveral a la fábrica: cambio social en Puerto Rico*, ed. Eduardo Medina and Rafael L. Ramírez (Río Piedras: Huracán-Academia, 1985); and Gerardo Navas Dávila ed., *Cambio social y desarrollo en Puerto Rico: la transformación ideológica del Partido Popular Democrático* (Río Piedras: Editorial de la Universidad de Puerto Rico, first edition 1980, 1985). For an analysis of the cultural implications of populism on the island, see *Del nacionalismo al populismo: cultura y política en Puerto Rico*, ed. Silvia Álvarez-Curbelo and María Elena Rodríguez Castro (Río Piedras: Ediciones Huracán, 1993).

43. María Elena Rodríguez Castro, "La 'escritura de lo nacional' y los intelectuales puertorriqueños" (Ph.D. diss., Princeton University, 1988) 26. See Rodríguez Castro for a detailed and encompassing study of the discourses on the nation formulated in the early part of the twentieth century and how they converge and diverge from those put in place by later generations of writers.

44. Rodríguez Castro, "La 'escritura de lo nacional,'" 291–302.

45. Guillermo A. Baralt, *Esclavos rebeldes: conspiraciones y sublevaciones de esclavos en Puerto Rico (1795–1873)* (Río Piedras: Ediciones Huracán, 1982). Francisco Scarano, *Sugar and Slavery in Puerto Rico: The Plantation Economy of Ponce, 1800–1850* (Madison: University of Wisconsin Press, 1984). Jalil Sued-Badillo and Ángel López

Cantos, *Puerto Rico Negro* (Editorial Cultural: Río Piedras, 1986). Of great interest also is the catalog that accompanied the exhibit on African presence in Puerto Rico, *La tercera raíz: presencia africana en Puerto Rico* (San Juan: Centro de Estudios de la Realidad Puertorriqueña, Instituto de Cultura Puertorriqueña, 1992). Arlene Torres, "Blackness, Ethnicity, and Cultural Transformations in Southern Puerto Rico" (Ph.D. diss., University of Illinois Urbana-Champaign, 1995). See also the special issue dedicated to the question of race in Puerto Rico, *Centro: Journal of the Center of Puerto Rican Studies* 8, 1–2 (1996).

46. The obsession with the land as a theme has been, in recent years, very ably and convincingly discussed by José Juan Beauchamp, "La literatura de la crisis social y cultural de la identidad nacional puertorriqueña (1925–1949): un ensayo de apertura," *22 Conferencias de la literatura puertorriqueña*, ed. Edgar Martínez Masdeu (San Juan: Librería Editorial Ateneo, 1994) 295–369.

47. See the many studies of peasant displacement by Fernando Picó especially, *Libertad y servidumbre.* Ángel López Cantos, *Los puertorriqueños: mentalidad y actitudes* (siglo XVIII) (San Juan: Ediciones Puerto y Editorial de la Universidad de Puerto Rico, 2000). Ángel G. Quintero Rivera, "El tambor camuflado," *Salsa sabor y control: sociología de la música tropical* (Mexico City: Siglo Veintiuno Editores, 1999) 201–251. See also Guerra, *Popular Expression*, 67–121.

48. See Sued-Badillo, *Puerto Rico Negro*, and Quintero Rivera, "El tambor camuflado," 201–251.

49. Eileen J. Suárez Findlay, *Imposing Decency: The Politics of Sexuality and Race in Puerto Rico, 1870–1920* (Durham and London: Duke University Press, 1999). See also Félix V. Matos Rodríguez, "'¿Quién Trabajará?': Domestic Workers, Urban Slaves, and the Abolition of Slavery in Puerto Rico," *Puerto Rican Women's History: New Perspectives*, ed. Linda C. Delgado and Felix V. Matos Rodríguez (Armonk and London: M. E. Sharpe, 1998) 62–82.

50. Fray Iñigo Abbad y Lasierra qtd. in *Puerto Rico negro.* 244.

51. The poetry, riddles, and sayings Lillian Guerra examines were collected in the second decade of U.S. colonial rule on the island. See Guerra, *Popular Expression*, chapters 4, 5, and 6. For his part, Arcadio Díaz Quiñones's study of the poetry of Llorens Torres, Poet Laureate and one of the foremost exponents of *jibarista* poetry, shows how it idealized the Creole past in its depiction of the peasant world. Arcadio Díaz Quiñones, "La isla afortunada: sueños liberadores y utópicos de Luis Lloréns Torres," *El almuerzo en la hierba* (Río Piedras: Ediciones Huracán, 1982) 19–70.

52. Santiago-Valles, *"Subject People" and Colonial Discourses*, 44.

53. Santiago-Valles, *"Subject People" and Colonial Discourses*, 46.

54. Guerra, *Popular Expression*, 160–248.

55. Isabel Picó, "Apuntes preliminares para el estudio de la mujer puertorriqueña y su participación en las luchas sociales de principios del siglo XX," *La mujer en la sociedad puertorriqueña* (Río Piedras: Ediciones Huracán, 1980) 23–25.

56. Picó, *La mujer en la sociedad puertorriqueña*, 23–24.

57. Quintero Rivera, *Conflictos de clase*, 42–51.

58. See Yamila Azize's well-researched book on Puerto Rican women's history, *La mujer en la lucha* (Río Piedras: Editorial Cultural, 1985) 82–88.

59. There are striking parallels between Capetillos's use of the body as a site of resistance to patriarchy and the ethos and strategies of the British suffragists who, among other things, championed the use of bloomers and more comfortable attire. For a study of the body as site of suffragist resistance see Martha Vicinus, "Male Space and Women's Bodies: The English Suffragette Movement," in *Women in Culture and Politics: A Century of Change*, ed. Judith Friedlander, Blanche W. Cook, Alice Kessler-Harris, and Carol Smith-Rosenberg (Bloomington: Indiana University Press, 1986) 209–222.

60. Suárez Findlay, *Imposing Decency*, 161.

61. One such incident is reported by Margot Arce de Vázquez to Norma Valle Ferrer in her pioneering biographical study of Luisa Capetillo. Arce recounts to Valle Ferrer that when Capetillo would visit her father's law practice, the women of the family would hide from view. Norma Valle Ferrer, *Luisa Capetillo, historia de una mujer proscrita* (Río Piedras: Editorial Cultural, 1990) 14. See this still invaluable resource for the study of working-class Puerto Rican feminism.

62. Azize, *La mujer en la lucha*, 32.

63. Azize, *La mujer en la lucha*, 32.

64. Azize, *La mujer en la lucha*, 33. See Lydia Milagros González "Tras el mundillo de la aguja" *Revista Homines* 10, 2 (1986–1987): 166–172. See also the more extensive study done under the auspices of Centro de Estudios de la Realidad Puertorriqueña and Centro de Investigación Para la Acción Femenina by Lydia Milagros González García, *Una puntada en el tiempo: la industria de la aguja en Puerto Rico 1900–1929* (Santo Domingo: Editora Taller, 1990).

65. Picó, in *La mujer en la sociedad puertorriqueña*, 27, points out that by 1930, women constituted 66 percent of all typists and secretaries as well as 94 percent of all nurses.

66. Azize, *La mujer en la lucha*, 137–147.

67. Margarita Ostolaza Bey, *Política sexual en Puerto Rico* (Río Piedras: Ediciones Huracán, 1989).

68. Francisco Manrique Cabrera, *Historia de la literatura puertorriqueña* (Río Piedras: Editorial Cultural, 1969) 288.

69. Cabrera, *Historia de la literatura*, 288. Emphasis added.

70. Cabrera, *Historia de la literatura*, 288.

71. Santiago-Valles, *"Subject People" and Colonial Discourses*, 166.

72. Santiago-Valles, *"Subject People" and Colonial Discourses*, 166.

73. See Carlos Altamirano and Beatriz Sarlo, *Ideología/Sociedad* (Buenos Aires: Hachette, 1983) 84.

74. Pierre Bourdieu, "Campo intelectual y proyecto creador," *Problemas del estructuralismo* (Mexico City: Siglo Veintiuno Editores, 1973) 135–182.

75. For an extensive discussion of Bourdieu's ideas as they would apply to the Latin American context, see Carlos Altamirano and Beatriz Sarlo, *Ideología/Sociedad*, 83–96.

76. Terry Eagleton, *The Ideology of the Aesthetic* (Oxford: Basil Blackwell, 1990) 9.

77. As an example, Altamirano and Sarlo document the effect that Jorge Luis Borges's consecration in Europe had on his status in the Argentine cultural field in the late sixties and beyond. Borges is, so to speak, "rediscovered" after his European success.

78. "Poesía y recitación negras." *Revista Bimestre Cubana* 37–38 (1936): 24.

79. The concept of a cultured elite who would be intellectually and professionally trained to lead and speak for the masses also influenced the thinking of W. E. B. du Bois on the necessity of a black cultured elite in the United States. See "The Talented Tenth," in W. E. B. du Bois, *Writings* (New York: The Library of America, 1986) 842–861.

80. See, for example, John King's *Sur: A Study of the Argentine Literary Journal and Its Role in the Development of a Culture* (Cambridge: Cambridge University Press, 1986).

81. María Cristina Parodi Lisi, *El proyecto cultural de la revista 'Sur' (1931–1970) en la obra de Victoria Ocampo* (Berlin: Freien Universität Berlin, 1987).

82. Concha Meléndez, *El arte del cuento en Puerto Rico* (San Juan: Editorial Cordillera, 1975) 9.

83. Emilio S. Belaval, "Los problemas de la cultura puertorriqueña," *Ateneo Puertorriqueño,* 1 (1935): 223.

84. Belaval, "Los problemas," 223.

85. Edward Said, "Yeats and Decolonization," in *Nationalism, Colonialism, and Literature,* ed. Terry Eagleton, Fredric Jameson, and Edward Said (Derry, Ireland: Field Day, 1988) 13.

86. Lizabeth Paravisini, "Las novelistas puertorriqueñas 'inexistentes,'" *Cupey: Revista de la Universidad Metropolitana* 6, 1–2 (1989): 90–112.

87. Mary Louise Pratt, "'Don't Interrupt Me': The Gender Essay as Conversation and Countercanon," *Reinterpreting the Spanish American Essay: Women Writers of the 19th and 20th Centuries* (Austin: University of Texas Press, 1995) 10–26.

88. See Concha Meléndez's introduction to *El arte del cuento en Puerto Rico* (San Juan: Editorial Cordillera, 1975) 9.

89. See Aida Negrón de Montilla's *La americanización en Puerto Rico y el sistema de instrucción pública 1900–1930* (Río Piedras: Editorial Universitaria, 1977). See also José Juan Beauchamp and José Luis Méndez's *La agresión cultural norteamericana en Puerto Rico* (Mexico City: Editorial Grijalbo, 1980).

90. Isabel Picó de Hernández, see the chapter "La protesta estudiantil en la década del treinta," in "Los estudiantes universitarios y el proceso político puertorriqueño 1903–1948" (Ph.D. diss., Harvard University, 1974) 135.

91. Picó de Hernández, "La protesta estudiantil," 143–148.

92. Picó de Hernández, "La protesta estudiantil," 158.

93. Thomas E. Benner, *Five Years of Foundation Building: The University of Puerto Rico, 1924–1929* (Río Piedras: Editorial Universidad de Puerto Rico, 1967) 89.

94. Cecilia Arnaldi de Olmeda, *Concha Meléndez: vida y obra* (Río Piedras: Editorial de la Universidad de Puerto Rico, 1972) 17.

95. Benner, *Five Years of Foundation Building,* 90.

96. Luis Ángel Ferrao, "Nacionalismo, hispanismo y élite intelectual en el Puerto Rico de los años treinta," in *Del nacionalismo al populismo: cultura y política en Puerto Rico,* ed. Silvia Álvarez-Curbelo and María Elena Rodríguez Castro (Río Piedras: Huracán, 1993) 60. For a fuller account of Ferrao's argument see also his *Pedro Albizu Campos y el nacionalismo puertorriqueño* (Río Piedras: Editorial Cultural, 1990) 43–148.

97. Jorge Font Saldaña, "Margot Arce: un valor de nuestra cultura," *Puerto Rico Ilustrado* 28, 1494 (1938): 19.

98. Ferrao, *Pedro Albizu Campos,* 112. Another such case is that of Emilio S. Belaval whose father was an actor and commercial expert originally from La Coruña, Spain.

99. Ferrao, *Pedro Albizu Campos*, 58–59.

100. Benner, *Five Years of Foundation Building*, 94. Emphasis added.

101. Benner, *Five Years of Foundation Building*, 97.

102. Ferrao, *Pedro Albizu Campos*, 255. Ferrao includes Nationalist Party leader Toro Nazario in this group.

103. Julia de Burgos, *Mairena* 7, 20 (1985): 150. Emphasis added.

104. Julia de Burgos, *Mairena* 7, 20 (1985): 150.

105. Julia de Burgos, *Mairena* 7, 20 (1985): 150. Emphasis added. Some years earlier in her poem, "Ay, ay, ay de la grifa negra," she had spoken of the shame the white master should feel for the enslavement of the slave. She did not see her admiration for Spain as contradictory.

106. Frantz Fanon's *The Wretched of the Earth* (New York: Grove Press, 1968) explicates at length the complex effects that racism has on the colonized. His works form part of the indispensable literature of emancipation that has informed the struggle against colonialism all over the world.

107. Julia de Burgos, *Mairena* 7, 20 (1985): 150.

108. Richard Handler, *Nationalism and the Politics of Culture in Quebec* (Madison: University of Wisconsin Press, 1988). The Mohawk's demands for their ancestral homeland in much of what is today French Canada is not without a certain irony.

109. See the introductory essay in Eric Hobsbawm, "Inventing Traditions," *The Invention of Tradition* (Cambridge: Cambridge University Press, 1983) 1–14.

110. Ferrao, "Nacionalismo, hispanismo y élite intelectual, 37–60.

111. Margot Arce de Vázquez, *Obras Completas*, ed. Matilde Albert Robatto, vol. 3 (San Juan: Editorial de la Universidad de Puerto Rico, 2001) 384.

112. Arce de Vázquez, *Obras Completas*, 383.

113. Arce de Vázquez, *Obras Completas*, 384.

114. Arce de Vázquez, *Obras Completas*, 384.

115. Arce de Vázquez, *Obras Completas*, 384.

116. Arce de Vázquez, *Obras Completas*, 385.

117. Arce de Vázquez, *Obras Completas*, 385.

118. Arce de Vázquez, *Obras Completas*, 385.

119. The anti-Franco movement surges with more strength in the regions where economic development is greatest. See Yvonne Lassalle-López, "The Limits of Memory and Modernity: The Cultural Politics and Political Culture of Three Generations of Andalusians" (Ph.D. diss., City University of New York, 1997).

120. This should not surprise us given the heavy influence of German scholars at the Centro de Estudios Históricos of Madrid when Arce studied there in the late 1920s.

121. Arce de Vázquez, *Obras Completas*, 385–386.

122. Arce de Vázquez, *Obras Completas*, 386. Emphasis added.

123. See Richard Handler for detailed analysis of the purist assumptions of cultural nationalism in his *Nationalism and Politics.*

124. *Casticismo* is a type of Castilian-centrist or Hispanist regionalism that challenges Basque, Catalan, or Galician regenerationisms or nationalisms.

125. Arce de Vázquez, *Obras Completas*, 387.

126. Arce de Vázquez, *Obras Completas*, 387. Emphasis added.

127. Arce de Vázquez, *Obras Completas*, 387. Emphasis in the text.

128. See Ángel Quintero Rivera, *Conflictos de clase.*

129. In legal terms, the "gag law" dates strictly from 1948 to 1957. One could affirm, however, that the "gag era," in other words the period of repression of militant nationalism, lasted twenty years, from 1937 to 1957. Ivonne Acosta, *La mordaza: Puerto Rico 1948–1957* (Río Piedras: Edil, 1989).

130. Arce de Vázquez, *Obras Completas*, 388.

131. Arce de Vázquez, *Obras Completas*, 390–391.

132. Arce de Vázquez, *Obras Completas*, 391.

133. Arce de Vázquez, *Obras Completas*, 391.

134. Arce de Vázquez, *Obras Completas*, 391.

135. Arce de Vázquez, *Obras Completas*, 391.

136. Arce de Vázquez, *Obras Completas*, 383.

137. On this particular point, see the study by Arlene M. Dávila, *Sponsored Identities: Cultural Politics in Puerto Rico* (Philadelphia, Temple University Press, 1997).

138. Antonio Gramsci, "The Intellectuals," in *Selections from the Prison Notebooks* (New York: International Publishers, 1971) 5.

139. Quintin Hoare and Geoffrey Nowell Smith, "Introduction" to *Selections from the Prison Notebooks*, 3.

Chapter 2

1. Quoted in Isabel Andreu de Aguilar, "Reseña histórica del movimiento feminista en Puerto Rico," *Puerto Rico* 1, 3 (1935): 255–266, emphasis in the original. All translations in this chapter, unless otherwise noted, are by Nina Menéndez and the author.

2. Latin American interest in suffrage and women's rights is evidenced in the many meetings and conferences that confront these questions; for example, in 1916 in Merida, on the Yucatan peninsula, Mexican women converged for a congress on women's rights. See Shirleen Ann Soto, *Emergence of the Modern Mexican Woman: Her Participation in Revolution and Struggle for Equality, 1910–1940* (Denver: Arden Press, 1990) 72–81. See also Francesca Miller, "Latin American Feminism and the Transnational Arena," *Women, Culture, and Politics in Latin America* (Berkeley: University of California Press, 1990) 10–26. Miller reports that in 1910 two hundred women from Peru, Chile, Uruguay, Paraguay, and Argentina met in Buenos Aires at the Congreso Femenino Internacional to discuss questions of international law, married women and work, health care, and divorce. See Gladys Jiménez Muñoz for a perspicacious analysis of Muna Lee de Muñoz's participation as the representative of Puerto Rican women at the Sixth Pan American Conference in Havana, "A Storm Dressed in Skirts: Ambivalence in the Debate on Women's Sufrage in Puerto Rico" (Ph.D. diss., State University of New York, 1993) chapter 5. Muna Lee was born in Mississippi and was a member of the National Women's Party. Her marriage to Luis Muñoz Marín gave her an ambivalent status as the dual representative of Puerto Rican women and of American white womanhood, as Jiménez Muñoz explains.

3. Andreu de Aguilar, "Reseña histórica del movimiento feminista," 261. Emphasis added. For more on *La Mujer del Siglo Veinte* and Roqué's other suffragist newspapers see also Yamila Azize, *La mujer en la lucha* (Río Piedras: Editorial Cultural, 1985) 98–104.

4. Andreu de Aguilar, "Reseña histórica del movimiento feminista," 261.

5. On the importance of teachers as organizers of demands for better working conditions and advancement opportunities for women, and as promoters of reforms in the school system, see Yamila Azize, *La mujer en la lucha,* 45–47.

6. Julio Ramos, Introduction to the anthology of works by Luisa Capetillo, *Amor y anarquía: los escritos de Luisa Capetillo* (Río Piedras: Editorial Huracán, 1992) 15–16.

7. Pierre Bourdieu, *Distinction: A Social Critique of the Judgement of Taste* (Cambridge: Harvard University Press, 1984).

8. See Andreu de Aguilar, "Reseña histórica del movimiento feminista," 258. Azize, *La mujer en la lucha,* 45, gives 1894 as the founding date for this newspaper.

9. María de Fátima Barceló Miller, *La lucha por el sufragio femenino en Puerto Rico, 1896–1935* (Río Piedras: Ediciones Huracán, 1997) 84–99. Though no woman of her class wrote more copiously than Capetillo on women's rights, Azize, *La mujer en la lucha,* 78, informs us that some feminist trade unionists like Gregoria Molina and Juana Cofresí left brief writings on the topic.

10. See especially Azize's *La mujer en la lucha,* chapters 1 and 2.

11. Azize, *La mujer en la lucha,* 46–47.

12. Azize, *La mujer en la lucha,* 47.

13. Aixa Merino Falú in her study of Afro-Puerto Rican women analyzes the situation of black school teachers during this period. See her "Raza, género y clase social: los efectos del racismo en las mujeres puertorriqueñas negras (siglo veinte)" (Ph.D. diss., University of Puerto Rico, 2002). Additionally, Gladys Jiménez Muñoz has advanced the theory that a number of the suffragists from the *Liga Social Sufragista* were the educated daughters of illiterate working-class mothers. These teachers wanted the vote extended to their mothers and aunts. Jiménez Muñoz, "Re-reading Womanhood, Race and Labor in Early-Twentieth Century Data," Puerto Rican Studies Association Conference, Chicago, October 2002.

14. I rely on María M. Solá's excellent introductory biographical and critical essay on Julia de Burgos. *Julia de Burgos: yo misma fui mi ruta* (Río Piedras: Ediciones Huracán, 1986) 13.

15. For new critical approaches to the study of her poetry, as well as biographical information, see the 1985 edition in homage of Julia de Burgos in the journal *Mairena* 7, 20 (1985). For an assessment of Julia de Burgos's "afridentidad" see Jessie Dixon's "A Self-Defining Dawn: 'Afridentity' in the Poetry of Julia de Burgos," *Cincinnati Romance Review* 20 (2001): 62–77.

16. María de F. Barceló Miller, "Estrenando togas: la profesionalización de la mujer en Puerto Rico, 1900–1930," *Revista del Instituto de Cultura Puertorriqueña* 99 (1992): 62. Some of these doctors were Blanca Dimas, Josefina Villafañe, Marta Robert de Romeu, Anita Janer, Palmira Gatell, and Dolores M. Piñeiro.

17. Barceló Miller, "Estrenando togas," 63.

18. Barceló Miller, "Estrenando togas," 65.

19. Gladys Jiménez Muñoz, "Literacy, Class, and Sexuality in the Debate on Women's Suffrage in Puerto Rico during the 1920s," in *Puerto Rican Women's History: New Perspectives,* eds. Félix V. Matos Rodríguez and Linda C. Delgado (Armonk, London: M.E. Sharpe, 1998) 144.

20. Jiménez Muñoz, "Literacy, Class, and Sexuality," 144.

21. Jiménez Muñoz, "Literacy, Class, and Sexuality," 144.

22. Jiménez Muñoz "Literacy, Class, and Sexuality," 154–158.

23. Nina Menéndez, "*Garzonas y feministas* in Cuban Women's Writing in the 1920s: *La vida manda* by Ofelia Rodríguez Acosta," in *Sex and Sexuality in Latin America*, eds. Daniel Balderston and Donna J. Guy (New York and London: New York University Press, 1997) 187.

24. Menéndez, "Garzonas y feministas," 187.

25. *Unión Obrera*, qtd. in Jiménez Muñoz "Literacy, Class, and Sexuality," 162.

26. Eileen Suárez Findlay, *Imposing Decency: The Politics of Sexuality and Race in Puerto Rico 1870–1920* (Durham and London: Duke University Press, 1999) 168.

27. Suárez Findlay, *Imposing Decency*, 173.

28. Suárez Findlay, *Imposing Decency*, 186–187.

29. Suárez Findlay, *Imposing Decency*, 194.

30. Suárez Findlay, *Imposing Decency*, 195.

31. Jiménez Muñoz, "Literacy, Class, and Sexuality," 147–148.

32. Azize, *La mujer en la lucha*, 101. Additionally, Jiménez Muñoz in chapter 6 of *A Storm* gives a penetrating analysis of the April 25, 1928 congressional hearing on women's suffrage in Puerto Rico. Representing the *Liga Social Sufragista*, Dr. Marta Robert de Romeu and Miss Rosa Emanuelli testified in the deposition sponsored by the National Women's Party.

33. Jiménez Muñoz 139–163. This is also one of the central arguments made by Kelvin A. Santiago-Valles in his *"Subject People" and Colonial Discourses: Economic Transformation and Social Disorder in Puerto Rico 1898–1947* (Albany: State University of New York Press, 1994).

34. See Barbara Ehrenreich, *Fear of Falling: The Inner Life of the Middle Class* (New York: Pantheon Books, 1989) 12.

35. Ehrenreich, *Fear of Falling*, 12.

36. Ehrenreich, *Fear of Falling*, 14.

37. Ehrenreich, *Fear of Falling*, 14.

38. Ehrenreich, *Fear of Falling*, 15.

39. Mercedes Solá, *Feminismo: estudio sobre su aspecto social, económico y político* (San Juan: Cantero, Fernández y Co., 1922) 13.

40. Solá, *Feminismo*, 14.

41. Solá, *Feminismo*, 15.

42. Solá, *Feminismo*, 16. Emphasis in the original.

43. bell hooks, *Yearning: Race, Gender, and Cultural Politics* (Boston: South End Press, 1990) 18.

44. Solá, *Feminismo*, 17. Emphasis in the original.

45. Solá, *Feminismo*, 17. Emphasis added.

46. Solá, *Feminismo*, 19. Emphasis added.

47. Solá, *Feminismo*, 23.

48. Solá, *Feminismo*, 24. Emphasis added.

49. Jiménez Muñoz, *A Storm*, 86. See also Suárez Findlay, *Imposing Decency*.

50. Jiménez Muñoz, *A Storm*, 88–91. Though they were recognized *de jure*, Jiménez Muñoz cautions that these rights were not always enforced and suffragists had to bring these issues up again as part of their demands. Jiménez Muñoz puts the figure of consensual unions at 20 to 30 percent of the population.

51. Suárez Findlay, *Imposing Decency,* 121. Emphasis in the original.

52. Solá, *Feminismo,* 24. For a comparative perspective with Cuban feminism and its discussion of "free love" see Menéndez, "Garzonas y feministas," 174–189.

53. Solá, *Feminismo,* 26. Emphasis in the original.

54. Solá, *Feminismo,* 27.

55. Solá, *Feminismo,* 28.

56. Solá, *Feminismo,* 28.

57. Solá, *Feminismo,* 30. Emphasis in the original.

58. Here I more than agree with Suárez Findlay's assertion that white women saw Afro-Puerto Rican women as sexual competition, a situation that hindered alliances between the two groups. As she puts it, "Women of the laboring classes were generally too African, too public, and believed to be too frankly sexual to be included, even rhetorically, in the early feminists' community of women," 68.

59. Margot Arce in Angela Negrón Muñoz, *Mujeres de Puerto Rico desde el período de colonización hasta el primer tercio del siglo,* (San Juan: Imprenta Venezuela, 1935) 256.

60. Arce in Negrón Muñoz, *Mujeres de Puerto Rico,* 256. English in the original.

61. Arce in Negrón Muñoz, *Mujeres de Puerto Rico,* 255.

62. Arce in Negrón Muñoz, *Mujeres de Puerto Rico,* 255.

63. Arce in Negrón Muñoz, *Mujeres de Puerto Rico,* 255. Emphasis added.

64. Arce's antifeminist views are repeated in other essays during that decade. In a 1935 graduation speech at a private school for girls she expressed similar views. See "Colegio Blanche Kellog: discurso de graduación," Margot Arce de Vázquez, *Obras Completas* vol. 3 (San Juan: Editorial de la Universidad de Puerto Rico, 2001) 104–110. Additionally, in a 1938 interview with *Puerto Rico Ilustrado* she reiterated her idea that men are superior to women. Jorge Font Saldaña, "Margot Arce: un valor de nuestra cultura," *Puerto Rico Ilustrado* 28,1494 (1938): 19, 22–24, 27.

65. Suffragist leader Andreu de Aguilar was accompanied by María L. de Ashford and Milagros Benet de Mewton. For a complete account of the relationship between Puerto Rican and U.S. suffragists, see Gladys Jiménez Muñoz, *A Storm.* See also Azize, *La mujer en la lucha,* 101.

66. Azize, *La mujer en la lucha,* 110–122.

67. Azize, *La mujer en la lucha,* 130.

68. Another proposal underwritten by the *Liga social sufragista* favored universal suffrage and aligned itself with a working-class proposal on this issue. Azize, *La mujer en la lucha,* 137–138.

69. Roqué de Duprey qtd. in Azize, *La mujer en la lucha,* 103.

70. Barceló Miller, "Halfhearted Solidarity: Women workers and the Women's suffrage Movement in Puerto Rico During the 1920s," in *Puerto Rican Women's History: New Perspectives,* eds. Félix V. Matos Rodríguez and Linda C. Delgado (Armonk, London: M.E. Sharpe, 1998) 133.

71. Jiménez Muñoz, *A Storm,* 167. Barceló Miller, "Halfhearted Solidarity," 132. Barceló Miller gives 1920 as the date of the creation of the working-class feminist group.

72. Emphasis in the original. Pilar Pacheco qtd. from Azize, *La mujer en la lucha,* 138–139.

73. Azize, *La mujer en la lucha,* 137–147.

74. Santiago Iglesias qtd. in Azize, *La mujer en la lucha,* 146.

75. Margot Arce, who had graduated the previous year, taught the freshman courses in Spanish at the time of the survey.

76. I rely on a survey of students reported in Thomas E. Benner's memoirs, *Five Years of Foundation Building: The University of Puerto Rico 1924–1929* (Río Piedras: Editorial de la Universidad de Puerto Rico, 1965) 68. Emphasis added.

77. Benner, *Five Years of Foundation Building*, 69.

78. The "lack" was also phallic; they did not have many of the symbols of male power and prestige that elite men define as solely theirs.

79. Soto, *Emergence of the Modern Mexican Woman*, 72–81.

80. *Revista* 5, 2 (1943): 32.

81. Margot Arce, Concha Meléndez, Nilita Vientós Gastón, "In memoriam, Isabel Andreu de Aguilar," *Asomante* 4, 4 (1948): 6.

82. A study of how cinema and other mass media helped shape their Puerto Rican public, especially women, is sorely needed. It would provide many clues to the process of modernization or, as some call it, Americanization in the first half of the twentieth century. For excellent studies of modernization and women in Latin America see, Francine Masiello, "Women, State, and Family in Latin American Literature of the 1920s," and Kathleen Newman, "The Modernization of Femininity: Argentina, 1916–1926," in *Women, Culture, and Politics in Latin America* (Berkeley: University of California Press, 1990).

83. Vientós Gastón, *Asomante* 1 (1948): 8. Emphasis added.

84. From 1969 on, the number of females enrolled in school including universities have exceeded that of males. Nonetheless, the labor market remains relatively segregated and salaries remain low, 70 percent of the male average. For more details see Marcia Rivera, "El proceso educativo en Puerto Rico y la reproducción de la subordinación femenina," in *La mujer en Puerto Rico* (Río Piedras: Ediciones Huracán, 1987) 136.

85. V. Y. Mudimbe, *The Invention of Africa: Gnosis, Philosophy, and the Order of Knowledge* (Bloomington and Indianapolis: Indiana University Press, 1988) 1–23.

Chapter 3

1. The *Biblioteca de Autores Puertorriqueños* was the brainchild of Manuel García Cabrera, a lawyer by profession whose enthusiasm for literature attracted the most important writers of the time. García Cabrera enlisted the services of caricaturist Carmelo Filardi, responsible for the most memorable book jackets of BAP.

2. Not properly a class, but a contradictory class with a hegemonic vocation.

3. See Raymond Williams, *The Sociology of Culture* (New York: Schocken Books, 1982) 68, emphasis added. For a Puerto Rican critique of the generational concept see also José Juan Beauchamp, "La literatura de la crisis social y cultural de la identidad nacional puertorriqueña (1925–1949): un ensayo de apertura," *22 Conferencias de Literatura Puertorriqueña*, ed. Edgar Martínez Masdeu (San Juan: Librería Editorial Ateneo, 1994) 295–369.

4. Francis Mulhern, *The Moment of Scrutiny* (New York: Schocken Books, 1987) ix.

5. Mulhern, *The Moment of Scrutiny*, ix.

6. Carlos Altamirano and Beatriz Sarlo, *Literatura/Sociedad* (Buenos Aires: Hachette, 1983) 97. Unless otherwise noted this and other translations from the Spanish throughout this chapter are by Nina Menéndez.

7. Vicente Géigel Polanco, prologue to facsimile edition of *Índice* (San Juan: Editorial Universitaria, 1979).

8. Géigel Polanco, prologue, no page.

9. Both Concha Meléndez and Margot Arce contributed significantly to fostering the de Diego cult with books and articles published throughout the years. In recent studies José de Diego's nationalism has been reevaluated in the light of its glaring class biases.

10. Rafael W. Ramírez, "El bando del general Prim," *Índice* 12 (1930): 188. Emphasis added.

11. In the very last issue of *Índice* there is a note welcoming her to the staff of the journal.

12. Margot Arce, *Índice* 24 (1931): 389–390. Language as a marker of nationality is at best an ambiguous proposition, especially if it is simultaneously a marker of class. The experience of Puerto Ricans in the United States has forced Puerto Rican scholars to reexamine the language question from the point of view of the class struggle. This issue is by no means settled.

13. See Arcadio Díaz Quiñones, *El almuerzo en la hierba* (Río Piedras: Huracán, 1982) 198.

14. Josefina Rivera de Álvarez, *Diccionario de literatura puertorriqueña*, 2 vols. (San Juan: Instituto de Cultura Puertorriqueña) 1 (1971–1974): 1075.

15. For an excellent analysis of the "Aterrizajes" as the blueprint of *Insularismo*, see Juan José Beauchamp's "Los aterrizajes de Antonio S. Pedreira: el pretexto de *Insularismo*," *Revista de Estudios Hispánicos* 22 (1995): 253–267.

16. "Aterrizaje," *Índice* 1, 1 (1929). Emphasis added.

17. Juan Martínez Capó, "Las pequeñas revistas literarias," *Asomante* 11, 1 (1955): 104–105. For an account of the small cultural journals available in the 1930s, see Capó's article.

18. Martínez Capó, "Las pequeñas revistas literarias," 105.

19. *Índice* and Antonio S. Pedreira's *Insularismo* have been the subject of copious critical analysis in the past years. It is beyond the scope of this study to account for the many important approaches to this work that enrich our knowledge of Pedreira's oeuvre.

20. Other student periodicals besides Ámbito are: ABC universitario (1930), Vórtice (1930), and El cuko (1938–1939). Isabel Picó de Hernández's doctoral thesis is an in-depth study of the rise of political militancy in the 1930s. She convincingly explains how the development of cultural nationalism gives rise to the students' political militancy. Picó de Hernández links this movement with the political evolution of Puerto Rican society in the first half of the twentieth century. "Los estudiantes universitarios y el proceso político puertorriqueño" (Ph.D. diss., Harvard University, 1974) 161–162.

21. *Boricuismo*, from Borinquen or Borikén, the Taino name of Puerto Rico.

22. Martínez Capó, "Las pequeñas revistas literarias," 107–109.

23. In 1940 the ideological leaders of the populist coalition—all members of the *Generación del treinta*—would discuss their cultural program compiled under the title *Foro del Ateneo.* The conference papers were published in a commemorative edition, *Foro del Ateneo* (Río Piedras: Editorial Universitaria, 1976).

24. The *Revista* overlaps as far as the year of publication. For example, the first year of the journal includes October 1938, December 1938, April 1939, and July 1939. As a rule, publication of the journal agreed with the academic year. All citations are from the original issues of the *Revista.* Generally, the editorials cited in this chapter can also be found in Margot Arce de Vázquez, *Obras Completas*, ed. Matilde Albert Robatto, vol. 3 (San Juan: Editorial de la Universidad de Puerto Rico, 2001) and *Obras Completas*, ed. Hugo Rodríguez Vecchini, vol. 1 (San Juan: Editorial de la Universidad de Puerto Rico 1998). At times, the original versions of these editorials differ slightly from their reprints in Arce's complete works.

25. Arce, "No es el propósito de esta revista," editorial, *Revista* 1, 1 (1938). Emphasis added.

26. Arce, editorial, *Revista* 1, 1 (1938).

27. Arce, editorial, *Revista* 1, 1 (1938).

28. Arce, editorial, *Revista* 1, 1 (1938).

29. Arce, editorial, *Revista* 1, 1 (1938).

30. The Circle of Spanish Teachers had suspended the publication of its journal *Brújula* the year before.

31. Carmen Gómez Tejera, "Breves palabras con motivo del homenaje ofrecido por el Círculo de Maestro de Español a Alejandro Casona," *Revista* 1, 1 (1938): 6–11.

32. Acevedo, *Revista* 1, 1 (1938): 13.

33. Discussed in Chapter 1. There is a full page advertisement for the Banco Popular de Puerto Rico, an "Institución que debe ser orgullo y patrocinada por todo buen puertorriqueño."

34. See Rubén Dávila Santiago's anthology of working class theater, *Teatro obrero en Puerto Rico (1900–1920)* (Río Piedras: Editorial Edil, 1985). See also Dávila's *El derribo de las murallas: orígenes intelectuales del socialismo en Puerto Rico* (Río Piedras: Editorial Cultural, 1988).

35. See Chapter 1 of this book.

36. See Julio Ramos's introductory essay to *Luisa Capetillo, amor y anarquía: los escritos de Luisa Capetillo* (Río Piedras: Huracán, 1992) 11–58.

37. Berta Cabanillas, "Problemas económicos del ama de casa," *Revista* 1, 1 (1938): 25.

38. See Carol Asher, "Selling to Ms. Consumer," *American Media and Mass Culture* (Berkeley: University of California Press, 1987) 43. Additionally, María de Fátima Barceló Miller has an interesting study of the advertisements that appeared in the photo magazine *Puerto Rico Ilustrado* during the 1910s. Pages dedicated to advertizing of American products were considerable. She explains that since no such ads were seen before 1898, the magazine represented a veritable shift on the Puerto Rican scene. The trends she described had intensified by the 1930s. See Barceló Miller's "Ojos soñadores, gracia hechicera y existencia seductora: imagen social de la mujer en la revista *Puerto Rico Ilustrado* en la década del 1910," *Revista Cupey* 11, 1–2 (1994): 102–113.

39. Included among these goods are: Elizabeth Arden beauty products, toothpaste, soaps, over-the-counter medicines (which promised strength and health to a highly anemic population), cars, telephone services, pleasure trips, powdered milk (with pictures of healthy Puerto Rican children raised on Klim), electric appliances and services, and banking services.

40. Cabanillas, "Problemas económicos del ama de casa," *Revista* 1, 1 (1938): 25.

41. Mistral was awarded the Nobel in 1945. In light of recent research on women writers in Latin America, we could reflect on the implications in Mistral's works of the strictures imposed by the role of the *maestra rural,* a persona that broadened the appeal of her poetry and her prestige all over Latin America, while at the same time prescribing limited readings of her oeuvre. In "The 'Schoolteacher of America': Gender, Sexuality and Nation in Gabriela Mistral," in *¿Entiendes? Queer Readings, Hispanic Writings,* eds. Emilie L. Bergmann and Paul Julian Smith (Durham and London: Duke University Press, 1995), Licia Fiol Matta argues that "Mistral herself set the process in motion early in her life. She invested a tremendous amount of energy and time (approximately twenty years) in creating this persona." 201.

42. These three essays were reprinted by *Alma Latina,* another magazine published in San Juan.

43. Arce, "La patria es mucho más," editorial, *Revista* 1, 2 (1938).

44. Arce, editorial, *Revista* 1, 2 (1938).

45. Arce, editorial, *Revista* 1, 2 (1938).

46. Arce, "La dirección de esta revista se complace," editorial, *Revista* 1, 3 (1939). Emphasis added.

47. Carrión collaborated with José Colombán Rosario, considered by many to be the dean of Puerto Rican sociology, in a number of research projects, especially the work on racial prejudice *Problemas sociales: el negro (Haití, Estados Unidos, Puerto Rico)* (San Juan: Negociado de Materiales, Imprenta y Transporte, 1940).

48. Justina Carrión, "Modelo 1939," *Revista* 1, 4 (1939): 7.

49. Carrión, *Revista* 1, 4 (1939): 8.

50. Carrión, *Revista* 1, 4 (1939): 9.

51. Carrión, *Revista* 1, 4 (1939): 9.

52. This article is a reprint from a publication of a charitable institution called the *Asociación Pro Salud Maternal,* that understood contraception as eugenics, a way of controlling "las serias cargas que presenta el cuidado de delincuentes, enfermos mentales y su población desvalida en general." *Revista* 1, 4 (1939): 35.

53. Arce, "Gabriela Mistral y el premio Nobel de la literatura," editorial, *Revista* 2, 3 (1940). The *encanto apacible de nuestro ambiente moral* is a wish expressed by Arce more than a social reality. Emphasis added.

54. Arce, "La crisis," editorial, 2, 4 (1940).

55. Arce, "María Zambrano," *Revista* 2, 4 (1940): 14. Emphasis added. Zambrano was very influential for the Cuban group *Orígenes.* She resided in Havana where she taught at the university.

56. Juan Ramón Jiménez had also come to the island as a visiting professor. He would return to live there permanently.

57. Picó de Hernández, "Los estudiantes universitarios," 224.

58. Picó de Hernández, "Los estudiantes universitarios," 225.

59. Picó de Hernández, "Los estudiantes universitarios," 224.

60. Arce, "El desarrollo de los acontecimientos políticos europeos," editorial, *Revista* 3, 2 (1941).

61. This position became available after the sudden death of Pedreira.

62. Arce, "La ley de la Universidad," editorial, *Revista* 3, 3 (1941). In the original journal this essay appears in *Revista* 3, 3 (1941): 3–4 while in the *Obras Completas* it appears

as 3, 1 (1941): 3–4. The journal would later dedicate a whole issue to university reform in April, 1942.

63. For a detailed analysis of the Foro del Ateneo see María Elena Rodríguez Castro, "Foro de 1940: las pasiones y los intereses se dan la mano," in *Del nacionalismo al populismo: cultura y política en Puerto Rico*, ed. Silvia Álvarez-Curbelo and María Elena Rodríguez Castro (Río Piedras: Ediciones Huracán, 1993) 61–105.

64. Arce, "Con especial devoción y hondo recuerdo," editorial, *Revista* 4, 1 (1941). Emphasis added.

65. Arce, "Nuestro deber," editorial, *Revista* 4, 2 (1942).

66. Julita Córdova Infante, "Lo que la asociación de mujeres graduadas significa para Puerto Rico," *Revista* 4, 2 (1942): 28.

67. Arce, "El status de Puerto Rico y la Carta del Atlántico," editorial, *Revista* 5, 1 (1943).

68. Arce, editorial, *Revista* 5, 1 (1943).

69. Arce, editorial, *Revista* 5, 1 (1943).

70. Arce, editorial, *Revista* 5, 1 (1943).

71. Dávila Santiago, *El derribo de las murallas: orígenes intelectuales del socialismo en Puerto Rico* (Río Piedras: Editorial Cultural, 1988),134–135.

72. Dávila Santiago, *El derribo de las murallas*, 135.

73. Of the popular compositors, Gómez Tejera mentions only Rafael Hernández.

74. Arce, "Reflexiones en torno a *Insularismo*," *Revista* 5, 1 (1943): 20.

75. Arce, "Reflexiones en torno a *Insularismo*," *Revista* 5, 1 (1943): 24.

76. Arce, "Reflexiones en torno a *Insularismo*," *Revista* 5, 1 (1943): 25.

77. Arce "La reforma universitaria," editorial, *Revista* 5, 2 (1943). There is a discrepancy regarding my journal citation of "La reforma universitaria" and attribution in Margot Arce de Vázquez's Complete Works. They situate this editorial in *Revista* 3, 4 (1942). I have not been able to find the issue they mention. The confusion is due to the fact that Arce wrote an earlier editorial 4, 3 (1942) entitled simply "Reforma universitaria." We briefly discussed that issue of the journal earlier in this chapter. The editorial "La reforma universitaria" corresponds to 5, 2 (1943).

78. Arce, "La reforma universitaria," editorial, *Revista* 5, 2 (1943).

79. Arce, editorial, *Revista* 5, 2 (1943).

80. Arce, editorial, *Revista* 5, 2 (1943). Emphasis added.

81. Arce, editorial, *Revista* 5, 2 (1943).

82. Arce, editorial, *Revista* 5, 2 (1943).

83. Jaime Benítez, "Discurso del rector de la univerdidad D. Jaime Benítez, ante el claustro, administración y estudiantes, el 15 de febrero de 1943," *Revista* 5, 2 (1943): 20.

84. Nilita Vientós, "Con emoción y gratitud . . . Llorens Torres," editorial, *Revista* 5, 3 (1944).

85. Prior to the last issue of the journal another issue appeared with no editorial essay. It is mistakenly labeled year 5, 1944, when it should be labeled year 6, 1944. This uncertainty is a sign that a reorganization of the editorial board was under way.

86. Some of Vientós Gastón's collaborators in the *Asomante* enterprise have referred to the first *Revista* with the pejorative "revistilla" because it was not a proper literary journal.

87. A study of *Asomante* is outside the scope of this book.

Chapter 4

1. "Cartel" *Ateneo Puertorriqueño* 1 (1935): 4. All translations in this chapter are mine.

2. "Cartel" *Ateneo Puertorriqueño*, 5.

3. "Cartel" *Ateneo Puertorriqueño*, 5.

4. They speak as people quite familiar with the symbols of the new capitalist consumer culture in their statement of intent. Quintero Rivera reports that the first radio station was established in San Juan in 1922. Ángel G. Quintero Rivera, *Salsa, sabor y control: sociología de la música tropical* (Mexico D. F.: Siglo Veintiuno, 1998) 302.

5. Juan Flores, "'Bumbúm' and the Beginnings of *Plena* Music," in *Divided Borders: Essays on Puerto Rican Identity* (Houston: Arte Público Press, 1993) 85–86. Flores also delineates a third moment, that comprises the 1950s and 1960s, representing a "return to those roots, both in the working-class point of reference and in the renewed moorings in *bomba* and Afro-Caribbean rhythms."

6. Flores, "'Bumbúm,'" 87.

7. Flores, "'Bumbúm,'" 88.

8. See Ruth Glasser, *My Music Is My Flag: Puerto Rican Musicians and Their New York Communities 1917–1940* (Berkeley: University of California Press, 1995).

9. Tomás Blanco "Elogio de *la plena:* variaciones boricuas," *Ateneo Puertorriqueño* 1 (1935): 99.

10. Blanco, "Elogio de *la plena,*" 99.

11. Blanco, "Elogio de *la plena,*" 99.

12. See Felix Echevarría Alvarado, *La plena: origen, sentido y desarrollo en el folklore puertorriqueño* (Santurce: Express, 1984).

13. Blanco, "Elogio de *la plena,*" 100.

14. Blanco, "Elogio de *la plena,*" 100.

15. Emphasis in the original. Blanco uses ñama, the colloquial rendition of llama.

16. Blanco, "Elogio de *la plena,*" 100.

17. Blanco, "Elogio de *la plena,*" 100–101.

18. Ray Pratt, *Rhythm and Resistance: Explorations in the Political Uses of Popular Music* (New York: Praeger, 1990) 86. See in addition, Halbert E. Barton, "The Drum-Dance Challenge: An Anthropological Study of Gender, Race, and Class Marginalization of Bomba in Puerto Rico" (Ph.D. diss., Cornell University, 1995).

19. Pratt, *Rhythm and Resistance*, 86.

20. Flores, "'Bumbúm,'" 89.

21. Flores, "'Bumbúm,'" 89.

22. Quintero Rivera, *Salsa, sabor y control*, 201–251.

23. It is hard to do justice to the author's complex arguments here. Please see Quintero Rivera, *Salsa, sabor y control*, 252–299.

24. Quintero Rivera, *Salsa, sabor y control*, 285.

25. For more on this interesting phenomenon, see Bernice Johnson Reagon's interview with Bill Moyers, "The Songs Are Free," Gail Pellett, producer (New York: Mystic Fire Video, 1991) 58 minutes.

26. Blanco, "Elogio de *la plena,*" 106.

27. Blanco, "Elogio de *la plena*," 102–103. One of the curious symbols of *burundanga* or dissonance that Blanco uses is that of a Hottentot in a top hat. The Khoi-khoi of Southern Africa were converted into the "Hottentots" by a racist propaganda that construed them to be some of the most backward humans on earth. Let us not forget the tragic episode of Sarah Barthman, the "Hottentot Venus," who was paraded around Europe as a curiosity for the amusement of thrill-seekers interested in her anatomical proportions. The expropriation, hunger, and impoverishment of the indigenous peoples of the Southern region of Africa were accompanied by vicious propaganda that circulated all over the world. For an illuminating discussion of one such example see Robert J. Gordon, *The Bushman Myth: The Making of a Namibian Underclass* (Boulder, San Francisco, and Oxford: Westview Press, 1992).

28. Blanco, "Elogio de *la plena*," 105.

29. Blanco's essay ends with an admonition: the *plena* should not imitate "jazz's purely exotic qualities," and it should not plagiarize Cuban music. These were prophetic words, for decades later, what Blanco feared became manifest in the musical form known as *salsa*, a Puerto Rican musical language that expresses the basic values of an alternative culture.

30. See the provocative essay by Arcadio Díaz Quiñones, "Tomás Blanco: racismo, historia, esclavitud," introduction to *El prejuicio racial en Puerto Rico* (Río Piedras: Ediciones Huracán, 1985) 15–83.

31. Díaz Quiñones, "Tomás Blanco," 55.

32. Díaz Quiñones, "Tomás Blanco," 36.

33. Mercedes López-Baralt, *Sobre ínsulas extrañas: el clásico de Pedreira anotado por Tomás Blanco* (San Juan: Editorial Universidad de Puerto Rico, 2001) 17.

34. This is an idea developed by Rubén Ríos Ávila in "La raza cómica: identidad y cuerpo en Pedreira y Palés," *La Torre: Revista de la Universidad de Puerto Rico*, 7, 27–28 (1993): 559–576.

35. Dieter Woll, "Esp. *criollo* y port. *crioulo:* volviendo a la cuestión del origen y la historia de las dos palabras," eds. Annegret Bollée and Johannes Kramer, *Latinitas et Romanitas* (Bonn: Romanistischer Verlag, 1997). Additionally, see Woll, "Esp. *criollo* y port. *crioulo*," 525–530, for his detailed historical-morphological and historical-phonetic arguments that contest the theory of a Portuguese origin of the Spanish *criollo.*

36. Woll, "Esp. *criollo* y port. *crioulo*," 532. Woll's emphasis.

37. Woll, "Esp. *criollo* y port. *crioulo*," 532. Woll's emphasis.

38. Woll, "Esp. *criollo* y port. *crioulo*," 522.

39. Qtd. in José Juan Arrom, "Criollo: definición y matices de un concepto," *Hispania* 34 (1951): 173.

40. Arrom, "Criollo," 174.

41. Arrom, "Criollo," 175.

42. Luis Ángel Ferrao, *Pedro Albizu Campos y el nacionalismo puertorriqueño* (Río Piedras: Editorial Cultural, 1990) 55–57.

43. Emilio S. Belaval, "Los problemas de la cultura puertorriqueña," *Ateneo Puertorriqueño* 1, 3(1935): 225. This essay was published in two installments. Part one appeared in *Ateneo Puertorriqueño* 1, 2 (1935): 172–188 and part two in 1, 3 (1935): 191–247.

44. Belaval, "Los problemas," 224.

45. Concurrently, other Latin-American intellectuals were in the midst of formulating their own brands of *criollismo.* In places with large indigenous populations some looked toward "indigenismo." A number of Cuban Creoles wrestled with "negrismo," in order to organize their bid for hegemony. All these cultural nationalist ideologies, however, are parts of strategies of containment or partial incorporation that sought to manage non-white and other subaltern populations.

46. The metaphor of the nation as an edifice would be further elaborated decades later by José Luis González in *El país de cuatro pisos.* Though he has been harshly criticized for the rigidity of the edifice metaphor, González's interpretation had the consciousness-raising effect of contesting the notion of Spanish supremacy.

47. Belaval, "Los problemas," 177.

48. Belaval, "Los problemas," 178.

49. Belaval, "Los problemas," 178.

50. Belaval, "Los problemas," 178.

51. Belaval, "Los problemas," 183.

52. Belaval, "Los problemas," 192.

53. Belaval, "Los problemas," 193.

54. Belaval, "Los problemas," 193.

55. Belaval, "Los problemas," 195.

56. Belaval, "Los problemas," 186.

57. Belaval, "Los problemas," 187.

58. Belaval, "Los problemas," 188.

59. Belaval, "Los problemas," 198.

60. Belaval, "Los problemas," 218.

61. Belaval, "Los problemas," 227

62. Belaval, "Los problemas," 228.

63. Belaval, "Los problemas," 233.

64. Belaval, "Los problemas," 230.

65. The term *blanchitude* was suggested to me by Kelvin Santiago-Valles.

66. Belaval, "Los problemas," 238.

67. See Luis Ángel Ferrao, *Pedro Albizu Campos,* for a detailed study of the effects of immigration on the formation of an elite Creole class and their descendents in the early twentieth century.

68. Belaval, "Los problemas," 235. In English in the original.

69. Belaval, "Los problemas," 239.

70. Belaval, "Los problemas," 235.

71. Belaval, "Los problemas," 222.

72. Belaval, "Los problemas," 238.

73. Belaval, "Los problemas," 238.

74. Belaval, "Los problemas," 238.

75. Belaval, "Los problemas," 238.

76. Bolívar Pagán, *Historia de los partidos políticos puertorriqueños,* vol. 2 (Barcelona: M. Pareja, 1959) 79.

77. Belaval, "Los problemas," 239.

78. Belaval, "Los problemas," 239.

79. Belaval, "Los problemas," 239.

80. Belaval, "Los problemas," 241.
81. Belaval, "Los problemas," 219.
82. Belaval, "Los problemas," 219. Emphasis in the original.
83. Belaval, "Los problemas," 221.
84. Belaval, "Los problemas," 226.
85. Belaval, "Los problemas," 224.
86. Belaval, "Los problemas," 246.
87. Belaval, "Los problemas," 242.
88. Belaval, "Los problemas," 245.
89. Belaval, "Los problemas," 247.
90. Margot Arce, "El paisaje de Puerto Rico," *Horizontes* 1,1 (1939): 43–56. The essay appeared in the inaugural issue.
91. Arce, "El paisaje de Puerto Rico," 43.
92. Arce, "El paisaje de Puerto Rico," 43.
93. Arce, "El paisaje de Puerto Rico," 44. This bold introductory passage in which the author encapsulates her anti-colonial thesis vis-à-vis the United States is excised in *Impresiones: notas Puertorriqueñas* (San Juan: Editorial Yaurel 1950). Some of the changes are simply stylistic, but others are more profound and have a greater ideological impact.
94. Arce, "El paisaje de Puerto Rico," 44.
95. Arce, "El paisaje de Puerto Rico," 44.
96. Arce, "El paisaje de Puerto Rico," 45.
97. See chapter two of George M. Fredrickson, *Racism: A Short History* (Princeton and Oxford: Princeton University Press, 2002).
98. Arce, "El paisaje de Puerto Rico," 45.
99. Arce, "El paisaje de Puerto Rico," 46. Capitalist exploitation is not so directly mentioned in the later version of the essay.
100. Juan José Beauchamp, "La literatura de la crisis social y cultural de la identidad nacional puertorriqueña (1925–1949): Un ensayo de apertura," in *22 Conferencias de literatura puertorriqueña*, ed. Edgar Martínez Masdeu (San Juan: Librería Editorial Ateneo, 1994) 313.
101. Beauchamp, "La literatura de la crisis social y cultural," 344. Within the literature of the land Beauchamp further differentiates between, on one hand, that which deals with the theme of the coffee *hacienda* or desirable life, and on the other, that of sugar plantations and the degradation by foreign monopolies.
102. Richard Handler, *Nationalism and Politics of Culture in Quebec* (Madison: The University of Wisconsin Press, 1988) 47.
103. Arce, "El paisaje de Puerto Rico," 45.
104. Arce, "El paisaje de Puerto Rico," 45.
105. Arce, "El paisaje de Puerto Rico," 45–46.
106. Arce, "El paisaje de Puerto Rico," 44.
107. Arce, "El paisaje de Puerto Rico," 53.
108. Arce, "El paisaje de Puerto Rico," 53.
109. Arnaldo Cruz-Malavé gives us an ingenious reading of the fear of "queerness" in *Insularismo* and subsequent works of Puerto Rican literature. See Arnaldo Cruz-Malavé, "Toward an Art of Transvestism: Colonialism and Homosexuality in Puerto Rican Literature," *¿Entiendes? Queer Readings, Hispanic Writings*, eds. Emilie L. Bergmann and Paul Julian Smith (Durham and London: Duke University Press, 1995) 137–167.

110. Beauchamp,"La literatura de la crisis social y cultural," 344.
111. Arce, "El paisaje de Puerto Rico," 49.
112. Arce, "El paisaje de Puerto Rico," 45.
113. Arce, "El paisaje de Puerto Rico," 56.
114. In the 1950 version Arce chose other less obviously political verses by Mistral to give closure to the essay.

Chapter 5

1. For an analysis of these metaphors see Richard Handler, *Nationalism and Politics of Culture in Quebec* (Madison: The University of Wisconsin Press, 1988). One of the salient presuppositions of nationalist discourses conceives the nation as a male entity striving to assert itself in opposition to forces that threaten its integrity. During times when women were not legally considered adults, this metaphor could put them at a great disadvantage vis-à-vis citizenship in the nation.
2. Isabel Picó de Hernández, "Los estudiantes universitarios y el proceso político puertorriqueño 1903–1948" (Ph.D. diss., Harvard University, 1974).
3. *Los cuentos de la Universidad* (San Juan: Biblioteca de Autores Puertorriqueños, 1935). The second reprint is also by the Biblioteca de Autores Puertorriqueños, 1945; the revised and expunged edition by Editorial Rumbos of Barcelona was published in 1967, and reprinted by Editorial Cultural of Río Piedras in 1977.
4. The University of Puerto Rico was founded in 1903 as a teacher's college.
5. Emilio Belaval, "Lohengrin ha perdido su cisne," in *Los cuentos de la Universidad* (San Juan: Biblioteca de Autores Puertorriqueños, 1935) 9. All citations unless otherwise noted are from the first edition. The pagination of the various editions may differ. All Spanish citations were translated by Susan M. Dever and the author.
6. Belaval, "Lohengrin ha perdido su cisne," 9.
7. Belaval, "Lohengrin ha perdido su cisne," 9–10.
8. Belaval, "La termópila en la plaza del mercado," 165. Emphasis added.
9. Belaval, "La termópila en la plaza del mercado," 165–166. Emphasis added.
10. The humorous and satirical tone of many of the short stories will be accentuated in his next, and best known, collection: *Cuentos para fomentar el turismo* (San Juan: Biblioteca de Autores Puertorriqueños, 1946).
11. José Luis González provides a very convincing account of the cultural motivations of the professional elite's nationalism in his essay, "Literatura e identidad nacional en Puerto Rico," in *Puerto Rico, identidad nacional y clases sociales (Coloquio de Princeton).* (Río Piedras: Ediciones Huracán, 1979) 45–79.
12. I discuss some of these theories in relation to his generation in "Race, Gender and the Generación del Treinta: Toward a Deciphering of Puerto Rican National Identity Discourse" (Ph.D. diss., Stanford University, 1993) chapter four.
13. For a discussion of student activism and the political implications of the struggles for university reform, see Picó de Hernández, "Los estudiantes universitarios," chapters two and three.
14. The caricature is by Filardi, the foremost Puerto Rican satirist. The typography used on the 1935 jacket of the book has a definite avant-garde flavor. Later editions do not reproduce this bold image.

15. Belaval, "Lohengrin ha perdido su cisne," 18. Emphasis added.
16. Belaval, "Tony Pérez es un niño flan," 20–21.
17. Belaval, "Tony Pérez es un niño flan," 24.
18. Belaval, "Tony Pérez es un niño flan," 21.
19. Belaval, "Exaltación de Bebé Pacheco," 30.
20. Belaval, "Exaltación de Bebé Pacheco," 30.
21. Belaval, "Exaltación de Bebé Pacheco," 31. Emphasis added.
22. Belaval, "Exaltación de Bebé Pacheco," 35.
23. Belaval, "Exaltación de Bebé Pacheco," 35.
24. Belaval, "Exaltación de Bebé Pacheco," 35.
25. Belaval, "Exaltación de Bebé Pacheco," 36.
26. Belaval, "Exaltación de Bebé Pacheco," 36. Emphasis added.
27. Belaval, "Exaltación de Bebé Pacheco," 37.
28. Belaval, "Tony Pérez es un niño flan," 27.
29. Emilio Belaval, "Mi señoría el boticario de mi pueblo," 60. Emphasis added. In the revised 1967 version "juncales mulaticas" is replaced by "juncales obrericas," or slender laborers.
30. See Lydia Milagros González, "Tras el mundillo de la aguja," *Revista Homines* 10, 2 (1986–1987): 166–171. González explains that, in its apogee, the needlepoint industry was extremely exploitive of its workers.
31. Belaval, "Mi señoría el boticario de mi pueblo," 60–61.
32. Belaval, "Mi señoría el boticario de mi pueblo," 61. Emphasis added. In the revised edition of 1967 Belaval would change the racial term "trigueñas," which translates as black or dark-skinned girls, for "casquivanas," flighty girls or feather-brained girls, thus crucially altering the meaning of the passage.
33. Such a mayoral staff, adorned with flowers, has decidedly phallic overtones.
34. Belaval, "Mi señoría el boticario de mi pueblo," 61. Likewise, as with the previously quoted section, Belaval substitutes "casquivana" and "casquivanitas" for the racial terms "mulata" and "mulaticas."
35. Belaval, "Un cráneo chato se arrima a la luna," 64.
36. Belaval, "Un cráneo chato se arrima a la luna," 64–65.
37. Belaval, "Un cráneo chato se arrima a la luna," 65.
38. Belaval, "Un cráneo chato se arrima a la luna," 73. Emphasis added.
39. St. Clair Drake, *Black Folk Here and There*, vol. 1 (Los Angeles: Center for Afro-American Studies, 1987) 80.
40. Belaval, "Un cráneo chato se arrima a la luna," 66.
41. Belaval, "Un cráneo chato se arrima a la luna," 71.
42. Belaval, "Un cráneo chato se arrima a la luna," 71. Baldomero becomes a "Snow White" awaiting the kiss that will rescue him from social death.
43. Belaval, "Un cráneo chato se arrima a la luna," 69. Emphasis added.
44. Belaval, "Un cráneo chato se arrima a la luna," 69.
45. This could well have been José Vasconcelos, whose *La raza cósmica* was published in 1925. He had written that out of the mixing of the four races a new one, the cosmic race, would emerge. Vasconcelos had been Mexico's minister of education from 1920 to 1924. He visited Puerto Rico in 1927 where he lectured and cemented relationships with Nationalist leader Pedro Albizu Campos.

46. Belaval, "Un cráneo chato se arrima a la luna," 68.

47. See Arcadio Díaz Quiñones's introductory essay, "Tomás Blanco: racismo, historia, y esclavitud," in Tomás Blanco, *El prejuicio racial en Puerto Rico* (Río Piedras: Ediciones Huracán, 1985).

48. Belaval, "Un cráneo chato se arrima a la luna," 70.

49. Belaval, "Un cráneo chato se arrima a la luna," 71.

50. Belaval, "Un cráneo chato se arrima a la luna," 70.

51. Belaval, "Un cráneo chato se arrima a la luna," 71.

52. Belaval, "Un cráneo chato se arrima a la luna," 71–72.

53. Belaval, "Un cráneo chato se arrima a la luna," 72.

54. Belaval, "Un cráneo chato se arrima a la luna," 72.

55. Belaval, "Un cráneo chato se arrima a la luna," 72. Emphasis added.

56. George Fredrickson reports that Kipling's poem, written in 1899 on the occasion of the Cuban–Spanish–American War, was a way of urging the United States to rise as a conquering nation, " . . . to encourage the victorious Americans to establish colonial rule over the Philippines." *Racism: A Short History* (Princeton and Oxford: Princeton University Press, 2002) 107.

57. Calabar is a seaport in South Eastern Nigeria. Slaves from this region of Africa were reputed to take a very rebellious stance against enslavement. Belaval, "Un cráneo chato se arrima a la luna," 72.

58. At the time, many whites were uneasy with the charismatic social movement of the Jamaican Marcus Garvey, or the work of black intellectuals like W. E. B. Du Bois, or the athletic prowess of the boxer Jack Johnson.

59. Belaval, "Un cráneo chato se arrima a la luna," 72.

60. J. A. de Gobineau was one of the many authors who tried to give a veneer of legitimate science to the most blatant ethnocentric xenophobia. J.A. de Gobineau qtd. in Martin Bernal, *Black Athena: The Afro-Asiatic Roots of Classical Civilization*, vol. 1 (New Brunswick: Rutgers University Press, 1987) 241.

61. Belaval, "Un cráneo chato se arrima a la luna," 74.

62. Belaval, "Un cráneo chato se arrima a la luna," 74. Curiously, Baldomero goes from fellow student to slum dweller.

63. Luis Rafael Sánchez, *Fabulación e ideología en la cuentística de Emilio S. Belaval* (San Juan: Instituto de Cultura Puertorriqueña, 1977) 93–94. This study is an indispensable analysis of Belaval's short stories.

64. Even though this is Luis Rafael Sánchez's term, he does not elaborate on the gender implications of this point of view. See Sánchez, *Fabulación e ideología*, 101.

65. Linda Hutcheon, *Irony's Edge: The Theory and Politics of Irony* (London and New York: Routledge, 1995) 12. Emphasis in the original.

66. Hutcheon, *Irony's Edge*, 37.

67. According to Hutcheon, irony's continuum of functions can be reinforcing, complicating, ludic, distancing, self-protective, provisional, oppositional, assailing, and aggregative.

68. Belaval, "La pasión rural de Tintagiles Bermúdez," 120.

69. Belaval, "La pasión rural de Tintagiles Bermúdez," 121.

70. Belaval, "La pasión rural de Tintagiles Bermúdez," 115. This passage does not appear in the later version. The author also deletes a comment made by one of the students who admiringly declares "¡Caballeros, que nodriza para un niño aprovechado!" as he praises Tintagiles's beloved, or rather, his desire for her big—wetnurse—breasts.

71. María E. Rodríguez Castro, "La escritura de lo nacional y los intelectuales puertorriqueños" (Ph.D. diss., Princeton University, 1988) 64.

72. Hutcheon, *Irony's Edge*, 94.

73. The proverbial bohemian opium den is a marijuana den in this story.

74. Belaval, "Se enciende la lámpara de Aladino," 159. Emphasis added. For the purpose of my discussion, I use the term "mulatto" to indicate the race mixture known as *grifo*, or high yellow, used by Belaval to describe Antoñón, the brothel keeper. In the 1967 revision racial references are excised from this story also, softening the very serious racialized class conflict at the base of the story. Here Antoñón is not a "grifo," a high yellow man, but a "chivo," a rascal. Interestingly, by exchanging "grifo" for "chivo" Antoñón becomes a scapegoat—what is known in Spanish as a "chivo expiatorio"—for the white gentlemen.

75. Belaval, "Se enciende la lámpara de Aladino," 163. In the heat of struggle the epithets thrown at Antoñón are "grifo carnicero," "negro bozal," "puerco espín." The narrative voice refers to him as "grifo asado al palo," "grifo emparejado."

76. Belaval, "Se enciende la lámpara de Aladino," 162.

Chapter 6

1. Sylvia Wynter, "Beyond Miranda's Meanings: Un/silencing the Demonic Ground of Caliban's 'Woman,'" in *Out of the Kumbla: Caribbean Women and Literature*, eds. Carole Boyce Davies and Elaine Savory Fido (Trenton: Africa World Press, 1990).

2. Peter Hulme and William H. Sherman, preface to *The Tempest and Its Travels* (Philadelphia: University of Pennsylvania Press, 2000). See also Gerald Graff and James Phelan, preface to *The Tempest: A Case Study in Critical Controversy* (Boston: Bedford/St. Martin's, 2000). Additionally, see R. S. White, introduction to *The Tempest* (New York: St. Martin Press, 1999).

3. *The Tempest* is represented prominently in the literature of a great number of colonized nations in the world. In my discussion I refer to some of the recent studies of this master text of Western culture, characterized and reconstructed from a post-colonial perspective. Many more are available.

4. William Shakespeare, *The Tempest*, ed. Frank Kermode, 5th ed. (Cambridge: Harvard University Press, 1954) 32.

5. Eric Cheyfitz, *The Poetics of Imperialism: Translation and Colonization from* The Tempest *to* Tarzan (New York, Oxford: Oxford University Press, 1991) 163. Cheyfitz proposes that, in the Elizabethan cultural context, eloquence is a technology of power. Prospero is a magician of the word who, as scholar and master of the art of eloquence, is capable of subduing and entreating with the skillful use of the word.

6. Wynter, "Beyond Miranda's Meanings," 365.

7. I am aware of the dangers of interchanging indigenous Amerindian with African. However, given that in the Caribbean women of African descent came to occupy early on the ontological place of usable native, this analysis stands.

8. See Marie Ramos Rosado, *La mujer negra en la literatura puertorriqueña* (San Juan: Editorial Universidad de Puerto Rico, 1999), for a detailed study on the theme of the representation of black womanhood. As for self-representation, it would be interesting to

reexamine the production of Afro-Puerto Rican women writers—that of authors who have not emphasized this self-identification as well as that of those who have underlined it, such as Mayra Santos Febres. See also Gladys Jiménez Muñoz, "Carmen María Colón Pellot: mujer y raza en Puerto Rico entre las dos guerras," in *Contrapuntos de género y raza en Puerto Rico* (San Juan: Ediciones Callejón, forthcoming). Her enlightening essay about the poet Carmen Colón Pellot gives us new ways of approaching the subject more accurately. Additionally, see Elizabeth Crespo, "Domestic Work and Racial Divisions in Women's Employment in Puerto Rico, 1899–1930," *Centro: Journal of the Center for Puerto Rican Studies* 8, 1–2 (1996): 31–41, and Félix V. Matos Rodríguez, "¿Quién trabajará?: Domestic Workers, Urban Slaves and the Abolition of Slavery in Puerto Rico," in *Puerto Rican Women's History: New Perspectives*, eds. Félix V. Matos Rodríguez and Linda C. Delgado (Armonk and London: M.E. Sharpe, 1998) 62–82.

9. Josefina Guevara Castañeira offers an interesting biographical essay on Cadilla de Martínez where she enumerates her publications and professional affiliations. Josefina Guevara Castañeira, *Del Yunque a los Andes* (San Juan: Editorial Club de la Prensa, 1959) 155–176.

10. Isabelo Zenón Cruz, *Narciso descubre su trasero: el negro en la cultura puertorriqueña*, 2 vols. (Humacao: Ediciones Furidi, 1974, 1975). José Luis González, "Literatura e identidad nacional en Puerto Rico," in *Puerto Rico: identidad nacional y clases sociales. Coloquio de Princeton* (Río Piedras: Ediciones Huracán, 1979).

11. María Cadilla de Martínez, *Raíces de la tierra: colección de cuentos populares y tradiciones* (Arecibo: Tipografía Hernández, 1941) 14–21. The author gives us a detailed retelling of the genre of *tradiciones* in her book *Raíces de la tierra*.

12. Magali Roy-Féquière, "Race, Gender and the Generación del Treinta: Toward a Deciphering of Puerto Rican National Identity Discourse," (Ph.D. diss., Stanford University, 1993). See also Magali Roy-Féquière, "The Nation as Male Fantasy: Discourses of Race and Gender in Emilio Belaval's *Los cuentos de la Universidad*," in *Ethnicity, Race and Nationality in the Caribbean*, ed. Juan Manuel Carrión (San Juan: Institute of Caribbean Studies Universidad de Puerto Rico, 1997) 122–158.

13. Miriam Jiménez Román, "Un hombre (negro) del pueblo: José Celso Barbosa and the Puerto Rican 'Race' Toward Whiteness," *Centro: Journal of the Center for Puerto Rican Studies* 8, 1–2 (1996): 8–29. Frank Guridy, "Historicizing Race in the Spanish Speaking Caribbean: Radicalization in Cuba and Puerto Rico during the Early Twentieth Century," Puerto Rican Studies Association Conference, University of Massachusetts, Amherst, 26–28 Oct. 2000.

14. Kelvin A. Santiago Valles, *'Subject People' and Colonial Discourses: Economic Transformation and Social Disorder in Puerto Rico 1898–1947* (Albany: State University of New York Press, 1994). Additionally, see Eileen Suárez Findlay, *Imposing Decency: The Politics of Sexuality and Race in Puerto Rico 1870–1920* (Durham and London: Duke University Press, 1999).

15. María Cadilla de Martínez, *Hitos de la raza: cuentos tradicionales y folklóricos* (San Juan: Imprenta Venezuela, 1945) 49. Emphasis in the original. Unless otherwise noted, all Spanish translations in this chapter are by Jacqueline F. Roy and the author.

16. Crespo, "Domestic Work and Racial Divisions," 31–41, provides us with insightful information from oral interviews with women who worked as domestics. See also the pioneering article of Angela Davis, "Reflections on the Black Women's Role in the Community

of Slaves," *The Black Scholar: Journal of Black Studies and Research* 12, 9 (1981): 2–16. Judith Rollins, *Between Women: Domestics and Their Employers* (Philadelphia: Temple University Press 1986). Barbara Omolade, "Hearts of Darkness," in *The Rising Song of African American Women* (London: Routledge, 1994) 3–19. In addition to Crespo see Matos Rodríguez, "¿Quién trabajará?," 62–82, for a study specific to Puerto Rico.

17. Cadilla de Martínez, *Hitos de la raza*, 51.

18. This *hacienda* in fact really existed. Historian Astrid T. Cubano Iguina reports that Montegrande was a very solvent sugar estate in the jurisdiction of Arecibo that was able to transform itself into a large sugar plantation at the end of the nineteenth century. Astrid T. Cubano Iguina, "Economía y sociedad en Arecibo en el Siglo XIX: los grandes productores y la inmigración de comerciantes," in *Inmigración y clases sociales en el Puerto Rico del siglo XIX*, 3rd ed. (Río Piedras: Ediciones Huracán, 1989) 77.

19. Cadilla de Martínez, *Hitos de la raza*, 52

20. Cadilla de Martínez, *Hitos de la raza*, 60.

21. Cadilla de Martínez, *Hitos de la raza*, 52.

22. Fernando Picó, *Libertad y servidumbre en el Puerto Rico del siglo diecinueve* (Río Piedras: Ediciones Huracán, 1981). See also, Matos Rodríguez, "¿Quién trabajará?" 62–82.

23. Cadilla de Martínez, *Hitos de la raza*, 53.

24. It is worth mentioning that the way Fortunato Vizcarrondo represents the black woman in his poem "¿Y tu agüela, a' onde ejtá?" from *Dinga y Mandinga*, 1942, is more attuned to the aesthetic project of *négritude* than to the *negrismo* practiced by Creole authors. Fortunato Vizcarrondo, *Dinga y mandinga: poemas* (San Juan: Talleres Tipográficos Baldrich y Co., 1942).

25. In this vein, see the outstanding study of slavery in the city of San Juan by Raúl Mayo Santana, Mariano Negrón Portillo, and Manuel Mayo López, *Cadenas de esclavitud y solidaridad: esclavos y libertos en San Juan, siglo XIX* (San Juan: Centro de Investigaciones Sociales, Universidad de Puerto Rico, 1997).

26. Cadilla de Martínez, *Hitos de la raza*, 7.

27. Cadilla de Martínez, *Raíces de la tierra*, 25.

28. Cadilla de Martínez, *Raíces de la tierra*, 25.

29. Such influences might have been at work also among those she describes as "whites."

30. Jalil Sued-Badillo and Ángel López Cantos report these groups already in seventeenth-century Puerto Rico in *Puerto Rico Negro* (Río Piedras: Editorial Cultural, 1986) 167. We must caution, however, that slaves often received their designations from port cities from which they were shipped. Nonetheless, these are still helpful in tracing the history of the enslaved groups. Ana Mirem Villamil, for her part, confirms these regional identifications of the enslaved with the Congo, Angola, Guinea, Sudan, and Sierra Leone. See her "Los vejigantes de Ponce," in *La tercera raíz: presencia africana en Puerto Rico* (San Juan: CEREP and Institute of Puerto Rican Culture, 1992) 66.

31. María Cadilla de Martínez, *La poesía popular en Puerto Rico* (Cuenca: Imprenta Moderna 1933) 25.

32. Cadilla de Martínez, *La poesía popular*, 25–26.

33. Cadilla de Martínez, *La poesía popular*, 26.

34. Fernández de Oviedo, *The Conquest and Settlement of Borinquen or Puerto Rico by Captain Gonzalo Fernández de Oviedo y Valdez: Chronicler to His Sacred, Caesarean,*

Catholic, and Royal Majesty, The King-Emperor Charles V, trans. and ed. Daymond Turner (Avon, Connecticut: Cardamon Press, 1975) 46. Gonzalo Fernández de Oviedo, *Historia general y natural de las Indias*, Biblioteca Histórica de Puerto Rico 2nd ed. (San Juan: Instituto de Literatura Puertorriqueña, 1945) 51. Alejandro Tapia y Rivera annotated and published the first edition of these documents.

35. Fernández de Oviedo, *The Conquest*, 48, and Fernández de Oviedo *Historia General*, 52. The problems of narrative license and projection, often present in the accounts of the conquest, have merited that they be read as texts with a strong fictional component as well as texts of factual description. These questions have been studied exhaustively by scholars of the Spanish conquest.

36. Fernández de Oviedo, *The Conquest*, 48, and Fernández de Oviedo, *Historia General*, 52.

37. Fernández de Oviedo, *The Conquest*, 48, and Fernández de Oviedo, *Historia General*, 52.

38. Fernández de Oviedo, *The Conquest*, 48, and Fernández de Oviedo, *Historia General*, 52–53.

39. Fernández de Oviedo, *The Conquest*, 49, and Fernández de Oviedo *Historia General*, 53.

40. Cadilla de Martínez, *Hitos de la raza*, 17.

41. Cadilla de Martínez, *Hitos de la raza*, 18–19.

42. Cadilla de Martínez, *Hitos de la raza*, 20.

43. Cadilla de Martínez, *Hitos de la raza*, 20.

44. Jalil Sued-Badillo, *Los caribes: realidad o fábula* (Río Piedras: Editorial Antillana, 1978). Peter Hulme, *Colonial Encounters: Europe and the Native Caribbean, (1492–1797)* (London and New York: Methuen, 1986). Samuel M. Wilson, ed., *The Indigenous People of the Caribbean* (Gainesville: University Press of Florida, 1997). Jalil Sued-Badillo, *La mujer indígena y su sociedad* (Río Piedras: Editorial Cultural, 1989).

45. Cadilla de Martínez. *Hitos de la raza*, 21.

46. Cadilla de Martínez, *Hitos de la raza*, 11.

47. Cadilla de Martínez, *Hitos de la raza*, 11. Emphasis in the original.

48. Handler proposes that "if the nation is a species, then it is a natural entity whose boundaries can be fixed by a scientific description of its qualities." Richard Handler, *Nationalism and Politics of Culture in Quebec* (Madison: The University of Wisconsin Press, 1988) 43–44.

49. Juan Flores, *From Bomba to Hip-Hop: Puerto Rican Culture and Latino Identity* (New York: Columbia University Press, 2000).

50. Handler, *Nationalism and Politics*, 69. Emphasis mine.

51. Cadilla de Martínez, *Hitos de la raza*, 126.

52. The character is right to point this out. Tremendous changes in production had taken place after 1898.

53. Cadilla de Martínez, *Hitos de la raza*, 128.

54. Cadilla de Martínez, *Hitos de la raza*, 131.

55. Cadilla de Martínez, *Hitos de la raza*, 132.

56. Cadilla de Martínez, *Hitos de la raza*, 133.

57. Cadilla de Martínez, *Hitos de la raza*, 136.

Chapter 7

1. Her talk, which, as the caption reads, "garnered the warmest applause from the distinguished and intelligent public," ("mereció los aplausos más cálidos de la concurrencia distinguida e inteligente") was part of the homage to Palés Matos held on May 20, 1938; Juan Bosch, Tomás Blanco, and Ramón Lavandero also participated. *Puerto Rico Ilustrado* 28, 1473 (June 4, 1938), special issue dedicated to tourism.

2. Historian George M. Fredrickson would add to our discussion that racism proper was the child of Enlightenment ideologies that separated church from state, as well as of economic struggles that made it convenient to stigmatize a competing economic group or a group whose labor those in power needed. See his *Racism: A Short History* (Princeton and Oxford: Princeton University Press, 2002) 51–95.

3. St. Clair Drake, *Black Folk Here and There*, vol. 1 (Los Angeles: Center for Afro-American Studies, University of California, 1987) 25.

4. See Mary Louise Pratt's "Scratches on the Face of the Country; or, What Mr. Barrow Saw in the Land of the Bushmen," in *Race, Writing, and Difference*, ed. Henry Louis Gates (Chicago: The Chicago University Press, 1985) 138–162.

5. Drake, *Black Folk Here and There*, 25.

6. Drake, *Black Folk Here and There*, 25.

7. As historian Martin Bernal has shown, a discourse of white supremacy erased the true history of ancient Greece's heavy cultural borrowings in the sciences and arts from the Egyptians and the Phoenicians, both darker-skinned peoples. Then, German and French nineteenth-century scholarship, especially the discipline of philology, strove to find the origins of Western cultures as far from Africa as possible. The Germans around the University of Göttingen "whitened" the Ancient Greeks and their civilization, and constructed the mythical Aryan origins of Germans as prefigured in the Greeks. See Martin Bernal, *Black Athena: The Afro-Asiatic Roots of Classical Civilization*, 2 vols. (New Brunswick: Rutgers University Press, 1987) vol. 1.

8. Gobineau qtd. in Bernal, *Black Athena*, 241.

9. Gobineau qtd. in Bernal, *Black Athena*, 241.

10. Cuvier qtd. in Drake, *Black Folk Here and There*, 27.

11. For a detailed account of the debate on the "nature" of Amerindian peoples from the European perspective, see Anthony Pagden, *The Fall of Natural Man: The American Indian and the Origins of Comparative Ethnology* (Cambridge: Cambridge University Press, 1982).

12. Fredrickson points to a 1412 law so discriminatory against Jews and Moors that it created a mass of converts. See Fredrickson, *Racism*, 32.

13. For an illuminating discussion of the relationship between ideologies of *mestizaje*, *mulatez*, and national identity in the Latin American context see Lourdes Martínez-Echazábal "*Mestizaje* and the Discourse of Cultural/National Identity in Latin America (1845–1959)," *Latin American Perspectives* 25, 3 (1998): 28.

14. Martínez-Echazábal, "*Mestizaje*," 30–32.

15. See José Joaquín Blanco, *Se llamaba Vasconcelos: una evocación crítica.* (Mexico City: Fondo de Cultura Económica, 1977). See additionally, Susan Dever's introduction to *Celluloid Nationalism and other Melodramas: From Post-Revolutionary Mexico to* fin de siglo *Mexamérica* (Albany: State University of New York Press, 2003).

16. The foremost novelist of the *Generación*, Enrique Laguerre, is visibly mulatto. It is interesting that his works indulge less in the *hispanismo* so dear to his peers. Another case of a black intellectual is José Ferrer Canales. It is fitting that Ferrer Canales studied the works of the "great liberators" of the nineteenth century, Martí, Bolívar, and Hostos. Though they do not mute their African ancestry, neither Laguerre nor Ferrer Canales overtly asserts it.

17. The controversy surrounding José Celso Barbosa, a dark-skinned medical doctor and politician who favored annexation to the United States points to the racist structuring of Puerto Rican society. It is no coincidence that Barbosa studied in the United States where other professional blacks formed a cohesive group. Unlike Barbosa, none of the intellectuals of the *Generación* could be said to be "hombres del pueblo." See also, Miriam Jiménez Román, "Un hombre (negro) del pueblo: José Celso Barbosa and the Puerto Rican 'Race' Toward Whiteness," *Centro: Journal of the Center for Puerto Rican Studies* 8, 1–2 (1996): 8–29.

18. Silvia Álvarez-Curbelo, "El color de la guerra: los soldados puertorriqueños en la Segunda Guerra Mundial y el racismo," Puerto Rican Studies Association, Chicago, Congress Hotel, October 2002. On this question see also Jiménez Román, "Un hombre (negro) del pueblo,"8–29.

19. Juan Antonio Corretjer, "Spengler: una proyección criolla," *El Mundo* (25 Jun. 1936). Unless otherwise noted, all English translations in this chapter are by Nina Menéndez and the author.

20. Corretjer, "Spengler."

21. See Aníbal González, "La (sín)tesis de una poesía antillana: Palés y Spengler," *Cuadernos Hispanoamericanos*, 451–452 (1988): 64. Aníbal González's essay proposes a careful reading of Palés's poetry in relation to the poet's pronouncements on Caribbean culture made in the famous interview with Ángela Negrón Muñoz and in the short essay "Hacia una poesía antillana."

22. For an Afrocentric and very illuminating reading of Palés's poetry, see G. R. Coulthard, *Race and Colour in Caribbean Literature* (London: Oxford University Press, 1962). See also Richard Jackson, *The Black Image in Latin American Literature* (Albuquerque: The University of New Mexico Press, 1976).

23. Palés Matos, "El arte y la raza blanca," *Poliedro*, 1, 16 (1927): 5.

24. See Sylvia Wynter's "Beyond Miranda's Meaning," *Out of the Kumbla* (Trenton: Africa World Press, 1991) 355–366.

25. Palés Matos, *Poliedro*, 5.

26. Palés Matos, *Poliedro*, 5.

27. On the date of this trip to New York there is a certain uncertainty. Mercedes López-Baralt gives August 7 to November 2, 1950 as the dates of his sojourn in New York. Palés Matos attended an homage in his honor at Columbia University sponsored by the *Instituto Hispánico*. There is also a photograph of the poet taken, perhaps in 1952, at the Brooklyn dock with a Puerto Rican delegation that consisted of Benjamín Arnaldo Meyners, Eloisa Rivera, Bobby Quintero, Juan Avilés, and other unidentified well-wishers that can be found in the archives of the Center for Puerto Rican Studies at Hunter College. This might well be the same trip.

28. *El Mundo* interview, November 13, 1932, given to Ángela Negrón Muñoz, "Hablando con Don Luis Palés Matos." A reprint of this text can be found in Margot

Arce's edition of *Luis Palés Matos: poesía completa* (Caracas: Biblioteca Ayacucho, 1978) 213–218.

29. Palés Matos, "Hablando con Don Luis Palés Matos," interview, *El Mundo* 13 Nov. (1932).

30. Palés Matos, "Hablando con Don Luis Palés Matos," interview.

31. Palés Matos, "Hablando con Don Luis Palés Matos," interview.

32. Isabelo Zenón Cruz, *Narciso descubre su trasero: el negro en la cultura puertorriqueña*, vol. 1 (Humacao: Ediciones Furidi, 1974) 47.

33. Zenón Cruz, *Narciso descubre su trasero*, 47–48.

34. Julio Marzán, *The Numinous Site: The Poetry of Luis Palés Matos* (Madison and Teaneck: Associated University Presses, 1995) 15.

35. Marzán, *The Numinous Site*, 20.

36. I follow Marzán's translation of the verses with a small modification of my own. Marzán, 20.

37. Marzán, *The Numinous Site*, 26.

38. Marzán, *The Numinous Site*, 29.

39. J. I. de Diego Padró, "Antillanismo, criollismo, negroidismo," *El Mundo* 19 Nov. (1932). Reprinted in J. I. De Diego Padró, *Luis Palés Matos y su trasmundo poético* (Río Piedras: Ediciones Puerto, 1973) 93–107. See also de Diego Padró's "Tropicalismo, occidentalismo, sentido de la cultura," *El Mundo* 18 Dec. (1932). Reprinted in J. I. De Diego Padró, *Luis Palés Matos y su trasmundo poético* (Río Piedras: Ediciones Puerto, 1973) 109–121. J. I. de Diego Padró's book is of great interest to anyone interested in his personal history of the controversy.

40. de Diego Padró, "Antillanismo."

41. de Diego Padró, "Antillanismo."

42. Luis Palés Matos, "Hacia una poesía antillana," *El Mundo* 26 Nov. (1932).

43. Palés Matos, "Hacia una poesía antillana."

44. Palés Matos, "Hacia una poesía antillana."

45. Luis Antonio Miranda, "El llamado arte negro no tiene vinculación con Puerto Rico," *El Mundo* 26 Nov. (1932).

46. Miranda, "El llamado arte negro."

47. Miranda, "El llamado arte negro."

48. Miranda, "El llamado arte negro." Emphasis in the original.

49. Graciani Miranda Archilla, "La broma de una poesía prieta en Puerto Rico," *Alma Latina*, 1933.

50. It is customary for Puerto Rican literary criticism to stress that a number of Palés's black poems predate Nicolás Guillén's *negrismo.* It is of little value for my arguments to engage in a discussion regarding who was first, Palés or Guillén. A more important project would be to compare the anxiety at the base of the *negrista* projects of both *criollo* Cubans and *criollo* Puerto Ricans. What is the level and quality of influence that the Cubans might have exerted on the Puerto Rican scene in the 1930s? A writer like Juan Marinello was very well known in Puerto Rico. But, by the same token, it is not clear that a writer like Carpentier had an audience in Puerto Rico before the Cuban Revolution.

51. Her talk "Los poemas negros de Luis Palés Matos" was sponsored by the Phi Eta Mu fraternity in September 1933. The entire essay was later published in *El Mundo*, a major San Juan daily, on January 21, 1934.

52. "Pueblo de negros," an earlier composition in prose, reflects more judgmental and ethnocentric attitudes toward blacks.

53. Margot Arce, "Los poemas negros," *El Mundo* 21 Jan. (1934).

54. Arce, "Los poemas negros."

55. Arce, "Los poemas negros."

56. Even Palés's vision of the black experience is narrow. Palés says nothing of the history of black resistance to racism and oppression, nothing of black people's humanity.

57. Arce, "Los poemas negros."

58. Arce, "Los poemas negros."

59. Margot Arce de Váquez, *Impresiones: notas puertorriqueñas* (San Juan: Editorial Yaurel, 1950), 45.

60. Arce, "Los poemas negros." Emphasis added.

61. Arce, *Impresiones*, 46. Emphasis added.

62. *Culteranismo* can be considered the Spanish equivalent of *Mannerism*, a Baroque style known for its cultivation of syntactic obscurity, neologisms, and affectation.

63. Arce, "Los poemas negros." The statements are identical in both versions. Ballagas was also a white man whose poems imitated a black popular voice.

64. One of the constants of Arce's critical style is this criticism by analogy.

65. Palés, "Hablando con Don Luis Palés Matos," interview.

66. Palés, "Hablando con Don Luis Palés Matos," interview. Emphasis added.

67. Arce, "Los poemas negros."

68. Arce, "Los poemas negros."

69. Arce, "Los poemas negros."

70. Arce, "Los poemas negros."

71. Arce, *Impresiones*, 48.

72. Arce, "Los poemas negros." Emphasis added.

73. Arce, *Impresiones*, 48. Emphasis added.

74. Arce, *Impresiones*, 49. Emphasis added.

75. Arce, "Los poemas negros."

76. Arce, *Impresiones*, 51.

77. Arce, "Los poemas negros."Emphasis added.

78. Arce, "Los poemas negros."

79. Arce, *Impresiones*, 50.

80. Arce, "Los poemas negros," and *Impresiones*, 51. This statement is identical in both versions. Emphasis added.

81. Tomás Blanco, "Refutación y glosa,"*Ateneo Puertorriqueño* 1, 4 (1935): 302–309. Tomás Blanco's remarks were sent in a 1934 letter from Madrid to Margot Arce. The letter was published as "Refutación y glosa" in the journal of the Ateneo. Later it was reprinted in a section entitled "Poesía y recitación negras" of the *Revista Bimestre Cubana* 37–38 (1936): 24–30. My quotations are from the *Ateneo Puertorriqueño* version.

82. Blanco, "Refutación y glosa," 303.

83. In 1937, four years after the publication of Arce's first essay on Palés, her cousin and colleague Tomás Blanco visited Cuba and gave a talk on Palés Matos, reprinted in his collection *Sobre Palés Matos* (San Juan: Biblioteca de Autores Puertorriqueños, 1950). Blanco also dedicated his *El prejuicio racial en Puerto Rico* to Ortiz with the following words: "Al habanero don Fernando Ortiz, maestro en antillanismo dinámico y creador."

This essay was first read in Havana in 1937, and later to the *Asociación de Mujeres Graduadas de la UPR.* A copy of this essay was also sent to every member of the *Asociación.*

84. Blanco, "Refutación y glosa," 305.

85. Blanco had commented on Palés's poetry as early as September of 1930 in an article for *The American Mercury* of New York.

86. Blanco, "Refutación y glosa," 307.

87. This essay, "Más sobre los poemas de Luis Palés Matos," was published first in *Ateneo Puertorriqueño* 2 (1936) and shortly after by the *Revista Bimestre Cubana* together with the Tomás Blanco's objections to Arce's "Los poemas negros." All quotations are from the *Revista Bimestre Cubana* 37–38 (1936).

88. Arce, "Más sobre los poemas," 32.

89. Arce, "Más sobre los poemas," 32, and in *Impresiones*, 54.

90. Arce, "Más sobre los poemas," 32, and in *Impresiones*, 54. Emphasis added.

91. The affective bonds that may or may not exist between servants and employers is much in need of study, especially in the Caribbean setting. Questions of relative power and powerlessness must be taken into account, as we saw in Cadilla de Martínez's story "Tate."

92. Arce, "Más sobre los poemas," 32. Emphasis added.

93. Arce, "Más sobre los poemas," 32.

94. One would have to think of the culture of resistance produced by mulatto and black artisans, as well as the participation of mixed-race and black people in the political arena of the late nineteenth and first decades of the twentieth century, to counteract Arce's happy mammy image with that of the striking tobacco worker. See Ángel Quintero Rivera and Gervasio García's *Desafío y solidaridad: breve historia del movimiento obrero puertorriqueño* (Río Piedras: Ediciones Huracán, 1986). We should also remember the coastal black culture that produced leaders and cultural workers such as José Celso Barbosa and Arturo Schomburg and even the mulatto nationalist leader Pedro Albizu Campos.

95. Arce, "Más sobre los poemas," 33. Emphasis added.

96. Of course, the exploitation of dispossessed peasants regardless of race also contributed to *criollo* enrichment.

97. Arce, "Más sobre los poemas," 35. Emphasis added.

98. Arce, *Impresiones*, 56. Emphasis added.

99. Arce, "Más sobre los poemas," 35. Emphasis added.

100. Arce, *Impresiones*, 57. Emphasis added.

101. Arce, "Más sobre los poemas," 34.

102. Tomás Blanco quoted in Arce, *Impresiones*, 56. Emphasis added.

103. One should not forget that a number of French took refuge in Puerto Rico after the Haitian Revolution and were aided by the Spanish government who feared a repeat of revolutionary upheaval in Puerto Rico and Cuba. After the overthrow of the French, Europe and the United States proceeded to isolate Haiti economically and politically, in order to teach free or enslaved black people everywhere a lesson in humility. The United States would invade Haiti from 1915 to 1934, as part of its expansionist crusades to secure further sources of cheap labor and markets for its goods.

104. Some will argue that *negrito* is a term of endearment. I see this as very problematic. For a trenchant analysis of semantic slippage and racial context, see Isar P. Godreau,

"La semántica fugitiva: 'raza,' color y vida cotidiana en Puerto Rico," *Revista de Ciencias Sociales* 9 (2000): 52–71.

105. Margot Arce, "Recitales de Eusebia Cosme en Puerto Rico," *Carteles*, 1936. There is also a picture of Cosme with Palés, Arce, Dr. Ramón Lavandero (also a performer of Palés's poems), Dr. Tomás Blanco, and Dr. Leopoldo Santiago documenting her "triúnfo ruidoso en la capital borinqueña." Among some of the other people to review Cosme's visit were Nilita Vientós Gastón, Carmelina Vizcarrondo, A. J. Colorado, and Pedro Juan Labarthe.

106. Antonio J. Colorado, "El recital de Eusebia Cosme," *El Mundo*, 1936.

107. Colorado, "El recital de Eusebia Cosme."

108. Pedro Juan Labarthe, "Eusebia Cosme, reina recitadora," *El Mundo*, 1936.

109. Labarthe, "Eusebia Cosme, reina recitadora."

110. Palés Matos, "Hacia una poesía antillana."

111. Palés Matos, "Hacia una poesía antillana."

112. bell hooks, *Black Looks: Race and Representation* (Boston: South End Press, 1992) 25.

113. bell hooks, *Black Looks*, 27.

114. This essay first came out as "Los adjetivos en la 'Danza negra' de Luis Palés Matos" in the journal *Ateneo Puertorriqueño* in 1939.

115. Margot Arce, "El adjetivo en la 'Danza negra' de Luis Palés Matos," *Impresiones*, 61.

Chapter 8

1. See Aníbal González, "La (sín)tesis de una poesía antillana: Palés y Spengler," *Cuadernos Americanos* 451–452 (1988): 70. See also Arcadio Díaz Quiñones's "La poesía negra de Luis Palés Matos: realidad y conciencia de su dimensión colectiva," in *El almuerzo en la hierba* (Río Piedras: Ediciones Huracán, 1982).

2. Wole Soyinka, "Ideology and the Social Vision (2): The Secular Ideal" in *Myth, Literature and the African World* (Cambridge: Cambridge University Press, 1976) 126.

3. See Audre Lorde's essay on the limitations feminists of color face when they uncritically adopt the conceptual tools of a white feminism that has not divested from racist understandings of the world. Audre Lorde, "The Master's Tools Will Never Dismantle the Master's House," in *This Bridge Called My Back: Writings by Radical Women of Color* (New York: Kitchen Table Women of Color Press, 1983) 98–101.

4. Soyinka, "Ideology," 127.

5. Soyinka, "Ideology," 129.

6. Soyinka, "Ideology," 129.

7. Soyinka, "Ideology," 129.

8. Soyinka, "Ideology," 130.

9. The Kalahari desert region in Southern Africa was known as the home of the so-called Bushman, the quintessential primitive in European eyes. All the quotes from Palés's poems are from the excellent critical edition of the complete poems of Palés Matos by Mercedes López-Baralt, *La poesía de Luis Palés Matos: edición crítica* (San Juan: Editorial

de la Universidad de Puerto Rico, 1995). The reader may also consult *Luis Palés Matos, poesía completa*, ed. Margot Arce de Vázquez, (Caracas: Biblioteca Ayacucho, 1978).

10. The indigenous inhabitants of the Kalahari region were undergoing severe repression and forced labor in the early decades of the twentieth century. The Kalahari represented in the Western media and in political and missionary propaganda was meant to obfuscate these brutal realities. See Robert J. Gordon, *The Bushman Myth: The Making of a Namibian Underclass* (Boulder, San Francisco, and Oxford: Westview Press, 1992).

11. Josaphat Kubayanda, *The Poet's Africa: Africanness in the Poetry of Nicolás Guillén and Aimé Césaire* (New York: Greenwood Press, 1990).

12. Kubayanda, in another context, provides us with the following information: Timbuktu has been for centuries an important sub-Saharan cultural center. He also says of the baobab tree that, "This towering multipurpose tree of voices of African ancestors holds out no uncertain promises to its beneficiaries: its leaves can be used to make sauce, its fibers can make cord; its fruit has a lemon-like taste and can be used as a food and water preservative. In addition, in precolonial Africa the tallest baobab trees could be used as lookout posts in searching for stray animals, or as sentinel posts in warfare, and making public announcements. Hence the baobab is a potent symbol of independence." Kubayanda, *The Poet's Africa*, 49.

13. Emphasis added.

14. González, "La (sín)tesis de una poesía antillana," 70.

15. Emphasis added.

16. Kubayanda, *The Poet's Africa*, 23.

17. See especially Kubayanda, *The Poet's Africa*, 17–32.

18. Kubayanda, *The Poet's Africa*, 23. Kubayanda includes in this assessment other *negrista* works: Emilio Ballagas's *Antología de la poesía hispanoamericana* (1935), *Mapa de la poesía negra americana* (1946), Ramón Guirao's *Órbita de la poesía afro-cubana 1928–1937* (1938).

19. Kubayanda, *The Poet's Africa*, 23.

20. Kubayanda, *The Poet's Africa*, 23.

21. Kubayanda, *The Poet's Africa*, 23–24.

22. Kubayanda, *The Poet's Africa*, 24.

23. Kubayanda, *The Poet's Africa*, 24.

24. Kubayanda, *The Poet's Africa*, 24. Though African cultural expressions are not transferred to the Caribbean unchanged, but rather are modified and refashioned, Kubayanda's arguments stand.

25. Kubayanda, *The Poet's Africa*, 39.

26. Jerome Branche, "Negrismo: hibridez cultural, autoridad y la cuestión de la nación," *Revista Iberoamericana* 65, 188–189 (1999): 484.

27. Branche, "Negrismo," 487.

28. Branche, "Negrismo," 487.

29. Branche, "Negrismo," 488.

30. Branche, "Negrismo," 488.

31. Branche, "Negrismo," 488.

32. These are just a few names. There are many more.

33. Alba Lía Barrios, "Ese negro fantasmal de Palés Matos," *INTI: Revista de Literatura Hispánica* 29–30 (1989): 71.

34. Barrios, "Ese negro fantasmal," 72.
35. Barrios, "Ese negro fantasmal," 75.
36. Barrios, "Ese negro fantasmal," 75.
37. Barrios, "Ese negro fantasmal," 72.
38. See Eric Lott, *Love and Theft: Blackface, Minstrelsy, and the American Working Class* (New York: Oxford University Press, 1993).
39. Branche, "Negrismo," 492–493.
40. Branche, "Negrismo," 493.
41. See Montejo, Estaban Montejo, *The Autobiography of a Runaway Slave*. ed. Miguel Barnet and trans. Jocasta Innes (New York: Pantheon Books, 1968). For a historical account of Afro-Cuban struggles for civil rights see, Aline Helg, *Our Rightful Share: The Afro-Cuban Struggle for Equality, 1886–1912* (Chapel Hill: The University of North Carolina Press, 1995). See also Branche, "Negrismo," 494.
42. Branche, "Negrismo," 495.
43. Carmen María Colón Pellot, *Ámbar mulato: ritmos* (Arecibo: 1938) prologue.
44. Colón Pellot, *Ámbar mulato*, prologue.
45. Colón Pellot, *Ámbar mulato*, prologue.
46. Gladys Jiménez Muñoz, "Carmen María Colón Pellot: mujer y raza en Puerto Rico entre las dos guerras." in *Contrapuntos de género y raza en Puerto Rico* (Río Piedras: Ediciones Callejón, forthcoming, 2003) 19. I quote from a photocopy of her essay.
47. Jiménez Muñoz, "Carmen María Colón Pellot," 20.
48. Jiménez Muñoz, "Carmen María Colón Pellot," 21.
49. Mercedes López-Baralt, "El erotismo pionero de Palés: en 'Las voces secretas' de *El palacio en sombras*," *Nómada* 3 (1997): 13
50. López-Baralt, "El erotismo," 18–19.
51. Arcadio Díaz Quiñones, "La poesía negra de Luis Palés Matos: realidad y conciencia de su dimensión colectiva," in *El almuerzo en la hierba* (Río Piedras: Ediciones Huracán, 1982) 78.
52. Díaz Quiñones, "La poesía," 86.
53. Díaz Quiñones, "La poesía," 83.
54. Díaz Quiñones, "La poesía," 85. Emphasis added.
55. Díaz Quiñones, "La poesía," 86.
56. bell hooks, "Eating the Other: Desire and Resistance," in *Black Looks: Race and Representation* (Boston: South End Press, 1992) 21–39.
57. Díaz Quiñones, "La poesía," 88.
58. Díaz Quiñones, "La poesía," 88–89. Emphasis added.
59. Arcadio Díaz Quiñones, "Notas para el estudio del Tuntún de pasa y grifería," *El almuerzo en la hierba*, 114.
60. Díaz Quiñones, "Notas para el estudio," 114.
61. Palés Matos, qtd. in Arcadio Díaz Quiñones, "Luis Palés Matos en la biblioteca Ayacucho," in *El almuerzo en la hierba*, 126.
62. Palés Matos, qtd. in Díaz Quiñones, "Luis Palés Matos," 126.
63. Díaz Quiñones, "Notas para el estudio," 115.
64. Díaz Quiñones, "Notas para el estudio," 117.
65. Díaz Quiñones, "Notas para el estudio," 118. See also Gerald Guinness, "Here and Elsewhere, (One), Luis Palés Matos: Thoughts on Rereading the *Poesía Completa*," in

Here and Elsewhere: Essays on Caribbean Literature (Río Piedras: Editorial de la Universidad de Puerto Rico, 1993) 1–26.

66. Guinness, "Here and Elsewhere," 18–19.

67. See Mary Ann Caws, "Ladies Shot and Painted: Female Embodiment in Surrealist Art," in *The Female Body in Western Culture: Contemporary Perspectives*, ed. Susan Rubin Suleiman (Cambridge: Harvard University Press, 1986) 262–287.

68. Jorge Font Saldaña, "El negro lírico de Luis Palés Matos," *Puerto Rico Ilustrado* 28, 1474 (1938): 58.

69. Pratricia Hill Collins, *Black Feminist Thought: Knowledge, Consciousness, and the Politics of Empowerment* (New York, London: Routledge, 1991).

70. Hill Collins, *Black Feminist Thought*, 7.

71. González, "La (sín)tesis de una poesía antillana," 59.

72. González, "La (sín)tesis de una poesía antillana," 71.

73. González, "La (sín)tesis de una poesía antillana," 71.

74. Miriam Jiménez Román, "Un hombre (negro) del pueblo: José Celso Barbosa and the Puerto Rican 'Race' Toward Whiteness," in *Centro: Journal of the Center for Puerto Rican Studies* 8, 1–2 (1996): 25.

75. See Isabelo Zenón Cruz, *Narciso descubre su trasero: el negro en la cultura puertorriqueña*, vol. 2 (Humacao: Ediciones Furidi 1975) 137.

76. Zenón Cruz, *Narciso descubre su trasero*, 137.

77. See Juan A. Giusti Cordero for a perceptive critique of *negrismo* as an expression of "cultura negroide," a precursor of a more modern "antillanismo" practiced today. "AfroPuerto Rican Cultural Studies: Beyond *cultura negroide* and *antillanismo*," *Centro: Journal of the Center for Puerto Rican Studies* 8, 1–2 (1996): 56–77.

78. My reading of a number of her other essays in her anthology *Impresiones: notas puertorriqueñas* (San Juan: Editorial Yaurel, 1950) shows a continuum in her thinking on race and national culture.

79. The anthology, published in 1950 by Editorial Yaurel, is prefaced by Cesáreo Rosa-Nieves, one of Arce's colleagues and collaborators. The publishing house was an editorial venture of the *trascendentalista*s, a literary group dedicated to the cultivation of narrowly Puerto Rican themes. The book is divided into three parts. The first section, *Marco y figuras*, includes Arce's well anthologized "Paisaje de Puerto Rico," as well as essays on exemplary figures of Puerto Rican cultural life. Hostos, Pedreira, María Cadilla de Martínez, and Isabel Andreu de Aguilar are featured prominently. The second part, *Figuraciones*, deals with the works of five Puerto Rican poets. It includes four essays on Palés Matos, and essays on Lloréns Torres, Samuel Lugo, Carmen Alicia Cadilla, and Eugenio Rentas Lucas. The last part, *Perspectivas*, opens with a re-reading of Pedreira's *Insularismo*, and closes with "La salvación por el lenguaje," a review of Antonia Saez's book for the teaching of Spanish in elementary schools. This section of the anthology also includes an essay on Abelardo Díaz Alfaro's *Terrazo*, a review of Cesáreo Rosa Nieves's drama *Román Baldorioti de Castro*, and a review of Navarro Tomás's *El español de Puerto Rico*.

80. Arce, prologue to *Luis Palés Matos: Poesía completa* (Caracas: Biblioteca Ayacucho, 1978) xi.

81. Arce, prologue, xii.

82. Arce, prologue, xiii.

Index